CHRISTIANS AND THE HOLY PLACES

Christians and the Holy Places

The Myth of Jewish-Christian Origins

JOAN E. TAYLOR

CLARENDON PRESS · OXFORD
1993

Oxford University Press, Walton Street, Oxford OX2 6DP
Oxford New York Toronto
Delhi Bombay Calcutta Madras Karachi
Kuala Lumpur Singapore Hong Kong Tokyo
Nairobi Dar es Salaam Cape Town
Melbourne Auckland Madrid
and associated companies in
Berlin Ibadan

Oxford is a trade mark of Oxford University Press

Published in the United States
by Oxford University Press Inc., New York

British Library Cataloguing in Publication Data
Data available
ISBN 0–19–814785–6

Library of Congress Cataloging in Publication Data
Taylor, Joan E.
Christians and the holy places: the myth of Jewish-Christian
origins/Joan E. Taylor.
Revision of the author's thesis (Ph.D.—University of Edinburgh,
1989), published under title: A critical investigation of
archaeological material assigned to Palestinian Jewish-Christians of
the Roman and Byzantine periods.
Includes bibliographical references and index.
1. Christian shrines—Palestine.   2. Christian pilgrims and
pilgrimages—Palestine.   3. Christian antiquities—Palestine.
4. Jewish Christians—Palestine.   5. Sacred space.   6. Palestine—
Antiquities.   7. Palestine—Church history.   8. Excavations
(Archaeology)—Palestine.   I. Title.
BV896.P19 T39   1993
263'.0425694—dc20
ISBN 0–19–814785–6

Typeset by Hope Services (Abingdon) Ltd.
Printed in Great Britain by
Biddles Ltd, Guildford and King's Lynn

For Paul, for our little daughter Emily,
and for my parents, Robert and Birgit

Preface

DURING a visit to Jerusalem in 1988, I was lucky enough to be shown the Greek Orthodox archaeological excavations on and around the Rock of Calvary in the Church of the Holy Sepulchre. Excited by what was uncovered, I asked to take a few photographs, and, upon being given permission, I advanced a couple of steps on to the Rock. I was about to take a photograph when my guide whispered, 'Quickly! This is a holy place . . . and you are a woman!'

His words struck many chords. At once I realized he had not expected me to walk on to the surface of the rock. I had seen men walking there the day before and had presumed that this was normal practice. However, I was not only a scholar but also 'a woman'. I did not press him on why 'a woman' should take special care in the holy places, but suspect it goes far back to Old Testament ideas about the uncleanness of a woman during her menstrual period (Lev. 15: 19–30). Perhaps this should not be a surprise, for the Old Testament is part of the Christian Bible, and its concepts have actively informed Christianity at every stage of its growth.

The idea of a holy place being in danger of contamination by those who may be unclean lies at the heart of why it is deemed necessary by Christians, Jews, and Muslims today to keep hold of such places. The holy site is supposed to be kept pristine. Cleanliness is truly next to godliness in these circumstances, but the cleanliness is not physical but spiritual. It is horror at spiritual pollution that comes across in the Christian writers of the fourth and fifth centuries when they consider how sites sacred to Christians have been used by pagans. In order to guarantee the spiritual cleanliness of the holy places, they must be in the hands of those who worship God correctly: those who can recognize what is unclean and guard against it.

What struck me even more forcefully about my guide's comment, however, was the strength of his conviction that the very rock on which I stepped was holy. The proscriptions for the ancient priests serving in the Jewish Temple and visitors to that sanctuary could apply in some way to this site, because it was so very sacred; but it was sacred in a way that the Temple was not. The Temple was the house of God, where his presence rested, but the Rock of Calvary was holy because of an historical event that was supposed to have taken place there. On this rock, according to my guide, Jesus was crucified and died. The rock itself had then become hallowed ground. The material and the divine met beneath my feet.

For myself, I was interested in the site out of historical and archaeological concerns. I found myself a little irritated by my guide's attitude. If I had challenged him and asked what he meant by the place being 'holy', he would have answered that this rock had been touched by Jesus or that his blood had fallen and sanctified it. We are here not in the realm of Old Testament notions, but in a primitive and superstitious universe of ideas. The distance from the idea of the holiness of a sacred stone or tree to the belief in the sacredness of the Rock of Calvary is not as long a jump as some might wish to think.

Nevertheless, it is a primitive and superstitious universe from which few today can claim complete immunity, not even myself. In the course of my research I had become convinced that the so-called Rock of Calvary was not the precise place where Jesus died, and therefore I felt no sense of awe standing there. On the other hand, I formed the view from my examination of the Gethsemane Cave on the Mount of Olives that this was a place that was very likely used by Jesus and his followers and was probably where Jesus was arrested. For most contemporary tourists and pilgrims, this cave is a rather uninspiring one; Christian tradition has invented the idea of a Garden of Gethsemane, and it is in this that most Christians imagine the arrest taking place.

I found myself in the Cave of Gethsemane picturing Jesus and his followers on the night he was betrayed . . . and then caught myself being alarmed by a noisy party of tourists who did not know why they had been brought to this rather bare cavern. Clearly, even without any conscious belief in the sanctity of place, I had some feelings towards a site in which momentous events may have taken place. This was more than an historian's wish to preserve and respect ancient sites of historical significance. My imagination had been at work in the Cave of Gethsemane, and I was moved to recall events that led to Jesus' death. This process of using one's imagination to recall biblical events is, in fact, yet another aspect of why Christians respect the holy places. A visit to a holy place nourishes faith by stimulating the minds of pilgrims to imagine biblical events taking place, which provides an opportunity for deep prayer and contemplation.

The early Christian pilgrims combined both a belief in the sacredness of the physical places with a practice of travelling around Palestine in order to recollect the great events of the Old and the New Testaments and to pray. Despite their devotion and piety, they were not as worried as the custodians of the places today about tampering with the sites; bits of rock from Calvary, or bits of the Tomb of Christ, were chipped off and taken home. A bit of holiness could be pocketed. Likewise, they could leave a mark by scratching a name or, if they could not write, a symbol or drawing, to show that they had been in the place. Christian holy sites are frequently covered in ancient graffiti of this kind. Modern pilgrims, of course, would not dare make a mark, and to chip off any rock would be an act of vandalism. Even so, sand and old potsherds from the Holy Land are profitably sold to tourists.

For many who visit the holy places today there is an interest not only in recalling the events of the Bible and praying, but in knowing whether the sites are genuine. If a site is spurious, then for many it loses its claim to holiness. It can still be a place of silent contemplation—like the pavement on the Via Dolorosa which we now know dates from the time of Hadrian and cannot therefore have been the pavement ('Lithostrotos', see John 19: 13) where Christ stood at his trial—but something of the divine is lost.

The origin of the Christian holy places is a controversial subject. It is beneficial to the Christian communities in charge of existing sites if all of them are thought in some way to be genuine. The greater the claim for a given site's authenticity, the more likely it is that Christian tourists will be attracted to visit and thus provide a source of revenue for the community which owns it. Moreover, a community in possession of a site which has strong claims to authenticity gains a measure of prestige. Up until this century, Church tradition was proof enough for the genuineness and antiquity of the Christian holy places. Recently, archaeological data have been called as evidence.

Many of the important early Christian holy places have been identified by the Franciscan scholars Bellarmino Bagatti and

Emmanuele Testa as being venerated by Jewish-Christians of the first century onwards. Their hypothesis, based on archaeology and interpretations of patristic literature, is in fact an argument for the authenticity of these sites, for in positing the existence of a group of Jewish-Christians who descended from Christ's first followers, Bagatti and Testa are able to fill the gap between mention of certain places in the New Testament and their identification and development in the Byzantine period.

This study presents an argument about the origins of Christian holy places. It is also an attempt to refute the claims made by Bagatti and Testa. It will be suggested that their hypothesis concerning the Jewish-Christian foundation of many holy places is dubious. The evidence about who the Jewish-Christians were and where they lived will be reviewed. The demography of Palestine during the Late Roman period will be considered in order to provide a background to the development of Christian holy places and a context for archaeological remains. The archaeology and history of important Christian holy sites will then be examined, site by site. The purpose of this examination is to determine whether they are likely to be where New Testament events took place and to see how they came to be developed as centres for pilgrimage. We shall also look at the origins of the Christian concept of the holy place. Fundamental to this examination is the question of the beginnings of Christian pilgrimage and the development of Palestine as the Holy Land.

In combining detailed archaeological analyses with historical investigations mainly based on texts, the method of argumentation adopted here may at first seem strange to those familiar either with pure archaeological reports of excavations or with historical writing founded on surviving literature. However, both literary and archaeological material needs to be assessed together for the proper understanding of the origins and early development of Christian holy places in Palestine. It is simply not adequate to look at one portion of the available data without a thorough considera-tion of the other. Very often, historians have taken the opinions of archaeologists as being final conclusions or indisputable facts. Frequently too, archaeologists have adopted the views of one school of historical study, and attempted to fit all the material evidence into a particular reconstruction of history, especially if this endorses Church tradition. Archaeology, however, may disprove a particular reconstruction of history and, equally, texts can disprove interpretations of material remains. Both historian and archaeologist have felt an understandable reticence to tamper with the other's discipline. The way out of this impasse is, of course, to be both historian and archaeologist, although this has its own dangers.

How and why did Christians come to venerate sites where it was thought that biblical events took place? In answering this we will explore only the first stage of the history of Christian sanctification of places and artefacts. From this time onwards, through the Middle Ages and until today, Christian holy places and relics have been a significant factor at many turns in Western history. A desire to liberate the holy places from the perceived pollutions of Muslim domination was one of the sparks which led to the Crusades. Reaction against the traffic of relics associated with indulgences gave impetus to the Reformation. Moreover, the development of the idea of the physical as sacred did not stop in the early Byzantine period, but has continued. This study will not deal with the icon theology of the Eastern Orthodox Church, or with holy places of Africa or South America created after missionaries established the Church there, or with the modern sanctuaries, often associated with a healing cult, established as a result of an 'appearance' of the Virgin Mary. All these later developments are outside the present field of study, but may be borne in mind when considering the origins of the Christian holy places in Palestine, for the dynamics at work at the beginning have informed subsequent processes to the present day.

The basis of this study is my Ph.D. thesis, 'A Critical Investigation of Archaeological Material Assigned to Palestinian Jewish-Christians of the Roman and Byzantine Periods' (Edinburgh, 1989). I would therefore like to thank all those who helped me write the thesis, and also those who gave me advice on how it could profitably be altered to form a book.

At the outset, I wish to express my gratitude to Peter Matheson, Professor of Church History at Knox Theological Hall, Dunedin, New Zealand, for encouraging me to pursue early Christian studies and for throwing me in at the deep end by giving me classes to tutor before I had completed my Bachelor of Divinity degree. The numerous questions and challenges of the students were invaluable in stimulating my thinking about many aspects of the development of the early Church.

I would like to thank my excellent supervisors at Edinburgh University, Peter Hayman and David Wright, who were assiduous in pointing out errors in my thesis and in providing advice on how my work could be improved.

I owe very special thanks to Fergus Millar, Camden Professor of Ancient History at Oxford, who was external examiner of the thesis. His criticisms and observations were extremely valuable in numerous ways, and enabled me to shape the present study. Moreover, I am additionally grateful for his notes after reading the typescript of this book. The finished product has greatly profited from the wealth of his knowledge and insights.

I am indebted to the British School of Archaeology in Jerusalem for providing me with the means to do research 'on the spot' as their annual Scholar in 1986, and also to the Palestine Exploration Fund and the Anglo-Israel Archaeological Society, who granted me funds for additional site research in 1988.

Whilst I was in Jerusalem, advice, information, and assistance was given freely by very many people, but I would like to thank especially: Michele Piccirillo of the Studium Biblicum Franciscanum; Richard Harper of the British School of Archaeology in Jerusalem; Magen Broshi, Director of the Shrine of the Book, Israel Museum; George Hintlian and Bishop Guregh Kapikian of the Armenian Orthodox Patriarchate; Émile Puech of the École Biblique et Archéologique Française (Couvent des Dominicains St Étienne Bibliothèque); Amos Kloner and Yitzhak Magen of the Israel Department of Antiquities.

I am grateful to Vasilios Tzaferis and the team for permitting me to participate, albeit briefly, in the 1986 Capernaum excavation on the Greek Orthodox site, and to Mary June Nestler for discussing the Capernaum and Sepphoris excavations with me at length.

Thanks are also due to Shimon Gibson, with whom I have worked closely in regard to aspects of Golgotha not discussed here; these will be examined in a jointly-written forthcoming book. His archaeological knowledge has helped many parts of the present study. I am indebted to Greville Freeman-Grenville who provided pertinent observations on drafts of the thesis text. Thanks also to Graham Stanton and Robert Murray, who made room in their busy schedules to discuss the Jewish-Christians.

I am grateful to John Wilkinson for his critique and advice. Thanks must also go to Robert Milburn, who pointed out a number of mistakes that otherwise may have slipped through the net.

I am indebted to many with whom I have been in correspondence, who have generously replied sharing their expertise and opinions, in particular Sebastian Brock, Charles Dowsett, Michael Stone, Zvi Maoz, Dan Barag, Michael MacDonald, Stephen Goranson, and Rafael Frankel.

Thanks also go to Rupert Chapman of the Palestine Exploration Fund for finding certain books and references, and for sending photocopies of relevant articles to my various addresses abroad.

JOAN E. TAYLOR

August 1992

Contents

List of Plates

I would like to thank the Studium Biblicum Franciscanum for the use of all these photographs.

List of Figures

List of Maps

Abbreviations

AASOR	*Annual of the American Schools of Oriental Research*
AJA	*American Journal of Archaeology*
AJBA	*Australian Journal of Biblical Archaeology*
ANT	M. R. James, *The Apocryphal New Testament* (Oxford, 1924)
ATR	*Anglican Theological Review*
BA	*The Biblical Archaeologist*
BAIAS	*The Bulletin of the Anglo-Israel Archaeological Society*
BAR	*Biblical Archaeology Review*
BASOR	*Bulletin of the American Schools of Oriental Research*
CBQ	*Catholic Biblical Quarterly*
CCSL	Corpus Christianorum Series Latina (Turnhout, 1953–)
CIJ	J.-B. Frey, *Corpus Inscriptionum Iudaicarum*, 2 vols. (Vatican City, 1936, 1952).
CIL	*Corpus Inscriptionum Latinarum* (Berlin, 1862–)
CSCO	Corpus Scriptorum Christianorum Orientalium (Louvain, Paris, etc., 1903–)
CSEL	Corpus Scriptorum Ecclesiasticorum Latinorum (Vienna, 1866–)
CSHB	Corpus Scriptorum Historiae Byzantinae (Bonn, 1828–78)
DACL	F. Cabrol and H. Leclercq (eds.), *Dictionnaire d'archéologie chrétienne et de liturgie*, 15 vols. (Paris, 1907–1953)
EAEHL	M. Avi-Yonah (ed.), *Encyclopaedia of Archaeological Excavations in the Holy Land*, 4 vols. (London, 1975–8)
EI	*Eretz Israel*
EJ	*Encyclopaedia Judaica*, ed. C. Roth, G. Wigoder, *et al.* (Jerusalem, 1971–2)
ET	*Expository Times*
GCS	Die griechischen christlichen Schriftsteller der ersten (drei) Jahrhunderte (Leipzig and Berlin, 1897–)
GRP	M. Avi-Yonah, *A Gazetteer of Roman Palestine* (Jerusalem, 1976)

HTR	*Harvard Theological Review*
HUCA	*Hebrew Union College Annual*
IEJ	*Israel Exploration Journal*
JAC	*Jahrbuch für Antike und Christentum*
JBL	*Journal of Biblical Literature*
JEH	*Journal of Ecclesiastical History*
JJS	*Journal of Jewish Studies*
JPOS	*Journal of the Palestine Oriental Society*
JQR	*Jewish Quarterly Review*
JRS	*Journal of Roman Studies*
JSJ	*Journal for the Study of Judaism*
JSS	*Journal of Semitic Studies*
JTS	*The Journal of Theological Studies*
LA	*Studium Biblicum Franciscanum Liber Annuus*
LS	C. T. Lewis and C. Short, *A Latin Dictionary* (Oxford, 1879)
LSJ	H. G. Liddell, R. Scott, and H. S. Jones, *A Greek–English Lexicon*, 9th edn. with suppl. (Oxford, 1968)
MRP	M. Avi-Yonah, *Map of Roman Palestine*, 2nd edn. (Jerusalem, 1946)
NT	*Novum Testamentum*
NTA	E. Hennecke, *New Testament Apocrypha*, W. Schneemelcher (ed.) Eng. trans. and ed. R. McL. Wilson, 2 vols. (London, 1963–5)
NTS	*New Testament Studies*
PEFQSt	*Palestine Exploration Fund Quarterly Statement*
PEQ	*Palestine Exploration Quarterly*
PG	Patrologia Graeca, ed. J. Migne *et al.* (Paris, 1857–)
PGM	H. D. Betz (ed.), *The Greek Magical Papyri in Translation* (Papyri Graecae Magicae), Chicago and London, 1986
PL	Patrologia Latina, ed. J. Migne, *et al.* (Paris, 1844–)
PO	Patrologia Orientalis, ed. R. Graffin, F. Nau, *et al.* (Paris, 1907–)
QDAP	*Quarterly of the Department of Antiquities in Palestine*
RA	*Revue archéologique*
RAC	*Rivista di Archeologia Cristiana*
RB	*Revue biblique*
RSR	*Recherches de science religieuses*
SC	Sources chrétiennes (Paris, 1940–)

SEG	*Supplementum Epigraphicum Graecum* (Leiden, 1923–)
ST	*Studia Theologica: Scandinavian Journal of Theology*
TLL	*Thesaurus Linguae Latinae* (Leipzig, 1900–)
TS	*Terra Santa*
TU	Texte und Untersuchungen zur Geschichte der ältchristlichen Literatur (Leipzig, 1882–)
VC	*Vigiliae Christianae*
ZDPV	*Zeitschrift des Deutschen Palästina-Vereins*
ZNTW	*Zeitschrift für die neutestamentliche Wissenschaft und die Kunde der Älteren Kirche*

I

The Bagatti–Testa Hypothesis

How and when did the veneration of Christian holy places in Palestine begin? The Franciscan scholars Bellarmino Bagatti and Emmanuele Testa have developed an hypothesis which attempts to answer this question.[1] They argue that many Christian holy places are genuine because Jewish-Christians identified and preserved sites which were meaningful in the life of Jesus, from the time of his ministry without interruption until the fourth century. These sites were then appropriated by the mainstream 'Gentile' Church when the emperor Constantine began establishing Christian shrines in Palestine. Before proceeding to answer this question differently, we shall begin by looking at the theories of Bagatti and Testa in order to establish why there may be grounds for thinking they are mistaken.

According to the Bagatti-Testa school, the Jewish-Christian church was centred in Jerusalem and headed first by Peter and then by James, Jesus' brother. The Jewish-Christians practised the Mosaic law and opposed Paul's mission to the Gentiles. In the war preceding Titus' destruction of the Jewish Temple in AD 70, the Jewish-Christian community fled to Pella in the Decapolis, where an important Jewish-Christian community was established. Many Jewish-Christians then returned to Jerusalem after the war ended and established themselves on Mount Zion. The community was headed by Simeon, son of Cleopas, another of Jesus' relatives. The relatives of Jesus themselves constituted an important hierarchy in the Jewish-Christian church. After AD 135, when all Jews were evicted from Jerusalem, the Jewish-Christians avoided eviction because they were not counted as Jews. However, they considered themselves to be Jews, and the other (Gentile) Christians of Palestine condemned them as heretics. The two

---

[1] For a summary, see Bagatti (1971c), 3–14. The history of the Jewish-Christians, according to the Bagatti-Testa school, is also found in Briand (1982), 10–17.

effect on archaeologist and lay person alike, who have little Palestine. The Jewish-Christian church developed its own distinctive theology, closely connected with the veneration of holy places and caves. Bagatti has argued that it is simply logical to presume that the Jewish-Christians of Palestine accredited importance to the sites which they found in their religious literature. These sites have 'una base storica poggiata sulla transmissione di une tradizione antica.'[2] Noting the large number of caves found in later Christian holy sites, Testa proposed that Jewish-Christians employed caves for certain sacred mysteries,[3] particularly for baptismal rites and special meals. Moreover, Jewish-Christians, according to Bagatti and Testa, used a complex system of cryptic signs and symbols to illuminate their theology. Some of these were used in the iconographical repertoire of the Church as a whole, and some were peculiar to the Jewish-Christians of Palestine.[4]

For those belonging to the Bagatti-Testa school there is no doubt that Jewish-Christians must have existed in Palestine prior to the Peace of the Church; these are the *minim* referred to in rabbinic literature. Their history is traced by recourse to many references in patristic sources to Ebionites, Nazoraeans, Elchasaites, and, sometimes, Gnostics. There is equally no doubt expressed that the Jewish-Christians must have possessed a recognizable theology distinct from that of developing orthodoxy. The foundations of this notion are, again, to be assembled from wide-ranging patristic references. The existence of Jewish-Christians in Palestine, their maintenance of Christian holy places and their distinctive theology and practice are all presented together as part of a closely argued package which can at first appear plausible, and has been seen as such by many. However, this hypothesis appears to be wrong in its basic assumptions about Jewish-Christians and its analysis of historical and archaeological material is often inadequate.

The question of who the historical Jewish-Christians were and how they should be defined will be examined in the following chapter. For the moment, the Bagatti-Testa school's analysis of historical and archaeological material will be reviewed. This forms an introduction to how its methodology functions.

In the work of the Bagatti-Testa school, there is frequently a wealth of references to patristic literature. This has a convincing

[2] Bagatti (1964b), 33.   [3] Testa, (1962a), (1964a).
[4] Bagatti (1971c), 137–236; Testa (1962b).

ethnically distinct churches existed in mutual enmity side by side in knowledge of the writings of the Church Fathers. In relating archaeology to biblical and patristic literature at every turn, Bagatti, Testa, and their followers set themselves in the tradition of the so-called 'Roman school' of Christian archaeology, which has its foundations in the early studies of the Christian catacombs in Rome by Giuseppe Marchi and Giovanni B. de Rossi.[5] As Graydon Snyder has pointed out, the Roman school presupposes a continuity of tradition, evidenced in biblical and patristic literature. This has led scholars to assign archaeological material to earlier centuries than might be appropriate. The Roman school has stressed the importance of first relating the subject to biblical and patristic literature to ground it in a literary milieu, which might appear to be sound methodology; but in practice this meant that archaeological data were used to supplement the Roman tradition of the development of the Church.[6] Scholars have become increasingly doubtful about the manner in which archaeological evidence has been used. The errors of methodology parallel those of the nineteenth-century biblical archaeologists who wished to 'prove the Bible true' by science; the science of archaeology, the physical remains of Palestine, would illuminate the theological world of the Bible. However, science's virtue as a discipline has always been, ostensibly, its determination to be empirically objective, so that the truth about the nature of a physical object or phenomenon is tested by experiments which require the fullest awareness of all contingencies. In seeking to endorse biblical or ecclesiastical tradition, both the early biblical archaeologists and the proponents of the Roman school of Christian archaeology fell into precisely the same methodological trap.

Bagatti and Testa may be seen to use the Roman school's methodology, with a slight twist. They too are fastidious in relating archaeological material to evidence found in biblical and patristic writings, but instead of using the archaeological evidence to bolster the orthodox ecclesiastical tradition, they use it to support an hypothesis of their own, based on an understanding of Jewish-Christianity gleaned from a select body of literary material.[7] The

[5] Marchi (1844); de Rossi (1864–7).

[6] For a history of the Roman school and an argument against its methodology, see Snyder (1985), 3–11, esp. 6. Snyder himself argues for a contextual methodology.

[7] Texts which the Bagatti–Testa school identifies as Jewish-Christian, and texts

same methodology is used, but with quite different results. Every literary source at their disposal is employed to support a definition of the archaeological evidence as being Jewish-Christian in character. On account of their understanding of an homogeneous Jewish-Christian tradition, they too are able to date material very early. It may be noted that Snyder uses the example of Testa himself to make his point about the dangers of using the *Roman* school's methodology: 'To be sure, there are still some scholars who insist on harmonizing the literary tradition with the archaeological data, or more pointedly, producing archaeological data that will confirm presupposed traditions. One thinks here of P. E. Testa on the presence of the cross in early Palestinian remains . . .'[8] As Roland de Vaux has stressed, literary and archaeological material must be evaluated separately and used together to reconstruct history.[9] Any approach which at its outset seeks to prove a view of history by using archaeology is biased and prone to produce tendentious results.

Today, we are also more aware of the difference between popular religion and the literature of the theologians. This insight is in great part the result of the work of the Bonn school, which stands over against the Roman school in its approach to early Christian archaeology. Founded by Hans Lietzmann and Franz Joseph Dölger, the approach of the Bonn school is to try to understand early Christian remains in terms of the context of the Mediterranean world, with Christianity seen as a *Volksreligion*.[10] When looking at sites in Palestine, particularly early pilgrim centres, it may then be necessary to consider the popular 'folkish' side of the Christian religion and allow symbols to remain ambiguous, or representative of a current popular iconography that has not been recorded in accounts by Church writers, whether orthodox or heterodox, that have been preserved. The orthodox 'Roman' ecclesiastical tradition, which sees the Church, pure in faith, beset by heresies and successfully fighting them, cannot be used exclusively in assessing the types of Christianity manifest in many of the early levels of Christian holy places. An unusual symbol does not by necessity indicate the existence of a heterodox

which show evidence of Jewish-Christianity have been collected and presented in Italian in Bagatti and Testa (1982).

[8] Snyder (1985), 6.   [9] de Vaux (1970).   [10] Snyder (1985), 5.

mind, let alone a sectarian group, but perhaps a popular faith in which certain pre-Christian elements have been preserved. It may well be the work of personal creativity.

The Ossuaries

As an example of how the Bagatti-Testa school has used its methodology to argue for the identification of a body of archaeological material as being specifically Jewish-Christian, the case of the ossuaries immediately presents itself. The roots of its identification of certain ossuaries are to be found in the nineteenth century. It was of some concern to biblical archaeologists at this time that while important Old Testament sites were being identified in many places, where interesting artefacts were coming to light, no evidence of first-century Christianity was found. Then, in 1873, Charles Clermont-Ganneau claimed that a collection of ossuaries discovered in a tomb on the Mount of Offence might now show evidence of the earliest Jewish-Christian fraternity of Jerusalem. There were thirty mainly Aramaic inscriptions scratched on a cache of about thirty ossuaries, and eight of these were thought by Clermont-Ganneau to be indicative of Christians, since there were names found in the New Testament: Judah, Salome, and Jesus, for example (see Figures 1 and 2). He was equally convinced of their Christian character by the rough crosses and symbols reminiscent of crosses incised close to their names.[11] There was also a clearly carved Latin cross with the Greek letters *HΔHA* (Figure 2.3, 4), probably spelling a name: Hedea.

Over the next century, much speculation ensued about ossuary use and burial customs. The early view was that first- and second-century ethnically Jewish Christians found a resting place in their Jewish family graves, their new faith being indicated only by a rough cross.[12] Perhaps ironically it was a later Israeli scholar, E. L. Sukenik, who made the strongest case for certain ossuaries being 'Jewish-Christian'.[13] Sukenik excavated a first-century tomb in Talpiot, west of Jerusalem, in September 1945 and concluded that two inscriptions, *Ιησους Ιου* (Figure 3.1) and *Ιησους Αλωθ* (Figure 3.2) represented lamentations over the crucifixion of Jesus by

[11] Clermont-Ganneau (1883), (1899).   [12] See Kaufmann (1922), 143.
[13] Sukenik (1947).

1.1

1.2

1.3

1.4

FIG. 1. Graffiti scratched on ossuaries found on the Mount of Offence, Jerusalem

some of his disciples. *Iov* he translated as 'woe', and in *Αλωθ* he saw the Semitic root *alah*, 'to wail'.[14] Crosses on another ossuary, he thought, 'were placed there with some definite purpose'.[15] As comparative material for the early employment of the cross as a Christian symbol he pointed to the Casa del Bicentenario in

---

[14] Sukenik (1947), 363.   [15] Ibid. 364.

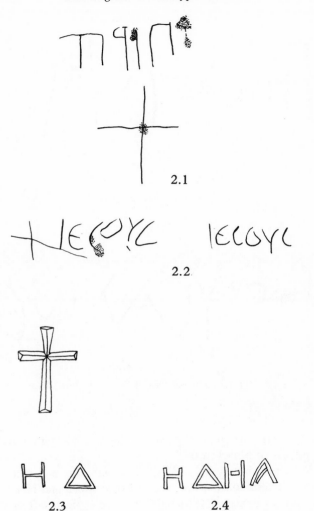

FIG. 2. Graffiti scratched on ossuaries found on the Mount of Offence, Jerusalem

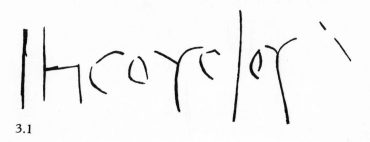

3.1

3.2

FIG. 3. Graffiti scratched on ossuaries found in Talpiot, Jerusalem

Herculaneum, where a shape something like a Latin cross is cut in the plaster of a back wall.[16]

However, already in 1946, Carl H. Kraeling had come to the sobering realization that the 'crosses' of Pompeii and Herculaneum were not evidence of Christians, but were the result of wooden wall brackets which had since decomposed.[17] He was also one of the first to point out that the names in the ossuaries, so like those of the people found in the New Testament, were extremely common in the first century, as was the name 'Jesus' itself.[18] A cursory survey of the names found in Josephus' works confirms this impression.

---

[16] See Maiuri (1939).   [17] (1946), 19.   [18] Ibid. 18.

The clearly carved Latin cross with the Greek letters *HΔHA* in Clermont-Ganneau's cache probably comes from the Byzantine period, drawn by a Christian hand. The cave in which the ossuaries were found was not their original resting-place. It was a rock-hewn chamber without loculi, and looked to Clermont-Ganneau as if it was a storehouse for ossuaries brought from other tombs. The ossuaries were piled up one on top of the other in a disorderly fashion, so that their lids did not match, and bones were randomly placed with vases and other debris.[19]

Over the past thirty years Clermont-Ganneau and Sukenik have been proved wrong. Even Bagatti saw that Sukenik's *Ιησους Ιου* was a misreading of the graffito, which should be read *Ιησους Ιουδ(ο)υ*, Jesus, (son) of Judah.[20] The word *Αλωθ* is not a lament, but probably a name transcribing a Hebrew name *Ahalot*, meaning 'aloes'.[21] Furthermore, the purpose of the cross marks and other symbols was without doubt to show which way the lid should be placed on the ossuary box.[22] As Pau Figueras writes: '. . . not only prudence, but scholarly objectivity should restrain us from forcing a Christian interpretation where a Jewish one is acceptable. This is not an a priori position as we *know* . . . that secondary burial and the use of ossuaries were the norm among Palestinian Jews during this period'.[23] Figueras is in this case arguing not so much against Sukenik but against Bagatti, for ten years after Sukenik had published his findings at Talpiot, Bagatti, with J. T. Milik, proposed that another cache of Jewish-Christian ossuaries had been discovered.

Bagatti had been interested in uncovering early Christian remains in Jordan[24] and Israel[25] for some years. In 1953, when workmen by chance discovered a Jewish cemetery in the Franciscan Dominus Flevit property, on the western slope of the Mount of Olives, he was given the task of making an archaeological examination of the site. For precisely the same reasons as Clermont-Ganneau, Bagatti identified ossuaries in the first- and second-century *kokhim* tombs as being Jewish-Christian.[26] He

---

[19] Clermont-Ganneau (1899), 381.   [20] (1950), 118–20.

[21] For an examination of both these inscriptions, see Kane (1971).

[22] R. H. Smith (1974).

[23] Figueras (1984–5). For further clarification about these ossuaries and ossuaries in general, see id. (1974); Kane (1978); Fishwick (1963–4).

[24] Bagatti (1940), (1948).   [25] Bagatti (1950), (1952).

[26] Bagatti (1953*b*); Bagatti and Milik (1958), 166–82.

admitted that the majority of signs scratched on the sides and lids of the ossuaries were for practical purposes, so that the lid would be placed the right way round, but he remained convinced that the cross shapes had religious significance. He believed these crosses represented the ancient Hebrew letter *tau*, which was written as a small cross or Greek letter *chi*. According to Bagatti, the *tau* became a Jewish-Christian symbol.[27]

Bagatti summarizes his understanding of Church history in the excavation report[28] and it is helpful to review this in order to comprehend why he fought against the developing scholarly consensus about the Jewish (and perhaps exclusively Pharisaic) use of ossuaries. The key component in his historical summary is a stress on the numbers of converts in the Acts of the Apostles. He notes that in the early period, there were many 'cristiani di razza ebraica'; he takes the numbers converted in Acts 2: 41 (3000) and Acts 4: 4 (5000) as precise head counts, and uses Eusebius to support his view (*Hist. Eccles.* iii. 33, 35). To Bagatti's mind there simply had to be some archaeological record of this vast movement.

While Bagatti enjoyed some initial support during the 1960s, his hypothesis on the ossuaries is now almost entirely discredited. Antonio Ferrua, who was among those critical of his approach, responded to his preliminary reports by noting that it would have been better to establish the religious nature of the tomb and then to deduce the cryptography, rather than to argue for the presence of Christianity on the basis of cryptic symbols.[29] Michael Avi-Yonah took issue with Bagatti's assumptions about the numbers of converts, and maintained that the chances of finding tombs of the tiny minority of Jewish-Christians in Jerusalem were exceedingly slim.[30] Even if the reading of the letter *tau* were to be credited with some validity, the rare symbolic value of the Hebrew letter is based on Ezekiel 9: 4, where the elect of God are marked with this sign, and it could therefore have been the property of any of the sects, which existed in Judaea at the end of the Second Temple period, who claimed to be the elect. Furthermore, we do not have to look so far as these sects. Avi-Yonah did not point out that there is good evidence for the importance of the Hebrew *tau*, written like a Greek *chi*, in the rabbinic tradition (*b.Shab.* 55a;

[27] Bagatti and Milik (1958), 177.
[28] Ibid. 166–9.   [29] Ferrua (1954).   [30] Avi-Yonah (1961*b*).

b.Men. 74b; cf. *b.Ker.* 5b). Avi-Yonah did note, however, that Bagatti's reasoning was itself faulty in using the invalid syllogism:

> The *tau* is a Jewish symbol
> The early Christians were Jews
> *ergo*: The *tau* is a Christian symbol[31]

The names of a Christian character are, as has been stated already, ordinary Jewish names of the first and second centuries AD. Avi-Yonah pointed out that no specifically Christian onomasticon existed before the latter part of the third century AD, when Gentiles in Egypt appear to have taken names from the Old and New Testaments upon baptism.[32]

Another matter was the problem of what appeared to be a *chi-rho* monogram drawn on ossuary no. 12 at Dominus Flevit, which belonged to 'Judah the son of Judah the proselyte'.[33] It was this sign that provided a key reason for Bagatti to identify the whole of Chamber 79 at Dominus Flevit as Jewish-Christian.[34] It is very doubtful, however, that this sign should be considered Christian, since it was in use in the ancient world long before Constantine adopted it as a symbol heralding Christianity. Figueras notes that here the *chi-rho* may be short for either χαράκτεον or χαράσμενος,[35] but it could have been an abbreviation for any word, or name, with a Greek *chi* and *rho* prominent within it.[36] It is axiomatic that a *chi-rho* found in a Jewish setting should be interpreted in the light of its Jewish context. It would not appear to be methodologically sound to interpret it in the light of a much later, religiously alien, symbol.

The case of the Dominus Flevit ossuaries demonstrates the manner in which Bagatti and, soon after him, Testa, would approach a wide variety of archaeological data. An important feature of Bagatti's aim was to find on the ossuaries definite symbols which might illuminate the thought of the 'Jewish-Christian' church of Judaea, which he was sure existed from the first to the fourth century. It was Bagatti's firm belief that such a

---

[31] Ibid. 93–4.   [32] Ibid. 94.
[33] Bagatti and Milik (1958), 64–5, photo 75, fig. 17.
[34] Ibid. 178–9.
[35] (1984–5), 49. See also Colella (1973); Avi-Yonah (1940), 111–12.
[36] For example, the *chi-rho* abbreviation found in a synagogue inscription from Sepphoris would need to be interpreted in the light of other similar abbreviations used in Jewish or Semitic contexts. Avi-Yonah (1940: 111) has proposed that this *chi-rho* should be interpreted as *lamprotatos*, *pace* Meyers (1988), 71.

church must have left some material evidence. The perceived symbols were the way into the minds of these Jewish-Christians, but even more they were the earliest evidence of Christian iconography itself.[37] Bagatti was indebted to Jean Daniélou for many primary identifications of so-called Jewish-Christian symbols, but Bagatti and Daniélou soon became mutually influenced by each other. Daniélou's *Théologie du judéo-christianisme* (Paris, 1958) provided Bagatti with the foundations upon which he could build a grander hypothesis. Daniélou, on the other hand, sought justifications for his notions of a specific Jewish-Christian theology by appealing to Bagatti's work, for example on the ossuary scratchings. In his *Les Symboles chrétiens primitifs* (Paris, 1961), Daniélou lauds Bagatti with praise over his discoveries of a number of ossuaries in which their Jewish-Christian character is certain.[38] Daniélou continued to reserve high praise for the work of the Bagatti–Testa school in many reports.[39] It may be argued, however, that in one sense Bagatti and Daniélou misunderstood one another. Daniélou was attempting to distinguish a Jewish theology within early Christianity, but not necessarily any historical Jewish-Christian groups. Bagatti, on the other hand, read Daniélou's work as a textbook for the beliefs of historical Palestinian Jewish-Christians.

The Stelai of Khirbet Kilkish

A further example of how alleged Jewish-Christian remains began to proliferate on slender and contentious evidence, by means of an approach that was prone to make erroneous assessments by its very nature, may be seen in the case of the Khirbet Kilkish funerary *stelai*. Ignazio Mancini, in his review of Jewish-Christian archaeology in Palestine, provides a compact outline of the discovery of the *stelai* which will not be repeated here.[40] It will suffice to note that in 1960 a quantity of inscribed stone slabs were brought to the attention of Augustus Spijkerman, then director of

[37] Bagatti (1954).
[38] Daniélou (1961), 8. This book collects together nine articles written about early Christian symbols. See also id. (1949), (1951*b*), (1952), (1954).
[39] Daniélou reported on the theories of Bagatti and Testa in *RSR* 51 (1963), 117–22; 55 (1967), 92–6; 56 (1968), 119–20; 58 (1970), 143–5.
[40] Mancini, (1984).

the Museum at the Studium Biblicum Franciscanum, by a dealer in antiquities on the Via Dolorosa who later showed Spijkerman the freshly ploughed field in Khirbet Kilkish, near Hebron, from which the objects originated. Excavation of the field eventually uncovered over 200 of these *stelai* (which Bagatti thought were stone amulets) within a metre of the surface of the ground (see Figure 4 for examples). In fact, it is unnecessary to publish a detailed refutation of the archaeological authenticity of the *stelai*, for a trained eye will see that the inscriptions are relatively fresh, and the stones unhurt by the ravages of time. The location of the *stelai* just below the surface of a ploughed field (which was equipped with a hoard of diverse Roman sherds), along with the very probable conspiracy of the antiquities' dealer and the landowner, all indicates rather strongly that the Franciscans were in this case shamefully deceived.[41] Michele Piccirillo, present director of the Museum, has accordingly removed all but two of these *stelai* from display.[42] However, the iconography of the *stelai* has formed a basis for Testa's extensive discussion of Jewish-Christian symbolism in *Il simbolismo dei giudeo-cristiani* (Jerusalem, 1962), from which many conclusions were drawn about the details of Jewish-Christian theology.

Bagatti believed that Hebron was the centre of a fourth-century sect, the so-called Archontics, described by Epiphanius (*Pan.* xl, xli),[43] which it may well have been; but Epiphanius nowhere indicates that the Archontics were a Jewish-Christian sect. Rather, it is quite clear from his description that they were Gnostics. For example, they believed in seven heavens, each presided over by an archon, at the top of which, in an eighth, was the shining Mother (*Pan.* xl. 2. 3); they believed in the resurrection of the soul, but not of the flesh, and rejected Christian baptism (*Pan.* xl. 2. 4–9). Nothing is said about their ethnic origins, or about any Jewish customs. They were found in Palestine in a place named by Epiphanius as Καφαρβαρίχα (*Pan.* xl. 1. 3), three miles from Hebron, which Bagatti identifies with Bene Naim.[44] Epiphanius says that a certain Peter, the originator of the sect, was expelled by

---

[41] Prof. Dan Barag has now kindly informed me that he has found a man in Hebron who admits to faking the *stelai*, and has recorded the details in correspondence with Prof. Morton Smith.

[42] I understand that these remain out of respect for Father Bagatti.

[43] Bagatti (1964a).   [44] (1971c), 38.

FIG. 4. Examples of the Khirbet Kilkish *stelai*

Bishop Aetius, and fled to Kochaba, which Epiphanius considered to be a centre for Ebionites and Nazoraeans (*Pan.* xl. 1. 5), but he was clearly not an Ebionite or a Nazoraean. He returned to Kaphar Baricha as an old man and, having told certain people about his views, he was anathematized by no less a person than Epiphanius himself, after which Peter became a hermit in a cave where he would receive a few devotees (*Pan.* xl. 1. 6–9). Peter does not appear to have had any interest in Jewish praxis, and the ideas of the Archontics are quite unlike those that Epiphanius associated with his 'Ebionites'.[45]

The closest group to the Archontics were the Sethians. Both groups used the *Ascension of Isaiah* and believed in the power of Seth (*Pan.* xl. 6. 9–7. 5; cf. xxxix. 1. 3–2. 7), son of Adam and Eve. H. C. Puech accordingly sees the Archontics as nothing more than a ramification of the Sethians.[46] Seth is also found in Jewish haggadic material, which was a source of ideas for both Gnostic and catholic Christians, but, as A. F. J. Klijn has noted, we should not come to hasty conclusions about the origins of Gnostic groups simply because haggadic elements are present in Gnostic treatises.[47] Seth was an attractive figure capable of a variety of interpretations.

The Bagatti–Testa school has made an error in identifying the Archontics as Jewish-Christians. The *stelai* were interpreted by Testa in the light of Archontic theology, which was then considered to be representative of Jewish-Christian theology. His extensive study of the *stelai* then formed the foundation for subsequent analyses of possible Jewish-Christian material found in holy sites in Palestine. However, since the *stelai* are undoubtedly fraudulent,[48] and the identification of the Archontics as Jewish-

---

[45] Epiphanius' 'Ebionites' may have been Elchasaites. It is striking that in Epiphanius' *Panarion* alone do we find references to Ebionites as being vegetarian, having purificatory baths, rejecting the Temple and sacrifices, being obliged to marry, or having other characteristics which are otherwise found distinctively among the *Elchasaites* and in the Pseudo-Clementine literature. See the comparative table in Klijn and Reinink (1973), 78–9 (app. II).

[46] (1950), 634–43.

[47] (1977), 119. Moreover, many of the Hebrew- and Aramaic-sounding names found in Sethian (and other Gnostic) writings come not from Jews but from the field of syncretistic magic; see Jackson (1989).

[48] This is a sensitive matter discussed amongst archaeologists in Jerusalem but, in the cautious climate there, no one has published a work designed to prove the *stelai* are frauds. Prof. Dan Barag, who has privately investigated the *stelai* and

Christians is erroneous, it is not too strong to say that Testa's work based on the *stelai* is entirely valueless in illuminating the symbolism or the possible theology of Jewish-Christians. Any analysis of possible Jewish-Christian remains which relies on Testa's conclusions about the Khirbet Kilkish material is also invalidated.

By the middle of the 1960s, Bagatti and Testa had assembled a large body of archaeological data that were considered by them to be Jewish-Christian in nature. Already in 1955, Bagatti had begun work on excavating a section of ancient Nazareth, on land belonging to the Franciscan Custody of the Holy Land, and had soon developed the theory that it had been a Jewish-Christian cult centre prior to the fourth century.[49] Testa argued that sacred rites of baptism were administered in the main caves there, the 'mystic grottos'.[50] The judgements passed on Nazareth by Bagatti and Testa have not yet been assessed in detail, unlike those on Dominus Flevit. It is now no simple task to examine the site, as it has been covered over by the erection of the Basilica of the Annunciation, which has turned the caves into parts of the church used for worship. Other important remains are accessible to visitors only with the permission of the authorities there.

It would appear that the conclusions reached by Bagatti and Testa influenced the work of their fellow Franciscans, Virgilio Corbo, Stanislao Loffreda, and Augustus Spijkerman, in excavations in Capernaum, which began in 1968. While a four-volume report of the excavations was produced on the basis of results from nine campaigns,[51] work still continues at the Franciscan part of the site, although the area of a Byzantine octagonal church is now enclosed in a modern church which, like that in Nazareth,

---

established that all but two are forgeries, was strongly urged to delay publishing his findings until after Father Bagatti's death (personal communication).

It may also be noted that Testa has fared badly in regard to another fraud. In 1973 Testa published a bought stone inscription which he thought came from Samaritan Christians and indicated a Samaritan Christian regeneration myth; see Testa (1973). Pummer (1979: 109) thought the identification of the letters as being Samaritan very questionable. Then Naveh (1982a) conclusively showed that the letters derived from the coins of the Bar Kochba Revolt and that the stone 'amulet' was a forgery; cf. Shanks (1984).

[49] Bagatti (1955), (1969).
[50] Testa (1962a); cf. Bagatti (1957a), (1957b).
[51] Corbo (1975); Loffreda (1974a); Spijkerman (1975); Testa (1972).

incorporates the archaeological evidence into its design. Corbo argued that under the octagonal church there was a house-church belonging to the Jewish-Christian community of Capernaum, which in turn was created out of the original house of Peter, the apostle. Therefore, yet another important Christian holy site is alleged to have been the property of Jewish-Christians. A number of Franciscan scholars joined with Bagatti and Testa in supporting the idea that at Nazareth and Capernaum, as well as in many other places, Jewish-Christians preserved the memory of important sites in Jesus' life.[52]

From this brief survey of the work of the Bagatti–Testa school, it would appear that the methodology it deploys in assessing finds made at Christian holy places is open to serious question. It has already been shown to have made errors of judgement in regard to archaeological material—as in the case of the ossuaries, and also with the Khirbet Kilkish *stelai*—but the ideas of the school are widely available, especially at a popular level, to visitors to Christian holy sites and through the Franciscan Printing Press.[53] It may be added that certain archaeologists who seem to be not wholly conversant with the known development of Christianity in Palestine, have found the theories of the Bagatti–Testa school convincing and have publicized these.[54]

Fundamental to the hypothesis is the belief that there were heterodox Jewish-Christians who were present in Palestine and who actively sustained, in a deviant way, the holy places of Christendom. It is, then, to the subject of the definition of Jewish-Christianity, and the question of whether any Jewish-Christians existed in Late Roman Palestine, that we shall now turn.

[52] The output of the Bagatti–Testa school may be seen in the list supplied in Manns (1979), 190–5, though others writing on the subject are also included in this bibliography. It should be noted that while many books and articles are the products of the Franciscan Printing Press in Jerusalem, the views of the Studium Biblicum Franciscanum there should not be equated with the Bagatti–Testa position. The Studium is made up of scholars with various opinions. It engages in a broad spectrum of biblical and archaeological work. Its library acts as a focus for scholars from all over the world and its journal, the *Liber Annuus*, provides a forum for debate on numerous subjects.

[53] The guidebooks to Christian holy places owned by the Franciscans—Capernaum and Nazareth for example—frequently give the Bagatti–Testa school's opinion without offering any other views.

[54] See Cornfeld (1976), 269, 283–5, 291–2, 294, 308–9; also, to some degree, Strange (1983); Meyers and Strange (1981), 107, cf. 110–15, 130–9; Meyers (1988); Groh (1988).

Jewish-Christians in Palestine?

In this chapter, we will explore the question of who the Jewish-Christians were (and who they were not) and also look at literary and archaeological evidence that might testify to their presence in Palestine and Syria in the Roman and Byzantine periods. If the Bagatti–Testa hypothesis has Jewish-Christians as the conservators of holy places, does the evidence for this hypothetical group stand up to cross-examination?

Jewish-Christianity: Term and Definition

'Jewish-Christianity' and 'Judaeo-Christianity' are synonymous terms used in modern scholarship to refer to a supposed religious phenomenon which spans the period from the very beginnings of Christianity to some time in the fifth century, when it is perceived to be extinct. Jewish-Christians are generally understood to have been marginalized, accepted neither by church nor by synagogue, because they intended to be both Jewish and Christian at one and the same time.

One of the reasons why it has been possible for the Bagatti–Testa school to develop the hypothesis that early Jewish-Christians preserved and venerated many important Christian holy sites is the climate of uncertainty that has surrounded studies of Jewish-Christianity. Recently, however, progress has been made in many aspects of these studies, so that we are better equipped to understand Jewish-Christianity's nature and diversity.[1] The Bagatti–Testa school has relied almost exclusively upon the theories of the last generation of historians working on the subject and has applied these to archaeological data, but it is questionable whether these

---

[1] For a discussion on the current scholarly positions and an argument for a better definition of the term 'Jewish-Christianity' see Taylor (1990).

theories are reliable for determining actual historical groups which may or may not have left material remains.

As it was shown in the last chapter, in concentrating on the ethnic and theological characteristics of a conjectural group of Jewish-Christians, the Bagatti–Testa school rests on the work of Jean Daniélou.[2] Daniélou attempted to define a first form of Christian theology, which he labelled 'Jewish-Christian', that expressed itself in Jewish/Semitic terms. The main criteria which he used to establish a piece of literature as Jewish-Christian were: a date prior to the middle of the second century, a literary genre popular in Judaism, and the presence of ideas, notably those of apocalyptic literature, which he thought characteristic of Jewish-Christianity.[3] Since it was not necessary to apply all criteria simultaneously, Daniélou was able to classify a text as Jewish-Christian simply on the basis that it showed, for example, liberty in its use of biblical citations, an allegorical exegesis, and an angelomorphic Christology.[4] This approach may be helpful in tracing strands of thought, but, as R. A. Kraft has pointed out, it was undertaken without consideration of whether any historical groups consciously adhered to such a theology.[5] Daniélou's argument was in danger of being read as circular: the theology became the evidence for positing the existence of historical groups, while the groups' existence became the rationale for introducing the theology. Many scholars now ask whether Daniélou's approach has obscured historical realities rather than illuminated them. Should Jewish-Christians be defined, primarily, on the basis of a peculiar theology?

In the world of Jewish-Christian scholarship, terminological chaos abounds, although numerous scholars have sought to clarify terms and definitions.[6] While it cannot seriously be doubted that patristic and rabbinic sources testify to the existence of Christians who were also 'Jewish' (or Jews who were in some way 'Christian'), most scholars today reject the notion that there were two definite streams of early Christianity, one Jewish and one Gentile. Those belonging to the Bagatti–Testa school are among

---

[2] Daniélou (1964).   [3] Ibid. 11.   [4] Daniélou (1971).
[5] (1972), 86.
[6] For a survey of what has been written about Jewish-Christianity up to 1972, see Malina (1973); also id. (1976); Riegel (1977–8); Murray (1974), (1982); Quispel (1968); Munck (1959–60); Gager (1972); Klijn (1973–4); Kraft (1972) and his review in *JBL* 79: 91–4; Simon (1965), (1975).

the minority who believe that the Church soon split into two clear factions, with separate and distinct theologies which can be adduced from surviving texts and archaeological remains.

The idea of there being two streams originated 160 years ago in the work of the Tübingen school. F. C. Baur distinguished, behind the gloss of Acts, a grave conflict between a 'Jewish' Christianity, led by Peter, and a Gentile Christianity, led by Paul.[7] But already in 1886, W. A. Hilgenfeld had modified Baur by pointing out the varieties of thought among the *Urapostel*.[8]

As R. E. Brown has recently argued, Jewish culture and Hellenistic culture were not mutually exclusive milieux, and consequently a distinction between a Jewish and a Gentile Christianity on cultural, or even theological, terms is a false one.[9] Indeed, the beliefs and practices of Jews within the early Church would have varied as much as did Christian Gentiles' belief and practices, and there is no reason to doubt that both ethnic groups participated in the full spectrum of possible attitudes. There is no sure way of dividing the Christian Jews from the Gentiles in theological terms. Simply in regard to the Jewish law, some Jews and their Gentile converts appear to have steadfastly followed Jewish praxis, the *dat Mosheh vihudit* (*m.Ket.* 7. 6): Sabbath observance, customs, festivals, food laws, circumcision of sons (following the 'circumcision party' of Gal. 2: 12); other Jews and their Gentile converts rejected most Jewish praxis as being obsolete under the new covenant (Paul); still more stood somewhere in between the two positions (Peter and James).

If Jewish-Christianity were to be defined as encompassing all Jews who were also Christians, then the term would in fact be meaningless.[10] For it to have any real meaning, the term must refer not only to ethnic Jews but those who, with their Gentile converts, upheld the *praxis* of Judaism. Jewish-Christians, in this

---

[7] Baur (1831). Baur's understanding of the dichotomy is reflected by some modern writers. J. B. Tyson (1973), for example, distinguishes between Jewish Christians, who believed Jesus became Messiah only at the time of his resurrection, and Gentile Christians, who understood him to be the Son of God who descended to earth and was at his resurrection restored to divine status. Such simplifications owe much to Baur.

[8] Hilgenfeld (1886).

[9] R. E. Brown (1983); Brown and Meier (1983), 1–9.

[10] It is easily replaced by the simple term 'Christian', since the adjective 'Jewish' serves no useful purpose, see Klijn (1973–4), 426.

definition, were those Jews who maintained a Jewish life-style beyond the point, early in the second century, when most Jews in the Church found it unnecessary to sustain this life-style. As Ignatius wrote, *c*.110-15: 'we have seen how former adherents of the ancient customs have since attained to a new hope; so that they have given up keeping the Sabbath, and now order their lives by the Lord's Day instead' (*Magnes.* ix). Certainly, some Christians did not abandon the Sabbath as blithely as these words might suggest, as Ignatius well knew, but major theological differences between groups that maintained Jewish praxis and those that abandoned it are impossible to determine at the beginning of the second century. Until the middle of the century, Jewish-Christians appear to have been generally accepted in the Church despite their increasingly marginalized position, and despite factional fighting. For example, Justin Martyr (*c*.160) finds no quarrel with Jewish-Christians who do not attempt to *Judaize* communities that do not practise a Jewish lifestyle (*Dial.* xlvii, cf. xlvi. 1–2), though he admits that some of his colleagues object to them.

After Justin, Jewish-Christians, defined as groups of Christian Jews and their converts who upheld the Mosaic customs, are no longer found in surviving literature as being accepted within the catholic Church. Celsus (*c*.178) would characterize Jews who believed in Christ as having left the ancestral law, deserting to another name and another life (Origen, *Contra Celsum* ii. 1).

In abandoning a Jewish life-style, Jews within the Church followed Paul. His campaign against the maintenance of Jewish praxis was a leitmotiv of his mission. To Paul, the praxis was irrelevant under the new covenant in which 'there is neither Jew nor Greek' (Gal. 3: 24). He would understand the Church as the new Israel in which all were Abraham's seed (Gal. 3: 29) but he would also speak of his 'former life in Judaism' (Gal. 1: 13); the Judaic law was obsolete. Paul was therefore not a Jewish-Christian, properly speaking, even though he was a Christian of Jewish ethnic origin. Ethnicity alone cannot be a criterion for determining whether a person is a Jewish-Christian. The history of Christianity is littered with examples of Jews who converted to Christianity and ceased to maintain their Jewish identity or life-style. Jerome speaks of 'a believing brother who had been a Jew' (*Ep.* cxxv. 12). The Theodosian Code records laws which forbid harassment of Jews who fled Judaism 'and resorted to the worship of God' (e.g. xvi. 8. 1, AD 315/339; cf. xvi. 8. 5, AD 335; xvi. 8. 28, AD 426).

Furthermore, any attempt to define Jewish-Christianity by theology alone is doomed to fail. The theological positions of Jewish-Christian groups varied considerably. A distinctive 'Jewish' theology defined by some modern scholars is, moreover, arbitrary, since all the main beliefs of early Christianity are grounded in post-exilic Jewish thought. Christianity is the child of Judaism. The very idea of a Christ is a Jewish one. The Christian God is the Jewish God.

From the late second to the fourth century the Church Fathers condemned groups who sustained Jewish praxis, but the Fathers tended to be loose in their descriptions of such groups. A. F. J. Klijn and G. J. Reinink's analysis of the relevant patristic texts shows that these writers tended to refer to any observance or belief that was perceived as in some way 'Jewish' as 'Ebionite', and went much by hearsay and what others had written before them.[11] This makes heresiological study of the groups mentioned in such texts an extremely complex field, since what might be termed 'Ebionite' by one writer is not necessarily what is referred to as 'Ebionite' by the next. While a Jewish-Christian sect of the Ebionites probably did exist in the late Roman world, we have to allow for Jerome's pejorative use of the term (*in Esa.* cxvi. 20) to refer to Christian millenarians (cf. *in Esa. Prol.* xviii; *in Zech.* xiv. 9–11; *in Zeph.* iii. 8–9), a category which includes such notables as Tertullian, Irenaeus, Victorinus, Lactantius, and Apollinaris.[12] They were by no means Jewish-Christians, but simply Christians who believed that God's holy ones would be physically gathered together in Jerusalem in the time of peace which would last a thousand years. Since this was perceived by the orthodox of the fourth and fifth centuries as a 'Jewish' idea, Jerome would label them *Ebionitae*.

Behind the patristic term 'Ebionites' lurk the 'Jewish-Christian' groups of modern scholarship, and yet the tendency manifested by the Church Fathers to mass these groups together to form a precise identifiable heresy needs today to be resisted. Jewish-Christians were not all sectarian Ebionites; they may not have given themselves a sectarian name. Some of the 'heretics' described in the third-century *Didascalia Apostolorum* are, for example,

---

[11] Klijn and Reinink (1973).   [12] See Wilken (1985), 450.

clearly Jewish-Christians (*Didasc.* xxiii–xxvi) but their opponents in the 'catholic church, holy and perfect' (*Didasc.* ix) know of no neat title under which they could be defined and no founding heresiarch who could be denounced—only that they were wrong to observe Jewish praxis: food laws, circumcision of sons, and hygiene laws.[13]

Other groups described by the Church Fathers under different titles but with the common attribute of somehow following Jewish customs (or being influenced by Ebionites) may not have been Jewish-Christian or have even existed at all. Frank Williams has pointed out that a 'sect' to Epiphanius meant anything from an organized church to a school of thought, or a tendency manifested by some exegetes.[14] He can then speak of 'Origenists' when there was no 'Origenist' church. Klijn and Reinink suggest that the 'Jewish-Christian' groups labelled by Epiphanius as 'Cerinthians', 'Symmachians', 'Sampsaeans', and 'Ossaeans' were largely the product of polemic.[15]

The Elchasaites, once thought to have been a Jewish-Christian sect, have had to be reclassified after the work of G. P. Luttikhuizen,[16] who has concluded that the group arose after an Aramaic book of revelation, written in a Parthian Jewish community at the turn of the first century, was adopted almost a hundred years later by a Christian group headed by Alcibiades of Apamea. The book may have been called *The Revelation of Elchasai*, where 'Elchasai' is a Greek transliteration of *hel kassi*,

---

[13] See Strecker (1971), 244–57. Strecker notes the argument by W. C. van Unnik (1939) that the heretics are Judaizing Christians who adopted only some Jewish praxis, but Strecker rightly suggests that the term 'heretics' would then be too harsh for the group. Certainly, Christians who adopted a few Jewish customs and participated in festivals were considered to be in error, but not exactly heretics. Strecker's view that in this part of Syria the Jewish-Christians occupied the 'orthodox' position superior to 'catholicism' (p. 257) does, however, push the evidence somewhat. The reference to 'believing Hebrews' (*Didasc.* xxi), with whom the catholic church is in communion, surely does not refer to the Jewish-Christian 'heretics' but to Jews who had converted to the 'catholic' type of Christianity.

[14] (1987), p. xviii.   [15] (1973), 3–19.

[16] Luttikhuizen (1985). Much the same conclusions about the Elchasaites were reached by Klijn and Reinink (1973: 66–7), who describe them as 'an apocalyptic syncretistic missionary movement which originated during the Roman invasion of Parthia within a Jewish community which tried to show its allegiance with the Parthians'. The relationship between the *Kerygmata Petrou* and the Elchasaites has not been satisfactorily established, but see Klijn and Reinink (1973), 78–9 (app. II).

Aramaic for 'the hidden power/God' (cf. Epiphanius, *Pan.* xix. 2. 2). The Elchasaites were therefore influenced by Jewish apocalyptic writings, and possibly by Jewish-Christians, but were not actually Jewish-Christian themselves.

This serves as an example of how complex the origins of so-called 'Jewish-Christian' groups might be (even without venturing into the problems of Pseudo-Clementine research). Certainly, it is almost impossible to see in the plethora of possible Jewish-Christian groups any real case for their being a unified movement. The Jewish-Christian Nazoraeans[17] of Syria, for example, appear to have been theologically orthodox. According to Epiphanius (*Pan.* xxix. 7. 2–5; xxix. 9. 4), the Nazoraeans used both the Old and New Testaments, including a Gospel of Matthew in Hebrew, believed in the resurrection of the dead, and proclaimed one God and his son Jesus Christ. The only difference between them and the vast majority of other churches was that they maintained Jewish praxis: Hebrew language, circumcision of sons, keeping the Sabbath, and so on (cf. *Pan.* xxix. 5. 4; xxix. 8. 1 ff.). From Jerome's quotations from a Nazoraean interpretation (*pesher?*) of the prophet Isaiah (*in Esa.* viii. 14, 19–22; ix. 1–4; xxix. 17–21; xxxi. 6–9) it appears that they accepted the apostle Paul and were deeply suspicious of the 'scribes and Pharisees', the rabbis.[18]

The Nazoraean sect, however, is not reported as being found in the heartland of Palestine. There is, in fact, no literary evidence whatsoever for Jewish-Christians existing in Galilee, Samaria, or Judaea past the beginning of the second century, as we shall see in the following chapter.

[17] The name 'Nazoraeans' is unlikely to be a sectarian self-reference; instead, it appears to indicate that a group with this name spoke a dialect of Aramaic or Syriac. The Aramaic term, transliterated into Greek as Ναζωραῖος or Ναζαρηνός was that by which the Aramaic-speaking church referred to itself from the beginning, but it carried no implication of theological separation. The Aramaic-derived word and its cognates (as opposed to the Greek-derived term 'Christians') became the normative reference to believers in Christ in Persia, Arabia, Armenia, Syria, and Palestine, providing a clue to the extent of the success of missions from the Aramaic-speaking Palestinian church; see H. H. Schaeder, in Kittel (1964–76), iv. 874–9. The rabbis referred to all Christians as *Notserim*: cf. (sing.) *b.Sanh.* 43a; *b.A.Z* 6a, 16–17a; (plur.) *b.Taan.* 27b; *b.Ber.* 17b; *b.Sota* 47a; *b.Sanh.* 103a, 107a. The *waw* in this Hebrew term may have arisen from a *plene* spelling, since the word *natserim* in Jer. 4: 16; 31: 6(5) was pronounced *notserim*; see Weinberg (1975) 473 n. 49. For a recent examination of (some) Nazoraeans as constituting a Jewish-Christian sect, see Pritz (1988).

[18] Klijn (1972); Klijn and Reinink (1973), 49–50.

The Bagatti–Testa school argues that for evidence for Jewish-Christianity in the heartland of Palestine we must look to rabbinic references about *minim* and to a description of relatives of Jesus, called *desposunoi*, living in Galilee in the second century.

Minim

Rabbinic sources mention four specific places in Galilee in which a group of Jews called '*minim*' were present: Diocaesarea/Sepporis (*t.Hull*. 2. 24), Kefar Sikhnin/Samma (*t.Hull*. 2. 22; *b.A.Z*. 16b–17a, 27b), nearby Kefar Neburaya (*Qoh. Rab*. 7. 26), and Capernaum (*Qoh. Rab*. 1. 8).

To take the last first, it may be noted that Stanislao Loffreda, in his most recent guidebook to the Franciscan excavations at Capernaum, writes: 'From the context it is clear that those Minim of Capernaum were Jews converted to Christianity, i.e. Jewish Christians.'[19] Loffreda then quotes the story of Hanina, the nephew of Rabbi Joshua, who was apparently put under a spell by *minim* in Capernaum and made to transgress the Sabbath by riding an ass. Hanina then goes to Rabbi Joshua who, after anointing his nephew with oil to heal him, says: 'Since the ass of that wicked one has roused itself against you, you cannot remain in the land of Israel any longer.' Hanina duly goes to Babylon. Loffreda informs us that the 'wicked one' is Jesus, when the reference is quite clearly to Balaam. 'The ass of Balaam' is a standard epithet in rabbinic Judaism. Balaam was the Gentile accuser of Israel (Num. 22–4) whose ass saw the angel of the Lord on the road before Balaam was able to do so (Num. 23: 21–35). Balaam in rabbinic literature mouths blasphemous arguments in general, but never specifically Christian ones.[20] Rabbi Issi's explanation of this story, that Hanina is good and the people of Capernaum evil (*Qoh. Rab*. 7. 26), would prima facie indicate that the story was understood as a conflict between a righteous man of God and wicked people (for whom the symbol was Balaam) hostile to rabbinic Jews. This tells us that the Capernaum population were viewed with disdain by the rabbis, but it does not tell us why.

---

[19] (1985*a*), 29–30; cf. (1974*b*); Bagatti (1971*c*), 21–2.

[20] *Pace* Lachs (1969–70). I am grateful to Dr Peter Hayman for this observation.

The Bagatti–Testa school would appear to believe that the term *minim* refers to Jewish-Christians, but this is an identification that has long been superseded.[21] Indeed, Jerome states that the 'Pharisees' call the 'Nazarei' 'Minaei' (*Ep.* cxii. 13), but the information provided is far from self-evident. While Jerome's anachronistic use of the word 'Pharisees' probably refers to the rabbis, it is to be remembered that the Hebrew word *Notserim*, transliterated by Jerome to refer to the Jewish-Christian sect of the Nazoraeans, was used by Jews to refer to *all* Christians. Jerome is aware of this himself, for he mentions that the Jews curse Christians three times a day 'sub nomine Nazarenorum' (*in Amos* i. 1. 11 f.; cf. *in Esa.* ii. 5. 19; xiii. 49. 7; xiv. 52. 4–6). Jerome may have mistaken the rabbis' use of the term as a reference to a Jewish-Christian sect, when it in fact referred to all Christians of the late fourth century, or else he may be saying that the Nazoraeans of Syria were indeed referred to as *minim* by the rabbis. If the first possibility is the case, then the category of *minim* had become very broad. If the second is correct, it demonstrates only that a Jewish-Christian sect was included in the category. In no way does Jerome say that *minim* are to be identified as *Notserim*. It would appear that the *Notserim* are a group to be classified as being among the *minim*, but should not be equated with them.

The word *minim* is the plural form of the word *min*, meaning 'kind, species' (cf. Gen. 1: 12—*leminehu*, 'according to its kind').[22] One of the most enlightening passages for the rabbinic use of the word is in the Babylonian Talmud, tractate *Rosh ha-Shanah* 17a, where it is said that *minim* 'have deviated from the communal norms'. *Minim* were therefore a species of Jews (or even Christian Gentiles) who did not accept the norms of the group to which they belonged (cf. *b.A.Z.* 65a). *Minut* may therefore mean 'waywardness'.

Much debate about the identity of the *minim* has focused on the *Birkat ha-Minim* in the Eighteen Benedictions, part of the daily *Amidah*. The text of this was supposedly written by Rabbi Samuel ha-Katan and approved by Rabban Gamaliel II in the last decades of the first century AD (*b.Ber.* 28b). The scope of the reference is

---

[21] For the old view that the term *minim* frequently referred to Jewish-Christians, see Herford (1903), esp. 255 f. Cf. Freyne (1980), 344–91.

[22] Jastrow (1950), 775.

not easy to determine. In its early form it may have been a curse against the *Notserim* rather than all the *minim*. William Horbury points out that Justin (*Dial.* xvi, xciii, xcvi, cxiii, cxxiii, cxxxiii) and Tertullian (*Adv. Marc.* iv. 8. 1) believed that the curse applied to Christians,[23] which would indicate that the word *Notserim* was found in the curse by the middle of the second century, when Justin wrote, and that Justin and Tertullian understood the word *Notserim* to refer to Christians as a whole and not just the Nazoraean sect (as Epiphanius thought, cf. *Pan.* xxix. 9). The word *Notserim* is found in two texts of the old Palestinian rite in the Cairo Genizah, but scholars have recently begun to doubt the antiquity of this evidence, the originality of which was advocated by H. L. Strack.[24] It is just possible that Justin and Tertullian may have heard that the term *minim* included Christians by implication, but this seems unlikely; it is more probable that they knew that Christians were called *Notserim* by Jews. Reuven Kimelman has gone so far as to support Epiphanius' understanding of the word *Notserim*, claiming that the reference to *Notserim* in the Cairo Genizah is meant to refer to the fourth-century Nazoraeans,[25] but again this seems unlikely. Whenever the curse included the *Notserim* and the *minim* together, it would appear most probable that the rabbis really did wish to curse all Christians as such, adding at the same time a general curse against people with whom they did not agree theologically. Christianity was, after all, derived from Judaism; of all Jewish sects and offshoots, Christianity would have seemed the most offensive.

We have other literary evidence that *Notserim* were hated by at least one Jewish group in the second century: those who followed Bar Kochba. Hegesippus writes that, according to Justin Martyr, Bar Kochba commanded that Christians should be punished severely if they did not deny that Jesus was Messiah and blaspheme him (Eusebius, *Hist. Eccles.* iv. 8. 4). Bar Kochba probably viewed Christians as *minim*. Rabbi Akiba, whose name is associated with Bar Kochba, decries *minim* when he says that those reading 'outside' books, interpreted in the Babylonian Gemara as 'books of the *minim*' (*b.Sanh.* 100b), would have no share in the world to come. He may have included Christians in this category; the writings that would compose the New Testament

---

[23] Horbury (1982). [24] (1910), 31.
[25] Kimelman (1981). See also Flusser (1983–4), 32–4.

were certainly 'outside' those approved of by Rabbi Akiba. However, the animosity felt by Bar Kochba towards the Christians in Jerusalem was probably not to do with *minut* pure and simple, but also because they did not support his revolt (see below).

References to *minim* in rabbinic literature are impossible to fit into one neat category. Nicolas De Lange writes that the word was 'a convenient term to refer to different antagonists at different times and perhaps even at the same time'.[26] Martin Goodman sees a development in the scope of the term, so that in the early days *minut* referred to Jewish sectarianism, but later, in the Amoraic period, texts about *minim* might refer to (Gentile) Gnostics and orthodox Christians.[27] Rabbi Abahu's discussions with *minim* in Caesarea, some of whom are clearly Christian, gives us no proof of *Jewish*-Christianity, as these Christians inhabited a Graeco-Roman city whose population was mixed. Moreover, their views exhibit Marcionite or Gnostic beliefs[28] which would be very surprising to find amongst Jewish-Christian groups; the former sect rejected what it perceived as a Jewish contamination of the Gospel message, and Gnostic sects were generally concerned with more esoteric considerations than Jewish praxis.

Kimelman distinguishes between Palestinian and Babylonian usage of the word *min*. In the latter case *min* could apply to a Gentile but not in the former. This radical assertion lacks sure proof. He does, however, use as an illustration the one case where we do have a *min* who seems to have been a Christian and ethnically a Jew (*b.A.Z.* 16b–17a; *t.Hull.* 2. 22–24). Rabbi Eleazar, arrested once for *minut*, is coaxed by Rabbi Akiba into remembering why he might be thought to have been a *min*. Eleazar remembers that he was walking in Sepphoris when a man named Jacob from Kefar Sikhnin/Samma told him about *minut* in the name of Yeshu ben Pantiri. Yeshu ben Pantiri is a known reference to Jesus.[29] One version has it that Jacob cured Eleazar in the name of Yeshu ben Pantiri, but when Kimelman concludes that 'Jewish-Christians figured prominently'[30] in the Palestinian

---

[26] (1976), 44.   [27] (1983), 105.
[28] See Lachs (1969–70) for a survey of these texts.
[29] Cf. Neusner (1973), i, 400–3; ii, 366 f. Bagatti (1956) has argued for the *min* Jacob to be considered a Christian.
[30] (1981), 232.

understanding of *minim* on the basis of this illustration he is overstating the case.

It may be more helpful to note that magic is found as a component of *minut*. As with the *minim* of Capernaum, the *min* here displays magical powers, in this case to heal Eleazar. Use of the name of Jesus in spells does not automatically indicate that the user was a Christian. Magicians using the name of Jesus are found in rabbinic literature (*b.A.Z.* 28a; *j.Sanh.* 14. 19–25d), but this indicates only that Jesus' name was considered effective by magicians. In this instance, the magician Jacob appears to have been a Christian, since he is speaking *minut* in the name of Jesus; and in the Babylonian Talmud version he utters what seems to be an apocryphal saying: 'For the hire of a harlot she has gathered them, and to the hire of a harlot they shall return. From the place of filth they have come, and to the place of filth they will go.' This impressed Eleazar and, being impressed (perhaps the implication being that he was bewitched), he was later arrested. The practice of magic does not mark Jacob as being a heterodox Christian. Orthodox Christians were also interested in magic. Julius Africanus, for example, was interested in the craft, and recorded some of his knowledge.[31] Jesus himself could be seen to be a magician.[32] It is not known whether Jacob should be classed precisely as a Jewish-Christian, though it is possible. As regards dating, if the story is based on any real event, it should be assigned to the turn of the first century and beginning of the second.[33] Eleazar ben Hyrkanos is recalling an incident from long ago.[34]

If Jacob was a *min* because he was a Christian, this does not mean he was a Christian because he was a *min*. Christianity can in no way be identified as being the same phenomenon as *minut*. *Minut* may have meant different things to different people at different times. Even Goodman's definition of *minim* as Jews who

---

[31] See Thee (1984).   [32] See M. Smith (1978).

[33] Pritz (1988), 96–7. Bagatti believed the tomb of this *min* Jacob should be identified with the mausoleum of a Saddiq Yacub in the village of Sakhnin, but this is more likely to be the alleged tomb of Rabbi Joshua; see Bagatti (1961), 302–4; (1967); (1971b), 145–53.

[34] The historicity of the story is impossible to determine, but its general setting is consistent with what we know. Sepphoris was a market centre for pottery manufactured in Kefar Sikhnin and therefore a meeting between a villager and a rabbi in the commercial district of the city was not improbable; see Adan-Bayewitz and Perlman (1990).

absorbed Greek ideas from the coastal cities of Palestine[35] is in the end too narrow. *Minut* was anything which deviated from the community norms laid down by the rabbis. The *minim*, of course, need not have consciously thought of themselves as belonging to any sorts of sects. As Goodman has convincingly argued, the rabbis struggled for authority in Galilee and attained it, after some compromises, only as late as the fourth century.[36] The story about the *minim* of Capernaum may better be seen as part of this struggle for authority. It should be remembered that the story is polemical, and its historicity is suspect, since it was written almost 500 years after the events it purports took place. Perhaps, nevertheless, it preserves some folk memory of the Capernaum population of the second century being resistant to rabbinic authority.

It should be noted that the narrative itself tells us by implication that, since they forced Hanina to transgress the law by riding an ass on the Sabbath, the population of Capernaum were not Jewish-Christians. The careful observance of Jewish law is the characteristic feature of Jewish-Christian groups.[37] Even the so-called *am ha-arets* ('people of the land') in Galilee, of whom the rabbis did not always approve, kept the Sabbath.[38] It is hard to imagine that either the Jewish-Christians or the *am ha-arets* would have wished to make Hanina offend God so grossly by transgressing the Sabbath, even to make him look a fool, and the fact that they themselves would have been 'working' by casting a malicious spell on the Sabbath would have shown that they had little regard for the day themselves. It was people who had become lax in Jewish praxis, people who were influenced by the practices of Gentile pagans, that neglected to observe the day.

Bagatti's assertion that cities such as Capernaum, Tiberias, Sepphoris, and Caesarea had large Jewish-Christian populations because rabbinic writings make references to *minim* in or near these

---

[35] (1983), 106. See also A. F. Segal (1977), 121; Vermes (1975), 169 ff; Büchler (1956), 243–74. Büchler argued that in the 2nd to 3rd cents. in Galilee, the word *min* already denoted non-Jewish sectarians.

[36] (1983), 180.

[37] Eusebius, *Hist. Eccles.* iii. 27. 5; Epiphanius, *Pan.* xix. 5. 1; xxix. 7. 5; xxx. 2. 2, 17. 5; Jerome, *Ep.* cxii. 2; Filaster, *Div. Her. Lib.* xxxvi; Ps.-Hieronymus x; Augustine, *Contra Faust.* xix. 4; *Ep.* xvi. 16. 1; Rufinus, *Exp. Symb.* xxxvii; Theodoret of Cyr., *Haer. Fab.* ii. 1; Nicephorus Callistus, *Hist. Eccles.* iii. 13.

[38] Goodman (1983), 51, 104, 107, 177, 181.

areas is, therefore, quite unfounded.[39] As it will be argued in the next chapter, two of these four cities—Tiberias and Sepphoris—appear to have had a fair proportion of Gentile inhabitants, and one—Caesarea—was a cosmopolitan city (and formally, from the early 70s, a Roman *colonia*)[40] in which Jews formed a large minority ethnic group. The presence of *minut* in such environments, given the close proximity of Gentiles, is hardly surprising.

The Relatives of Jesus

Two other towns in Galilee, Nazareth and Kochaba, are identified by Bagatti as being predominantly occupied by Jewish-Christians from the first to the beginning of the fourth century; this stems from the mention of Jesus' relatives living in these towns in the late second century in the letter to Aristides by Julius Africanus (in Eusebius, *Hist. Eccles.* i. 7. 14).

Julius Africanus states that the relatives of Jesus went around the country expounding their genealogy. This genealogy was, according to Bagatti, an outline of their descent from David which would demonstrate 'their right to preside over the churches'.[41] In fact, Julius Africanus does not say that those relatives of Jesus who were known to him were Christians, nor does he link their actions with the Church. He uses their methods of calculating their descent from David, mainly by means of recourse to levirate marriage, to explain the discrepancies between the genealogy of Jesus in Matthew (1: 1–17) and Luke (3: 23–38). Having argued the case for the veracity of both Gospel genealogies, Africanus writes: 'Indeed, this is not undemonstrated or written off-hand; at least, the relatives of the Saviour according to the flesh, either loving ostentation or simply teaching thoroughly, but at any rate telling the truth, handed on these things also' (*Hist. Eccles.* i. 7. 11).

The genealogy supplied by Africanus is Joseph's, and it is quite possible that relatives of Joseph used precisely what Africanus outlines to determine their descent from David; but whether the genealogy was worked out before Jesus' messianic claims were made, or after the genealogies of Jesus were published in the Gospels and he was accepted as being a 'son of David' by

---

[39] (1971*c*), 21–2.   [40] See Millar (1990*b*).
[41] (1969), 15. See also id. (1966).

Christians, is a moot point. Africanus writes what reads as an apology on the relatives' behalf. Apparently, Herod burnt the records of all the noble families of the land; these were all stored in one convenient location, which explains why there were no 'official' records of the connection with the Davidic line. Had Herod really committed such an act of arson, it is surprising that Josephus does not mention it. At any rate, the relatives of Jesus claimed that a few, like them, who were diligent, collected together scraps of the genealogy and preserved the genuine record of their descent (Eusebius, *Hist. Eccles.* i. 7. 14).

In the passage that Eusebius records, Africanus uses the uncommon word δεσπόσυνοι to refer to the relatives of Jesus. It is the usual practice amongst translators of Eusebius to leave the term untranslated,[42] taking their cue from Rufinus' fifth-century translation into Latin, where the word is, mysteriously, left in Greek. The general consensus of opinion, however, is that the word δεσπόσυνοι means 'belonging to the Lord',[43] 'belonging to a lord/master',[44] 'the Master's People',[45] or 'kinsmen of the Lord'.[46] The master is understood to be Jesus, since he is twice called δεσπότης in the New Testament (Jude 4 and 2 Pet. 2: 1). G. Bardy even goes so far as to identify the relatives of Jesus as Jewish-Christians.[47]

The word δεσπόσυνος can mean 'belonging to a master', where there is a sense of *possession*, as in the case of a slave, for example; it is found in the neuter to specify the master's property (τὰ δεσπόσυνα χρήματα).[48] However, it would be difficult to argue that Jesus actually *possessed* all his relatives; they cannot be counted as his 'belongings'. The word is never used in other cases in which a family 'belonged to' a lordly ancestor. As consultation of the *Concise Oxford Dictionary* will show, the English word 'belong' carries a variety of meanings. A person can 'belong' as a possession (a slave), or as a member of some group or clan. It would seem that the proprietary sense of the Greek has not been fully realized by those who have read the definition 'belonging to a

---

[42] Crusé (1838), 20; McGiffert (1890), 93; Lawlor and Oulton (1927), i. 21; Bardy (1952), 28; Lake (1949), i. 63; Williamson (1965), 55.

[43] Lampe (1961), 339.

[44] Crusé (1838), 21; McGiffert (1890), 93; LSJ, 381.

[45] Williamson (1965), 55.

[46] Meyer and Bauer (1963), 424.   [47] (1952), 28.   [48] LSJ 381.

master', and the second of the English senses given here has been understood, when the Greek does not permit it.

There is, moreover, a perfectly reasonable alternative understanding of δεσπόσυνος: that it was simply another way of saying δεσπότης.[49] This meaning is rare, which may account for Rufinus' hesitation in translating the curious word, but nevertheless it is attested from the seventh century BC until the sixth century AD.[50] Perhaps the best confirmation that this was Africanus' understanding of the word comes from the earliest translation of Eusebius' text, which is almost universally ignored: the Syriac version of AD 462, now in Leningrad.[51] The Syriac text[52] has the word *marawata*, an honorific title used to address lords and masters, sometimes found with a possessive ending (sing. *maruteh*, 'his lordship').[53] On balance, it seems that the fifth-century Syriac translators of Eusebius understood the text better than more recent scholars. One should note that Africanus says that the relatives of Jesus were *called* δεσπόσυνοι, as if this was a form of address. A translation of δεσπόσυνοι as 'lords' would, moreover, fit with the context; the relatives of Jesus were boasting of their descent from *David*, not of their relationship with Christ. The passage may then be translated:

However, a few of the careful ones, who had personal records of their own, either having a recollection of the names or otherwise getting them from copies, are vain about[54] the memory of noble descent being preserved; among these were the aforementioned[55] called 'lords' because of their connection with the line[56] of the Saviour. From the Jewish villages

[49] Ibid. This is Liddell and Scott's sense II.

[50] Sophocles (1870), 352.

[51] A 6th-cent. copy exists in the British Museum (BM 14639). The 5th-cent. Armenian version is a translation from the Syriac; see McGiffert (1890) 53. Rufinus' Latin translation was made shortly after.

[52] See Wright and McLean, with Merx (1988), 36.

[53] See Payne-Smith (1891), cols. 2209–10; Prof. S. Brock, personal communication.

[54] In Syriac, the text clearly reads that the relatives of Jesus 'boast' or 'glorify themselves', with an implication that they were arrogant. The sense is more derogatory than is plainly evident in the Greek. The pejorative overtones of Africanus' description of Jesus' relatives appears also to have been noted by Rufinus, who translated the Greek here as 'in primis gloriabantur'.

[55] 'The aforementioned' are 'the relatives of the Saviour according to the flesh' (*Hist. Eccles.* i. 7. 11).

[56] Γενός is a word of numerous meanings. I have used 'line' in order to avoid an emphasis on Jesus here; it is the family tree that is of key interest to the relatives of Jesus, not their relationship to him in itself.

of Nazareth and Kochaba they went around the rest of the country and, so far as they were able, they narrated the above-mentioned genealogy, and (the one) from the Book of Days. (Eusebius, *Hist. Eccles.* i. 7. 14)

It would seem likely that they travelled around the country reciting their Davidic genealogy not because they wished to claim authority over the churches, which are not mentioned, but because they vainly (in both senses of the word) wanted to be considered aristocrats in Israel; truly this was a high-minded aspiration for a group of lowly villagers from Galilee.

The genealogy is traced from Joseph, and therefore it might be asked whether the relatives of Jesus display 'Ebionite' ideas in their belief that Jesus was descended from Joseph rather than, physically, only from Mary.[57] However, it should be remembered that the canonical Gospels also trace Jesus' physical descent from Joseph, not Mary. Luke has: 'Jesus . . . being the son (as was supposed) of Joseph' (3: 23), and then lists Joseph's descent from David, and Adam. Matthew has the genealogy down from David, to 'Joseph, the husband of Mary of whom Jesus was born' (1: 16). Moreover, a multitude of early versions of Matthew 1: 16 have: '. . . Joseph, to whom was betrothed Mary the virgin, begot Jesus who is called Christ'.[58] Hegesippus (see below) and Africanus both indicate that it was the physical brothers of Jesus, sons of Joseph, who were descended from David. The development of orthodox theology would later find this a problem. The idea of Mary's descent from David is first found in the third-century *Protevangelium of James*. There is in the second century nothing necessarily 'Ebionite' about the tracing of Jesus' descent from Joseph: it was an early belief of the Church which was soon discarded. Bagatti has suggested that the later evidence of two Davidic genealogies, one from Joseph and one from Mary, shows that 'two different branches in Nazareth had preserved their own house and their own records,'[59] tying his hypothesis down to Byzantine physical edifices (for which, see Chapter 11).

It would be reckless to suggest that all Jesus' relatives were, during the first century, Christians. The Gospel evidence which sees

---

[57] Cf. Irenaeus, *Adv. Haer.* v. 1. 3.

[58] Manuscripts O, f¹³; l⁵⁴⁷ᵐ; it.ᵃ, ⁽ᵇ⁾, ᶜ, ᵈ, ᵍ, ⁽ᵏ⁾, ᑫ This reading is also attested by Ambrosiaster (4th cent.) and in the Syriac Sinaitic version (3rd cent.).

[59] (1969), 15.

Jesus' relatives as being hostile to his mission undoubtedly reflects a situation in which some of them were against him. John makes a pointed reference to the unbelief of Jesus' brothers (John 7: 5). Luke has Jesus almost cast over a cliff for claiming to be the Messiah after preaching in the synagogue of Nazareth (Luke 4: 16–30; cf. Mark 6: 1–6; Matt. 13: 53–8). The Synoptic Gospels preserve a pericope which is at best ambiguous, and which would seem to imply that Jesus spurned his unbelieving family in favour of his true family, namely those that believed in him (Matt. 12: 46–50; Mark 3: 31–5; Luke 7: 19–21).

Bagatti's theory that the grandchildren of Jesus' brother Jude, who, according to Hegesippus, were arrested during the reign of Domitian (81–96) as being descendants of David (*Hist. Eccles.* iii. 20. 1–5), were bishops of Nazareth and Kochaba respectively seems to push the evidence. The Roman authorities were apparently worried about people who claimed Davidic descent, since they were possible messianic pretenders, and there was concern about their capacity to raise an army of rebellion. The line of questioning of the two who were arrested concerns their financial resources, their property, and their concept of a Messiah and his Kingdom. It was determined that they owned only thirty-nine *plethra* (about twenty-five acres) of land on which they paid taxes, farming it by their own labour, and that they possessed 9,000 *denarii* between them, which was the value of the land. From their response, it would seem that their understanding of a future Messiah was eschatological and heavenly, but nothing is said of Jesus. Their interrogator, called 'Domitian Caesar' for the purpose of the story, then dismisses the pair as being contemptibly lower class. Hegesippus adds that upon their release they 'came and presided over every church' as witnesses and members of the Lord's family, and lived on until the time of Trajan (Eusebius, *Hist. Eccles.* iii. 32. 6; cf. iii. 20. 6).

The language may be formulaic, a way of according the grand-nephews of Jesus a nebulous authority, but it does not make them actual bishops. Jude himself is traditionally considered a Christian, and the letter of Jude in the New Testament is traditionally thought to have been written by him.[60] Certainly, there is some reason to consider that his grandsons believed in Jesus as Messiah,

[60] See Bauckham (1990).

since Eusebius considers their interrogation to be an instance of the early persecution of the Church (*Hist. Eccles.* iii. 20. 5), but the historicity of the tale is doubtful. Not only does it employ the emperor Domitian as a protagonist, which seems to be poetic licence, but the names of the two men are not remembered. One might ask to what extent they could have been significant church leaders if their names were soon forgotten. Furthermore, a century had elapsed between the time this event took place and the date when Hegesippus began to record the history of the Church; quite enough time for legendary elements to have crept into the story.[61]

Nazareth and Kochaba

The two towns in Galilee from which, according to Africanus, the relatives of Jesus came, are not definitively linked with Jewish-Christianity. Africanus himself writes that they are 'Jewish towns' (cf. Epiphanius xxx. 11. 10, on Nazareth). A list of priestly courses found in Caesarea, dated to the third or fourth century, mentions Nazareth as one of the places where priestly families lived.[62] Preserving the tradition, the priestly family Hapizzez (cf. 1 Chron. 24: 15) is recorded as living there in a ninth-century liturgical poem by Eleazar ha-Kalir.[63] It would certainly be odd for Nazareth to have been known as a Jewish village inhabited by priestly stock if it was in fact populated by Jewish-Christian sectarians. There is no mention of *minim* or *Notserim* living in Nazareth in any surviving Jewish literature.

Africanus' Kochaba, however, has not yet been identified with absolute certainty, and some would connect his attestation of a place named Kochaba with attestations by fourth-century writers of a town with the same name inhabited by Jewish-Christians. According to Epiphanius, for example, Κωκάβα, or Χωχάβα (in 'Hebrew'), was the name of a town located in the Bashan which was occupied by Nazoraeans (*Pan.* xxix. 7. 7; cf. xxx. 2. 8–9,

---

[61] John Chrysostom, commenting on John's Gospel, notes that the 'lords' were admired everywhere for a long time, but that their names were not known: a simple deduction from what is preserved in Eusebius' text (*Hom. in Joh.* xxi. 3, *PG* 59, 132).

[62] Avi-Yonah (1962), 139.   [63] Klein (1909), 5.

18. 1). Since Epiphanius addresses his *Panarion* to priests from Coele Syria, who would presumably know the region well, his information stands a good chance of being correct. Moreover, he is quite specific about the town's location. He places it near two towns which can be pin-pointed on the map—Karnaim (map ref. 242250) and Ashtaroth (245246), in the southern part of today's Golan (see Map 1). Michael Avi-Yonah has accordingly identified Kokaba/Chochaba with the remains of a town close to these places, twenty-seven kilometres east of the Sea of Galilee (at map ref. 237248).[64]

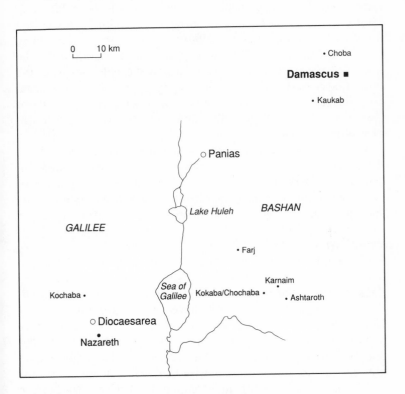

MAP 1. Possible towns named Kochaba during the Roman and Byzantine periods in the regions of Galilee and the Bashan

---

[64] *GRP* 50; Schumacher (1886), 83.

Almost a century before Epiphanius, Eusebius wrote of a village named Χωβά, in which 'those of the Hebrews who believe in Christ, called Ebionites' lived (*Onom.* 172. 1–3; cf. Jerome, *Lib. loc.* 112). He describes this village as being in the same region as another Choba 'to the left of Damascus' (cf. Gen. 14: 15). He may be referring to the Kokaba/Chochaba that Epiphanius would later mention, since Χωβά and Χωχάβα would have been pronounced similarly, or else his evidence may suggest that Jewish-Christians lived in yet another village in the region of the Bashan, close to Damascus. A reason to believe that his Jewish-Christian Choba corresponded with Epiphanius' Chochaba would be if his other Choba 'to the left of Damascus' corresponded with the remains of Kaukab, fifteen kilometres south-west of Damascus, adjacent to the hill of Mar Boulos (St Paul). In the late Roman period, the town was pagan, and a temple stood on the hill, though in the Byzantine period the site became known as the place where Paul was converted.[65] There is, however, another contender for this Choba, a modern village of the same name ten kilometres north-west of Damascus.

Kochaba was in fact quite a common name for villages throughout the Semitic east. Aramaic *kokheba*, Syriac *kawkeba*, and Hebrew *kokhba* all translate 'star' or 'planet'. The names of towns called 'star' probably originated from their association with the ancient Semitic star-god mentioned by the prophet Amos (5: 26).[66] The feminine form of the name in Syriac indicates the planet Venus.

We may be justified in looking for Africanus' Kochaba not in the Bashan, but closer to Nazareth, since he gives us no reason to think that the village was composed of Jewish-Christians. Indeed, there was a village named Kochaba very near Nazareth, in central Galilee (map ref. 173248).[67] We know that Rabbi Dositai was born in a town named Kochaba (*Pesikta rabbati* 16), which may be this one, but otherwise we know nothing about it. At any rate, it does not appear to have been Jewish-Christian. If we have any worthwhile evidence for the location of Jewish-Christians, it comes from the fourth century, and relates to the area of the Bashan.

---

[65] Meinardus (1980).   [66] *EJ* ii. col. 884; cf. Testa, (1962*b*), 182–8.
[67] *GRP* 50; Bagatti (1961), 300–4; (1969), 19.

The Golan

There is archaeological evidence which may point to the most western extent of possible Jewish-Christian groups in the Bashan, but as yet it is inconclusive. Claudine Dauphin, in a survey of a Roman-Byzantine village named Farj, located in the southern Golan, noted inscriptions with both the Jewish candle-holder (menorah) and Christian symbolism together. Similar inscriptions were found by Schumacher at Khan Bandak and Butmiyeh,[68] as well as by W. F. Albright at nearby Nawa.[69] Dauphin argues that the inscriptions in Farj show that Jews, Jewish-Christians, and later Monophysite Christians lived together here in the Roman and Byzantine periods.[70] What is clear is that the village was originally Jewish.[71] At some point, Christian inscriptions were drawn by people from a Jewish iconographical tradition. They therefore used the symbol of the menorah along with the standard crosses, fishes, and palm branches used by Christians everywhere. Dauphin herself wonders whether the inscriptions were drawn by descendants of Jewish-Christian refugees from Pella and cites Bagatti's theory that the existence of two synagogues in a Jewish community shows a split between Jews and Jewish-Christians.[72]

Farj had two synagogues, one of which was later converted into a Christian church. However, a drawing on the lintel from this church (Figure 5.2) probably shows the cross on the Rock of Calvary, which dates the inscription to the middle of the fourth century at the earliest. The type of menorahs depicted in the inscriptions in one Christian inscription is Byzantine (Figure 5.3); A. Negev has dated menorahs with the horizontal bar at the top to the second half of the fourth century onwards. The menorah without a bar on top then became rare from the fifth to the seventh century.[73] This type is also found at Farj. In addition, there is at Farj a peculiar kind of cross-menorah (Figure 6) with a bar at the top, similar to one found by G. Schumacher at Breikah, ten kilometres north of Farj.[74]

---

[68] (1888) 116, fig. 27 (Butmiyeh); 183, figs. 74–6, on different slabs (Bandak).
[69] (1925), 14.
[70] Dauphin (1984). See also ead. (1982).   [71] Dauphin (1984), 240–1.
[72] Ibid. 243; cf. Bagatti (1971c), 23; (1965), 292.   [73] Negev (1963).
[74] (1888), 114–15, fig. 23; also see Z. U. Maoz (1985). For a general survey of the Golan in antiquity, see Urman (1985).

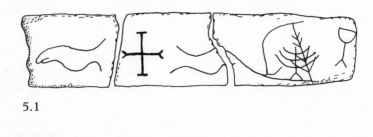

5.1

5.2

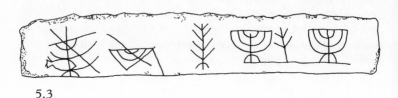

5.3

FIG. 5. Farj: inscriptions on masonry

If all the inscriptions were produced for a Christian building at more or less the same time, they may then be placed between the latter part of the fourth century and the early fifth. This dating would fit with the known datable features. Since there was an orthodox church presence in the area of the Bashan (Aere Bataneae) at the beginning of the fourth century and probably earlier,[75] the possibility that the Jews of Farj were converted to orthodox Christianity is equally as likely as their being Nazoraeans. The presence of multiple synagogues in a community is not in general indicative of different theological persuasions but of the

[75] We know this because a bishop from this area went to the Council of Nicaea in 325; see Chapter 3 below.

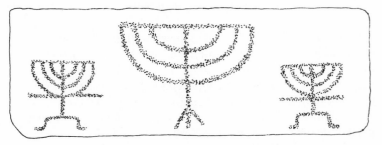

FIG. 6. Farj: inscriptions on masonry

size of the community.[76] The people who made these inscriptions were almost certainly ethnic Jews who had become Christians. Whether they were Jewish-Christians, however, is not shown conclusively by the evidence. The presence of a menorah with Christian symbols does not immediately indicate Jewish-Christians; a tombstone dated to 551 in the southern church at Eboda, for example, has both crosses and the menorah.[77] The menorah, seen as a candle-holder, a source of light, was a good symbol for Christians who might wish to indicate Christ.

Without excavations that might provide further clues, it is impossible to define the group with any accuracy. An important indication of the group being Jewish-Christian would have been if Hebrew was used to express a Christian message, but the language of the Farj inscriptions is Greek (Figure 5.2). Nevertheless, in the absence of further material that would absolutely confirm the situation one way or another, the Farj material is just possibly the work of converts to the Nazoraean sect, since Farj lies in an area geographically close to Epiphanius' Kokaba/Chochaba, as it has been positioned by Avi Yonah (see Map 1).

Jerusalem and Pella

The Jerusalem church itself is never denounced by the Church Fathers as having fractured into 'Ebionite' sectarianism. According

[76] Two or three synagogues have been found in Sepphoris and two in Tiberias, although literary sources report that the regions of Sepphoris and Tiberias had 18 and 13 respectively; see Levine (1981*a*).
[77] *EAEHL* ii. 353.

to Eusebius (from Hegesippus), the members of this church were 'Hebrews in origin, who had received the knowledge of Christ with all sincerity' (*Hist. Eccles.* iv. 5). Jewish ethnicity alone does not make a church Jewish-Christian, but most people in the church may have continued to maintain a Jewish life-style. As it was argued above, this was not considered to be a mark of heresy until after the middle of the second century. There is no indication that the dispute recorded in Acts 15 and Galatians 2 continued to plague dealings between the Jerusalem and Pauline churches anywhere in the Empire or beyond. Acts itself indicates that the situation was settled. It is probably best to imagine that there continued to be frequent exchanges between the Jerusalem church, the churches founded by missionaries from Jerusalem (such as the church of Rome), and the Pauline churches. As stated above, the Jerusalem Christians were persecuted by Bar Kochba during the Second Revolt (Eusebius, *Hist. Eccles.* iv. 8. 4), though one can but speculate on the reasons for this. Certainly, it is unlikely that the Christians would have supported the revolt. Moreover, it is probable that Bar Kochba viewed with deep suspicion a community who had dealings with the very Gentiles whom he wished to remove from authority in Israel. It would appear from Eusebius that Bar Kochba did not ask the Christians to return to the praxis of Judaism, from which we may infer that they had not in general abandoned it by *c.*130.

After the suppression of the Second Revolt, Hadrian banned Jews from Jerusalem (now Aelia Capitolina), and the Jerusalem church became Gentile; bishops of the church henceforth had Greek names (cf. Eusebius, *Hist. Eccles.* iv. 5. 1–4; cf. *Dem. Evang.* iii. 5).

Nevertheless, it would be going too far to imagine that there was an absolute break between the 'Jewish' Jerusalem church before the war and the 'Gentile' one that followed it.[78] We do not need to assume that all the Jewish-Christians packed their bags and fled,

[78] The notion that there was absolutely no continuity between the Jerusalem church of before 135 and the church subsequent to that date was propounded by Turner (1900) and has been widely accepted. It should probably be remembered that any church in Jerusalem between the years 70 and 135 would have been very small. Excavations show that, not just the Temple, but many other parts of Jerusalem in these years lay in ruins, and very few Jewish tombs were used at this time. Settlement in Jerusalem was then sparse. I am grateful to Prof. D. Barag for this observation.

leaving an empty space for entirely alien Christians from other places to step into. If there had been friendly contacts between the church of Jerusalem and other Palestinian churches prior to the Revolt, then it is very likely that efforts were made to maintain the continuity of traditions and customs, even though the personnel of the church may have changed. Moreover, we do not need to assume that all the members of the church fled. They need only have declared themselves no longer Jews to stay. If it is probable that during the middle of the second century many ethnically Jewish Christians were abandoning the praxis of Mosaic law, and thereby becoming 'Gentile', then it is very possible indeed that certain members of the Jerusalem church dropped Jewish praxis after the Revolt and thereby stayed in their ancestral city. It would have been a very tempting option. After persecution by Bar Kochba and his supporters, they may have felt unease at being still linked with Judaism, and it would have been natural if members of the church began to think of themselves as quite separate from other Jews, having more in common with the universal church, which had largely abandoned Judaism. It may be significant that there is no legend of a 'flight from Jerusalem' after the Bar Kochba Revolt, only one which tells of a flight to Pella after the Jewish War, in AD 70 (see below). At any rate, we can surely imagine that at least one or two members of the church abandoned Jewish praxis, declared themselves no longer Jews, stayed in the city, and passed on the traditions of the church to new members from outside. The transition from 'Jewish' to 'Gentile' church may have been as smooth as it appears to have been elsewhere. Those who did not wish to forsake Mosaic law would have had to go to Caesarea, or other places; perhaps even to the Bashan.

Some scholars have sought to find continuity between the fourth-century groups of 'Ebionites' east of the Jordan rift and the Jerusalem church by arguing for the historicity of the so-called Pella tradition[79] recorded by Eusebius (*Hist. Eccles.* iii. 5. 3) and Epiphanius (*Pan.* xxix. 7. 7–8; xxx. 2. 7; *De Mens. et Pond.* xv). Epiphanius makes a clear connection between these Jewish-Christian groups and refugees from Jerusalem. In this tradition the Jerusalem church fled to Pella, across the Jordan in the region of

---

[79] Simon (1973); Koester (1989); Pritz (1981), and see the bibliography and discussion in id. (1988), 122–7.

the Decapolis, during the revolt of 66–70. According to Epiphanius it was in Pella that the heresy of the Nazoraeans and the Ebionites had its beginning—strangely, not in Jerusalem—but he also states (*De Mens. et Pond.* xv) that those who went to Pella returned to Jerusalem after the war was over. It would be rash to assume from this that the entire Jerusalem community went to Pella, descended into sectarianism there, and then returned to Jerusalem *en masse* as a substantially changed church. Perhaps a few returned, but it is possible that Epiphanius simply drew this conclusion to account for Hegesippus' report, used by Eusebius, of a church in Jerusalem during the Bar Kochba Revolt.

Some scholars have rejected the tradition outright as being completely lacking in historical foundation.[80] Others have sought to find the origins of the tradition in the foundation history of the Pella community.[81] At most, it would be possible to say that some Jerusalem Christians who were maintaining the praxis of Judaism, as were most of the members of this church at the time, fled to Pella. Some members of this group remained in Pella and steadfastly opposed changes in the church which culminated in the abandonment of Jewish praxis by the majority of Christians. From Pella they may have influenced a number of Christian communities east of the Jordan, and have founded new ones. Some may have returned to Jerusalem after the war. Whatever the case, the watershed date as regards the Jewish, including Jewish-Christian, presence in Jerusalem is 135. The Roman ban included not only the city but also the hill country, Gophna and Herodium (*j.Ned.* 38a) and Acraba (*j.Yeb.* 9d).[82] As will be seen from the next chapter, archaeology confirms that from this time onwards the city of Jerusalem, renamed Aelia Capitolina, was pagan.

For the Bagatti–Testa school, Jewish-Christianity is identified by race and by heterodox theology, the latter proved in some way by graffiti and symbols found at the Christian holy places. Bagatti claimed to base his own ideas about the Jewish-Christians on the human context of the first Christians and believed that archaeology itself constituted an essential source for our understanding of Jewish-Christianity.[83] He asserted that the excavations of sites

[80] Strecker (1958), 229–31; Brandon (1957), 168–71; (1967), 208–10.
[81] Lüdemann (1980).   [82] Avi-Yonah (1976*b*), 17.
[83] Manns (1979), 5.

such as Nazareth and Capernaum down to levels before the fourth century have exposed the liturgical objects and inscriptions of the Jewish-Christians who lived in these places, so that we can now better determine elements of their theological thought.[84] In defining this thought, Bagatti made extensive use of apocryphal literature, in which, like Jean Daniélou, he distinguished a Jewish-Christian theology. Without this initial identification of the literature as Jewish-Christian, Bagatti had nothing on which to base his ideas about the nature of the archaeology. Furthermore, Bagatti wrote of 'the first Christians', 'pre-Constantinian Christians', and 'Jewish-Christians' as if they were all one and the same group in Palestine. He was apparently unaware of the questions of continuity between the earliest Jewish-Christian communities of Jerusalem and elsewhere and later manifestations of Jewish-Christianity, so-called, within the early Church as a whole. Despite many references to patristic and apocryphal texts, the Bagatti–Testa school is highly selective in what it uses from the field of Jewish-Christian scholarship and has ignored recent studies that have radically altered the general perception of who the historical Jewish-Christians were. I have argued that Jewish-Christians may best be defined as Christians who were ethnically Jewish and who continued to maintain a Jewish life-style by practising the Mosaic law, celebrating Jewish festivals, circumcising their sons, and so on. The Bagatti–Testa school defines them too loosely.

From the above examination, it would seem that there is no literary evidence of Jewish-Christians living in central Palestine past the middle of the second century. Nothing supports the notion that a multifibrous strand of heterodox sectarianism unravelled itself from Jerusalem and spread throughout Palestine and the regions east of the Jordan rift. There is no literary attestation of Jewish-Christians at any later Christian holy places.

The *minim* of rabbinic literature are rarely specifically identified in a way that indicates that they are Jewish-Christians. It is well known that the category of *minim* appears to include orthodox Christians, along with almost anyone of whom the rabbis disapproved theologically. The people called *desposunoi* were not Jewish-Christians, even though they were related to Jesus. They

---

[84] Ibid. 6–7.

were interested in propounding the acceptance of their Davidic ancestry, and were not missionaries. The towns from which they came, Nazareth and Kochaba, were Jewish villages in Galilee. Another village named Kochaba in the Bashan, however, probably was inhabited by Jewish-Christians in the fourth century, and there may have been other Jewish-Christian villages in this region, perhaps as far north as Damascus and as far south as Pella. There is archaeological evidence that may have been left by Jewish-Christians in the Golan.

The Jewish-Christian church in Jerusalem appears to have been broadly orthodox in theology. After the cataclysmic events of 135, many members of the church probably fled, to where we do not know. Some members of the church may have renounced Judaism and continued to live in Aelia Capitolina. This is important when we come to consider the question of the authenticity of later holy sites in Jerusalem.

If there is no literary evidence of Jewish-Christians living in Palestine from the middle of the second century onwards, this is not to say that Jewish-Christians cannot have existed there. There may well have been Jewish-Christian pockets in villages and cities, as there may well have been such pockets all over the Empire, but if one is to identify archaeological remains as being specifically Jewish-Christian, it would be necessary to argue that these remains show incontrovertible proof of Jewish praxis being maintained by the community which left them. Symbols and strange graffiti would have to be such that no other interpretation is possible. One would need to find examples of Hebrew language, or symbols in which Jewish iconography alone is used to propound a Christian message, or inscriptions which mention Jewish customs and festivals and give a clear indication of Christian belief.

Already, however, one may be sceptical about the assertion that Christian holy places were kept safe by Jewish-Christians. To propound this hypothesis on the basis of archaeology alone would be extremely difficult, even if the archaeology did seem to indicate a Jewish-Christian presence at some of these sites during the Roman period. In looking at the origins of Christian holy places, it may be better to take a completely different approach, namely to set the archaeology of these sites in the context of what we know about the general history and demography of the land of Palestine from the middle of the second century onwards. What do we know about the population of Palestine and their religious beliefs before the emperor Constantine wrought momentous changes there? If there is no surviving evidence of Jewish-Christians past the middle of the second century, how much evidence is there for Jews or Christians in general? Where did they live? Were there sacred places in Roman Palestine? If so, to whom did they belong? These questions will now be addressed.

The Distribution of
Religious Groups in Palestine
from AD 135 to 324

BEFORE looking at developments in the early part of the fourth century that would in time establish Palestine as a holy land to which pilgrims came from the farthest corners of the Empire, it is useful to consider the centuries preceding these developments. The period from the quashing of the Bar Kochba Revolt until Constantine has often been viewed as a 'dark age' in the history of the land as a whole. Studies tend to concentrate on Galilee, where the Jewish rabbis were engaging in debates that would culminate in the formulation of the Jerusalem Talmud. Historians are often vague about the rest of the country.

Archaeology has helped to clarify the demography of Palestine considerably during these years. We are now in a position in which it is possible to determine with some accuracy where the main religious and ethnic groupings of Palestine lived.

Jews

The Jews of Palestine in the century before Constantine were conscious of shrinking in both power and distribution, and of being hedged about by other peoples with religious beliefs very different from their own. The weak Jewish position in Palestine owed much to the disastrous failure of the Second Revolt (135), and the exclusion order put upon Jews, so that they were not permitted to live in a large part of former Judaea.[1] Many towns and cities in Judaea were completely destroyed, and later Christian pilgrims

---

[1] Tertullian, *Adv. Jud.* xiii; Justin Martyr, *Dial.* xvi; *Apol.* i. 77; Eusebius, *Hist. Eccles.* iv. 6. 3. See Avi-Yonah (1976b), 50–1, and also p. 17 for a map showing the exclusion zone.

would remark upon the ruins.[2] Jews were employed in the date and balsam plantations in the southern Jordan Valley, around Jericho (*b.Shab.* 26a) where there were Jewish villages, as well as in an area between Eleutheropolis and Hebron, called the Daromas (see Map 2). Some were to be found around Narbata (cf. 1 Macc. 5: 23), Samaria, and the Jezreel Valley, but the main centres of Jewish life and culture were the cosmopolitan Graeco-Roman cities of the coastal plain, especially Diospolis (Lydda), Jamnia, Azotus, and Caesarea. Jews lived in the former Decapolis region, the Golan and Bashan[3] and, particularly, rural Galilee.[4] Michael Avi-Yonah has estimated that more than a third of the Jewish communities were urban in character, and contained over half the Jewish population of Palestine.[5]

In Galilee, the situation was different. The 'indigenous' Galileans themselves were Jewish as a result of the forced conversions of 103 BC,[6] and the Judaean refugees of the post-Revolt period were not altogether impressed by these country-folk. The *am ha-arets* of Galilee were often thought of as inferior intellectually and theologically. Nevertheless, the centuries that followed brought about an acquiescence to the rabbis on the part of the agricultural Galileans, and compromises from the rabbis, which would result in a sense of Jewish solidarity centred in Galilee, with Tiberias as Palestinian Judaism's unofficial capital.

In the third century, there appears to have been a relaxation in practice, if not in law, of the Roman ban on Aelia and its environs. Simeon Kamtra, a Jewish donkey-driver whose course took him near the city, questioned rather wearily whether he had to rend his garments as an act of sorrow *every* time he passed it by.[7] Rabbis Hanina, Jonathan, and Joshua ben Levi visited Aelia,[8] while Rabbi Meir and a group of pupils managed to settle there briefly.[9] With the economic and political crises that beset the Empire in the third century, the Roman authorities appear to have had little

---

[2] Thedoret, *Cur. Affect.* xi. 71; Jerome, *Comm. in Soph.* i. 15–16; John Chrysostom, *Hom. in Psalm.* x. 9.

[3] See Z. U. Maoz (1981*a*), (1985), (1988); Dauphin and Schonfield (1983); Dauphin (1982).

[4] Avi-Yonah (1976*b*), 15–19.   [5] Ibid. 18.

[6] Aristobulus I appears to have been the agent of this change; see Schürer (1973), 217–18.

[7] Avi-Yonah (1976*b*), 80.   [8] *Gen. Rab.* 32. 19; 81. 4.

[9] Avi-Yonah (1976*b*), 79–81. See also Alon (1973), 55, 116–17 on the 'holy community which is in Jerusalem' (*b.Beizah* 14b; 21a); Safrai (1973).

MAP 2. Palestine in the third century AD

energy to guard Aelia against Jewish infringements of the ban. Rabbi Jonathan said, 'Anyone who wants to go up there can go' (*b.B.M.* 75b).

The Empire's crisis, which had allowed this to happen, also shook the Jewish communities of Palestine. The burdens of taxation and the hardship of rampant inflation were too heavy for many to carry, and emigration to Babylon could no longer be successfully discouraged.[10] As the economic depression became more and more severe, areas of Jewish settlement shrank. People could no longer make a living from the land. Jewish life outside Galilee became even more urban in character. There were only seven Jewish villages left in the Daromas at the end of the third century[11] and a handful in the lower Jordan Valley. The Jewish communities in Samaria disappeared, and those in the Golan, Bashan, Jezreel Valley, and western Galilee decreased.[12] Avi-Yonah estimates that in Galilee itself the Jewish population may not have been more than half the total.[13] The Jerusalem Talmud records that Rabbi Yohanon taught: 'most of the Land of Israel belongs to Israel', but his pupil, Rabbi Eleazar, said: 'most of the Land of Israel is in the hands of Gentiles' (*j.Dem.* 2. 1. 22c).[14] Rabbi Yohanon may have been optimistic, but his statement is evidence of some Jewish self-confidence. A wave of emigration shattered this confidence, and Jews saw themselves as a clear minority overall in the Promised Land.[15]

Third- and fourth-century authors stress the smallness of Jewish occupation in Palestine. Celsus wrote that the Jews were 'bowed down in some corner of Palestine' (Origen, *Contra Celsum* iv. 36),[16] a matter that Origen did not dispute. The emperor Julian's version of Jewish history (*Contra Galilaeos* 209d–213a) seems to be influenced by the Jews' depressing present as much as by their

[10] Avi-Yonah (1976*b*), 123–4. For the economic plight of third-century Palestine, see also Sperber (1978), 526–38.
[11] Avi-Yonah (1976*b*), 16.   [12] Ibid. 132.   [13] Ibid.
[14] For the extent of the territory perceived as Eretz-Israel at this time, see *t.Shev.* 4; *Sifre Deut.* 10; *j.Shev.* 6. 36c. The approximate boundary ran from the Waters of Gaaton, 9 km. north of Ptolemais, to the area of Paneas, and then went south-east to the borders of Bostra, south of Petra, and west to Ascalon. It thereby included the Golan, where there were a number of Jewish settlements, but excluded much of *Palaestina Tertia*, which was almost entirely populated by Gentiles. See also J. Sussman (1981). It is highly probable that the Samaritans were included with the Jews in 'Israel' in estimates of population proportions from the Palestinian Talmud, which preserved more of the accepting attitude towards the Samaritans reflected in parts of the Mishnah (e.g. *m.Ket.* 292; *m.Dem.* 9: 'A Samaritan is like a fell Jew') than did the Babylonian Talmud; cf. Schur (1989), 47–8.
[15] Answering a question on the meaning of the term *terra repromissionis*, Jerome says, 'The Jews assert that it is this land Palestine that is the land of promise' (*Ep.* cxxix. 3); see Wilken, (1985), 446.
[16] Chadwick (1953), 211.

past. According to Julian, their fortune was miserable: 'one small tribe which, hardly two thousand years earlier, had settled in one portion of Palestine' (*Contra Galilaeos* 106c–d).[17]

Despite Avi-Yonah's estimate, however, there is little literary or archaeological evidence for pagan worship in Galilee itself. Goodman's observation that the rabbis may have called people 'Gentiles' who nevertheless thought of themselves as Jews (or Samaritans?) warns us against taking rabbinic comments about the preponderance of Gentiles on face value.[18] There were, however, significant Gentile presences in the heartland of Galilee in the cities where Roman administration was centred: Diocaesarea (Sepphoris) and Tiberias. Through these district capitals the taxes were channelled to the Empire. The machinery that operated this important task was in the hands of pagans, the imperial officers and bureaucrats, who were supported by a pagan army.[19] However, these assertions must be reconciled with the fact that Epiphanius includes Diocaesarea and Tiberias in his list of places where no 'Hellene' (pagan), Samaritan, or Christian lived among the Jews (*Pan.* xxx.11. 9–10). He writes that no Gentile lived μέσον αὐτῶν, literally 'in the middle of them'. The solution may be that the Roman authorities ruled *over* the Jews, and that Diocaesarea and Tiberias were Jewish towns with a pagan ruling class which kept themselves socially separate, but this does not solve all the problems raised by Epiphanius' statement. Alternatively, it is possible that by the time Epiphanius was writing, in the late fourth century, the Roman administration had eroded away so that Jewish self-administration had replaced outside rule; Epiphanius then presumed this had always been the case. However, at the beginning of the century, Diocaesarea was a place in which ninety-seven Christians from the porphyry mines in Egypt would be tried by a Roman ruler.[20] Eusebius mentions that in his day in the 'large city' of Diocaesarea 'all the inhabitants are Jews' (*Mart. Pal.* (Syr) viii. 1), and it was they who watched the martyrdoms of the Egyptian Christians. In Eusebius' story of the events here, we would seem to have a clear case of a Jewish population governed by a stratum of Roman authorities.

The archaeological evidence from Sepphoris clearly attests a Gentile pagan presence in the Roman period, and literary sources

[17] See Rokeah (1982).   [18] (1983), 53.   [19] *EAEHL* iv. 1052–4.
[20] Eusebius, *Mart. Pal.* viii. 1, and see Barnes (1981), 357 n. 39.

apart from Epiphanius inform us of it. There was an impressively
large theatre,[21] which is evidence for the builders' expectations of
a correspondingly large audience, though a majority, if not all, of
the audience may have been Jews with few scruples about theatre
attendance. A temple of the Capitoline triad is recorded[22] and a
temple of Jupiter found on coins. The use of Roman sarcophagi,
found embedded in the walls of the present citadel, shows that
there were pagans there to be buried in the Roman manner. A
magnificent Dionysus mosaic, dating from the middle of the third
century, suggests that the god may have been revered here.[23] Two
statuettes from Greek mythology, one of Pan and one probably of
Prometheus, were found in a cistern.[24]

In Tiberias there was a Hadrianeum, which Epiphanius himself
mentions (*Pan.* xxx. 12. 1–2), apparently finding no reason to try
to reconcile this with his previous statement which has it that there
were no pagans to maintain such a temple. Goodman has
suggested that the structure was 'probably in ruins' in the middle
of the third century on the basis of the Jerusalem Talmud's tractate
Aboda Zara (4. 4. 24a), as interpreted by S. Appelbaum,[25] and
Avi-Yonah suggests the same.[26] Epiphanius says it was unfinished,
and yet still a ναὸς μέγιστος ('large temple'), and that people may
have started to restore it as a public bath (*Pan.* xxx. 12. 2).
Epiphanius admits to being rather unclear on the matter, as shown
by his repeated use of τάχα ('probably'). There were, he
understood, four walls standing made of huge stones. The
difficulty is that, from this fourth-century information, we cannot
know whether this was the state of the temple in the third century.

Furthermore, while it is true that we should sometimes be wary
of positing the existence of temples from coin types, when a mint
looked for local inspiration it tended to mark the significant cultic
features of a city. Goodman's view that numismatic evidence
shows a 'shaky indication of respect' for Zeus and Hygeia in
Tiberias[27] is therefore a trifle too weak. The gods were depicted on
coins not because there was a shaky respect for them, but because
the authorities in charge of the mint thought Zeus and Hygeia
fitting symbols for the city of Tiberias. It may be argued that

[21] Meyers, Netzer, and Meyers (1986), 13; comm. by eid., *IEJ* 35 (1985), 296.
[22] *GRP* 95.   [23] Meyers, Netzer, and Meyers (1987).
[24] Eid. (1986), 4–5.   [25] Appelbaum (1976), 6; Goodman (1983), 46.
[26] (1976*b*), 46.   [27] (1983), 46.

Hygeia is depicted simply because of the baths at Hammath, south of the town, but Zeus cannot be explained so easily. The representations of Zeus may be better seen as confirmation of the existence of the Hadrianeum. It is well known that Hadrian showed great reverence for Jupiter/Zeus. In the temple of Zeus Olympius at Athens the statues were of Hadrian. Sometimes, for example at Prusias, he was directly identified with the god.[28] The same may have been the case at Tiberias.

On the other hand, there may well have been some kind of disruption of Roman control over Tiberias in the middle of the third century. Rabbi Yohanan apparently ordered the destruction of statues of the gods in the public baths at Hammath (which also tends to suggest that it may well have been considered an Hygeian sanctuary).[29] The earliest synagogue at Hammath dates from the third century, under which a second-century building, resembling a gymnasium in plan, has been discovered. M. Dothan thinks this earlier building was a synagogue too, since later synagogues were frequently built on the ruins of earlier ones, but a significant find— a glass goblet shaped like a centaur—does not cohere well with this interpretation.[30] It seems more probable that we have a pagan public building, perhaps indeed a gymnasium, which was torn down and replaced with a synagogue in the third century. All this does at least argue against M. Simon's view that Tiberias was full of pagans at the end of the third century,[31] but prior to this there may well have been a significant Gentile pagan population.

At Diocaesarea (Sepphoris), the relationship between the Jewish leaders and the Roman administration appears to have been quite cordial. Coin legends from the reign of the emperor Caracalla (198–217) minted at Diocaesarea read: 'Diocaesarea, the Holy City, City of Shelter, Autonomous, Loyal, Friendship and Alliance between the Holy Council and the Senate of the Roman People'.[32] Talmudic stories about Rabbi Judah and the emperor seem to reflect a situation in which pagans and Jews,

---

[28] Ferguson (1970), 40–1. When Hadrian was planning his world journey some time after 120, he issued a coin depicting Jupiter, as lord of the world, placing it under the emperor's care. At the end of Hadrian's life coins were issued honouring Jupiter under the titles of Victor, Protector, and Guardian, while after his death a dedication to Jupiter Best and Greatest seems to honour Hadrian himself, identified with the god.

[29] Avi-Yonah (1976*b*), 47.   [30] (1981), 64.

[31] (1964), 49.   [32] Meyers, Netzer, and Meyers (1986), 7.

probably living as different social strata, undertook dialogue.[33] They were sometimes physical neighbours; the Jerusalem Talmud refers to a Roman living next to Rabbi Jonathan in Sepphoris in the late third century (*j.B.B.* 2. 11. 7b). Certainly, this warns us against taking Epiphanius' remarks about a fourth-century situation as being true for the third century. It is very likely that Gentile pagans and Jews did live together in Diocaesarea and Tiberias at this time.

The villages of Galilee cannot have been greatly threatened by Gentile settlement since, as Goodman points out, no disputes between village communities are recorded and the co-operation between villages attested in Jewish literature is good evidence for a basic similarity of outlook amongst the inhabitants.[34] Such accord also provides good evidence that there were no wholly Jewish-Christian villages in Galilee that might have caused disharmony.

Nevertheless, the Jewish heartland was tiny, and influence from the Gentile pagans was hard to guard against. Despite the rabbis' attitude to their own *minim*, there was a fairly liberal attitude towards the (non-Christian?) Gentiles. Jews were given licence to trade and interact with them, subject to certain controls.[35] Jewish artists and craftsmen adopted some of paganism's artistic repertoire. E. E. Urbach sees this development as pragmatic, and reflective of a new awareness of the distinction between idolatry and decoration,[36] as well as showing that Jews were being influenced by Gentiles overall.

The style of Galilean synagogues mainly came from Nabataean and Syrian architecture of the Roman period.[37] The iconography of synagogue decoration combined typically Jewish motifs: the menorah and the Ark, with fertility symbols (the palm tree); vine ornamentation that recalls Dionysiac motifs; oriental magical symbols like the pentagram ('the Seal of Solomon') and the hexagram ('the Star of David'); the sun-eagle of Syrian religion; winged victories, and fabulous animals.[38] From the fourth to the sixth century, Jews did not object to the depiction of Helios and

---

[33] Ibid. 6–8.   [34] (1983), 29.   [35] Ibid. 180.

[36] (1959). Rabban Gamaliel justified his visit to the Baths of Aphrodite in Ptolemais by saying that the image of the goddess was there only for adornment: *m.A.Z.* 3. 4.

[37] Amiran (1956), 244; Foerster (1981): the temple of Baal-Shamin at Sia and the Nabataean temple at Sahur are clear parallels.

[38] Avi-Yonah (1976*b*), 75.

the zodiac on their synagogue floors, such as at Beth Alpha, Na'aran, Hammath Tiberias, Husifa, or, without Helios, Susiya. The zodiac represented the cosmos.[39] They did not mind, either, King David being represented as Orpheus, as he was in the sixth-century mosaic in the synagogue of Gaza.[40] All this indicates that there is a possibility that material discovered at Jewish sites which might not fit into the distinctive norms of Jewish iconography may yet be Jewish and not, by default, Jewish-Christian.

Christians

If Epiphanius' fourth-century comments give unreliable evidence for population groups in third-century Diocaesarea and Tiberias, what should we make of his further statement that no Samaritans or Christians lived among the Jews in these places either? The context of this observation is a section dealing with the efforts of the Jewish convert, *comes* Joseph of Tiberias, who wished to build churches in Jewish strongholds in Galilee, *c*.335. Epiphanius writes that no churches had yet been erected in Jewish towns and villages of Galilee because of the rule that: 'neither Hellenes (pagans), nor Samaritans nor Christians are to be among them. This [rule] of permitting no other race is observed by them especially at Tiberias, Diocaesarea which is Sepphoris, Nazareth and Capernaum.' (*Pan.* xxx. 11. 9–10)[41]

While Epiphanius refers to a past event in telling the story of Joseph of Tiberias, he uses here the passive *present* tense φυλάσσεται, and not the past. This seems to emphasize that Epiphanius is writing of a situation in his own time. On the basis of what he knew of current Jewish attitudes in certain places, he must have reached the conclusion that Jews had not permitted other religious/ethnic groups to live amongst them at any earlier time. It might well have been true for the mid-fourth century, when Joseph was living, and true to a large degree even by the time of Eusebius (see above, *Mart. Pal.* (Syr) vii. 1), but we know that Gentile

---

[39] Foerster (1987).

[40] Ovadiah (1981a).

[41] The translation given by Williams (1987: 128) lists the towns in the way that makes Diocaesarea and Sepphoris seem like two different places, which was not the case.

pagans lived there as a governing class in most of the third century; what about Christians?

Those like Bagatti and Testa who have argued for a Jewish-Christian presence in the Jewish heartland of Galilee continuing into the fourth century maintain that Epiphanius did not consider Jewish-Christians as 'Christian' at all and therefore ignored them.[42] It is correct to say that Epiphanius considered Jewish-Christians to be heretical, but his discussions of specifically *Christian* heresies precludes us from thinking that he ruled them out as being non-Christian 'Jews' even if he greatly disagreed with them. It was precisely because the heretics were Christians that Epiphanius was so infuriated about their notions and practices.[43] While Epiphanius is careful to point out the geographical distribution of 'Ebionites' and Nazoraeans, he never once mentions that they were to be found anywhere west of the Jordan rift. An argument *ex silentio* for the existence of Jewish-Christians is then too great a licence to take with Epiphanius here, unless we have strong contradictory evidence, as in the case of Gentiles in third-century Diocaesarea. Moreover, since Epiphanius tended to include anything, hearsay or true, which outraged him about the Christian heresies, we can be reasonably sure that if he had heard of groups of Jewish-Christians living in the towns of Jesus' childhood and ministry he would have informed us of the scandal. What we cannot know precisely, however, is how long before the time of Epiphanius Christians left Galilee.

The first reliable evidence we have for the distribution of churches comes from the year 325, when bishops from Palestine attended the Council of Nicaea; none came from the Jewish towns of Galilee. We know that Christian communities existed in the following towns and cities: Paneas, Ptolemais, Maximianopolis/Legio, Caesarea, Sebaste, Diospolis/Lydda, Jamnia, Azotus, Ascalon, Gaza, Eleutheropolis, Nicopolis, Aelia Capitolina/Jerusalem, Jericho, Neapolis, Scythopolis, Capitolias, Gadara, Esbus, Philadelphia, and also the region of Aere Bataneae (the Bashan).[44] This list does not tell us how long Christians existed prior to the fourth century in these areas, nor does it inform us of the sizes of the groups. As

---

[42] So Bagatti (1969), 16–18, and see Manns (1977).

[43] Goodman (1983), 106.

[44] See the list found in *Patrum Nicaenorum Nomina*, and Van der Meer and Mohrmann (1958), map 4.

for the ethnic origins of these Christians, cities such as Jamnia, Jericho, Eleutheropolis, Diospolis, Azotus, and Caesarea all had sizeable Jewish populations, and it is, of course, very possible that some Christians were drawn from the Jewish communities. In Nicopolis and Neapolis, where there were large Samaritan populations (see below), some Christians may have been Samaritan in ethnic origin. However, ethnicity was not linked to any 'ethnic' theologies.

The church in Aelia appears in Eusebius' story of Narcissus and Alexander (*Hist. Eccles.* vi. 9–11). Eusebius also informs us that during a persecution in the reign of the emperor Valerian (253–60) three Christian men, Priscus, Malchus, and Alexander, were thrown to wild beasts in Caesarea (*Hist. Eccles.* vii. 12). They did not come from this city, but Eusebius does not give their native town. In the same passage, Eusebius mentions a Marcionite woman who suffered the same fate in Caesarea. Later a Roman soldier of Caesarea named Marinus was beheaded for failing to sacrifice to the emperor and for being a Christian (*Hist. Eccles.* vii. 15). Astyrius, a member of the Roman senate, may also have been a rare Christian believer from the upper classes, but this may be legend. It is said that Astyrius enacted a miracle by silent prayer at Paneas causing the sacrifice thrown into the springs there to reappear on the surface of the water when it normally disappeared into the depths. Astyrius himself may well have been as surprised as everyone else at the phenomenon. The material given by Eusebius seems to indicate only that Astyrius was sympathetic to Christians (*Hist. Eccles.* vii. 17).

Our most informative source for Christianity in Palestine at the end of the third century and the beginning of the fourth is undoubtedly Eusebius' *Martyrs of Palestine*.[45] Since only the governor of Palestine, resident in the provincial capital, Caesarea, had the legal power to punish Christians who refused to sacrifice after the edict of 23 February 303, Christians from throughout Palestine were sent to the city[46] where, conveniently for history,

---

[45] For the short Greek version, see G. Schwartz (ed.), *GCS* 11 (1908), and cf. *PG* 20, cols. 1457–1518. The complete long version survives in a Syriac manuscript from AD 411 (BM Add. MS 12,150), and was translated by W. Cureton (1861). The short version is frequently found included in translations of Eusebius' *Ecclesiastical History*, e.g. in McGiffert (1890) it appears as an appendix to Book 8 (pp. 342–56).

[46] Barnes (1981), 150.

Eusebius lived. As edicts against the Christians became progressively harsher, Eusebius recorded the martyrs' fates and usually their provenances. In doing so he has provided us with a rough indication of how Christians were distributed in Palestine.

T. D. Barnes believes that Eusebius did not intend to provide a complete list of Palestinian martyrs, but rather that he wished only to preserve the memory of those he knew personally.[47] In his *Ecclesiastical History* (viii. 13. 7) Eusebius writes that he would not try to give an account of the martyrdoms of Christians throughout the whole world since the records of martyrs belonged with those who had seen them 'with their own eyes'. Instead, 'for those coming after us, I will indeed record those well-known [struggles] to which I myself was near [παρεγενόμην] by means of another written work.' Perhaps this is an indication that Eusebius himself recorded only those martyrdoms he had witnessed with his own eyes, and the phrase in the Syriac unabridged manuscript, 'the deed also which is seen by our eyes bearing witness', as read by W. Cureton,[48] might also be used to bolster this interpretation. However, as Cureton notes in his introduction to the text, Eusebius records two events which took place on the very same day, the martyrdoms of Romanus in Antioch and Alphaeus and Zacchaeus in Caesarea.[49] He could not have been present at both. Eusebius says in the Syriac long recension that he has recorded the martyrs he knew about from 'the mouth of . . . those believers who were acquainted with them'. This suggests that Eusebius was not present to witness all the martyrdoms he reports. Eusebius emphasizes the fates of those he knew personally, like Pamphilus, but those he did not know are still mentioned. There are the shadowy figures of the 'three youths' (*Mart. Pal.* viii. 2–3), four members of Pamphilus' household (*Mart. Pal.* xi. 15–18), a group Theodosia spoke with (*Mart. Pal.* vii. 1–2), a group from Gaza (*Mart. Pal.* viii. 4), and others. Eusebius does therefore appear to have attempted to give a reasonably comprehensive account for posterity.

Table 1, which shows the martyrs and the churches to which

---

[47] Ibid. 154.

[48] (1861), 1. It may be argued that it is time for a new English translation of this important Syriac text.

[49] Cureton (1861), p. vii.

TABLE 1 *Eusebius'* Martyrs of Palestine *and their Churches*

Martyrs	Churches	Mart. Pal.
Procopius and companions	Scythopolis	i. 1–2
many local church leaders	whole province[a]	i. 3
Zacchaeus	Gadara	i. 5; Syr. 5
Alphaeus	Caesarea (formerly of Eleutheropolis)	i. 5; Syr. 5
Romanus	a village of Caesarea (killed in Antioch)	ii. 1–5
Timothy	Gaza	iii. 1
Agapius	Gaza	iii. 1; vi. 1–7
Thecla, a Montanist[b]	Gaza	iii. 2; Syr. 11
Montanist companions of Thecla	Gaza?	Syr. 11
Timolaus (Timotheus)	Pontus	iii. 2–4
Dionysius	Tripolis	iii. 2–4
Romulus	Diospolis	iii. 2–4
Paesis	Egypt	iii. 2–4
Alexander	Egypt	iii. 2–4
Alexander	Gaza	iii. 2–4
Apphianus (Syr. Epiphanius)	Caesarea (formerly of Lycia)	iv. 2–15
Theodosia	Caesarea (formerly of Tyre)	vii. 1–2
large group of Christians whom Theodosia spoke with	unknown	vii. 1–2
Silvanus and companions	Gaza	vii. 4; xiii. 1 ff.
Domninus	unknown	vii. 4
Auxentius	unknown	vii. 4
Pamphilus and others	Caesarea	vii. 4–5; xi. 1–19
some young men	unknown	vii. 4
some young women	unknown	vii. 4
97 Christians	Egypt (from mines in Thebais)	viii. 1
three youths	Palestine	vii. 4

TABLE 1 *Eusebius'* Martyrs of Palestine *and their Churches*

Martyrs	Churches	Mart. Pal.
a group of Christians	Gaza	viii. 4
Ennatha (Syr. Hatha)	Gaza	viii. 5–8
Valentina	Caesarea	viii. 5–8
Paul	unknown	viii. 9–12
130 Christians	Egypt	viii. 13
Antoninus	unknown	ix. 4–5
Zebinas	Eleutheropolis	ix. 4–5
Germanus	unknown	ix. 4–5
Ennathas	Scythopolis	ix. 4 ff.
a group, including Ares, Probus, Elias	Egypt	x. 1
Peter (Apselamus, Syr. Absalom)	Anaea (Syr. Aia)	x. 1–2
Asclepius, a Marcionite	unknown	x. 2; Syr. 39
Vales	Aelia	xi. 1–5
Paul	Jamnia	xi. 1–5
five Christians	Egypt	xi. 6–14
four members of Pamphilus' household, including Porphyry	Caesarea	xi. 15–18
Adrianus	Batanaea	xi. 29–31
Eubulus	Batanaea	xi. 29–31
Theodulus	Caesarea	xi. 24
Julian	Cappadocia	xi. 25
Seleucus	Cappadocia	Syr. 42

[a] McGiffert (1890) translated this as 'many rulers of the country churches', which implies rural parishes, but since οἱ ἐπιχώριοι refers to the native population of a country, τὸ ἐπιχώριον is the local custom, and as an adjective indicates something in or of a country or district (see LSJ 566), it would seem likely that 'local' is the best modern English word for the Greek. Eusebius means to indicate the churches of the province of Palestine, not 'country churches' in a pastoral landscape.

[b] Certain 'natives of Palestine' were condemned to pugilistic combat in the arena. This group probably included Agapius and Thecla (iii. 1; cf. v. 1–7) from Gaza. Thecla, however, is called a 'Phrygian' (Syr. MS, p. 11), and 'together with the rest of the Phrygians' (also from Gaza?) she is martyred in Caesarea. It seems unlikely that the term refers to the group's original provenance, as Eusebius implies they were all Palestinians, but rather to theology. Eusebius knows Montanism as 'the Phrygian heresy' (*Hist. Eccles.* iv. 27; v. 16, 18–19; vi. 20). The Phrygians here are therefore most likely to have been Montanists. Their identity as such is entirely omitted from the short Greek recension.

they belonged, helps to determine the geographical distribution of Christians at the beginning of the fourth century.[50]

Eusebius gives us twenty-four named individuals from Palestine, and numerous other Palestinians included in groups. Companions and others are said to come from Caesarea, Scythopolis, and, in particular, Gaza. In addition, there are six named individuals— Domninus, Auxentius, Paul, Antoninus, Germanus, and Asclepius —whose provenance is unrecorded, but since they are familiar by name to Eusebius and otherwise not noteworthy, it is likely they were friends or acquaintances of his from Caesarea. As mentioned above, there are also anonymous persons whose provenance is unknown. These were probably Palestinians not personally known to Eusebius, people whose fates he had heard about since they were sentenced in Caesarea. A striking feature of Eusebius' record is the number of named foreigners he includes: Paesis and Alexander from Egypt, Timolaus from Pontus, Dionysius from Tripolis, Apphianus from Lycia, Theodosia from Tyre, Julian and Seleucus from Cappadocia. All these people may well have been resident in Caesarea at the time of their arrest, as is explicitly stated with Apphianus and Theodosia. This would explain how Eusebius came to know them, and would correspond with what we know of Caesarea as a cosmopolitan city and an international port. In addition, there were groups of Egyptians passing through Palestine, and Egyptians in Palestinian mines.

The list suggests that the main concentrations of Christians were probably in Caesarea and Gaza. In addition, Eleutheropolis, Scythopolis, Gadara, Batanaea, Aelia, and Jamnia also had Christian churches. It is, then, not surprising to find that all these places sent bishops to the Council of Nicaea. Eusebius also mentions the village of Anaea as producing a martyr: Peter/ Absalom. In his *Onomasticon*, Anaea is listed by Eusebius as one of three Christian villages in Palestine (*Onom.* 26. 9, 13–14). With another, Jethira (*Onom.* 88. 3; 108. 1–4; 110. 18), it lay in the Daromas, in the territory of Eleutheropolis. While these villages were located in an area known to have been populated also by a proportion of Jews, Eusebius does not mention that they were 'Ebionite'. Eusebius admires the ascetic young man Peter/Absalom who was burnt on a pyre, and gives no indication that he was

---

[50] The Syriac manuscript pages are given only when the Syriac text supplies vital information not found in the short Greek text.

anything but orthodox. Both at Eleutheropolis and Mamre/
Terebinthus there were important pagan cult sites, and probably,
with shrinking Jewish landholdings, the majority of the population
in the region by the end of the third century was pagan. There is,
then, no reason to suggest that Peter/Absalom came from a
Jewish-Christian community. Another Christian village named
Cariatha (*Onom.* 112. 14–17) was located well into pagan territory
on the other side of the Dead Sea. This completes the record of
where Christians were known to have lived in the region of
Palestine prior to Constantine.

As mentioned above, some of the cities where Christians were
found also had large Jewish communities, so it is quite probable
that there were ethnically Jewish Christians in the churches,[51] but
an ethnic Jew who becomes a Christian is not the same as a Jewish-
Christian, properly defined. Eusebius does not mention the latter
at all in his account of the persecutions in Palestine, even though
he includes Marcionites (and cf. *Hist. Eccles.* vii. 12) and
Montanists. The presence of such sects in the country shows that
Palestinian Christianity did not develop in isolation, but was part
of the wider Church, even before Constantine turned his attention
to the province. The many foreign martyrs of Palestine known to
Eusebius reinforces the impression that the church of Palestine
kept close contact with churches of other lands. The Palestinian
church was influenced by the theological trends of the second and
third centuries, both heretical and orthodox, including, it would
seem from Jewish sources, Gnosticism,[52] but the overwhelming
impression we get from Eusebius' account is that most of the
martyred Christians in Palestine were within the bounds of
mainstream theology. There is absolutely no mention of any
Ebionites. Bagatti's idea that the Roman authorities could not
reach as far as places inhabited by Jewish-Christians[53] does not

---

[51] Several Tannaim and one of the Amoraim lived in Eleutheropolis (*GRP* 38;
EAEHL i. 19 f). The synagogue north of the Crusader city in Caesarea is from the
3rd cent. (*EAEHL* i. 271). Later synagogues and/or literary sources testify to
Jewish communities also in Scythopolis, Gaza, Diospolis, Ptolemais, Jamnia,
Azotus, Jericho, Batanaea. It should be noted that Scythopolis, Caesarea,
Nicopolis, and Neapolis had large Samaritan populations in their territory, and
smaller Samaritan populations existed in Diospolis, Ptolemais, Jamnia, and Gaza;
see Schur (1989), 52. So converts to Christianity may have come from Jewish,
Samaritan, or Gentile ethnic groupings; this provides us with no clues as to their
theology, *pace* Bagatti (1971c: 19).

[52] See Lachs (1969–70); also Basser (1981).   [53] (1971d), 41.

seem likely in view of the known comprehensiveness of the persecution. If it could reach as far as a little village like Anaea, it could reach anywhere.

So again, looking from the perspective of Christian distribution in Palestine, we do not find Jewish-Christians. What happened to Jewish-Christians that caused their probable disappearance from Galilee, Samaria, and Judaea, although they had lived in these places in the first century (cf. Acts 9: 31), is a matter for speculation. It may well be that when abandonment of Jewish praxis became the norm in the Church, and Jewish hostility toward them became extreme (perhaps during the Bar Kochba Revolt), Christians simply moved away from Jewish settlements and went to the cosmopolitan cities. Some of those who wished to maintain a Jewish life-style may have joined groups in villages east of the Jordan. Whatever the case, there is no evidence of Christians, let alone Jewish-Christians, living in Galilee by the time Eusebius was writing. Christians appear to have lived in areas of mainly pagan occupation.

Samaritans

According to Jewish tradition, the Samaritans were the outcome of intermarriage between Gentile pagan foreigners and the Hebrews of the Northern Kingdom, which took place after the Assyrians vanquished Israel in 721 BC; a process which corrupted the true faith of Yahweh.[54] The Samaritans, on the other hand, considered themselves to be the guardians of the pure religion of Moses, accepting the Pentateuch alone as inspired scripture. They continued to call themselves 'Israelites'[55] and spurned the Jerusalem-centred religion of Judaea and the Jews.[56]

[54] Cf. 2 Kgs. 17; Josephus, *Ant.* ix. 288–91. See Montgomery (1907), 48 ff.

[55] The Samaritans considered themselves the original Israelites from whom the Jews split in a schism after Eli moved the ark of the covenant from Shechem (Neapolis) to Shiloh; see Pummer (1987), 31; Schur (1989), 19–23. For use of the term 'Israelites', see Kraabel (1884); cf. Anderson (1989), 105. While Samaritans called themselves 'children of Israel' or 'observant ones', the Jews came to call them 'people from Samaria', 'lion converts', or *Kuttim* (Cuthaeans), regarding them as being intermixed with Cuthaeans from Mesopotamia who settled in Israel after the Assyrian invasion.

[56] In Ezra 4 the Samaritans' forebears are not permitted to help restore the Temple.

The Samaritan religion was not recognized as a *religio licita* in the same way as was Judaism, and Origen informs us that on account of circumcision they were persecuted (*Contra Celsum* ii. 13). During the third century, the Samaritans had a renaissance of sorts when Baba Rabba succeeded in gaining political autonomy for Samaria,[57] and there was a corresponding revival in worship, language, and literature. Samaritans would, however, suffer persecution under the Christian emperors from Constantine onwards, which prompted them to engage in repeated revolts.[58] In 484 a particularly fierce uprising was suppressed, with a loss of about 10,000 Samaritan lives,[59] and the emperor Zeno destroyed what may have remained of the Samaritan temple on Mount Gerizim, replacing it with a church.[60] Resentment again flared into violence thirty-eight years later; during this revolt Constantine's splendid church at Bethlehem was burnt. The Samaritans managed to seize Scythopolis and met with some success until their eventual defeat. This time about 20,000 Samaritans died and, for those that remained, severe persecution, fines, and slavery crippled the Samaritan communities in Palestine for good.[61] Their subsequent demise forms a striking contrast to the history of the Jews. However, it is necessary to put aside their poor situation in later centuries when considering the century before Constantine. In this period, Samaritans were a vigorous and significant population group in Palestine.

The focal point for the Samaritan religion was the holy Mount Gerizim (see Map 3) and the temple on its main peak, which had been, ostensibly, a temple to Zeus.[62] The temple, built in the fourth century BC, was apparently dedicated to Zeus Hellenios (Josephus, *Ant.* xi. 257) or Zeus Xenios (2 Macc. 6: 2), and was destroyed by John Hyrcanus in 128 BC. Another temple from the second century was built on the lower peak, Tel er-Rās, and was dedicated to Διὸς ὑψιστός.[63] Excavations at the site of this second

[57] I have adopted the dating of B. Hall (1989: 53–4) for Baba Rabba, but see Schur (1989: 66–7), who follows the suggestion by Cohen (1981: 225–6) that his dates should be c.308–28.

[58] For a history of the Samaritans in the Byzantine period, see Crown (1986); Schur (1989), 82–91.

[59] Avi-Yonah (1976b), 241–2.

[60] Montgomery (1907), 112 f.

[61] Avi-Yonah (1976b), 243.

[62] *GRP* 61.

[63] Anderson (1980). The reference to the sanctuary of Zeus Hypsistos comes from Marinus of Neapolis, see Stern (1980), ii. 673–75, no. 543.

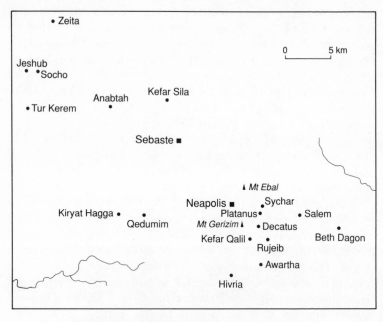

MAP 3. Region of dense Samaritan settlement

temple were conducted by R. Bull between 1964 and 1968. What was believed to be a temple of the second to third century AD was discovered (building A), and a podium of unhewn stones under it (building B) was dated to the third century BC.[64] Recently, however, the dating has been revised and it seems that both constructions distinguished by Bull are Roman. The temple was built in two stages: the first part under Antoninus Pius (138–61) and the second probably under Caracalla (198–217). It is now known that there was a fortified town on the main peak of Mount Gerizim, which may be identified as Louza, attested by Eusebius (*Onom.* 120. 11).[65] The site of the first temple probably continued to be the place of Samaritan worship, even though there was no significant building there, while the second-century temple may

[64] Bull (1968).

[65] For a summary of recent excavations and thought on the matter, see Pummer (1989), 166–9; Magen (1986), (1990b). For coins depicting the cult on Mount Gerizim, see Schur (1989: 45–6), who argues that there was a syncretistic form of worship here in which Samaritan and pagan elements were combined.

have been used only by pagans. It was, without doubt, on the site of the older temple that Zeno built the church, and his purpose in doing this was clearly to deliver a severe blow to the Samaritan faithful. Since Mount Gerizim was used by pagans as well as Samaritans, this might explain why the rabbis equated the two (cf. *j.Pes.* 1. 27b).

There was a 'Samaritan strip' according to rabbinic sources (*b.Hag.* 25a; cf. *Eicha Rabati* 3. 7) around ancient Neapolis and Sebaste, but it is difficult to determine how extensive this strip was. Literary sources attest that there were numerous Samaritan synagogues within a fifteen-kilometre radius of the mount. This literary evidence, combined with archaeological discoveries, informs us that Samaritan settlements probably existed in places such as: Awartha, Decatus, Hivria, Kiryat Hagga/Hajja, Kefar Qalil, Macher, Platanus (Balata), Rujeib, Salem (Sanim), and Sychar. At Platanus there was a Samaritan sacred tree next to a synagogue.[66] Identification of Samaritan remains is, however, controversial, especially if inscriptions are absent.[67] In Nablus there are the remains of an ancient Samaritan synagogue in the al-Hadra (Ḥuzn Yaʿqub) mosque; two Samaritan decalogue inscriptions have been used in its walls.[68]

Further Samaritan villages lay west and north-west of this centre near Mount Gerizim. Probable Samaritan sites include Silet edh-Dhar, Anabtah, Tur Kerem, Jeshub, Socho, Zeita, Qedumim. To the east, Beth Dagon (Beit Dejan) was also probably Samaritan.[69] Near Mount Carmel was the large village of Castra Samaritanorum.[70] A Samaritan village named Tharsila is known to have existed as far away as Batanaea.[71]

---

[66] Awartha: *GRP* 33, *MRP* 24—the tomb of a certain Pinhas has been found here; Decatus: *MRP* 24; Hivria: *GRP* 65; Kiryat Hagga/Hajja: *MRP* 25—there was a Samaritan synagogue here; Kefar Qalil: Anderson (1980), 220; Platanus: *GRP* 88, *MRP* 24; Rujeib: Anderson (1980), 220; Salem (Sanim): *GRP* 92, *MRP* 26; Sychar: Anderson (1980), 220.

[67] Pummer (1989), 136–40.

[68] Ibid. 145–7. The decalogue inscription placed upside down in the southern wall of the minaret was defaced beyond recognition during renovations to the mosque in 1980.

[69] Silet edh-Dhar/Kefar Sila: *GRP* 73; Anabtah: *GRP* 28; Tur Kerem: *GRP* 102; Jeshub: *GRP* 70; Socho: *GRP* 97; Zeita: *GRP* 103; Qedumim: Magen (1983); Pummer (1989), 162–5; Beth Dagon: *GRP* 37. For a further list of possible Samaritan sites, see Schur (1989), 51.

[70] *GRP* 48; Schur (1989), 51.

[71] *GRP* 100. This is attested in Euebius' *Onomasticon*.

The town of Nicopolis (Emmaus) was largely Samaritan (*j.A.Z.* 85. 45d); Samaritan inscriptions have been discovered there, including the earliest known inscription in the distinctive palaeo-Hebrew script used by Samaritans.[72] In the nearby village of Selebi (Salbit, Shaalvim) a Samaritan synagogue has been identified.[73] A Samaritan inscription has also been found at ancient Diospolis/Lydda.[74]

Samaritan sarcophagi have been found in the coastal region at Caesarea, Binyamma, Pardes-Hanna, Hadera, Giv'at-Haim, Pardes Hagdud, Netanya, Rosh Ha'ayin, and on the borders of Galilee at Ein Hasofet, Ar'ara, and Rehan, as well as in central Samaria at Arraba, Ajja, Kufeir, Khirbet Kheibar, Silet edh-Dhar, Nablus, Zuatha, Beit Iba, Khirbet Askar, Talluze, Khirbet el-Farua, and Akraba, and further south at Ammuriya.[75]

Lamps with Samaritan writing have been found all over Palestine. Large numbers have come from central Samaria, and from Tel Barukh on the northern boundary of Tel Aviv, Kfar Saba (Capharsaba), Tel Arshuf (Apollonia), Netanya, Caesarea, Habonim, Haifa, Kefar Ara, Ein Hashofet, Silet edh-Dhar, Beth Shean, Nahf, and Beth Shearim, the latter two places being in western Galilee. None has been found in the heart of Galilee.[76] Near Beth Shean a Samaritan synagogue has been identified.[77] While the presence of Samaritan lamps and sarcophagi indicate Samaritan manufacturers and not necessarily Samaritan use, it is generally presumed that in the majority of cases these objects were used by Samaritans.

There were significant Samaritan communities in the Graeco-Roman cities on the coast. Caesarea had a mixed population in which Samaritans were known until the sixth century AD.[78] Joppa's Samaritan community is indicated by the remains at Tel Barukh, where Samaritan amulets and lamps probably show that Samaritans

---

[72] *EAEHL* iv. 1070–1; see also Strugnell (1967), 556–9.

[73] *GRP* 97; Sukenik (1919). The building is probably 4th to 5th cent., but there may well be an earlier synagogue beneath it.

[74] See Pummer (1989), 154.

[75] R. Barkay (1987–8).

[76] V. Sussman (1978). For Tel Arshuf, see *EAEHL* iv. 1168; V. Sussman (1983).

[77] It is at Tel Istaba (197213). The Samaritan letters probably represent a Greek text, so Naveh (1981). The synagogue was built at the end of the 4th cent., but a Samaritan community may have been long in existence in Scythopolis.

[78] *EAEHL* i. 271.

were buried there.[79] A Samaritan synagogue from the sixth or seventh century AD was discovered at Ramat Aviv near the main entrance to the Ha'aretz Museum beside Tel Qasileh.[80] In Antipatris (Tel Aphek) the Samaritans formed a large part of the population.[81] A Samaritan talisman has been found in Ashdod (Azotus).[82] Six Samaritan inscriptions have been brought to light in Gaza.[83] Samaritan inscriptions discovered in the memorial to Moses on Mount Nebo (Rās Siyagha) indicate that it was probably a site venerated by the Samaritans before it became a place of Christian pilgrimage.[84]

This survey suggests that Samaritans were well distributed throughout Palestine in the period before Constantine and for some time after. It is therefore important to consider possible Samaritan origins for archaeological data that do not at once seem to be either Jewish or Christian, and to allow for the possible influence of Samaritan traditions on developing Christian ones.

Pagans

Apart from the concentrations of Jewish and Samaritan settlement, largely in Galilee and Samaria respectively, and a small Christian presence mainly in cities, the rest of the country was populated by Gentile pagans, and it was by no means an empty land. It must be remembered that there was never a time in which Judaism was the only religion of Palestine.[85] Indeed, the Hebrew scriptures are testimony to a running battle between the worshippers of Yahweh and those devoted to local or imported deities. Unfortunately for history, the descendants of the other ethnic groups in Palestine left

[79] For the lamps here, see: V. Sussman (1978), 238. For Samaritan amulets in general, see J. Kaplan (1967), (1975); *EAEHL* iv. 1074. Pummer (1987*a*) gives a complete list of Samaritan amulets which updates that of J. Kaplan (1980: 198), but argues that the existence of Samaritan amulets does not necessarily indicate the presence of Samaritans since these were worn by Christians and Jews as well. While this may be true, Naveh (1988) thinks there is no reason why Samaritan amulets were not produced primarily for Samaritans, even though other ethnic groups might have worn them on occasion.

[80] For the history of the debate about whether the building was a church or a synagogue, see Pummer (1989), 144–5.

[81] Kochavi (1981). [82] *EAEHL* i. 119.

[83] Anderson (1980), 219. [84] *EAEHL* iii. 925.

[85] Flusser (1976), 1065. For a discussion concerning an earlier period, see Schürer (1979), 85–183.

no records of their version of this conflict. By the third century AD, when Jewish power in the region had been seriously weakened, the traditions of the Gentile population of Palestine blossomed. This is attested in rabbinic writings, where the rabbis complain about 'Amorite ways' (e.g. *t. Ber.* 7. 2; *b. B. M.* 25b[86]) as well as in tractates which deal with paganism and Jews' interaction with Gentiles. The Gentiles were, in this period before Constantine, the largest and most influential segment of the population in Palestine.[87] The strength of paganism here parallels the strength of paganism everywhere during the third century.[88]

Palestine, lying on the trade route between Egypt and Mesopotamia, had been subject to many invasions, after which immigrants (from Hebrews to Phoenicians, Philistines to Romans) had settled, and had intermarried with the descendants of Canaanites and other peoples already resident in the land. After the Jews were forced to leave the area around Jerusalem, it would appear that Syrians and Nabataeans joined people from other parts of the country to settle the region (cf. Justin, *Dial.* xvi; Origen, *in Jos.* xxii. 1; Eusebius, *Dem. Evang.* vii. 1. 79; viii. 3. 10–12; Jerome, *in Esa.* i. 7). There was, of course, a Roman presence in the form of retirement colonies for Roman soldiers,[89] but the majority of the Gentile pagan population were probably native *Palestini*,[90] who had expanded their territories into former Jewish areas. They were not an homogeneous group. In the Bashan there were Ituraeans, in the south, Idumaeans, and in the east and further south, Nabataeans, while those in between preserved local characteristics consistent with their Canaanite, Amorite, Phoenician, Syrian, or other distant ancestry. All these had experienced some degree of Hellenization in the centuries following Alexander the Great's conquests, and they had thrived in the Seleucid Empire. Photius (*Bibl.* 242) records that the people of Palestine worshipped Greek gods, citing Asclepiodotus. The local gods were to varying extents equated with those of the Greek pantheon, and later that of the Romans. The local god Baal-Shamin, 'lord of the skies/heavens',

---

[86] Flusser (1976), 1080.
[87] Urbach (1959), 149–65.
[88] Geffcken (1978), 85.
[89] Mann (1983) notes that 800 veterans were settled in Emmaus, north-west of Jerusalem, after the first Jewish War (p. 41). See also Millar (1990*b*).
[90] The term was used from Ovid (*Met.* iv. 46) onwards.

appears to have been thought of as a form of Zeus.[91] Such Hellenization did not overwhelm local identity, or the identity of local gods: Resheph by any other name was still Resheph. Today, the site of ancient Apollonia corresponds to the modern town of Arshuf, which is the Arabic name for Resheph. The worship of Apollo at Apollonia appears to have been understood by the local inhabitants to be the worship of Resheph.[92]

The Canaanite traditions that had been so widespread in Palestine were long in dying, and some people may have considered themselves to be ethnically or religiously Canaanite. Augustine called Palestinians 'Canaanites' (*Ep. ad Rom.* xiii), which may be explained as polemic, but an inscription from Cirta, now Constantine, dating from before the Roman occupation mentions a certain 'Abdeshmun, son of Modir, Canaanite',[93] which is much harder to ignore.

Palestine was surrounded by entrenched paganism. Outside Galilee Jewish villages were frequently embedded in a landscape full of a variety of local and imported deities. For example, in the Bashan, where we know that both Jews and Christians lived prior to Constantine's victory, the local population was largely composed of pagan Ituraeans. A sculptured basalt lintel with a triad of two gods and a goddess was found at Mashara, along with three altars. M. Ben Dov identified the gods as the Heliopolitan triad: Jupiter-Zeus, Venus-Aphrodite, and Mercury-Hermes, but one can see, alternatively, the local deities of Hadad, Tanit-Astarte, and Melkart.[94] Lucian of Samosata (*De Syria Dea* iv) identified Astarte with Selene, which perhaps accounts for the crescent moon on her representation on the lintel. In the western part of the Bashan, the Golan, where most of the Jewish villages were located, no excavations have been undertaken, but surveys have noted pagan motifs scattered over the region. At Naʿaran, a spring was discovered with a design of an eagle, the symbol of Baal

---

[91] See Tarn and Griffith (1952), 341–2, but see also Millar's comments (1990*b*: 21–3) on the lack of correspondence between Hadad and Heliopolitan Zeus, and between Atargatis and Venus Heliopolitana. Syncretistic thinking was complex, and, while prevalent, it was not universally applied; some gods were simply not syncretized.

[92] Flusser (1976), 1070–1.

[93] Berthier and Charlier (1955), 83–4, no. 102; Teixidor (1977), 22 n. 10.

[94] G. Barkay *et al.* (1974); Ben Dov (1974).

Shamin. At Kafr Naffakh there was a statue of a man carrying a shield decorated with the Medusa head.[95]

Further south in the Hauran, the region was almost exclusively pagan. At Seeia, for example, there was a temple of Baal Shamin.[96] The same is true in the north around Mount Hermon; it was a pagan area. Hermon was considered sacred (cf. Eusebius, *Onom.* 20. 9–14) and was the home of numerous gods. Over twenty Hellenistic and Roman temples and cult sites have thus far been located, some in excellent repair, like that of Ein Harshah. At Har Senaim, fifteen kilometres east of Qiryat Shmoneh, a Roman temple has been discovered close to the ruins of one from the Hellenistic period; the altar bore the figure of the sun-god Helios. At Horvat Dura a small stone temple existed from the Hellenistic period until the sixth or seventh century AD.[97]

Even further north there were the cities of Damascus and Tyre, both of which were important cultic centres. Tyre bordered Galilee; the cultural weight of the city would thus have rested heavily on the area, and the attraction of its gods—Baal Shamin, Astarte, Heracles-Melkart, and possibly Apollo—may also have been felt.[98]

In the case of the Nabataeans, argument abounds as to the nature of their religion and the extent of their influence. Reputedly, they were Arab nomads who founded a kingdom in the second century BC in areas east of the Jordan rift in the Negev and Sinai.[99] However, according to Michael Avi-Yonah, the Arabs became a ruling stratum over a predominantly rural people whose roots were much more ancient in the region. This solution would make sense of the religious life of the Nabataean cities, for the iconography of the temples does not show us a pantheon appropriate to the nomadic, desert Arabs, but rather one which reflects the consciousness of a settled agricultural people.[100] On the other hand, Avraham Negev believes that these Arabs

---

[95] Dauphin and Schonfield (1983), 207; Schumacher (1888), 177–9; Kochavi (1973), 264.

[96] *GRP* 94.

[97] Dar and Mintzker (1987); comm. by S. Dar, *IEJ* 36 (1986), 99–100; id. (1988).

[98] See Jidejian (1969), 94 ff.

[99] For an introduction, see Bowersock (1983). On the identity of different Arab groups in Palestine and its borders, see Kasher (1988).

[100] Avi-Yonah (1961a), 57; cf. Bartlett (1979). For numismatic iconography, see Meshorer (1975).

themselves had very ancient roots in the area, particularly in the Sinai,[101] and considers that the nomads became urbanized and engaged in agriculture in the first century AD. Negev does not address the problem from Avi-Yonah's iconographical angle, but points to names as a clue to this society's origins and religious thought. He notes that 'Baal', 'Allah', and 'El', all common Semitic deities, are frequently employed in names, whereas peculiarly Nabataean gods like Dushara and Allat are rarely found. Since Dushara was the principal Nabataean god, his rare appearance in names is difficult to explain. Whatever the case, Nabataean influence was strong all around the east and south of Palestine.

The extent of Nabataean influence to the north can be seen at Hippos/Susitha, on the eastern side of the Sea of Galilee. There, the god Dushara may have been worshipped. A basalt fragment with the letters *ΔΟΥCΑΡΕΙ* was discovered here in 1974. Asher Ovadiah has suggested that Zeus and Hera, depicted on coins of the city, correspond with Nabataean Dushara and Allat. A marble panel depicting a dolphin was given a later Christian use as part of a Byzantine chancel screen. The dolphin was the symbol of Atargatis, which may point also to Syrian influence in the town.[102]

Whether influenced by Nabataean culture or not, all the cities east of the Jordan rift were powerful centres of pagan cult. In the north, close to Mount Hermon, was Paneas (Caesarea Philippi), and nearby Daphne (Dan). At Paneas a spring in a large cave which was sacred to Pan is one of the River Jordan's principal sources. A temple of Augustus was erected there by Herod the Great (Josephus, *Ant.* xv. 363), and niches in the cliff face where the cave is located were cut in the Roman period for cultic statues.[103] At Dan a Roman-period temple of a male deity has been discovered.[104] Already in the first century Josephus wrote that there was a temple to the golden calf at Daphne (*BJ* iv. 3). A bull was represented in the iconography of Baal, but Josephus may have been metaphorical, or referring to 1 Kgs. 12: 28–30. The people of the region of Daphne and Paneas were undoubtedly pagan, and there were probably pagan settlements well into the

---

[101] Negev (1986*b*).

[102] *GRP* 65; *EAEHL* ii. 522; Glueck (1965), 13–14, 24, 315–19, 359–60, 381, 392; Ovadiah (1981*b*), 103.

[103] *GRP* 44.   [104] Comm. by A. Biran, *IEJ* 26 (1976), 205.

region of upper Galilee. This has been confirmed by the recent discovery of a second-century temple and monumental tomb at Kedesh, ancient Cadasa. Two inscriptions to 'Holy God' and 'Holy God of the Sky' identify the deity worshipped there as Baal Shamin. The place may also have served as an oracular temple of Apollo.[105] Nearby, at Khirbet el-Harrawi, there may have been a temple of Athena.[106]

Like Hippos, the town of Gergesa was also located on the eastern side of the Sea of Galilee and was probably pagan, with a temple the rabbis called 'the house of Nebo' (*b.A.Z.* 11b).[107]

South of Hippos, there was a cluster of former Decapolis cities: Gadara, Abila, and Capitolias. In Abila and Capitolias, Helios was worshipped.[108] In the former city, there were a number of temples, and tombs have been found full of pagan motifs.[109] In Capitolias, there was probably a temple of the Capitoline triad.[110] Gadara had temples of Zeus, Astarte, and Hercules. A ring discovered here shows, on one face, a tetrastyle temple with Zeus on the throne accompanied by a small Nike and, on the other side, a temple with the Three Graces. Gadara also shows the Three Graces on coins from the times of Elagabalus and Gordian, which implies that it was a centre for their cult.[111]

Close by were the hot springs at Emmatha (modern Hammat Gader or el-Hamma), known as the Springs of Eros and Anteros. The therapeutic thermae and festivals held here were famous (cf. Epiphanius, *Pan.* xxx. 5. 7). The synagogue dates only from the fifth century, and while Jews before that date visited here to bathe and to determine the Sabbath boundaries between the baths and Gadara, Emmatha was markedly pagan.[112]

[105] *GRP* 44; *MRP*, 5; comm. by A. Ovadiah, M. Fisher, and I. Roll, *IEJ* 33 (1983), 110–11, 254; eid., *IEJ* 35 (1985), 189; eid. (1984); Aviram (1985); Magnes (1990).

[106] *MRP* 6.

[107] *EAEHL* ii. 459–60. Some 300 m. west of a Byzantine monastery compound there is a small, unexcavated mound known as Tel el-Kursi, occupied in the Roman and Byzantine periods as well as in the Crusader period. The Soncino edition of the Talmud identifies the House of Nebo in Gerasa rather than Gergesa, but this seems to be a rationalization. The Palestinian Talmud records that Gamaliel of Kounteh was burnt by the townspeople of Gergesa (*j.M.Kat.* 82c) which would be in keeping with Gergesa being a pagan town, and not a Jewish one; see Tzaferis (1983a), 41–6.

[108] Bowsher (1987), 66.   [109] *GRP* 25; comm. by W. H. Mare, *BA* 45: 57–8.

[110] *GRP* 47.   [111] *GRP* 58; Meshorer (1979).

[112] *GRP* 54; *EAEHL* ii. 469, 473; Hirschfeld and Solar (1981).

Moving south there were Pella,[113] Gerasa, and Philadelphia, all important towns and centres of pagan cult. At Gerasa there were temples of Artemis, Tyche, Zeus, Hera, Dionysus (Dushara), and Nabataean gods, as well as a nymphaeum. Hellenized local cults existed alongside a devotion to Isis and Serapis. There was also the universal cult of the emperor.[114] At Philadelphia there were temples of Heracles-Melkart, Zeus, and Astarte-Tyche, and a nymphaeum.[115]

In the south, in former Idumaea, was the town of Mampsis, where the necropolis has yielded three identical pendants in the form of dolphins, a small bronze bust of Zeus-Hadad, and the image of Allat-Aphrodite. Two representations of Eros carved in bone were also found here. A room with bands of frescos depicting Leda and the Swan, Eros and Psyche, and people walking with various cult objects in their hands, was also discovered.[116] These finds indicate well the diversity of pagan religious devotion amongst the Idumaeans, who probably spread north into former Jewish towns after the Bar Kochba War. Eleutheropolis (Beth Guvrin), for example, which had been Jewish in character, was released from paying tithes by Rabbi Judah the Prince (*j.Dem.* 2. 22c), because it was largely now pagan. It appears to have been a mixed town of retired Roman soldiers, other pagans, a Jewish community, and a small Christian one. The hippodrome was used for gladiatorial combats.[117]

Mamre/Terebinthus was a cult centre (for which, see Chapter 4). Bethlehem was located well into the area from which Jews were excluded (cf. Tertullian, *Adv. Jud.* xiii), and had a sacred shrine of Tammuz-Adonis (see Chapter 5). Encharim, a few kilometres south-west of Aelia, had a temple of Aphrodite.[118] As we have seen, the population of Aelia itself was almost entirely pagan, with a small Christian community. The new population was probably composed of a mixture of diverse ethnic groups by the end of the third century, though at the beginning Aelia Capitolina was a Roman *colonia*, with the camp of the X Fretensis legion. Accordingly, in the early third century, the gods of Aelia were

---

[113] *GRP* 86.

[114] *GRP* 61; *EAEHL* ii. 417–26; Ovadiah (1981b), 101–4; I. Browning (1982), 35–8; A. Segal (1986).

[115] *GRP* 87; *EAEHL* iv. 990.

[116] *EAEHL* iii. 728; R. Rosenthal (1976), 100; Negev (1971).

[117] Urman (1988); Kloner (1985a).   [118] Saller (1946).

Roman; there was a temple of the Capitoline triad—Jupiter, Juno, and Minerva—and another temple dedicated to Venus. Immigrants appear to have brought in the worship of other deities. At the site of Bethesda there was a healing sanctuary for Serapis. There are two pools connected by an underground passage decorated with frescos, and objects with dedicatory inscriptions and reliefs demonstrate the pagan nature of the site. A bone carving on a handle which depicts a partly clad female figure and a youth holding a bunch of grapes appears to have Dionysian associations. A mosaic found in 1901 near Damascus Gate may depict Orpheus.[119]

Samaria had two major pagan cities in its midst: Sebaste and Neapolis. As we have seen, the Samaritan temple on Mount Gerizim was no longer standing, and had been replaced by one further down, on Tel er-Rās, dedicated to Zeus. In the nearby city of Neapolis, Artemis and Tyche were worshipped, and there was a nymphaeum.[120] Sebaste had temples of Augustus, Kore, and Pan, and was an important centre of the imperial cult from the early third century. In the stadium there was a statue of Kore. Elsewhere, an altar with an inscription to Lady Kore has been found. A Roman mausoleum has been uncovered. Statues of Hercules, Dionysus, Apollo, and Kore-Persephone indicate where the city's religious devotion was directed. The synagogue mosaic of Rehov lists eighteen towns in the territory of Sebaste that were exempted from tithes by the rabbis: these must then have been pagan or Samaritan settlements. A stone relief showing a cap of the Dioscuri, the helmet decorated with a star over a wreath, is now in the Rockefeller Museum, Jerusalem, while an ivory of Zeus and Ganymede is exhibited in the Israel Museum (no. 35–3650).[121]

There is no doubt that Samaritans formed only part of the population of Samaria, and that Gentile pagans dominated these two major cities in the region. Pagans were probably also numerous in the countryside. At Aenam, a temple next to a spring

[119] *MRP* 8; *GRP* 69–70; comm. by N. Avigad, *IEJ* 20 (1970), 136–7; id. *IEJ* 21 (1971), 168–9; *EAEHL* ii. 612–13; Gath and Rahmani (1977); Meshorer (1989); Millar (1990*b*), 28–30; Margalit (1989); R. Rosenthal (1976), 100; Ovadiah and Mucznik (1981); cf. Friedman (1967); Rosen (1985).

[120] *GRP* 44; Flusser (1975).

[121] *GRP* 94; *EAEHL* iv. 1048; Smallwood (1976), 490; Flusser (1975); J. Sussman (1981), 153.

has been found.[122] At modern Turmus Aiya, the discovery of a third-century marble sarcophagus depicting Dionysus and the four seasons indicates a pagan presence in this vicinity.[123] Westwards, at Kfar Kesem, near Tel Aphek, there was a pagan holy tree.[124]

In Galilee, we have seen there was a pagan presence in Tiberias and Diocaesarea/Sepphoris. In the southern part of Galilee, there were numerous pagans in the territories of Scythopolis/Beth Shean and Maximianopolis/Legio.

Scythopolis had temples of Zeus (probably Zeus Akraios, 'of high peaks'), the Dioscuri, and possibly a large temple of Artemis. The place was associated with the birth of Dionysus. His wet-nurse, Nysa, was said to have been buried here. In fact, the well-known pottery figurine allegedly depicting a Madonna and Child is much more likely to be a representation of Nysa feeding Dionysus. Coins of the city show Nysa on a throne nursing the infant. The temples here indicate the existence of magnificent public cults, while the numerous figurines and statuettes found are testimony to private devotion. Two marble heads of monumental statues, one of Athena-Minerva (Israel Museum, no. 78–505) and one of Aphrodite (Israel Museum, no. 78–506) were found at nearby Tel Naharo, though their provenance was Scythopolis. A shrine of the emperor Hadrian and his consort was discovered near the city, along with a statue of the emperor. A maenad in motion and a large Hermes or Meleager with a sheep or dog were also found. Scythopolis, known to the rabbis as Beth Shean, was one of the four cities released from tithes by Rabbi Judah (*j.Dem.* 2. 22c). A Greek dedicatory inscription to the Semitic god Azeizos was recovered in the Beth Shean valley. A sarcophagus of the second century showing Leda and the Swan, hunting scenes, and a depiction of Achilles and Skyra, is now in the Rockefeller Museum, Jerusalem.[125]

Maximianopolis was a large station for Roman troops. An officer of the VI Ferrata legion set up an altar in the reign of Elagabalus. A bone carving of a male figure, possibly Dionysus,

[122] *GRP* 26; *MRP* 16.

[123] Although this is on display at the Rockefeller Museum, it does not appear to have been published.

[124] *GRP* 72; *MRP* 25.

[125] *GRP* 94–5; *MRP* 30; *EAEHL* i. 221; Schürer (1979), 38; Flusser (1976), 1066–7, 1084, 1086; Vermeule and Anderson (1981), 19; comm. by F. Vitto, *IEJ* 30 (1980), 214; Ovadiah and Roll (1987); Tsafrir (1987).

holding a cornucopia was discovered here. A Roman military *castra* was cleared on the small hill earlier this century, along with tombs dating from the third and fourth centuries. In a cave a bronze *patera* was found which depicts the face of Pan (Israel Museum, no. 43-377a).[126]

On the western borders of Galilee, the whole region of Mount Carmel was a powerful pagan holy place. Once sacred to the priests of Baal, Tacitus wrote that the name Carmel applied to both the mount and the god there, who had no statue or temple (*Hist.* ii. 78 f.). Iamblichus, the Neoplatonist, describes Carmel as a holy mountain (*Vita Pyth.* iii. 15, cf. Suetonius, *Vesp.* 5). Excavation has uncovered the base of a large statue on which is a dedication to Heliopolitan Zeus Carmelos. Forty-seven fragments of a casket carved in bone showing a Dionysian cycle were found in modern Haifa, also a Roman bath and tomb. The ruins of a temple have been found at Qod er-Rihan. A pagan holy tree existed somewhere on the mount (*t.A.Z.* 6. 8). A pottery statue of Venus with a small snake on her thigh, found in a cave in el-Wad, is now in the Israel Museum (no. 1-5156).[127]

Ptolemais, also bordering Galilee, appears to have had temples of Zeus, Tyche, Nemesis, Artemis, Hadad, Perseus, Atargatis, Pluto, Persephone, Serapis, Cybele. There were also the Baths of Aphrodite and an annual festival. The mausoleum of Memnon was located on the Belus River (Josephus, *BJ* ii. 188).[128]

All the coastal cities and towns were predominantly pagan, as they had been for centuries. At Dor there were temples of Zeus and Astarte.[129] Caesarea, the provincial capital, had many temples, including a Hadrianeum (Augusteum?) and Mithraeum, as well as a monument for Serapis and Isis. Statues of Asclepius, Zeus, and Apollo or Dionysus have been found. Coins of the city depict Zeus, Poseidon, Athena, Apollo, Tyche, Dionysus, Ares, Helios, Demeter, Hercules, Hygeia, Serapis. A statue of Artemis of Ephesus dates from the third century. A figure of a satyr is now in the Israel Museum (no. 64-490). A white marble figure of

---

[126] *GRP* 74; Negev (1986a), 220-1; R. Rosenthal (1976), 100; Rahmani (1981).

[127] *MRP* 7; R. Rosenthal (1976), 100; Flusser (1976), 1072; Avi-Yonah (1952), 118-24.

[128] *GRP* 89; *MRP* 6-7; Flusser (1976), 1094; Avi-Yonah (1959); Millar (1990b), 23-6.

[129] *GRP* 52; *MRP* 14; *EAEHL* i. 335; comm. by E. Stern, *IEJ* 36 (1986), 101; id. *IEJ* 30 (1980), 209-13.

Tyche, discovered in 1971, has been illuminated by another fragment of the same sculpture, which shows the headless torso of a male figure; this explains why many coins from Caesarea show an indistinct figure at the feet of Tyche. The Caesarea Maritima cup in the Louvre depicts 'Asklepios Leontoukhos' (lion-holder). A remarkable imported sarcophagus depicting an Amazonomachy, griffins, and trees of life is now in the Rockefeller Museum, Jerusalem, as well as a Roman funerary altar of the first or second century.[130]

Apollonia has already been mentioned as the sanctuary of the god Resheph.[131] Inland between Apollonia and Joppa was Antipatris (Tel Aphek), which had a temple dating from the beginning of the third century.[132] Joppa itself was famous for its role in the legend of Perseus and Andromeda. The fetters which bound Andromeda were exhibited here along with a spring which was tinged red, supposedly as a result of Perseus washing his bloodied hands in the water after slaying the sea monster. The bones of the sea monster had also been on display until they were removed to Rome by Scaurus (*c.*60 BC). A tomb door depicting a man with an actor's mask is now in the Israel Museum (no. 48–1421).[133]

Further south were Azotus, Ascalon, and Gaza. Azotus had a temple of Dagon, a Phoenician agrarian deity.[134] Ascalon was famous for the worship of Aphrodite Ourania (Atargatis?), also Baal (Apollo?). Coins of Ascalon have a goddess with the word Φανηβαλος (Pene-Baal), which refers to Tanit or Astarte. A small draped statue of Hercules (Heracles, Melkart) has been found here as well as reliefs of a winged Victory (Nike), a figure of Atlas, a depiction of Isis and Harpocrates, sculptures of Aphrodite kneeling, a bust and head of Pan, a relief of Pan and the nymph, a portrait of a Roman empress, and a painted tomb with pagan motifs including Pan playing a syrinx. Lead coffins made in Ascalon had Hermes on the side with vine tendrils.[135]

---

[130] Finkelsztejn (1986); Gersht (1984); *GRP* 44; *MRP* 12–13; Vermeule and Anderson (1981), 11; Levine (1975*a*), 57; (1975*b*), 18–23; Germer-Durand (1895), 75 f.; Avi-Yonah (1970), 203–8; cf. Diplock (1971); (1975), 165–6; *EAEHL* i. 271; comm. by R. Bull, *IEJ* 24 (1974), 280–2; Holum *et al.* (1988), 107 ff.; Millar (1990*b*), 26–8.

[131] Flusser (1976), 1070–2; *MRP* 18.

[132] Comm. by M. Kochavi, *IEJ* 27 (1977), 55; id. *IEJ* 35 (1985), 121; *EAEHL* i. 72–3.

[133] Flusser (1976), 1080–3.   [134] *GRP* 34; *MRP* 27.

[135] *GRP* 32; Flusser (1976), 1076; R. Rosenthal (1976), 100; *EAEHL* i. 127–9.

Gaza was a very important city, with temples of Helios, Aphrodite (Atargatis?), Apollo, Kore-Persephone, Athena, Hecate, Tyche, and Isis, but the chief god was Zeus Marnas, worshipped in the Marneion, a great temple which existed until the fifth century. Gaza had the largest known statue of Zeus in the world, which is now in the Archaeological Museum of Istanbul. North-east of Gaza, at Erez, a statue of a griffin with a six-pointed star or wheel dated to 210 has been discovered.[136] Gaza's port, Maiumas, was identified by the rabbis as the centre of a water festival which included orgiastic rites (*Sifre Num.* 131; *b.Sanh.* 67a). It is called Beth Marzeah on the Madaba mosaic map; *marzeah* means 'cultic feast' or 'revelry'.[137] In between Gaza and Ascalon, a temple has been found in Bitolium,[138] and at Diocletianopolis (Sarafia), there was a temple of Serapis.[139]

As this survey suggests, pagan occupation of Palestine in the late Roman period was extensive. It has been a strangely predominant view that Palestine during this time was rather sparsely populated, waiting for Christians to swoop in and develop it. Jewish occupation of the land certainly shrank, and, in general, times were hard amongst the rural population, but the life of the cities was thriving. Nevertheless, not all pagans lived in the cities, and this is where the above survey falters. A comprehensive summary which includes all the smaller towns and villages occupied by pagans cannot be produced. Such a 'map' would depend on a complex variety of evidence, both literary and archaeological, and neither can be complete. It is difficult to find evidence to illuminate the life of pagan villages. We are perhaps better equipped to determine the existence and religious life of Jewish communities in this period, since the rabbis recorded so much interesting information. The increasingly popular Jewish and Samaritan custom of building synagogues has also meant that we have material remains which can establish that these communities existed in certain places. On the other hand, the great religious monuments of the Graeco-Roman world are the tip of the pagan iceberg; paganism was also a matter of household observance as well as of temples. Only in the Nabataean regions have little

[136] *EAEHL* ii. 408, 417; Flusser (1976), 1073; Glucker (1987); Kasher (1982).
[137] Avi-Yonah (1954), 41.
[138] *GRP* 43; *MRP* 19.   [139] *GRP* 51; *MRP* 19.

temples been found in smaller towns and villages, pointing perhaps to some influence from Jewish and Samaritan practice.[140]

In Palestine, this household worship frequently employed small figurines, such as have been found in Beth Shean.[141] The rabbis' fear of pagan ways is to some extent justified if we remember, as Goodman has noted, that 'any house might have been used for idolatrous worship, whether custom-built and specially decorated or not, and any stone might have an idol set upon it, whether specially cut and shaped or just plastered and painted for the purpose'[142] (cf. *m.A.Z.* 3. 7).

It was characteristic of pagan religious life that very many sacred zones were venerated, whether they were temples or simply features of the land. In Palestine, it is very likely that the veneration of numerous high places (*bamot*) continued (cf. 1 Kgs. 12: 30; 2 Kgs. 21: 2–3; Deut. 12: 2). The remnants of this form of Canaanite religion may have been popular until the arrival of Islam in the area in the seventh century. This would account for the many *awliā* (sing. *weli*): domed Muslim chapels, often accompanied by trees. The word *weli* is supposed to refer to a Muslim saint who is buried under a pillar, but not every *weli* has a corpse. The *awliā* are a kind of 'Muslim disguise', as John Wilkinson puts it, for the ancient local Baals of Canaan.[143] It is then not surprising that we find the *weli* of Sheikh Ahmed el-'Areini on the acropolis of the important Bronze and Iron Age site at Tel Erani, or that a *weli* was located on the former acropolis of Gezer. Sometimes they are proximate to other venerated sites, such as the cave of Pan at Banyas (Paneas), where lies the *weli* of el-Hadr,[144] a kind of composite figure of Elijah and St George.[145]

Some pagan holy places may also have been venerated by Jews and Samaritans on a popular level. It may have been more difficult than we realize to distinguish at times between a pagan, Jewish, or Samaritan folk tradition. As we shall see in the next chapter, the

---

[140] Glueck (1965), 48–9, 56–62; *EAEHL* iii. 996, iv. 1152–9: Dhat Ras, Dibon, Er-Ramm, Kerak, Khirbet Brak, Khirbet edh-Dherih, Khirbet et-Tannur, Mahaiv, Main, Qasr Rabbah, for example. For Nabataean sites in general, see Wenning (1987).

[141] *EAEHL* i. 219.   [142] (1983), 48.   [143] (1977), 33.

[144] Tel Erani: *EAEHL* i. 89; Gezer: *EAEHL* ii. 438; Paneas: Murphy-O'Connor (1986), 155.

[145] In Palestinian folk tradition el-Hadr is a healing spirit of enormous power; see Canaan (1927), 120–5; Augustinovic (1971).

pagan site of Mamre was probably also visited by Jews. At Gilgal, twelve stones supposed by Jews to have been placed in the Jordan by Joshua (Josh. 4: 20; *t.Sota* 8. 6) were, according to Eusebius (*Onom.* 66. 5), also held in reverence by pagans. It may be significant that Samaritans appear to have venerated a sacred tree at Platanus, suggesting that they were influenced by pagan ways. While their continued veneration of Mount Gerizim had very ancient roots, their apparent veneration of Mount Nebo may have resulted from a cross-fertilization of traditions. Both Samaritans and Jews venerated tombs, which was quite a different phenomenon from the veneration of holy places as such, and will be discussed in the final chapter.

Tawfiq Canaan's extensive study of Muslim holy places in Palestine at the beginning of this century shows that the entire land was covered with innumerable sacred shrines: *awliā*, sacred trees and groves, sacred caves, sacred springs and wells, sacred stones or heaps of stones, and so on.[146] This was the deeply entrenched legacy of pagan life in Palestine. The proliferation of holy places in Palestine is not a recent phenomenon; Palestinians today have continued the religious beliefs of their ancestors, despite the change from paganism to Islam. The Gentile pagans of third-century Palestine would have perceived the land as similarly covered with sacred zones.

Worship of dolmens is mentioned by the rabbis (cf. *m.A.Z.* 1. 4) as is the veneration of *asherot*, which in rabbinic Hebrew referred to a living tree or grove of trees.[147] The practice of venerating groves is as ancient as the cults of *bamot* (Hos. 5: 13; Isa. 1: 19; 57: 5, 7; Ezek. 6: 13). Since trees are highly perishable, and all the ancient trees have perished, we do not know how predominant these *asherot* were in the third century. There were certainly hundreds of them in Palestine at the time Canaan wrote. Some clues about how the trees were viewed may be gleaned from the rabbis' rules on what a Jew should not do in regard to them. Like the pagans, the Jews were not allowed to use wood from such groves for cooking, or for making artefacts (*m.A.Z.* 3. 9). The 'Muslim' groves of trees today enjoy in the Muslim community the same inviolability.

---

[146] (1927), 1–84. A briefer catalogue of sites, though one which traces their very ancient roots, was provided by Paton (1919–20).

[147] Goodman (1983), 207 n. 105.

The gods of Palestine, apart from the introduced deities of the cities, were agricultural, and they were celebrated in agricultural festivals. Feasts were a chief characteristic of the local religions, There was a famous feast at Mamre/Terebinthus (*Onom.* 6. 13; 7. 20 f.; Sozomen, *Hist. Eccles.* ii. 4–54; George Syncellus, *Chron.* 1. 202; *j.A.Z.* 1. 4). Eusebius describes how many of the local people took part in such a feast, for example at Enaim (*Onom.* 8. 12), Gilgal (*Onom.* 66. 4), Areopolis (*Onom.* 36. 25), or Hermon (*Onom.* 20. 11). These feasts would take place around the *haram*, a sacred area belonging to a deity.[148]

Herms were found by roadsides, though these were probably introduced by Roman soldiers. These heaps of stones in honour of Hermes-Mercury were added to by passers by. The rabbis, aware of this habit, refer to any idol as 'Merkulis' (cf. *m.Sanh.* 7. 6). As Rabbi Isaac said, apparently in some consternation: 'if the names of idolatry were examined singly there would not be room in all the world for them'(*Sifre Deut.* 43).[149]

Palestine was heavily garrisoned, not only in provincial head-quarters, but also in the midst of towns such as Ein Geddi,[150] as well as by means of a plethora of forts. The Roman army's famous predilection for the worship of Mithras should not be forgotten, especially considering the evidence of a Mithraeum in Caesarea, and a Mithraic medallion.[151] There may also have been a Mithraeum in the vicinity of Diocaesarea for the use of the troops.[152]

This survey of pagan life in Palestine, as far as the present study is concerned, indicates that paganism was very prevalent indeed in Palestine prior to Constantine. Gentile pagans lived all over the country and had established many cult centres (where festivals attracted pilgrims from afar), including temples and sacred places in the form of trees, hills, springs, and caves. Many of these were

---

[148] Colledge (1986), 221. Colledge notes that throughout the East ancient Semitic forms of religion lived on: 'Any particular centre might possess all these forms, from the worship of stones and springs to a "Lord" and "Lady" or only some of them', (p. 225).

[149] Goodman (1983), 208 n. 147. Goodman is surely correct (n. 148) that Leiberman's suggestion that Mercury was identified with Hermes Trimegistus of the magical papyri is far-fetched; cf. Leiberman (1946), 46, 53–4.

[150] Avi-Yonah (1976*b*), 36.

[151] Comm. by R. J. Bull, *IEJ* 23 (1973), 260–2; id. (1974).

[152] *MRP* 32.

probably very ancient holy sites. Even in Jewish Galilee, there was a pagan presence in Diocaesarea and Tiberias. Galilee was, moreover, surrounded by pagan cult centres: Tyre, Ptolemais, Carmel, Maximianopolis/Legio, Scythopolis, Gadara, Emmatha, Hippos, Gergesa, Cadasa. No Jewish village in Galilee was over thirty kilometres away from one of these cultic centres, and if we include Diocaesarea and Tiberias in the list, the maximum distance is cut by half, at least for lower Galilee. Jews lived almost as closely with Gentile pagans as did the Samaritans. An intensive study of paganism in Roman Palestine has yet to be undertaken. But, in the meantime, this summary suggests that it is important to bear pagans in mind when we think about the possible origins of later Christian holy sites, and also when we consider how Constantine looked upon the province of Palestine at the beginning of the fourth century.

Furthermore, this chapter may provide a demographic and religious context in which one may view further information concerning Palestine in the second and third centuries. Only now can we look at the archaeology and history of Christian holy places. These should be seen as sites within certain inhabited areas and not in isolation. Pagans lived all over the country and were the main population group, while Jews were the most numerous group in Galilee, and Samaritans in Samaria. Christians, Jews, and Samaritans lived together with pagans in the cities, and there were also a few Christian villages in the south of the country. It is amongst the pagans and, to some extent, the 'paganized' Samaritans that one finds references to sacred trees or holy sites, including temples. Jews had lost their Temple in 70 and, under the influence of the rabbis, they were developing a religious life focused on the synagogue, but this was not a holy place as such. Pilgrimages had been made to the Jewish Temple in order to celebrate festivals there. In this, Jews had participated in a characteristic of religious life throughout the Empire and beyond. Without the Temple, and banned from Jerusalem, Jews no longer undertook pilgrimages to the city or, it would appear, to any other place.

As regards the Byzantine Christian holy places, it may be noted that most of them are located in areas in which we have no evidence for Christians in the second and third centuries. This may warn us that there is a constant danger of anachronism when considering the development of a site as holy to Christians. In

Christian texts, we have various chronological stages at which sites are mentioned in various genres of literature. We find, for example, mention of a site in New Testament material (mainly from *c*.50 to 100), references to New Testament sites in apocryphal literature (from *c*.150 onwards), places described or mentioned in the writings of the Church Fathers from the second and third centuries, and then descriptions of 'holy' places by pilgrims and Church Fathers from the fourth decade of the fourth century onwards. It must not be assumed that a reference to a site in the second century is a reference to a site that was understood to be holy then, or even to a site that was identified in contemporary Palestine. Places mentioned in the New Testament writings took on a mythic quality in apocryphal texts which could be utilized with effect.

We shall now look at the archaeological and historical evidence for the development of Christian holy places in Palestine, in order to determine whether there is any material which would point to the authenticity of sites, and to consider when, how, and why precisely they were identified by the Church as sacred. *En route*, we will note how the Bagatti–Testa hypothesis fails to analyse the evidence in a convincing way.

4

Mamre

CONSTANTINE is the first person known to have built churches in Palestine at places Christians regard as holy. These churches were begun shortly after he defeated his rival Licinius, on 18 September 324, and became emperor of the East as well as the West. Our examination of Christian holy sites in Palestine will therefore begin with the four places which were developed by imperial order: Mamre/Terebinthus (Ramat el-Khalil), Bethlehem, Golgotha in Jerusalem, and Eleona on the Mount of Olives. We will consider what we know about the history of these sites before their development by Constantine, and discuss the question of authenticity.

Mamre/Terebinthus was located two kilometres north of Hebron. The site of the sacred oak, or terebinth, of Mamre[1] is recorded by Eusebius in his *Demonstratio Evangelica*, which was written around the year 318, six years before Constantine's victory over Licinius. Eusebius describes it as a holy place for the local inhabitants (*Dem. Evang.* v. 9. 7), who revered it because of 'those who appeared to Abraham'.

According to Genesis 18: 1–22, these visitors were three messengers from God. They had dinner with Abraham and announced to him that Sarah, his wife, would bear a son. One would expect, because of the scriptural connection, that the site would have been Jewish or Samaritan in character, but Eusebius (*Onom.* 124. 5–7), Jerome (*Lib. loc.* 78. 4f.), and Sozomen (*Hist. Eccles.* ii. 4–54) indicate that it was overwhelmingly pagan. According to Eusebius, the people who worship Abraham's visitors are the 'ignorant' who just happen to believe the 'divine oracles' (*Dem. Evang.* v. 9) in this case. Eusebius also mentions a 'picture' depicting three figures, and suggests that the middle one is Jesus, but this means little. Christians reinterpreted pagan

[1] See Josephus, *Ant.* i. 186; *BJ* iv. 533; Jerome, *Com. in Jer.* xxxi; *Chron. Pasch.* xix; *m. Maasar Sheni* 5. 2; *Sifre Deut.* 306; *j.A.Z.* 1. 39d; *Judith* 1: 9; *Cant. Rab.* 4 f.

iconography to suit their own purposes and would use the norms of this iconography to illustrate Christian themes.[2] Eusebius is using this matter to show how ignorant the pagans were; only Christians had the wisdom to interpret the picture correctly. As far as the Christians were concerned, the place was the location of one of Christ's pre-incarnation epiphanies. Ever since Justin Martyr, in the second century, Christians had speculated that one of the messengers who came to Abraham was Christ (Justin, *Dial.* lvi. 1; cf. Eusebius, *Vita Const.* iii. 53; Sozomen, *Hist. Eccles.* ii. 4).

It appears from Sozomen's account of the festival at Mamre in the fifth century that Jews also attended, but it is difficult to determine how significant this practice was, or for how long it had been taking place. Mamre is not mentioned by the rabbis as a place where blessings should be made (cf. *b.Ber.* 54a), and they describe the town only as being an important market centre in the south (*j.A.Z.* 1. 4; 38d). Since the site appears to have been the focus of a pagan cult of Abraham, the rabbis may not have advocated attendance there, as it would have meant Jews mixing with pagans. If their attitude was negative, they would have been continuing the outlook of the editors of Genesis who, aware perhaps that the cult of the terebinth was more of a local phenomenon than a Hebrew tradition consistent with proper worship centred on Jerusalem, seem to have made an attempt to obscure the site by identifying Mamre with nearby Hebron (cf. Gen. 23: 19; 35: 27).[3] Some Jews may have attended the festival primarily to sell produce and, while there, they probably recited a blessing in recollection of the patriarch Abraham, but this seems to have taken place without the approval of the rabbis. Other Jews may have been continuing a practice which stretched back to the days before the Jerusalem Temple became the pre-eminent, and only, sacred shrine in Judaism. Whatever the case, if Jews visited the site in the fifth century, there is good reason to suppose they may have done so for centuries before this time, on a popular level; otherwise we would have to suppose that they only began to

[2] For example, it is well known that the Byzantine image of Jesus was a combination of the 'bearded philosopher' type and the image of Helios, or Sol, the sun-god, along with the sun's halo. For the myriad ways in which Christian art would plunder the iconographical norms of paganism, see the series edited by Dölger (1929–50).

[3] Murphy-O'Connor (1986), 277.

see the place as important after the Christian developments there, which seems unlikely.

Sozomen's fifth-century account of the festivities at Mamre is the most detailed we have. According to him, the site was visited by Jews, because of the patriarch Abraham, by pagans, because of 'the angels', and by Christians, because of Christ. Therefore, at this summer festival, where multitudes of people flocked from all over Palestine, Phoenicia, and Arabia, some of them prayed and some of them 'called upon the angels, poured out wine, burnt incense, offered an ox, a he-goat, a sheep, or a cock' (*Hist. Eccles.* ii. 4). Sozomen says that this latter group, the pagans, placed burning lamps near Abraham's well and offered wine, gold, myrrh, and incense. The festival was anything but orgiastic, as pilgrims kept themselves celibate during the course of the rites. This description of the practices of pagans in the fifth century gives us a fair picture of how they would have venerated the site for centuries.

Nevertheless, despite Sozomen's careful record, it is unclear how the pagans came to revere the site, or quite what their beliefs were. When Sozomen tells us that 'angels' were the reason for the pagan cult, we must of course understand him to mean 'pagan deities', but he gives us no further information. In general, Christians did not attempt to argue at this time that the pagan deities simply did not exist, rather that they were demons rendered powerless by faith in Christ. However, since the deities worshipped at Mamre were identified with the men who are the collective mouthpiece of God in the Genesis story, the term 'demons' would have been inappropriate, and therefore Sozomen makes them 'angels' in accordance with the Christian understanding of the story. The pagans, who were most likely Idumaean, and would therefore have traced their ancestry to Abraham, must have possessed some sort of legend which described three gods coming to speak with Abraham and Sarah. In the fourth century, one of these was probably identified with Dionysus, since among the fragments discovered during the excavations of 1926–8 was a sculpted head of this god.[4] A Hermes stele has also been found there.[5] It was probably Herod who built the impressive sacred enclosure (see Figure 7), the main door of which has recently been

---

[4] Mader (1957), pl. LXXIV. See also M. Smith (1975).
[5] Mader (1957), pl. LXXIII.

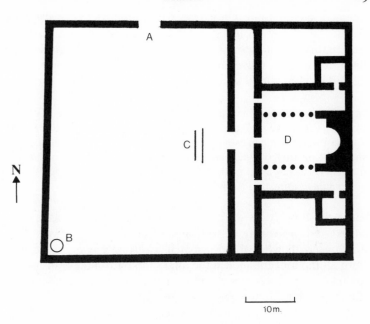

N

FIG. 7. The Constantinian sacred enclosure at Mamre

found on its northern side. According to Yitzhak Magen, the sacred enclosure was probably at the centre of a Roman town. The remains of a large Roman public house were found 200 metres to the west.[6]

Probably shortly after the year 324, Constantine's mother-in-law, Eutropia, arrived, observed, and wrote the emperor an outraged letter of complaint. Constantine immediately wrote to Macarius, bishop of Jerusalem, and the other bishops of Palestine. The contents of this missive are given in full by Eusebius (*Vita Const.* iii. 52–3), and provide us with a fascinating insight into the emperor's purposes and presuppositions.

Constantine writes that Eutropia 'has made known to us by letter that abandoned foolishness of impious men which had hitherto escaped detection by you' was taking place. This seems to imply that it had been the duty of Macarius and the other bishops of Palestine to detect pagan cult places at sites which might be

[6] Y. Magen, personal communication.

deemed 'sacred' to the Christians. Constantine does not attempt to disguise his extreme irritation at the presence of this festival at Terebinthus, this 'criminal conduct' which had 'eluded' the bishops. It was 'a grave impiety indeed, that holy places should be defiled by the stain of unholy impurities'. The emperor continues:

She assures me that the place which gains its name from the oak of Mamre, where we find that Abraham lived, is defiled by some of the slaves of superstition in every possible way. She declares that idols, which should be destroyed completely, have been set up on the site of that tree, that there is an altar near the spot, and that impure sacrifices are performed continually. (Eusebius, *Vita Const.* iii. 52)

Since these practices were 'inconsistent with the character of our times' and 'unworthy of the sanctity of the place', Constantine announced that he would dispatch a certain *comes*, Acacius, to burn all the idols, demolish the altar, and punish the transgressors 'in the severest manner'. Interestingly, Constantine's wrath was directed solely at the pagans. Jews, if involved, were ignored, perhaps because Constantine could not accuse the Jews of 'defiling' designated holy places, but it also points to the fundamentally pagan character of the rites.

Eutropia's visit and Constantine's letter beg a number of questions. Why was Constantine so outraged and so determined to have the site cleared of pagans? Was it because Christians once went there to pray before the pagans 'defiled' it? Had Christians ever venerated the terebinth at Mamre before Eutropia decided to make a specifically Christian pilgrimage there?

In his examination of the Christian holy places in Palestine, E. D. Hunt has pointed out that Eusebius presents Constantine as reviving the age of Abraham (cf. *Dem. Evang.* i; *Hist. Eccles.* i. 4): the age of Constantine entailed a return to the pure religion of the patriarchs.[7] This probably reflects the emperor's own views about his mission. The spread of Christianity through the Empire was a fulfilment of God's promise to Abraham that he would be the father of many nations. Therefore, Constantine, with his peculiar sense of destiny, may have seen the opportunity of pointing to the fulfilment of the promise to Abraham by converting the predominantly pagan terebinth shrine at Mamre into a Christian holy place.

[7] Hunt (1984), 102–3.

There is no literary or archaeological evidence which would support the notion that it was a site sacred to Christians before Constantine. However, it must also be noted that Constantine really believed that the place was holy; it was more than a cunning gesture. The site of Abraham's meeting with the pre-incarnate Christ had, he writes, an 'ancient holiness' ἀρχαίαν ἀγιοτῆτα (*Vita Const*. iii. 53) which had to be defended and preserved in its pristine state.

It is intriguing to speculate about how Eutropia came to be in this place at this time. As we have seen, in the fifth century the fame of Mamre was such that its festival attracted pilgrims (pagans, Jews, and Christians) from Phoenicia and Arabia, as well as Palestine. If it was famous, too, at the beginning of the fourth century, then she could not have been ignorant of its pagan character, unless she was misled or kept in ignorance for a reason. It would seem very likely indeed that Eutropia's visit was planned by someone who actually wanted her to be horrified by the sight of the pagan cult at this place. In fact, the shocked tenor of her letter to Constantine may have been no surprise to the emperor, who could then motivate the bishops of Palestine to action by implying that their negligence caused deep distress to the sensitivities of an imperial lady, as well as to himself. It may have been the bishops, who had not yet realized how great was their authority over pagan sites, who were the most dumbfounded. The beleaguered bishops of Palestine, fresh from persecution, may well have been perplexed by such admonitions, given their almost total lack of power and influence up until Constantine's triumph. The last thing they may have expected was that Eutropia would visit this site sacred to pagans, even if it was a place where Christ once manifested himself. As Eusebius might well have explained, there were many other sites she could have visited without being alarmed.

Constantine could have ordered the building of a church on the site without Eutropia's visit, but the speed of the operation would have been quickened by the knowledge of offence that had been caused. The incident would also have encouraged the bishops to search everywhere for places that might yet be visited by pious imperial ladies, in order to make sure that pagans were not in charge. We shall see in due course that this would fit perfectly with Constantine's plans for the East, in which he wanted to remove paganism altogether.

Christians, like Jews, may have visited the site of Mamre before Constantine; Eusebius' interpretation of the picture and his description of events may imply that he had visited the site, but this could also have been reported to him, and even Bagatti did not propose that there could have been any Jewish-Christian presence here to preserve some Christian activities. Despite their exegesis of Genesis 18, Christians appear to have kept their distance from the celebrations of Terebinthus. Certainly, Christians cannot have *owned* the property before Constantine, or administered it at any time before the fourth century. It is universally agreed that the veneration of this site must date at least to the time of the early Israelites.[8] The negative attitude of the editors of Genesis to the cult there tends to confirm its existence. A cult of some kind may have existed long before the Iron Age, if we interpret the pottery fragments from the Early Bronze period (2600–2000 BC) as being deposited by visitors at some kind of shrine. At any rate, Josephus' belief that the terebinth had continued alive since the creation of the world (*BJ* iv. 533) may be a hyperbole not completely wide of the mark. The tree was extremely old. Jerome confirms the legend that the tree dated from the beginning of time (*Lib. loc.* lxx. 2; cf. *Ep.* cviii. 11), but adds that it continued only up until the reign of Constantine, when it was covered over by a roof and subjected to the knives of Christian pilgrims who took mementoes of it home with them. Nevertheless, it continued to exist as a scarred stump through to the seventh century (cf. Adomnan, *De Loc. Sanct.* ii. 11. 3).

If the tree and the site around it were both subjects of very ancient veneration, and Christians had little to do with the area before the fourth century, it is interesting that the language Constantine employs is that of *restoration*.

It appears right to me that this should not only be kept pure from all defilement, through your diligence, but restored to its ancient holiness, so that, from now on, nothing may be done there apart from the performance of fitting service to him who is Almighty God and Saviour and Lord of all.

Sozomen summarizes this in his report of the letter: '. . . he rebuked the bishops of Palestine in no measured terms, because

---

[8] Mader (1957), 48.

they had neglected their duty, and had allowed a holy place to be defiled by impure libations and sacrifices' (*Hist. Eccles.* ii. 4).

The logic of Constantine's pronouncements appears to rest on the idea that a place was sanctified immediately at the time of the epiphany of God/Christ there, or even before; Constantine wrote in regard to Golgotha that it was a 'place which has been accounted holy from the beginning in the judgement of God' (Eusebius, *Vita Const.* iii. 30). It would follow, therefore, that if a place had been rendered holy then it belonged to God's chosen people, the Christians, who had inherited the promises made to Israel (cf. Rom. 9: 6–8; Gal. 3). Constantine clearly believed that sacred things had to be in the pure hands of the ecclesiastic authorities, who alone could guarantee the preservation of their holiness. This means, however, that we can never assume, on the basis of restoration language used by the Church Fathers, that a site was ever venerated by Christians before it was 'discovered' by them in the fourth century. If a site, formerly used only by pagans, Jews, or Samaritans, was deemed holy by fourth-century Christians and taken away, this was not thought by them to be an act of appropriation by the Church, but an act of restoration.

Constantine's wishes were, of course, carried out, and the remains of the church, which the Bordeaux Pilgrim of 333 described as 'exceptionally beautiful' (*Itin. Burd.* 599), can still be seen. The excavations of 1926–8 established that there had been since the time of Herod the Great an enclosure surrounded by a strong wall. The *haram*, or sacred enclosure, contained not only the tree, but also a well believed to have been dug by Abraham, and an altar. The Constantinian church was built into the Herodian shrine.[9] This church was not at all large, and does not compare with Constantine's splendid constructions at Bethlehem, Golgotha, or Eleona; it seems to have been tucked into one side of the sacred enclosure. Indeed, the Christian practice of visiting the site, as seen in Sozomen's description, seems itself to have been tucked into the pagan rites. Acacius may have been as ruthless as Constantine demanded, but it would seem that pagans continued to come to Mamre even though they had once been evicted and

---

[9] See *EAEHL* iii. 776–7; Ovadiah (1970), 131; Crowfoot (1941), 35–6; Murphy-O'Connor (1976), 277–8

the place had been given a nominal Christian stamp.[10] If so, then the relatively modest Christian construction there may have been a way of preventing a pagan backlash.

Whatever Acacius actually did in the way of retribution, it would appear that the pagans accommodated the new character of the place and continued as usual, and that the Church authorities there accepted this phenomenon, possibly on account of insufficient confidence that they could stamp the practices out, and possibly because they hoped that as the pagans continually came to the site they could be converted to believing in the Gospel. This kind of reasoning is given in an *inverted* way to argue why the pagans ostensibly 'stole' sites from Christians. As Sozomen writes of Golgotha: '. . . they supposed that those who went there to worship Christ would appear to bow the knee to Venus, and so the true cause of offering worship in that place would be forgotten in the course of time' (*Hist. Eccles.* ii. 1). In other words, the Christians hoped that in the course of time the pagans who went to Mamre, and would appear to be worshipping the Christian God, might forget their old traditions. In Chapter 6, on Golgotha, we shall see whether the restoration language applied to that site is any more significant than that applied to Mamre.

It would appear from the evidence concerning Mamre that it was a pagan sacred place, also venerated by some Jews, which Constantine believed was a Christian holy place which should therefore be administered by the Church. There was no time during which Christians possessed the site prior to the fourth century, even though restoration language was used as a justification for the appropriation of the area. If Christians visited the terebinth before the fourth century, there is no sure record of their having done so, although Eusebius may have been there. If Eusebius or others did go there before Constantine's innovations, it is significant that he does not say the place was holy to any Christians or that Christians worshipped at the spot, despite his theological interest in the theophany there.[11] It is the imperial lady Eutropia who is the first Christian known to have visited Mamre. The Christian church at the site is to be dated between 324 and 333.

[10] Magen has found pottery dating to the Mameluke period (personal communication), which shows that Mamre continued to be visited.
[11] Walker (1990), 276 n. 141.

It is clear that the site was venerated for 2,000 years or more before it was taken over by the Church. Many tribes who traced their ancestry to Abraham appear to have considered the terebinth holy. Among these tribes were the Idumaeans, the people who lived in this region. It came to be predominantly a place where a pagan, Idumaean cult of Abraham was celebrated with a famous agricultural festival.

5

Bethlehem

ACCORDING to Jerome, the Cave of the Nativity in Bethlehem,[1] believed by Christians to be the place where Christ was born, had been a pagan cult site. 'Bethlehem . . . belonging now to us . . . was overshadowed by a grove of Tammuz, that is to say, Adonis, and in the cave where once the infant Christ cried, the lover of Venus was lamented' (*Ep*. lviii. 3).[2] This attestation is fairly late, since the letter from which this comes is to be dated to 395. Eusebius does not mention any pagan veneration of the cave,[3] and the absence of other specific patristic references to the fact has prompted some scholars to doubt whether it is true.

In a recent study, Peter Welten has attempted to challenge the assumption that Tammuz-Adonis was worshipped here, arguing that there is no independent literary, numismatic, or archaeological evidence for any pagan cult in Bethlehem.[4] Welten himself believes that Jerome was predisposed to thinking of the cave as being connected with Adonis because he knew of the Venus temple in Jerusalem. The main evidence which he uses to support a case for Jerome's error is iconographical; that since the pagan motif of the wailing mother/woman and *Venus lugens*, found in Syrian and Phoenician contexts, was used in representations of 'the slaughter of the innocents',[5] Jerome subjected the latter to a kind of *interpretatio graeca* by suggesting there were lamentations for Adonis in the Nativity Grotto. Christian iconography, however, is not the most reliable evidence for the history of religious traditions, since it is very well known that Christian art adopted a

---

[1] For the history and archaeology of Bethlehem in general, with particular reference to the Church of the Nativity, see Bagatti (1952), (1968*b*); Hamilton (1947); W. Harvey (1937); Murphy-O'Connor (1986), 165–71; Vincent and Abel (1914*a*); Vincent (1936); Weir Schultz (1910); Wilkinson (1977), 151–2.

[2] Cf. *Ep*. cxlvii. 4.

[3] See *Dem. Evang*. iii. 2; vii. 2; *Vita Const*. iii. 42 f.; cf. Epiphanius *Pan*. li. 9; lxxviii. 15; Socrates, *Hist. Eccles*. i. 17; Sozomen, *Hist. Eccles*. ii. 2.

[4] (1983) esp. 200.   [5] See Kötzsche-Breitenbruch (1968–9).

large part of the iconographic repertoire of the pagan world. Simply in regard to Aphrodite, her birth in the waters was used as a motif for Christian baptism. In a Coptic stele of the sixth century, the orant even has the conch shell of Aphrodite to indicate she is newly baptized.[6] This does not mean that the origins of Christian baptism are to be found in the cult of Aphrodite.

The standard motif of the wailing mother/woman, found in both pagan and Christian art, cannot have been the foundation of Jerome's report. No one in the fourth century, let alone a man with Jerome's intellect and classical education, would have been so naïve as to believe that, because the iconographical form used for the depiction of a scene from the New Testament, the wailing mother/woman, was found in the classical representation of Aphrodite weeping for Adonis, an Adonis cult preceded Christian veneration at the site identified as the birthplace of Christ. One might equally argue that the Christian use of the form arose from the fact that a synonymous representation of Aphrodite bewailing her lover's death was known at Bethlehem before the Church adopted the site as its own, which would only serve to verify Jerome's observation.

As an example that might corroborate this latter proposition, one could consider the case of the Paneas statues. While it is never said by Eusebius, it is clear from his description of the bronze statues in Paneas (*Hist. Eccles.* vii. 18) that they represented Asclepius healing a sick woman. They were interpreted by Christians, including Eusebius, as showing Christ healing the woman 'with an issue of blood' (Mark 5: 25–34; Matt. 9: 20; Luke 8: 43–48).[7] As a result of this interpretation Paneas became a pilgrimage centre; it was so popular by the mid-fourth century that the 'born again' pagan emperor Julian had the statues replaced by one of Pan (Philostorgius, *Hist. Eccles.* vii. 3) or perhaps of himself (Sozomen, *Hist. Eccles.* v. 21), in a futile attempt to discourage Christian visitors. This is a good example of how the general tendency among Christians was to speculate on the earliest *Christian* use of a site, and to ignore its pagan past. Cyril of Jerusalem, for example, nowhere mentions that a temple of Venus stood anywhere near or on the site of Golgotha. Where certain Church Fathers do sometimes emphasize pagan 'desecration' of a

[6] See *Le monde de la Bible* 63 (1990), 28 (fig. 21), 38 (fig. 31).
[7] Maraval (1985), 53.

Christian holy place, for example at Mamre and Golgotha, it is probably because the pagan cults there were so well known that some explanation for their passing into Christian hands was necessary for apologetic reasons. They managed to make the pagan pasts of such sites serve their polemical purposes, but that any of the Fathers would have invented a pagan cult place antedating the Christian one, just for the sake of polemic, is extremely improbable and has no known parallel. A single patristic attestation of the existence of a pagan cult site at a Christian holy place is therefore weighty as evidence.

Moreover, by the time Jerome came to write of the pagan cult in Bethlehem, he had lived and researched there for almost ten years. We can surely take it for granted that the local population would have informed him of the use made of the cave fifty years before his arrival. The parents of the older members of the population would have participated in the cult, and there may have been one or two people still living who had done so. Some supporting evidence for there being a grove comes from Cyril of Jerusalem's *Catechetical Lectures* (xii. 20), written in about 348, where it is said that 'until lately' the district of Bethlehem was wooded. One may also conjecture from this that the Church dealt with the famous grove of Tammuz-Adonis by cutting it down.

Bagatti and Testa have advocated the early use of the Bethlehem cave by Jewish-Christians,[8] but it is also believed by many who come to the Nativity Grotto today that Christians venerated it as the birthplace of Jesus long before the site was made into a cult place for the dying-and-rising god Tammuz-Adonis. The basis for this idea comes from Jerome. The pagan cult is taken to prove the antiquity of the Christian veneration, because the pagans were apparently both curtailing Christian worship and establishing the cult of a god who shared certain common features with Jesus. The pagan cult was then a perverted continuation of the Christian, and after Constantine the Christians were able to reclaim the hallowed ground.

As we have just seen, however, restoration language used by the Church Fathers in no way implies that a site was ever in Christian hands before the fourth century. Jerome believed that this cave beside the grove was a place once sanctified by the manifestation

[8] Bagatti (1971c), 133–4; cf. id. (1963a); Mancini (1966); (1984), 162–5; Testa (1964a), 65–144.

of the Christ child, which the pagans then desecrated by worshipping Tammuz-Adonis, but the statement by Jerome is not useful as evidence for any early Christian veneration of the site. Given the model of Mamre, his remarks would indicate that the Bethlehem cave and grove were parts of a cult site appropriated by Christians, but nothing more.

However, there is literary evidence from the second and third centuries which would appear at first sight to connect the birth of Jesus with a cave somewhere in the vicinity of Bethlehem. The question is whether these refer to a specific cave which should be identified as the present Nativity Grotto, or whether the cave motif is a symbol. Was it these texts that influenced the identification of the cave in Bethlehem as the site of Christ's birth, or were they influenced by an existing venerated cave?

The earliest of the texts is Justin's *Dialogue with Trypho*, a work ostensibly reporting an actual conversation set before the end of the Bar Kochba War, although it was written down between 155 and 161, some twenty years later. Justin wrote, recalling his words to a group:

'About the birth of the child in Bethlehem: when Joseph could not find any lodgings in the village, he went to a nearby cave, and Mary gave birth to the child there and laid him in a manger, and there the Arabian magi found him. I have already quoted Isaiah's words in which he predicted the symbol of the cave, but I will repeat the passage for those of you who have joined today.' Then I repeated Isaiah's words, written above, and added that by these words the priests who enacted the mysteries of Mithras were prompted by the Devil to say that they were initiated by Mithras himself in a place they call a 'cave'. (*Dial.* lxxviii. 12–13)

The last part of this informs us of Justin's purpose in reporting the story. He wanted to endorse a certain interpretation of 'Isaiah's words' in order to show that the prophet foretold that the Messiah would be linked with 'the symbol of the cave'. The Septuagint text of Isa. 33: 16 has it that 'the righteous king' will dwell 'in a cave of mighty rock'. It is improbable that Justin could have derived the idea of Jesus' birth in a cave from this unlikely passage of Scripture,[9] but we are not told from where he gained the idea. It may have been Church tradition. It may also have been from an

[9] Weir Schultz (1910), 73.

apocryphal story which used the symbolic image of Christ (the light) born in a cave (the darkness, the world).

Having interpreted a passage in Isaiah to provide a type for a cave, Justin wished to set 'the symbol of the cave' in sharp relief against the pagan mysteries of Mithras, and thereby devised a dualistic paradigm: the birth of Jesus in a cave finds its prototype in the prophecy of Isaiah, and both of these act together as a good and true counterweight to the false and evil use of caves by the adherents of the Mithraic mysteries. In the legends of the latter, Mithras was born from rock, and his initiates were 'reborn' in secret ceremonies underground.[10]

There is some reason to suppose that Justin is employing some sort of apocryphal story as a basis for his explanation, for he gives us three details which are not found in the Gospels: the stable was a cave, the cave was outside the village, and the Magi were Arabs. These details are more than romantic additions, and come from somewhere other than the New Testament nativity stories as we know them. But Justin does not give his source, and indeed this may have been oral. However, it must also be said that the cave itself may have arisen as a motif in the story as a result of Justin's own assumptions. Justin was from Neapolis, born into a pagan family. He left Palestine while still a young man and went to Ephesus to study. It was probably there that he converted to Christianity, but he did not begin to propagate his faith until after 135, in Rome. Being a Palestinian, he would have found it only natural to assume that the stable of Luke 2: 7 was a cave. The employment of caves as places where animals, usually sheep and goats, could feed and sleep was as much a custom in the Palestine of Justin's time as it is in many Arab areas of the region today.[11] It was as easy for him to think of a stable as a cave as it is for us to think of it as a barn. For Justin, it would have been an obvious assumption. The idea of a cave may then simply have been Justin's identification based on his knowledge of Palestinian stables.

Justin gives no clue as to this cave's specific location. All he says is that the cave is somewhere nearby the village, σύνεγγυς τῆς κώμης, but nevertheless *outside* it. If we are to take Justin's knowledge of Judaean topography as sound, this implies a place

[10] Ferguson (1970), 47–8.
[11] Weir Schultz (1910), 73; Dalman (1935*b*), 40; Van-Lennep (1875), 417; Tristam (1894), 112.

further away than the Tomb of Rachel which, according to Justin
is '*in* Bethlehem' (*Dial*. lxxviii. 19). Either he is not interested in
the location, or he simply does not know, or he locates the cave
further away from the town than the Tomb of Rachel. The caves
used for the worship of Tammuz-Adonis, however, were *inside*
Bethlehem, probably at the western border of the ancient
village.[12] Moreover, Justin makes no mention of a specific cave
shown to Christian visitors.

It seems very likely that the evidence Justin provides is
illuminating in regard to the development of legend, but tells us
nothing about any actual cave. As a Palestinian Gentile with a
pagan background, he would have had no reason to visit Jewish
Bethlehem before he left the country, never to return.

The fact that the Magi are identified by Justin as Arabs will be
discussed below.

In the third century, an apocryphal work was produced called
the *Protevangelium of James*.[13] It purported to be an account of
Jesus' early life, but it shows an acute ignorance of Palestinian
geography and Jewish customs. In fact, it clearly arose in a Gentile
environment far from the Middle East.[14] Its reliability as an
historical source for information about the actual location of Jesus'
birth is, therefore, very limited. In chapter xvii a legendary
description of the circumstances of Jesus' birth is presented. Mary
sees a vision of two peoples, one weeping and lamenting and the
other rejoicing and exulting: the Jews and the Gentiles respectively
(xvii. 2). Then, before arriving at Bethlehem, Mary asks Joseph to
take her down from the ass because the child wants to be born.
Joseph replies, 'Where shall I take you and hide your shame, for
the place is desert?' Neither Bethlehem nor its immediate vicinity
is, or was, desert, although the Wilderness of Judaea lies several
kilometres to the east. The area around the cave of Tammuz-
Adonis was a wood. The legend fails to correspond with the
specific topography of the area of the Tammuz-Adonis shrine. The
writer clearly wishes to place the birth of Jesus in the desert
somewhere outside the town for symbolic reasons. Joseph, in the
story, finds a cave and brings Mary to it. He leaves her in the care
of his sons while he goes off to seek a Hebrew midwife 'in the
region of Bethlehem' (xviii. 1). It is clear from the text that Joseph

---

[12] See Benoit (1975).   [13] Oscar Cullmann in *NTA* i. 370–1.
[14] Ibid. 372.

and Mary have not yet reached this region. The story ends with meteorological events: a cloud overshadows the cave, vanishes, is replaced by light, and then a child appears (ix. 1 ff.). It is plain that all the details of the story, including the cave, are mythical and symbolic. As L.-H. Vincent and F. M. Abel have interpreted it, Christ born in an obscure cave is the light bursting into the shadows of the world; Christ born in an isolated grotto, away from human assistance, is a manifestation of divine power and the virginity of Mary.[15]

It may have been an archaic form of this story that was known by Justin. He refers to the things 'concerning the mystery of his birth' (*Dial.* xliii. 3) and, also for the writer of the *Protevangelium*, these are 'mysteries' (*Prot. Jac.* xii. 3). Alternatively, it is just possible that the *Protevangelium* utilized Justin's innovations. Unfamiliar with the Palestinian custom of using caves as stables, the writer may have accounted for Jesus' birth in a cave by providing a story of Jesus' premature delivery. Whatever the case, the *Protevangelium* should not be used as evidence for the early Christian veneration of the grotto inside Bethelehem; it is legend. Even if it were to be used as an historical source, it could only tell us of a cave in the Wilderness of Judaea over three kilometres distant from Bethlehem.

The *Gospel of Pseudo-Matthew*, composed in about the eighth century,[16] used the *Protevangelium*, and has substantially the same story. However, the writer tries to reconcile the legend with the Gospel accounts by having Mary go on to a stable proper on the third day after the birth (xiv) and to Bethlehem itself on the sixth day (xv). The *Story of Joseph the Carpenter*, written no earlier than the fourth century,[17] and probably considerably later, continues this tradition of Jesus' birth outside the village, and provides a specific location 'beside the Tomb of Rachel'. As was indicated above, the Tomb of Rachel is about a kilometre away from the Nativity Grotto. It may be added that it is unlikely that Christ was born beside the Tomb of Rachel. The excavations at Ramat Rahel[18] have shown that before the expulsion of the Jews by Hadrian, the area served as a cemetery, although there was a small village nearby. In the early part of the third century, the tiny Jewish community in Jerusalem appear to have buried their dead

[15] (1914*a*), 9.   [16] Cullmann in *NTA* i. 406.
[17] *ANT* 84.   [18] Aharoni (1962), 24–7; (1964), 38–40, 60–82.

here. The Tenth Legion then exploited the graves as cisterns and built a bathhouse as well as a large residential building in the latter part of the third century.

Some effort was made in the fifth century to provide a site to correspond to the apocryphal accounts of the birth beginning, at least, outside Bethlehem. A site became known as the *Kathisma*, 'place of sitting', since it was thought that Mary sat on a particular rock here after she dismounted from the ass, and a monastery was built between 451 and 458.[19] Early in the sixth century, Theodosius (*Itin.* xxviii) wrote that there was 'a stone in a place three miles from the city of Jerusalem which my lady Mary blessed when she dismounted from the ass on her way to Bethlehem and sat down on it'. This is the final, if modified, materialization of the entire tradition that has Jesus born in a cave outside Bethlehem, a literary tradition which began with Justin. It should be added that the fourth and fifth century veneration of this particular site has no likely origins prior to the fourth century.

The first piece of evidence for the existence of a specific cave actually *in* Bethlehem, identified as the place of Jesus' birth and shown to Christian visitors, is provided by Origen, writing *c*.247:

If anyone wishes to have further proof to convince him that Jesus was born in Bethlehem besides the prophecy of Micah and the story recorded in the Gospels by Jesus' disciples, he may observe that, in accordance with the story in the Gospel about his birth, the cave in Bethlehem is shown where he was born and the manger in the cave where he was wrapped in swaddling clothes. What is shown there is famous in these parts even among people alien to the faith, because it was in this cave that the Jesus who is worshipped and admired by Christians was born. (*Contra Celsum* i. 51)

In using 'the Jesus', I am following Henry Chadwick's translation[20] of this curious text, since it preserves the awkwardness of the last sentence in Greek: καὶ τὸ δεικνύμενον τοῦτο διαβόητον ἐστιν ἐν τοῖς τόποις καὶ παρὰ τοῖς τῆς πίστεως ἀλλοτρίοις, ὡς ἄρα ἐν τῷ σπηλαίῳ τούτῳ ὁ ὑπὸ Χριστιανῶν προσκυνούμενος καὶ θαυμαζόμενος γεγέννηται Ἰησοῦς. The Latin version by Rufinus keeps the final position of the proper name in the last clause: 'in illa spelunca natum esse eum, quem Christiani adorant et admirantur, Jesum': 'in this cave was born he whom the Christians

[19] Wilkinson (1977), 163.   [20] (1953), 47–8.

worship and admire, Jesus.' In Greek it is perfectly normal to have a definite article before a proper name, but the early Latin translation understood the letter 'o' in the original Greek text to be read as a relative pronoun, Ŏ, 'he whom'. If we read the Greek text in accordance with the Latin, the sentence would be better translated: 'And this (cave) which is shown is noised around these parts by those who belong to another faith, since in this cave he who is worshipped and admired by Christians, Jesus, was born'. All that need be changed in the edition of the Greek text is a single diacritic mark to indicate that it is a relative pronoun and not the definite article.

If this is what Origen wrote, and it seems very probable that he did, then he appears to preserve the actual words of the local population. They informed people that 'he who is worshipped and admired by Christians' was born in the cave. 'Jesus' would seem to be Origen's addition for the sake of clarity. Had he not meant to echo the words of the local inhabitants, he would have written 'in this cave, our Lord Jesus was born' or something similar. 'He who is worshipped and admired by Christians', on the other hand, is rather vague, especially when it comes from the mouths of polytheists with the syncretizing mentality of the age. If we know from Jerome that the people of Bethlehem worshipped Tammuz-Adonis in the cave in Bethlehem, then it is such worship that must have been famous. Origen is clearly referring to this cave, but far from this being proof of the actual birthplace of Jesus, all his words really tell us is that the pagan people of Bethlehem *believed* that Jesus was born there. The probability is that the pagans arrived at this notion by an identification of Jesus with Adonis, not from any ancient tradition. Origen's failure to mention the pagan worship is quite understandable. He wished only to enhance his proof that Jesus was born in David's city, and had he added that the pagans of the area honoured Tammuz-Adonis in the cave he would have given ammunition to his adversaries.[21]

The pagans may well have taken some delight in convincing the occasional Christian visitor of the third century that Christ was born in the sacred cave of Tammuz-Adonis. In the Syriac dialect, a cognate of that spoken in Palestine, the words *adana* (Heb. *adonai*), 'lord' and, more particularly, *adawni* (Heb. *adoni*),[22] 'my

[21] So Vincent and Abel (1914a), 13–14.
[22] See Payne-Smith (1891), i. cols. 35, 40.

lord' were extremely similar to the Greek Ἄδωνις. The rites of mourning for Adonis were called Ἀδώνια. The Greek words all derive from the Phoenician root.

One might conjecture that Origen, living in Caesarea, heard news of what was happening. He does not confirm that he personally visited Bethlehem, but he may well have done so. He knew that the Tomb of Rachel was on the road to Bethlehem (*in Matt.* xxxiv) and that the Tombs of the Patriarchs were at Hebron (*De Princ.* iv. 3. 4). He had seen the wells of Abraham in Ascalon (*Contra Celsum* iv. 4). Epiphanius mentions Origen preaching in Jerusalem (*Pan.* lxiv. 2). He embarked on a tour of Palestine at some stage during his sojourn in Caesarea, as his comments in relation to Bethany and Bethabara show (*in Joh.* xxiv).

To cater for such scholars as Origen, there appear to have been people willing to show sites of significance to Christians. Origen writes, speaking of his guides: 'They say [λέγουσι] that Bethabara is pointed out on the banks of the Jordan; they relate [ἱστοροῦσι] that there John baptized' (*in Joh.* xxiv). While it is clearly Christian guides of some kind who are the subjects of λέγουσι and ἱστοροῦσι, those who do the pointing out are a different group. They need not have been Christians at all. Bethabara, where the Roman road from Jericho to Livias forded the Jordan, was in Jewish tradition the place where the Hebrews made their entry into Palestine (cf. *b.Ber.* 54a; Origen, *Hom. in Iesum fil. Nave*, v. 1; Theodoret of Cyr, *in Josh.* i. 4). Bethabara would then have been pointed out to Christians on the banks of the Jordan by Jews. The identification of this place with the baptism of John, however, must have been made by local Christians, who appear to have been interested in knowing the spot so that they could use it for baptisms (cf. *Onom.* 74. 16–18). The Jews were not pointing out the site because of its Christian significance, but because of its importance in Jewish tradition; the Christians then made the identification that it was here that John baptized.

This was not the only place 'pointed out'. As regards Gergesa, Origen says: 'But Gergesa, from which come "the Gergesenes", is an ancient town on the lake now called "Tiberias", beside which is a steep place next to the lake, from which, it is pointed out the swine were cast down by the demons' (*in Joh.* xxiv). Eusebius confirms that someone was pointing out this cliff at the very beginning of the fourth century. In his *Onomasticon* (64. 1), he writes that at Gergesa the place where the Lord healed the demoniac 'is shown on the top of a mountain village very close to the lake of Tiberias'. In this case it was probably the local Christians who made the identification, since there were Christians in Gadara and Capitolias before the Council of Nicaea, as we saw above, and Batanaea had a Christian population. Guides could easily have brought their visitors to the spot, even though the local population of Gergesa was pagan.

If there was a tendency for persons to point out geographical features and associate them with biblical events deemed important by Christians in the third century, this does not necessarily mean that the guides made the right identifications, or that the places were considered to be holy. Certainly, Origen shows no signs of having believed he was seeing sacred sites. With regard to Bethabara it seems that a site important to Jews, and pointed out by them, was given a Christian significance by local Christians. As with Bethlehem, the original—in this case Jewish—significance of the site is not given by Origen in the place where he describes it as being where John baptized. Again, it seems that Christians tended to 'forget' a site's previous associations if it suited their particular case.

It is significant that Origen knew the popular *Protevangelium of James* (cf. *in Matt*. x. 17) and therefore the story of the cave near Bethlehem. In fact, he temporarily ignores the fact that the Gospels do not specifically mention a cave, but only a stable. This would demonstrate how influential the legend was at this time. It would perhaps have been natural for a Christian visitor from Jerusalem to ask the locals about a cave where 'my lord', *adawni*, was born. Origen says this cave was 'in Bethlehem', however, while the *Protevangelium* places it outside. It is important to stress here that for the first time in the Christian sources the cave appears within the town precincts.

Further evidence for the identification of the cave by the pagan local inhabitants as that of Tammuz-Adonis and the birthplace of Christ together is provided by Eusebius' *Demonstratio Evangelica*. As a Palestinian who was deeply interested in identifying biblical places, Eusebius cannot have been wholly dependent on Origen for his knowledge of Bethlehem. He writes: 'It is agreed by all that Jesus Christ was born in Bethlehem, as even a cave is shown by the local inhabitants there to those who come from elsewhere for a look' (*Dem. Evang.* iii. 2. 47). Eusebius says that people hurry from the other side of the earth to see the *famous* place of his birth in Bethlehem (i. 1. 2). Those who come are probably Christians, but Eusebius never says it is *only* those who believe in Christ that go there, in marked contrast to what he says concerning those who congregate on the Mount of Olives, where the assembly is identified specifically as faithful believers (*Dem. Evang.* vi. 18).

More particularly, he never says that *Christians*, or even Christian guides, in Bethlehem pointed out the cave: they are simply the local inhabitants.

To this day, the people who live at the place, the tradition having come down to them from their ancestors, bear witness to the [Gospel] account to those who come to Bethlehem, for the sake of an interpretation of the places, who believe the truth through the proof of the cave in which the Virgin bore and laid her child. (*Dem. Evang.* vii. 2. 14)

Eusebius may preserve a certain scepticism about the site. In his *Onomasticon* he makes no reference at all to the cave as the birthplace of Christ (cf. *Onom.* 42. 10–14; 82. 10–14).

The literary evidence taken as a whole is not, unfortunately, extremely clear, but one may conclude that the early Christian literature interpreted thus far as providing positive evidence for the early veneration of a specific cave can also be interpreted otherwise. Vincent and Abel believed that Justin knew of a real tradition of a cave and that the *Protevangelium* combined this true tradition with a symbolic one, while Origen preserved the kernel of truth.[23] However, we have seen that Justin may well have assumed the stable of the Gospels was a cave, and some sort of story like that in the *Protevangelium* lies behind his reference. This latter legend does not bear any relation to the actual topography of Bethlehem, but is symbolic in purpose. Origen knew that the local pagan population advertised a cave in Bethlehem where 'he who was worshipped and adored by Christians', in fact Tammuz-Adonis, was born. Eusebius also knew that the (pagan) local inhabitants advertised that Jesus was born in this cave, and that Christian visitors were attracted to the site.

Interestingly, a certain Jewish tradition also locates the birth of the Messiah in a specific place in Bethlehem, not simply in the

[23] (1914*a*), 4–5.

town in general. In the Palestinian Talmud (*j.Ber.* 5a), the
Messiah comes from 'the residence of the king which is in
Bethlehem'. Dating from around 400, the *Midrash Lamentations
Rabbah* (i. 16) has a story, set in 70, of an interchange between a
Jew and an Arab. The Jew is ploughing his field when the Arab
passes by and, magically understanding the lowing of the Jew's ox,
the Arab tells him that the Temple has been destroyed. The ox
lows again and the Arab says that the Messiah has been born 'in
Birat Arba/Araba which is in Bethlehem of Judah'.

In this tale, the Arab (*arabi*) claims that the Messiah of the Jews
was born in the fort or residence (*birah*), not of the king but of
'*Arba/Araba*'. If a pun is intended, the meaning of the place-name
would be 'Arab residence/fort'. On the other hand, if the word was
given slightly different vowels, so that it read as *Arba*, it would
mean 'willow', which could mean that the name of the place is
'willow residence' or even 'poplar residence', since in Mishnaic
times the word was used for the poplar (*b.Shab.* 36a) and in
Arabic it is the poplar that is called *arb*.[24] Poplars grew with oaks
and terebinths in Palestine (cf. Hos. 4: 13) which, coincidentally,
are three of the most likely constituents of a sacred grove. The yew
trees sacred to Aphrodite and Adonis are not native to the
country. There may just be some connection here between the
name of the tree and the appearance of the Arab. It is therefore
interesting that in Justin's story, *Arabs* come to Jesus in the cave,
while in *Lamentations Rabbah*, an Arab tells a Jew of the birth of
the Messiah in *Birat Arba/Araba*.

Certainly the puns would not have been lost on the editors of
Lamentations Rabbah, and it is worth remembering here that after
Hadrian evicted the Jews from Bethlehem, a fair proportion of the
population may have been Idumaeans and Nabataeans. There is a
possibility, then, that the story found in *Lamentations Rabbah*
derives from the time of pagan occupation of the town and
veneration of the sacred grove. Although, by the time the story
was recorded, Christians had taken over the site, there is no
possible allusion to anything pertaining to the Christian cult. One
might also wonder if there was some Jewish folk tradition
concerning the Messiah's birthplace at a particular place in
Bethlehem, which pre-dated the pagan developments. In the story

[24] *EJ* xvi. cols. 517–18.

in *Lamentations Rabbah*, the Messiah was born, and then taken away by the wind until the time came for the rebuilding of the Temple.

Whether a Jewish site important in local messianic folklore had been located there is impossible to prove. It is probably safer to assume that the development of a cave and grove of Tammuz-Adonis was an entirely spontaneous innovation of immigrants to Bethlehem after 135 (cf. Eusebius, *Hist. Eccles.* iv. 6. 4). The first wave of immigrants were more likely to have been Syrians than Arabs. Adonis was worshipped chiefly in Byblos, where annual feasts were held in his honour in Aphaca on the summit of Mount Lebanon, connected with a sacred cave and spring (cf. Eusebius, *Vita Const.* iii. 56).[25] The identity of the two gods Tammuz and Adonis is known from the euhemeristic *Oration of Meliton the Philosopher* (Pseudo-Meliton), dated to the third century,[26] and other writings.[27] Tammuz-Adonis was a vegetation god, both son and lover of Aphrodite.[28] The mourning rites from the cycle of Adonis parallel those of Hadad-Rimmon in the valley of Megiddo (Zech. 12: 11; 2 Kgs. 5: 18). The worship of the god was well established in Palestine in the sixth century BC; Ezekiel saw a vision of 'women weeping for Tammuz' in the Temple of Jerusalem (Ezek. 8: 14). In the Nabataean world, the divine pair of Aphrodite and Adonis was matched by Atargatis/Allat and Dushara, the power of the grape that dies and is reborn, and therefore Nabataean immigrants would certainly have found the cult attractive. In catering for immigrants from different ethnic groups, syncretistic language may have been common at the very beginning.

Tammuz-Adonis was a very appealing figure. Not only was he the dashing young consort to Aphrodite, but he was the power of regeneration. This god inspired love and a feeling of trust that came close to salvation.[29] Tammuz was also the shepherd who tends the flock, and in this aspect there was an emphasis on his death, with its corresponding mother's lament.[30] It is in this form that he most clearly parallels Adonis and Jesus, and it is interesting

[25] See Soyez (1977).

[26] For which see *Spicilegium Syriacum*, ed. Cureton.

[27] See Baudissin (1855), 22–35.

[28] See Graves (1955), i. 72–3; E. O. James (1958), 44–5; Langdon (1914); Moorgate (1949); Strong and Garstang (1913).

[29] Jacobsen (1970), 77, 80.   [30] Ibid. 87–8.

that Eusebius follows his mention of the cave in *Demonstratio Evangelica* iii. 2. 47 with a discussion of Jesus as 'the Lord of the Flock'. It is no wonder that many aspects of the cult of Adonis would soon find their way into Christian rituals and festivals.[31]

The enthusiasm of the pagan inhabitants of Bethlehem and the surrounding area, who may have told Christians that their god was born in the sacred cave, clearly backfired. Those whom everybody despised became rulers of the Empire. Constantine was no friend of Adonis, and the cave in Bethlehem was asking to be appropriated. The empress Helena soon accomplished the operation. She placed 'rare memorials' there and beautified the cave with 'all possible splendour', and the emperor donated silver, gold, and embroidered hangings (Eusebius, *Vita Const.* iii. 46). The basilica of the Nativity was dedicated some years after Helena's visit, on 31 May 339 (cf. *Itin. Burd.* 598. 5).

The cave complex (see Figure 8) has been subjected to numerous changes during its long history of use, and archaeology has as yet provided little that would illuminate its original form and function. The main cave (1) now measures approximately 12.3 by 3.5 metres and is connected to other caves which were used in the fourth and fifth centuries as graves for the pious. In the east of the main cave is a site identified as being the exact spot where Jesus was born, now marked by a star (2). Entrance to the main cave is afforded by steps in the north and south (4), but the Constantinian entrance was in the west. There was once an installation in the cave which, it seems, the pagans used to point out to the Christians as a manger (Origen, *Contra Celsum* i. 51). The remnants of this can be seen on the east side of the annex which contains the venerated manger. Unlike Cyril (*Cat.* x. 19; xii. 32), Eusebius does not mention it,[32] but Jerome says that the actual 'manger' was made of clay (*Nat. Hom.*, CCSL 78, 524 f.) which was replaced by one of silver and gold. At the place where the manger is thought to have stood, there is now a rocky ledge covered with marble (3). This rocky ledge continues in the remains to the east. In the centre of the 'manger' is a depression about 1 metre wide and 30 centimetres broad, which is open at the front.[33] The projection on the east side of the venerated cave was taken by Peter the Deacon (*Lib.* P1) to be the table at which the

[31] Vellay (1904), 177–92.　　[32] See Walker (1990), 175–7.
[33] Cf. Dalman (1935*b*), 102.

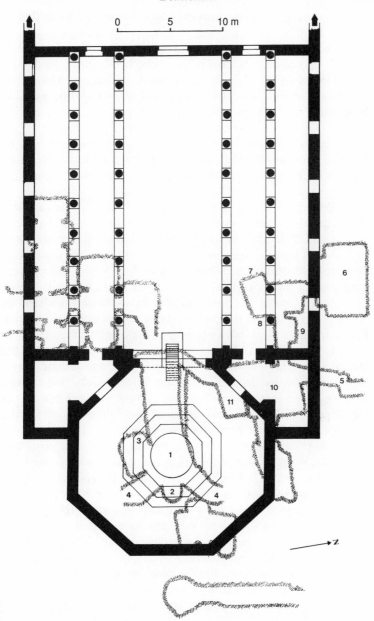

Fig. 8. The Constantinian basilica at Bethlehem, with subterranean areas

Virgin sat to have dinner with the Magi, which may mean that its present form is much reduced.

The northern part of the cave complex is entered by a medieval stairway and passage (5) and is comprised by 'Jerome's Study' (6), the 'Tomb of Jerome' (7), the 'Tombs of Paula and Eustochium' (8), the 'Tomb of Eusebius of Cremona' (9), the Chapel of the Holy Innocents (10), and the Chapel of St Joseph (11).

There is no evidence for the early Christian veneration of the Nativity Grotto in Bethlehem. The texts that are used to support a case for a Christian use of the cave prior to the fourth century fall into two categories. In the first place, there is the evidence of Justin Martyr, and the apocryphal stories, which place the birth of Christ somewhere outside Bethlehem in a cave. It has been argued that there are several possibilities that would explain why a cave should have been employed in this tradition, the most likely being that Justin assumed that the stable was a cave and perhaps made use of an apocryphal nativity story of a kind that utilized symbolic elements. The *Protevangelium* popularized this view by developing the idea of the cave as a symbol, and Christians visiting Palestine, who were influenced by apocryphal stories, came to presume that Christ's birth took place in a cave. There are, in the second place, the writings of Origen, Eusebius, and Jerome, which together show that by the end of the third century, the famous cave where the mysteries of Tammuz-Adonis were celebrated was identified with the birthplace of Jesus; these do not continue the tradition of Justin, in which the cave is located outside the town, but rather demonstrate a blending of pagan and Christian traditions. What pre-dated the pagan use of the site may have been some sort of Jewish folk cult of the Messiah's birthplace, but this is a purely hypothetical suggestion. There is no shred of evidence that might suggest that Jewish-Christians venerated the cave.

Whether the historical Jesus was actually born in Bethlehem is a debatable point that will not be explored here. If his birthplace was Nazareth, and the Bethlehem traditions of the Gospels were secondary, then 'the symbol of the cave', as Justin puts it, becomes a legend embellishing a legend which, by good fortune and some engineering, found its resting place on a pagan cult site.

6

Golgotha

WE will consider here the suggestion by the Bagatti–Testa school that Jewish-Christians employed an artificial cave in the side of the Rock of Calvary and venerated the Tomb of Christ before Hadrian built a temple of Venus[1] on the site. The fundamental question, however, is whether some of the area under the present Church of the Holy Sepulchre in Jerusalem is to be identified with Golgotha of the New Testament. Christian tradition holds that this is indeed the case, and that the church of Jerusalem handed on the fact, so that when Constantine decided to build a basilica on the site, the bishop of Jerusalem, Macarius, was able to direct the builders to precisely the right spot.

The Temple of Venus

The Church Fathers of the fourth and fifth centuries record that Hadrian built a temple to Aphrodite/Venus on the site where Jesus was crucified, buried, and rose again out of a malicious desire to smother holy ground, so that Christians were not able to worship there any longer and would lose their faith in Christ. We have already looked at the words of Sozomen (*Hist. Eccles.* ii. 1) in this regard, when it was argued that restoration language used by the Church Fathers was unhelpful for determining the history of sites. Jerome writes: 'Indeed, the original persecutors supposed that by defiling our holy places they could deprive us of our faith in the Passion and the Resurrection' (*Ep.* lviii. 3). The fifth-century

---

[1] The Greek Church Fathers refer to the goddess as Aphrodite, but the temple in Jerusalem was undoubtedly dedicated to the Roman form of the goddess, Venus (see Millar, 1990*b*), 28–30. Her temple had a 'Syrian' gable (see Kadman (1956), 23, 74), but it is unlikely that Venus was officially syncretized with Astarte. The image of Venus appears on 40% of the coin types from Aelia Capitolina, while Jupiter is found on only 6 types, 3 of which are unsure, see Kadman (1956), 36–43; cf. Meshorer (1989).

historian Socrates records: 'After the period of his Passion, those who embraced the Christian faith greatly venerated the tomb, but those who hated Christianity, not caring for the memory of the place, covered the spot with a mound of earth, erected a temple to Venus, and put up her image there' (*Hist. Eccles.* i. 17). All these (and see also Rufinus, *Hist. Eccles.* ix. 6; Ambrose, *Com. Ps.* xlviii) reflect Eusebius' account that the area around the tomb was covered with a fill of earth and a temple was built for the 'licentious demon Aphrodite': 'Moreover, with a great deal of hard work, they brought in earth from some place outside and covered up the whole area; thereafter raising the level and paving it over with stone. They concealed the sacred cave somewhere below by the great quantity of fill' (*Vita Const.* iii. 26).

With further hard work and an enormous excavation, Constantine's labourers managed to unearth the tomb of Christ, build a new mound of earth, and erect a Christian basilica where there had been the temple of Venus. This basilica was dedicated in September 335 and was known as the Martyrium (in Greek, Μαρτύριον, meaning 'witness'). We are told by Eusebius (*Vita Const.* iii. 25–40) that on the western side of this church was a vast courtyard which surrounded the Edicule, a small building which housed the supposed Tomb of Christ.[2] On the east side of the basilica, in front of its main entrance, was a courtyard which led on to the Cardo Maximus. This layout has been confirmed by archaeological excavations, which have uncovered portions of the Constantinian structure (proposed plan: Figure 9) and later Byzantine buildings.

There is no doubt that Hadrian's temple lay somewhere on the same site, on an area which is now mainly occupied by the Church of the Holy Sepulchre. Substructural walls built to support the Hadrianic *temenos* have been discovered in excavations in various parts of the church.[3] So we know that the Church Fathers are

---

[2] It seems very probable that the building constructed actually to house the Edicule was not part of Constantine's plan; see Wistrand (1952); Conant (1956), 47; Wilkinson (1981), 40–1. It was more likely completed in the latter part of the reign of Constantius II.

[3] For example: a wall on the eastern side of the Rock of Calvary (see below), a wall beneath the choir of the Katholicon, five walls south-east and six walls north-east of the Edicule; see Katsimbinis (1977), 209; Corbo (1981–2), pls. 10, 16, 19, 24, 40–4, 61:2a, 62:c, photos 30–1, 34, 44.1, 2, 45.1, 53, 88–90, 97 f, g; Díez Fernandez (1984), 28–36, fig. 48.8; Coüasnon (1974), 24.

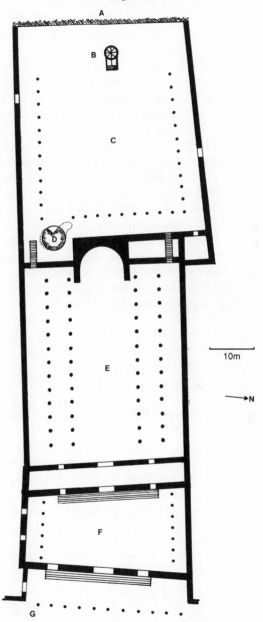

FIG. 9. Golgotha: the Constantinian basilica and its surroundings

correct when they tell us that Constantine built his basilica on top of the destroyed temple of Venus; but did Hadrian build the temple of Venus on Golgotha?

To begin with, it is helpful to consider what we know about the area immediately around the temple of Venus in the late Roman period. The seventh-century *Chronicon Paschale* (i. 224 *PG* 92, 613)[4] informs us that Aelia Capitolina had two civic centres, *demosia*. One of these has been found north of the Haram esh-Sharif.[5] It is very probable indeed that the second civic centre, or forum, was located immediately south of the temple of Venus, in the region of the present Muristan. The Muristan was known by the medieval period as the traditional market-place of Jerusalem. Evidence of Hadrianic filling and levelling operations have been discovered here and under the Church of the Redeemer (see Map 4).[6] These operations would have been undertaken to create a level space for the market region. Certainly a forum next to a temple would make sense. As with the temple, it would have been connected to the main north–south street of the city, the Cardo Maximus, in both late Roman and Byzantine times, and also to the east–west Decumanus I.[7]

The temple of Venus appears to have been composed of a multitude of small shrines, since Eusebius refers to numerous 'dead idols', and states that 'they were pouring out foul libations on profane and accursed altars' (*Vita Const.* iii. 36). Jerome makes a reference to a statue of Jupiter 'in the place of the resurrection', as well as a marble statue of Venus on 'the rock of the cross' (*Ep.* lviii. 3).

Given the probable location of the temple of Venus adjacent to the western forum, the evidence of Melito of Sardis' *Paschal Homily* is especially significant for the placement of biblical Golgotha. Late in the second century, after visiting Aelia Capitolina (cf. Eusebius, *Hist. Eccles.* iv. 26. 13–14), Melito wrote

[4] The text has been related to archaeological remains in Jerusalem by Margalit (1989). Since the citation of the *Chronicon Paschale* is problematic, references here are to the Patrologia Graeca edition, which is noted in the margin of Dindorf's text (CSHB, 1832). The English translation by Whitby and Whitby (1989) does not include this paragraph.

[5] Bagatti (1958); Loffreda (1985*b*); Benoit (1971).

[6] Lux (1972), 109, plans 1 and 6; Vriezen (1977), 76–81; Schein (1981), 23; Kenyon (1974), 26, fig. 37.

[7] For physical evidence of the Cardo Maximus, Decumanus I, and other nearby streets and features, see Margalit (1989), 48.

of Christ being crucified 'in the middle of Jerusalem' (*Paschal Homily* 93; cf. 94 'in the middle of the city').[8] In the New Testament, Golgotha appears to be located outside Jerusalem (Matt. 27: 32; Mark 15: 22–3; Luke 23: 26; John 19: 16). Certainly, given the close proximity of the tomb where Jesus was apparently laid, the execution place cannot have been inside. To Jews, tombs were unclean, and they were never located within Jewish cities (cf. *m. Baba Bathra* 2. 9). The area under the temple of Venus and the forum—a former quarry—had been outside first-century Jerusalem. During the years 41–4, however, under the reign of Agrippa I, the region was included within the city by Agrippa's Third Wall.[9] It has continued to lie within the city until the present day. If Christians were indeed pointing to the place where Christ died as being somewhere near where the temple of Venus was standing, then they would have given Melito the impression that Jesus was crucified in the middle of Roman Aelia Capitolina. He cannot have gained the impression that Jesus died in the middle of the city from the New Testament.

But Melito does not so much as hint that the place where Christ died was to be found under the *temenos* of the temple of Venus. In fact, he gives a location which would seem to place the crucifixion at a particular spot, but he fails to mention the temple at all. In his *Paschal Homily* (94) Melito writes that Christ suffered ἐπὶ μέσης πλατείας. If Melito had used the usual word ὁδός, 'road', instead of *plateia*, then it could be argued that he derived the reference from mention of 'passers-by' in the Gospel accounts (Matt. 29: 39; Mark 15: 29), which implies that there was a road near the place of Jesus' crucifixion. But, as L. Robert has shown in a study of the word,[10] *plateia* has a technical meaning: it particularly refers to a street in an avenue of colonnades.[11] The word would be appropriate as a reference to the colonnaded streets around the forum, especially to the Cardo Maximus or Decumanus. This is precisely Eusebius' use of the word *plateia* (*Vita Const.* iii. 39), when he is referring to the entrance to Constantine's

---

[8] Cf. A. E. Harvey (1966). For the most recent English translation, see S. G. Hall (1979).

[9] See Hamrick (1977).

[10] (1937), 532–6. See also Sauvaget (1941), 46; Martin (1956), 167. The Arabic word *al-Balat* traces its etymology from the Greek *plateia* to Aramaic *platia*; see Fränkel (1886), 281.

[11] Robert (1937), n. 3.

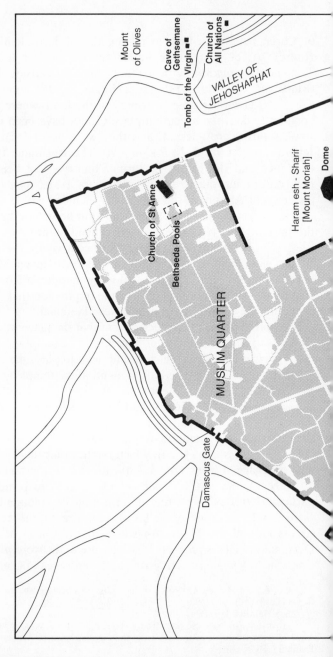

Map 4. Jerusalem: today's Old City and vicinity

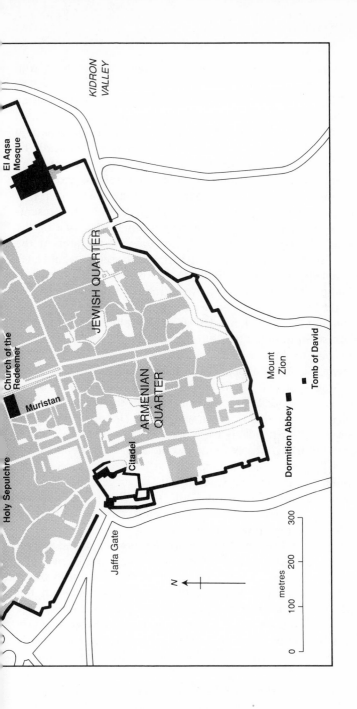

basilica off a colonnaded street, or more exactly the Cardo Maximus.

Eusebius' comments in his *Onomasticon* (74. 19–21), written before the Constantinian developments, that Golgotha was pointed out 'in Aelia near the northern parts of Mount Zion', would accord well with an identificiation of Golgotha as lying beneath the forum. It would be stretching the 'northern parts of Mount Zion' rather far if we were to assume that Eusebius is referring to the site of the temple of Venus. The topography of the area is such that Mount Zion descends into a shallow valley, north of the present-day Jaffa Gate, which runs east–west through the area of the Muristan. The ground level then rises towards the area of the Church of the Holy Sepulchre. Furthermore, Eusebius would later record that the basilica was built 'on the very site of the evidence for salvation' (*Laud. Const.* ix. 16), a reference to the finding of the wood of the cross, but he never names the place Golgotha.

'In the middle of a colonnaded street' is a phrase which may at first sight seem to imply that a rather small and specific area was pointed out to Melito. This is curious, because in the New Testament 'Golgotha' appears to have been an entire region rather than a little spot that could be pointed to in the middle of an avenue of colonnades. John records that 'in the place where he was crucified' there was a garden with tombs (John 19: 41), which suggests it was a reasonably large area.

The tradition of the early Church would also seem to understand the New Testament site of Golgotha as a large area. Eusebius' description in the *Onomasticon* appears to suggest that it was a certain region rather than one little spot. When the site was identified as lying under the temple of Venus, this idea of its being a fairly sizeable region was preserved.

The Bordeaux Pilgrim of 333 refers to Golgotha as the rise on which the Martyrium was built. Describing the scene s/he encountered walking northwards towards the Damascus Gate, along the Cardo, s/he wrote: 'On your left is the small hill Golgotha where the Lord was crucified; and about a stone's throw from it is the vault where they laid his body and he rose again on the third day' (*Itin. Burd.* 593–4). This passage has frequently been taken as a reference to the so-called Rock of Calvary,[12]

---

[12] For example, Wilkinson (1981), 322; cf. 158.

though it is hard to imagine that anyone would have called such a strange rocky protruberance a hill. The basilica, however, was built on a similar 'mound of earth' to the one laid for the temple of Venus.[13] It is 'there', on this small artificial hill, that the pilgrim locates the basilica: 'By order of the emperor Constantine there has now been built there a basilica' (*Itin. Burd.* 594).[14] The hill on which the basilica was built was slightly higher than Mount Moriah, and Eusebius would accordingly see it as the 'New Jerusalem' built over against the one celebrated of old (*Vita Const.* iii. 33).

Cyril of Jerusalem, writing *c*.348, seems also to have thought of Golgotha as the area on which the basilica stood (cf. *Cat.* i. 1; iv. 10, 14; v. 10–11; x. 19; xii. 39; xiii. 4, 22, 23, 26, 28, 32, 39; xvi. 4). The actual 'rocks' of Golgotha to which Cyril repeatedly refers (e.g. *Cat.* iv. 12; xiii. 34; xviii. 16) may have included the Rock of Calvary (cf. *Cat.* xiii. 39), but for him the Rock of Calvary was not exclusively Golgotha. Cyril could refer to the basilica on the site as itself 'Golgotha' (*Cat.* xvi. 4).[15] He understood Golgotha to have been in former times a garden (*Cat.* xiv. 5; cf. John 19. 41); Christ was, according to him, crucified 'in a garden' (*Cat.* xiii. 8). The Rock of Calvary can never have been a garden, only a geological formation.

The fourth-century pilgrim Egeria's use of the term is the same (cf. *Itin.* xxv. 1). According to her, the basilica built by Constantine, known as the Martyrium, is 'on Golgotha' (*Itin.* xxv. 1–6, 8–10; xxvii. 3; xxx. 1; xxxvii. 1; xli. 1). This terminology was continued until the sixth century, as we can see from its usage by Theodosius (*De Situ* vii), who refers to Constantine's basilica as 'Golgotha', but it became less popular during the course of the Byzantine period, when the tendency arose to identify the Rock of Calvary as the actual place of the crucifixion (see below).

In summary, if Melito is referring to a small specific locality lying in the middle of an avenue of colonnades, he would be a unique source, because up until at least the fifth century our other

---

[13] An argument for the minimum height of the hill will be presented in a forthcoming book: S. Gibson and J. E. Taylor, *The Church of the Holy Sepulchre in Jerusalem: Select Archaeological and Historical Problems* (Palestine Exploration Fund Monograph Series no. 2; London). Our conclusion is that the *floor* of the basilica must have been constructed at a height close to the level of the *top* of the Rock of Calvary.

[14] Trans. by Wilkinson (1981), 158.   [15] *Pace* Walker (1990), 254.

sources see Golgotha as a whole region, though how large a region is unknown; certainly it was all the land underneath the basilica. But Melito's evidence points to Golgotha as being understood to lie under a colonnaded street. The colonnaded streets were most likely around the forum, south of the temple of Venus. It seems very probable that Melito is using poetic licence in writing that Christ was crucified in the middle of a colonnaded street. Perhaps the elegant avenues of colonnades in this quarter struck the visitor as forming an extraordinary contrast to the atrocity of crucifixion. Nevertheless, Melito does not say that Golgotha was located where the basilica was later to stand, but in a place near by. It would be reading too much into Melito to argue that the Jerusalem church identified a spot in the middle of one particular street, and it would also be reading too much into his words to argue that he knew Golgotha as the same place as did the Christians of the fourth century and after. It may be that the Jerusalem church, aware that Golgotha was a sizeable region, identified its centre as being around the southern part of the forum, but with Constantine's developments this sense of where the centre was located was moved north to fit under the temple of Venus.

The Rock of Calvary and the Burial of Adam

What then of the Rock of Calvary? Egeria refers to the rock protrusion only as 'the Cross' (xxiv. 7; xxv. 9, 11; xxvii. 3, 6; xxx. 1, 2; xxxi. 4; xxxv. 2; xxxvi. 4, 5; xxxvii. 1, 4, 5, 8; xxxix. 2), the cross in question being the crucifix Constantine appears to have erected there as a special token. Since the Constantinian basilica was dedicated to 'the saving sign', i.e. the cross (Eusebius, *Laud. Const.* ix. 16), a cross would serve to remind those assembled in the western courtyard of this dedication. Fifth- and sixth-century literary evidence for the crucifix on the rock is curiously elusive. The garbled account of the *Breviarius* (A and B. 2), which is often read as referring to a gold and bejewelled cross on the rock, more likely refers to a reliquary box containing part of the wood of the cross, housed in an exedra of the courtyard. The first surviving pilgrim text to describe a crucifix, made of silver, on the rock is the account by Adomnan, written late in the seventh century (*De Loc. Sanct.* i. 5. 1).

The silence of pilgrims would appear to result from their perception of the crucifix as mere decoration. The early pilgrims were interested in relics and items which 'witnessed' biblical events, but they were remarkably vague about details of art or architecture. They would simply find a church 'very big' or 'splendid', and record facts about it only as these related to the matters which they considered important.

In a rather late (ninth-century) legend preserved by Theophanes (*Chron.* 86. 28), Theodosius II sends a gold, bejewelled crucifix to be placed on the Rock of Calvary. However, since both Egeria and Jerome refer to a cross as already existing on the rock before Theodosius II, this does not seem very credible. Theodosius II was very likely responsible for the depiction of a glorified, gold and bejewelled, 'True Cross' on an idealized Rock of Calvary in the apse mosaic of Sta Pudenziana in Rome, but not for an actual crucifix on the rock. The glorified True Cross was a popular motif in Byzantine art, but representations of it, even when placed on top of a semblance of the Rock of Calvary, are too diverse to be seen as actual depictions of the crucifix which physically stood on the Rock of Calvary in Jerusalem.[16]

It would not have been Constantine's intention that pilgrims should imagine that the crucifix on the rock marked the place of Christ's death, but pilgrims clearly began to believe this to be so. Later pilgrims tend to refer to the rock alone as 'Golgotha' or 'Calvary' (from the Latin: *calvarius locus*, 'place of a skull').[17] The Rock of Calvary became known as the place of Christ's crucifixion, but there is absolutely nothing to suggest that Christians of the fourth century or earlier saw this rock as anything special. However, judging from the many pagan artefacts and a small libation altar recovered in the recent excavations east of the rock,[18] it is clear that the pagans used the area as a shrine. As

---

[16] This point is convincingly made by Christine Milner in an unpublished paper, 'A Problem of Evidence: The Byzantine Jewelled Cross on the Rock of Golgotha', presented at 'The Peter Brown Seminar', Australian Byzantine Studies Conference, Canberra, April 5–7, 1991. I am grateful to her for sending me a copy of the paper and for corresponding about issues to do with the cross on the Rock. Milner's argument that the cross of the *Breviarius* must be the wood of the cross, because it is credited with miraculous powers (a crucifix could have had no such properties), is very strong.

[17] Theodosius, *De Situ* vii; Piacenza Pilgrim, *Itin.* xix–xx; Adomnan, *De Loc. Sanct.* i. 5. 1–2; Bernard Mon., *Itin.* xi; *Arm. Lect.* 42, 43, 44, 50.8.

[18] Illustrations of this altar are found in Díez Fernandez (1984), 34–5, fig. 55;

noted above, Jerome records that a marble statue of Venus stood at the top.

Archaeological discoveries east of the Rock of Calvary would also serve to support the notion that it was considered wholly devoid of Christian significance in the early fourth century. The area appears to have been used as a campsite. An oven (*a*, in Figures 10 and 11) was found connected to a small wall (*b*), which lay on an earth floor at the level used by the Constantinian workmen after they had laid the first fill for the basilica and western courtyard. Near by, foundation walls (*g* and *f*) for a small dwelling were found, which would have stood on this level.[19] The authorities in charge would not have permitted a site thought to be holy to be profaned by allowing workmen to use it as a camp, even if it was a pleasantly sheltered locality.

A tradition that has been used to argue for the early veneration of the Rock of Calvary, or Golgotha as a whole, is one which places the burial of Adam at the place where Christ rose from the dead. Bagatti and Testa have claimed that Jewish-Christians believed that Adam's burial place lay under the Rock of Calvary.

However, the first attestation of the belief in Adam's burial at Golgotha is not found in any writings that may be construed as being Jewish-Christian, but in Origen's *Commentary on Matthew*, written in the latter part of the third century. He writes:

Concerning the place of the skull, it came to me that Hebrews hand down [the tradition that] the body of Adam has been buried there; in order that 'as in Adam all die' both Adam would be raised and 'in Christ all will be made alive' (cf. 1 Cor. 15: 22). (*in Matt.* xxvii. 33)

This form of the paragraph is found only in the Greek catena of Origen. In the Latin, there is a reference to 'a tradition', but it is not specified that it is a Hebrew one; while the name 'the place of a

Freeman-Grenville (1987), 190, pl. VI. For a detailed analysis of the excavations east of the Rock of Calvary, see Taylor (1989), 217–22, which will appear in modified form in Gibson and Taylor (forthcoming; see n. 13 above). Suffice to say here that the common preconception that the Rock of Calvary was covered over in the Hadrianic period appears, on the basis of archaeology, to be wrong.

[19] I suggested in my Ph.D. thesis (Taylor (1989)) that the Constantinian workmen may have felt it a comfort to sleep and eat close to the Rock, if they perceived it as holy, but on further reflection this seems a weak apology for the use of the area.

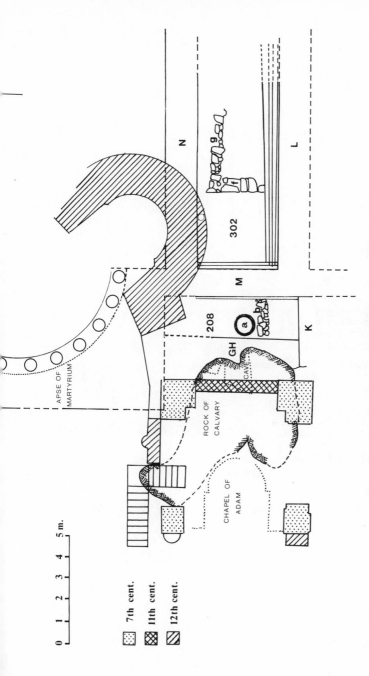

FIG. 10. Golgotha: the area around the Rock of Calvary

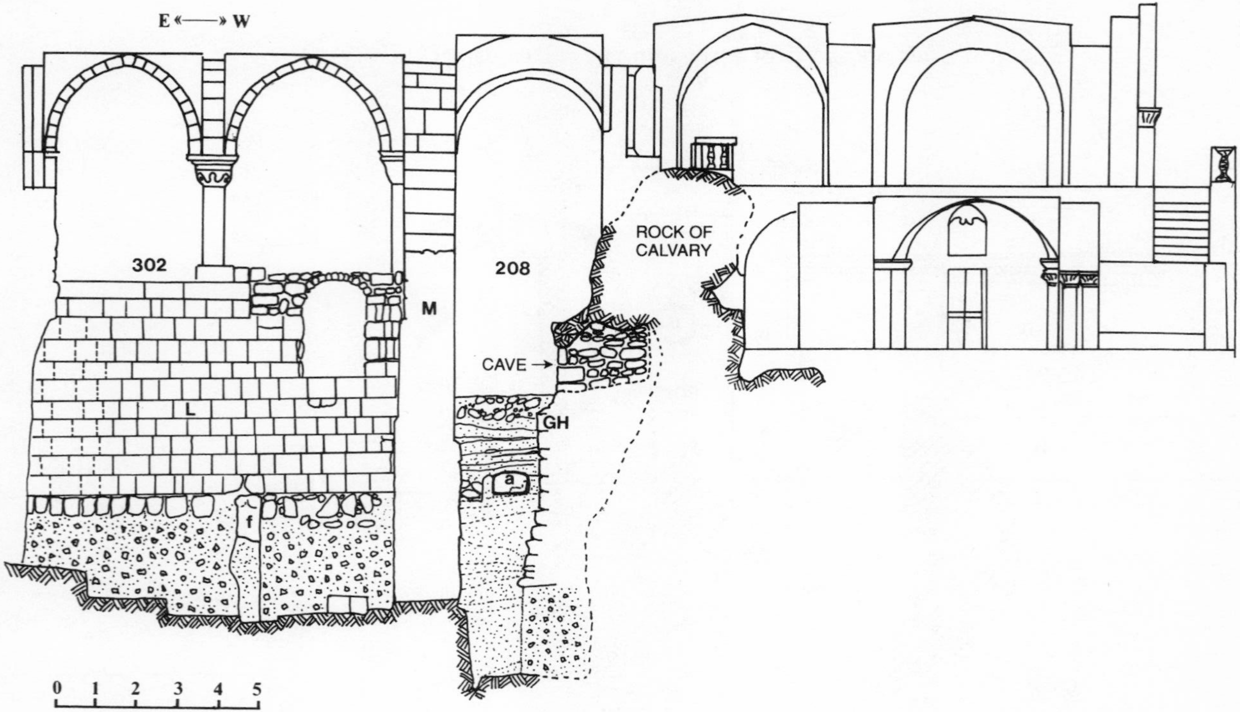

FIG. II. East–West section of the area around the Rock of Calvary

skull' is linked with the idea that the 'head' of the human race died and rose again.

According to the Bagatti–Testa school, the Hebrews referred to by Origen are Jewish-Christians. I. Mancini puts the argument concisely: 'these [Jews] . . . must have been Christians also, for the synagogue held that Adam was buried at Hebron or Mount Moriah'.[20] It is plainly an illogical piece of reasoning that would conclude that any Jewish tradition which the rabbis did not record or support is Jewish-Christian. As we saw above, Mamre was not recorded or supported by the rabbis as a site at which blessings might be made, but it was a place venerated by some Jews for a very long time.

It would cause us considerable difficulties if we were to believe Origen, because, if there was a Jewish tradition, preceding Christ's crucifixion, that Adam was buried under Golgotha, then the development of Paul's Adam Christology (Rom. 5: 12–21; Cor. 15: 22, 45–9) might be said to have derived from speculation concerning the place of Jesus' death. However, neither Paul nor any other New Testament writer even so much as hints that Adam lay buried beneath Golgotha. It is a profound silence.

Was Origen correct in reporting that a Hebrew tradition held that Adam was buried under Golgotha? His beliefs were certainly soon popular, and were reported by many other Church Fathers during subsequent centuries. As the name 'Golgotha' came to apply more and more to the Rock of Calvary alone, then so too the legend came to be confined to this locality.

Significantly, Eusebius does not mention the legend. Moreover, it appears that all the attestations to the belief ultimately derive from Origen. Pseudo-Athanasius' language clearly reflects his source: Christ suffered in the place of a skull 'which the Hebrew teachers declare was Adam's tomb, for they say he was buried there after the curse' (*De Passione et Cruce Domini*). Like others, Pseudo-Athanasius found the belief apposite in view of the fact that Christ was renewing the old Adam. Epiphanius embellished the tradition by suggesting that the skull of Adam was actually excavated on the site (*Pan.* xlvi. 1–9). From the end of the fourth century onwards the tradition that Adam was buried at Golgotha

[20] (1984), 167.

is well attested.[21] It is often found depicted pictorially in Byzantine and medieval art, a subject which Bagatti himself has discussed.[22] The popularity of a tradition, however, in no way proves its authenticity. It is interesting that out of all the literary references to Adam's burial at Golgotha, only Pseudo-Athanasius, Basil of Seleucia (*Oration* xxxviii. 3), and Ambrose (*Exp. of St Luke's Gospel* x) mention that it was a Hebrew tradition.[23]

Bagatti relied heavily on apocryphal texts to argue for the Jewish-Christian, as opposed to 'Hebrew', nature of the legend. Certain pertinent apocryphal writings are randomly deemed 'Jewish-Christian' or as having their origins in a Jewish-Christian milieu, the *Cave of Treasures*,[24] for example. In its present form, this is a sixth-century work.[25] The Christian author used a Jewish Syriac text written in the fourth century near Edessa, but while the work has a Jewish source and a Christian redaction, this does not make it a Jewish-Christian text as such. Furthermore, even the most ancient material in the text derives from after the time when Christians in general had advertised the burial of Adam at Golgotha.

The text of the *Cave of Treasures* preserves a story in which Noah takes the corpse of Adam in the ark during the Flood. The corpse is later replaced in 'the cave of treasures' at the centre of the world, at 'Golgotha'. The first thing to note here is that Eutychius (ninth–tenth century) preserves much the same story in his *Annales* (i. 918), which shows that the *Cave of Treasures* was employed in orthodox circles. The second point worth mentioning is that the Christians had a very different notion to the Jews of the 'centre of the world'. In the original Jewish story, used in the *Cave of Treasures*, Adam may well have been carried by Noah to this *omphalos*, but the centre of the world was *Mount Moriah*, not Golgotha. Jews believed that Jerusalem was the centre of the

---

[21] Basil of Caesarea, *Com. in Isaiah* v. 141; John Chrysostom, *Hom. in Joh.* xix. 16–18; Nonnus Panopolitanus, *Para. Joh.* xix; Ps.-Tertullian, *Carm. adv. Marcionem* ii. 4; Ps.-Cyprian, *Ad Cornelium*; Ambrose, *Ep.* lxx. 10; *Exp. Luc.* x; Ps.-Augustine, *Sermones Supposititii* iv. 5; Moses bar Kepha, *De Paradiso* i. 14; Basil of Seleucia, *Oration* xxxviii. 3; Eutychius, *Annales* i. 911–18; George Hamartolos, *Short Chronicle* iv. 236; Epiphanius Mon., *Itin.* i. 10–13.

[22] Bagatti (1977); Mancini (1965). Adam is shown coming out of a small coffin as Christ's blood strikes him.

[23] See also Walker (1990), 255 n. 58, for a similar sceptical view.

[24] Bagatti and Testa (1978), 27.

[25] Charlesworth (1981), 91; Budge (1927), xi, 21–3, 132, 230.

earth, and the Temple was the centre of Jerusalem (Ezek. 28: 12; cf. Ps. 74: 12; *Tanh. B. Lev.* 78; *b.Sanh.* 37a). In the writings of Cyril of Jerusalem (*Cat.* xiii. 27–8) and Jerome (*In Ezech.* xi. 5–6), however, the centre is Golgotha,[26] which shows that the Christians had appropriated a Jewish idea but relocated it, as the Muslims would do later; in Islam, the centre of the world is at the Kaaba in Mecca. At the end of the seventh century the Christian centre was marked in the middle of the courtyard which separated the circular construction around the Edicule, the Anastasis, from the Rock of Calvary.[27]

The appropriation of the Jewish idea of the centre of the world and its removal from Mount Moriah to Golgotha appears therefore to have happened in the fourth century. It is extremely likely indeed that the Jewish source material in the *Cave of Treasures* would have placed Adam's burial on Mount Moriah. This placement is well known in Jewish tradition, as L. Ginzberg has shown.[28] Origen simply got it wrong.

Another apocryphal work, the *Combat of Adam*, which Bagatti uses also as a 'Jewish-Christian' text,[29] is based on the final version of the *Cave of Treasures* and therefore dates from the sixth century at the earliest. Bagatti cites A. M. Denis's erroneous suggestion that the *Combat of Adam* comes from the second century[30] and then infers from this that the *Cave of Treasures* preceded it, thereby placing the latter text as early as the second century.

Despite its popularity, the tradition of Adam's burial at Golgotha (and later more specifically at the Rock of Calvary) was not uncontested in ancient sources. Jerome was initially taken by the notion (*Ep.* xlvi. 17), and incidentally provides us with a rare insight into how this tradition was passed on: someone discoursing in a church on St Paul's letter to the Ephesians (5: 14) told the story of Adam's burial at Golgotha, adding that Christ leaned over Adam's sepulchre and, paraphrasing the relevant verse, said, 'Rise

[26] See also Origen, *Comm. in Ps.* lxxiii. 12 (*PG* 12, 1532*b*). Origen refers to the Tomb of Jesus in 'the heart of the earth'. It is possible that this has some relationship to the idea of its burial at the centre of the earth, which increases the likelihood that it was Origen who was first to shift the centre from the Temple to Golgotha.

[27] Cf. Sophronius, *Anacreontica* xx. 29–30. See also Vincent and Abel (1914*b*), 224–5; Maraval (1985), 57.

[28] (1955), 117, 126–7; cf. Klijn (1977), 9; Jeremias (1926), 34–9.

[29] (1971*d*), 23.   [30] Denis (1970).

up, Adam, you that sleep, and arise from the dead' (*in Eph.* v. 14). However, around 398, Jerome vehemently dismissed the legend as fable (*in Matt.* xxvii. 33).[31] He repeated the reference to the person discoursing on Ephesians, but he went on to say that it was just a 'popular interpretation' which was 'pleasing to the ears' of people. Nevertheless, Golgotha did not gain its name because of Adam's skull, but because it was local jargon for 'execution place', or 'place of beheading'. He explained that outside the gate of Jerusalem there were areas where criminals were executed, and these were each called 'Golgotha', even in his day. Jesus was therefore killed in the 'field of the condemned', as a criminal among criminals. Furthermore, said Jerome, implicitly arguing against Origen, the Jews did not have a tradition that Adam was buried at Golgotha. Jerome knew of the tradition of Adam's burial at Hebron (cf. *Lib. loc.* 75. 23).[32]

Since Jerome was familiar with Jerusalem and its surroundings, his first-hand knowledge of the language of the local population provides weighty evidence for a proper understanding of the name 'Golgotha'. Perhaps, if there were other 'execution places' around Jerusalem, this would account for Cyril of Jerusalem's specification of the *Christian* Golgotha in his lectures as being 'pre-eminent' ὑπερανεστώς (*Cat.* xiii. 39, or ὑπερανεστηκώς x. 19), a *double entendre* of a word which appears to refer both to the physical height of the hill (part rock, part fill) of Golgotha and to its importance.[33]

If we know that Jews did not believe that Adam was buried under the temple of Venus, but under Mount Moriah or Hebron,

[31] It is interesting that few have followed Jerome's scepticism. A notable exception was Bede, *in Matt.* xxvi. The theological appeal of the story which had Adam buried at Golgotha was immense.

[32] Cf. *Ep.* cviii. 11. For the tomb of Adam at Hebron see *b.Sota* 13a; Josh. (Vulg.) 14: 15; Adomnan, *De Loc. Sanct.* ii. 9. 1–3. The placement of Adam's tomb here appears to be a late development based on the interpretation of the ancient name of Hebron, Kiryat Arba (Gen. 23: 2) or 'City of Four', to mean the three Patriarchs buried there and Adam, though local Christians believed that the fourth man was Caleb; cf. Jeremias (1958), 96–9.

[33] Lampe (1961), col. 1437, defines ὑπερανίσταμαι as literally meaning 'stand up or project over' with a metaphorical meaning of 'be superior to'. The words used by Cyril have been translated to refer to the Rock of Calvary which, according to Coüasnon (1974: 50), 'dominates'. Walker (1990: 252) writes that the Rock was 'conspicuous in its elevation' or 'rising on high'. Hunt (1984: 12) uses the passage to say that the Rock of Calvary 'stood above' the basilica . All these fail to realize that it was the basilica which towered over the tiny rocky outcrop (see n. 13 above).

how then did Origen come to make a mistake? Origen may have confused a 'temple' (the Jewish Temple) possibly referred to by his source[34] with the temple of Venus which had stood on the site of Golgotha since the days of Hadrian. Or else it is possible that his resiting of an event located by some Jews on the Temple Mount was polemical: it made the Adam Christology of Paul more poignant. If the centre or navel of the world was consciously transferred from Mount Moriah, it was certainly not the only Jewish localization to be thus removed. The sacrifice of Isaac also migrated from its original Jewish placement on Mount Moriah to Golgotha.[35] Since Isaac was a type of the Passion (Diodorus of Tarsus, *Frag. in Genesis* xxii. 2; cf. Gregory of Nyssa, *De Tridui Spatico*; Ps.-Augustine, *Serm. Sup.* vi (lxxi). 5[36]), the sacrifice of Isaac was moved to an altogether more appropriate place, to the Christian mind. Here, in the sixth century, an altar of stone was shown where Abraham apparently offered his son.[37] The ring of Solomon, which supposedly helped build the first Temple (*b.Gitt.* 7. 68a) was displayed at Golgotha in the fourth century (Egeria, *Itin.* xxxvii. 3). Even the place where Jesus cast out the people buying and selling in the Temple precincts was considered to be a court in the Golgotha complex (*Breviarius* A. 3).

It would seem very likely that with the developing popularity of the tradition of Adam's burial at Golgotha, and the gradual heightening of the sanctity of the place by means of these newly transferred localizations of biblical events, there came a marked tendency to isolate specific spots within the region as *the* actual sites where events took place. Golgotha was no longer seen as the site as a whole but as the rocky outcrop with the cross on its summit. It became one of the many sacred sites within a growing complex of shrines and buildings. Furthermore, the markings of different precise spots helped in the ordering of pilgrims during festivals and in the co-ordination of the liturgy. The actual form of the rock was obscured, and no one realized just how unlikely a place it would have been for a crucifixion: it was naturally hollow

---

[34] Whether the source was written is doubtful. It may even have been a case of hearsay.

[35] Maimonides, *Beit Abachria*, cap. 2; see Vermes (1961), 209.

[36] Ps.-Augustine says that it was Jerome who learnt from the Jews that Isaac was offered at the place where Christ was crucified, and that Adam was buried on the spot; a strange conflation of traditions.

[37] *Breviarius* A. 2; Theodosius, *De Situ* vii; Piacenza Pilgrim, *Itin.* xix.

and stood 12 metres above bedrock on the east, and 5 metres above bedrock on the west. In other words, any Roman soldiers who wished to crucify three people on top of this unstable spur would have had to overcome enormous logistical difficulties, to say the least.

A further point to consider is the cave created in the eastern side of the Rock of Calvary (see Figures 10 and 11, Plates 1 and 2). It is this artificial cave which Bagatti and Testa have suggested should be identified as the Tomb of Adam of the first century. According to their hypothesis, the cave pre-dates all the legendary material that would have Adam buried here, and also inspired Hadrian to create a pagan shrine on this precise spot.[38] The Jewish-Christians allegedly localized the 'descent into hell' here. Jesus went through the cleft in the rock, caused by the earthquake of Matthew 27: 51–2, and descended, spiritually, into the cave, the Tomb of Adam. This supposedly Jewish-Christian legend, based on speculations concerning the actual cleft in the rock (which was one of the reasons why the outcrop was not used for quarrying) is not found in any Jewish-Christian writings or writings about Jewish-Christians, but in orthodox writings such as Cyril's *Catechetical Lectures* (xiii. 39; xiv. 20), and the twelfth-century pilgrim accounts of Saewulf and Daniel the Abbot.

Bagatti's suggestion that the cave was used in pagan times for divination[39] is without foundation. There is no textual evidence for the present cave existing before the seventh century, and there are quite good reasons to believe it did not.

To begin with, it is very strange that no early pilgrim mentions the cave if it was there, and it is perhaps even stranger that the legends that have Adam buried at 'Golgotha' themselves fail to make mention of this remarkable feature. The first mention of a cave is in the sixth-century *Cave of Treasures*, which uses symbolic language to communicate theological themes, and, as stated above, derived its legend from a Jewish source which would appear to have had Adam buried on Mount Moriah. The source itself may have invented the motif of the cave.

The archaeological remains on the eastern side of the Rock of Calvary suggest that the cave, which is entirely artificial, was created after the Persian invasion (614) at the time when Abbot

---

[38] Bagatti and Testa (1978), 37–8.   [39] (1971*d*), 24.

PLATE 1. Cave cut in
the east side of the
Rock of Calvary

Modestus built a church around the rock. The wall labelled GH in
Figures 10 and 11 is Hadrianic. It appears to have been broken
down by Constantine's builders to a level about 70 centimetres
below the present cave's floor. A wall was built here to hug the
rock, covering up its irregularity and large hollow part.[40] The
irregular sides of the wall around the cave entrance (see Plates 1
and 2) indicate that the cave was not part of the Constantinian
design; rather, at some point later the Constantinian hugging wall
was breached to create the cave. Had the cave been part of the
Constantinian plan, then the entrance would have been constructed
in a neater manner. Prior to the Persian invasion, the rock was
covered with a silver screen,[41] but afterwards not. The cave is

[40] For a full discussion of the archaeology relating to the cave, see Taylor (1989),
224–8, which will also appear in Gibson and Taylor (forthcoming; see n. 13 above).
[41] For the screen, see the *Breviarius* A and B. 2.

PLATE 2.　Cave cut in the east side of the Rock of Calvary

mentioned first by Adomnan (*De Loc. Sanct.* i. 5. 1),[42] who wrote after the time of Modestus. After this, the whole church around the rock appears to have become known as 'The Tomb of Adam' (so Epiphanius Mon., *Itin.* i).

As for the Bagatti–Testa hypothesis, if the cave was not in existence before the time of Constantine, let alone Hadrian, it cannot therefore have been used in Jewish-Christian theology or cult. There is absolutely no evidence of any kind that the Rock of Calvary was venerated by Christians prior to Byzantine developments.

Authenticity and Veneration

We have seen that Golgotha was, in the fourth century, believed to be the general region on which Constantine built his basilica. The name probably applied also to the western courtyard and the

---

[42] Trans. by Wilkinson (1977), 97.

Tomb of Christ. During the late Roman period, the Rock of Calvary had been a shrine at the side of the temple of Venus. Constantine may have decided to employ it in his new Christian precinct partly as a special statement. The cross replacing the statue of Venus would have been a way of asserting the Christian victory over pagan belief.

Before we look more specifically at the question of the authenticity of the Tomb of Christ, let us consider the authenticity of the site under the Church of the Holy Sepulchre as a whole. Is it biblical Golgotha? It was argued above that Christians in Jerusalem prior to Constantine appear to have located Golgotha further south, towards the northern part of Mount Zion, probably under the western forum. In order that the forum could have become identified as the place of Jesus' death by the end of the second century, when Melito visited, it is tempting to credit the Christians in Jerusalem with some knowledge of the general area in which Jesus died and was buried. Had the Jerusalem church simply invented a site, then they might well have chosen one outside Aelia, for very few people would have known that the area of the forum was outside the walls of Jerusalem in Jesus' day, just north of the Gennath ('gardens') Gate. It would have seemed as strange a location for Jesus' crucifixion to Christians of the late second century as it does to many Christians of today, who prefer to imagine that Golgotha is situated outside the present Old City's Damascus Gate, in the area of the so-called Garden Tomb.

It is very possible that the Jerusalem church might have preserved the memory of the location of Golgotha, even given the radical disruptions that affected Jerusalem deeply. As it was argued in Chapter 2, the transition from Jewish to Gentile church in Jerusalem need not have meant a complete change in personnel, or a total break in the continuity of traditions and community memories.

Melito does not place Golgotha under the *temenos* of the temple of Venus. It is striking that no pre-Constantinian source makes anything of, or even mentions, the offensive conjunction of a temple of Venus and Golgotha. We may have to look to the emperor Constantine for bringing this point to the attention of Jerusalem's Bishop Macarius. It may well have been Constantine who had the brainwave that he could destroy Hadrian's temple and glorify Golgotha in one fell swoop, if he could convince the

Jerusalem church that this was an inspired decision; a point we will return to presently.

It is not completely astounding that the Constantinian workmen found an empty tomb in a place which was outside the city walls of Jesus' time, and then included inside, despite Eusebius' proclamation of the discovery as a testimony to the resurrection of the Saviour clearer than any voice could give (*Vita Const.* iii. 28). The area would have been cleared of corpses when it was included in Agrippa's city. Actually, it is interesting that Eusebius writes that the discovery of an empty tomb here was 'contrary to all expectation' (*Vita Const.* iii. 28). This rather argues against any idea that Christians were quietly sure that Christ's tomb lay buried here. It would certainly imply that Eusebius himself had been doubtful.

Did Christians venerate the Tomb of Christ before Hadrian's developments? This seems highly unlikely. In the first place, it is striking that there is no mention of Jesus' tomb in Paul's writings. From about the year 41, only a few years after Christ died, the probable region of Golgotha was included within the city. It would have been easy for any Christian living in Jerusalem to wander over there and say a blessing, and yet there is no record that such acts took place. It seems very probable that Christians' theology of Christ Risen (cf. 1 Cor. 15: 12–23) went sharply against any idea that the tomb in which his body had lain should be venerated. Jews of the time, particularly 'scribes and Pharisees' (Matt. 23: 29–30; Luke 11: 47–8), did honour the tombs of the righteous, as well as of prophets and Old Testament personalities (see Chapter 13), but the honour accorded these tombs was as a result of the corpses being still interred within them. According to one view, the righteous dead deserved to be physically in heaven, but instead chose to be buried below and thereby afford the faithful some measure of the power of mercy in which they may have rested in heaven (*Mid. Psalm.* 16. 2).[43] Christians too, heavily influenced by popular Jewish practices, would have given honour to the graves of their righteous, the saints. The Tomb of Peter in Rome, for example, was probably the subject of very early respect.[44]

---

[43] P. R. L. Brown (1983), 3. For Jewish venerated graves, see Jeremias (1958), and the discussion in Ch. 13 below.

[44] See Guarducci (1960), 87. There is a possible reference to Peter's tomb by Tertullian (*On Modesty* xxi).

However, they believed that Jesus Christ's body was not in his tomb but that he was physically alive and sitting at the right hand of God the Father in Heaven, the first-fruits of all who would be raised from the dead at the time of Judgement (1 Cor. 15: 20–8). The empty tomb was unimportant.

Moreover, there is good reason to believe that Eusebius' emphasis on the tomb gives an unbalanced picture of what Constantine considered important on Golgotha. It is striking that, despite Eusebius' description of the site as being focused on the tomb, Constantine did not build his grand basilica, 'finer than any other' (*Vita Const.* iii. 31), around this, but further east. As mentioned above, the basilica was built not to honour the tomb at all, but to honour the 'saving sign' (*Laud. Const.* ix. 16): the cross. The building was known by the writer of the *Chronicon Paschale* as 'the church of the Holy Cross' (PG 92, 713). The dedication festival of the Martyrium, and in time of the Anastasis building constructed around the Edicule, was celebrated on the day the alleged cross on which Christ had died had been found (Egeria, *Itin.* xlviii. 1–2). Indeed, thanks to a recent study by H. A. Drake, it now seems clear that Constantine believed that this cross had been recovered from under the temple of Venus.[45] Constantine's letter to Macarius, faithfully preserved by Eusebius (*Vita Const.* iii. 30–2) stresses the importance of the 'token of that most holy passion' and the 'clear assurance of the Saviour's passion', phrases which must refer to the cross rather than the tomb.

Tradition consistently confirms that the wood of the cross was believed to have been discovered on the site of the basilica.[46] As early as 348, Cyril notes that the 'whole world' had been filled with pieces from this cross (*Cat.* iv. 10), and refers to it on a number of occasions (*Cat.* x. 19; xiii. 4, 39; cf. *Ep. Const.* iii). Fourth-century sources repeatedly make mention of the pieces of the cross.[47] In

---

[45] (1985). See also Walker (1990), 127–30.

[46] For the cross being discovered under the basilica's apse: *Breviarius* A. 2, 'to the west is the great apse where the three crosses were found'; cf. Theodosius *De Situ* vii. For the discovery somewhere under the basilica: Egeria, *Itin.* xxvii. 3; cf. xxv. 1–6, 8–10; xxx. 1; xxxvii. 1; xlviii. 1; Piacenza Pilgrim, *Itin.* xx; Antiochus Mon., *Ep. ad Eustathium*; Epiphanius Mon., *Hag.* i; Adomnan, *De Loc. Sanct.* i. 2. 6–7 (and see Arculf's plans); Hugeburc, *Life of Willibald* xcvii. 12–15; Theophanes Isaurus, *Chron.* 18; Bernard Mon., *Itin.* 314.

[47] Gregory of Nyssa, *Vita Macrinae*, PG 46, 989; John Chrysostom, *Contra Judaeos et Gentiles, Quod Christus sit Deus* 9–10, PG 47, 826, cf. *Hom. in Johannem* lxxxv. For an examination of the cross phenomenon in the 4th century

Egeria's day, part of the cross was exhibited in the basilica ('Golgotha, behind the cross') on Good Friday (*Itin.* xxxvii. 1–3). Though late, the letter purportedly written by the emperor Leo to to Omar, king of the Saracens, may preserve accurately the imperial records on the matter, when it is stated that three crosses were found in a trench where Constantine's workmen were digging (PG 107, 315). Interestingly, in fifth-century accounts of the finding of the True Cross, the site of Golgotha is completely unknown to the Jerusalem church. It is revealed to Constantine's mother Helena, who is guided to the right place—which just happens to be the temple of Venus—by dreams and a heavenly sign (cf. Rufinus, *Hist. Eccles.* x. 7; Socrates, *Hist. Eccles.* i. 17; Sozomen, *Hist. Eccles.* ii. 1–2). The choice of site is justified by the discovery of the cross, which has miraculous powers of healing. We know from the evidence of Eusebius that the location of Golgotha had been remembered, but it seems to have suited both Constantine and the Jerusalem church that people should come to believe otherwise. Eusebius appears to avoid mentioning the discovery of the cross out of pure scepticism,[48] though it would not have been prudent to voice his views publicly, considering the discovery of the cross was meaningful, in numerous ways, to the emperor.

There is no doubt that the tomb was also meaningful, and honoured, but no structure was built to house the Edicule until perhaps the time of Constantius II, when the Anastasis was constructed. Furthermore, the basilica was not aligned to focus precisely on the tomb, but was offset slightly to the south. Constantine's letter to Macarius does not mention the tomb at all.

Both the cross and the tomb can only have been discovered after the temple of Venus had been torn down and the fill had been substantially dug away. If the tomb appears to have been an appendage to the basilica, which honoured the cross, then it seems

see Drijvers (1992), 81–93. As both Drijvers and Borgehammar (1991) have shown, the story of the finding of the True Cross was first written down in a (now lost) church history by Gelasius of Caesarea, *c.*390. Borgehammar (pp. 57–81) convincingly argues that an oral story originating in Jerusalem preceded the literary account, and that this was known to Ambrose (*De obit. Theod.* 40–50) and Paulinus of Nola (*Ep.* xxxi. 4–5). As Borgehammar suggests, it is highly probable that this story reflected historical events.

[48] Possible theological reasons for Eusebius' silence and change of emphasis are explored by Walker (1990), 129, and Borgehammar (1991), 93–122.

very likely that it was Constantine's intention at the very start that some such structure should be built. For Constantine, the 'saving sign' was that which had granted him victory over his rival at Milvian Bridge, and elsewhere, and secured him the rule of the entire Empire; it was perfectly fitting that he should build a temple to honour it. And what more fitting place for such a temple than Golgotha, where the cross was used to crucify Christ? The Jerusalem church could point to Golgotha as having been located somewhere around the forum, but, as suggested above, it would have seemed a much better plan to replace the temple of Venus, near by, than build on the forum. Proof that the emperor's judgement was superior to Jerusalem traditions would have been afforded by the discovery of Christ's cross, probably under the supervision of his agent Helena, and then the empty tomb. Indeed, Eusebius noted that Constantine's letter to Macarius which ordered the construction of a church on the site showed that it was 'as if he had this in mind for a long time and had seen with uncanny foresight what was to happen' (*Vita Const.* iii. 29). If Eusebius had held up his hands in horror at the audacity of the first discovery, then he appears to have softened and made room for the second. Such a softening was a wise move politically, and any reservations Eusebius continued to feel were expressed by silence rather than criticism.

Despite this, could the tomb uncovered by Constantine's workmen have been the one in which Jesus' body had rested? There was a burial cave dating from the early Roman period near by, now known as the Tomb of Joseph of Arimathea,[49] but there were tombs from other periods as well.[50] Eusebius may imply that other tombs were obliterated when the Tomb of Christ was cut away from the scarp to stand alone: 'It is indeed wonderful to see this rock standing out erect and alone in a level space and with just a single cave [tomb] in it; in case, had there been many, the miracle of the one who overcame death might be obscured' (*Theoph.* iii. 61; cf. Cyril, *Cat.* xiv. 9).[51] In other words, it may have been seen as a good idea to remove other tombs in case they distracted from the miracle of Christ's resurrection, especially

[49] For a discussion of the so-called Tomb of Joseph of Arimathea, see Clermont-Ganneau, in Warren and Conder (1884), 319–31; Kloner (1980), 145–6.
[50] See Walker (1990), 104.
[51] Wilkinson (1972), 84; Vincent and Abel (1914*b*), 246.

since they too will have been discovered to have been empty. The tomb identified as that of Christ may have been the first that Constantine's diggers uncovered. After it was heralded as belonging to the Saviour, it would not have done at all to have it as one among others which might be seen as having just as much claim to authenticity.[52]

Very little now remains of the tomb identified as that in which Christ was laid, since it was hacked down by Caliph Hakim's men in 1009. We cannot even establish that it was from the first century. It appears to have been rectangular, with an arcosolium bench on its northern side (cf. Adomnan, *De Loc. Sanct.* i. 2. 1, 9–12), but this type of tomb was used for many centuries prior to the time of Jesus. Given that the area of Golgotha was understood by the early Jerusalem church to have been further south than the site now occupied by the Church of the Holy Sepulchre, it would certainly have been miraculous if, given the history here outlined, Constantine's workmen had struck the right tomb.

Moreover, it is curious that if the basilica was the paramount structure, and was not designed to focus on the tomb, the tomb is nevertheless in such a convenient place. It is close to being aligned with the basilica. If it was secondary, as the evidence suggests, then one might well be justified in wondering whether it was not so much that this tomb was the first empty sepulchre to be recovered, but that it was the one in the most appropriate place for the arrangement of the architecture.

Constantine's Edicule was a modest structure, and confirms the impression that the tomb was something of an afterthought. Like the Rock of Calvary, it too was graced with a crucifix.[53] The saving sign was not forgotten here, and perhaps served to turn the attention back to the reason for the existence of the basilica.

This discussion suggests that the Jerusalem church was able to preserve an accurate memory of where Golgotha was situated, but only up until the fourth century. We do not know how large an

[52] There is a burial cave from the Iron Age in the area of the Coptic Monastery; see Vincent and Abel (1914*b*), pl. XII, and cf. Parrot (1955), 41 n. 2.

[53] We know of the crucifix on the top of the Edicule from representations on early pilgrim flasks and glass vessels, and the depiction on the 5th-cent. ivory reliquary box of Samagher; see Grabar (1958), Barag (1970–1), Guarducci (1978). As with the crucifix on the top of the Rock of Calvary, it is first mentioned in texts in the 7th cent.: Adomnan, *De Loc. Sanct.* ii. 1. 7.

area Golgotha was, but it may have been a sizeable region. We can deduce from the late second-century evidence of Melito of Sardis that the Jerusalem church pointed out Golgotha as lying under the colonnaded streets of the forum or the adjacent Cardo Maximus or Decumanus. This location is confirmed by the evidence of Eusebius, writing in his *Onomasticon*. The site of Golgotha was close to the temple of Venus, built by order of the emperor Hadrian, but further south.

With Constantine came a relocation of Golgotha. The emperor made the identification of the site as actually lying under the temple of Venus. He wished to destroy this and replace it with a new Christian temple in honour of the 'saving sign', the cross, which had proved the instrument of his success. Proof of his having chosen the correct site, for those who may have been doubtful amongst the Jerusalem church, came with the finding of the wood of Christ's cross in the course of excavating the Hadrianic fill. The matter was clinched when an empty tomb was discovered and heralded as being that belonging to Christ. Further tombs which came to light were simply cut away.

The Martyrium basilica was built in honour of the cross, and large crucifixes were also affixed to the roof of the Edicule, built around the tomb, and the top of the Rock of Calvary. The rock had been a shrine in the cult of Venus, and it was utilized as a podium for the cross as a statement which proclaimed the victory of Christianity over paganism. Crosses may have been a decorative feature of the entire architectural setting of the basilica, and would have served to remind visitors of the sign to which it was dedicated, but the crucifix on the Rock of Calvary must have been by far the largest. The rock was known as 'the rock of the cross'; the crucifix was simply 'the cross'. In the course of time, various specific localities were identified for biblical events, and these began to accrue in parts of the complex. Christians began to see the rock of the cross as being the precise place where Jesus' cross had been positioned; the decorative cross was believed to have replaced the cross of wood on which the Saviour had died. The rock of the cross, the former Venus shrine, became Golgotha itself.

It may well have been that the belief that Hadrian built a temple on Golgotha led to the idea that pagans wished to annihilate sites with Christian significance in general, so that it was precisely for this reason that the Christians were inclined to accept that the birthplace of Christ was in the cave of Tammuz-Adonis in Bethlehem. But the evidence suggests that Hadrian did not build his temple exactly over Golgotha, and that neither the Rock of Calvary nor the supposed Tomb of Christ was venerated by Christians before the fourth century.

7

Eleona

THE fourth and final site of a Constantinian basilica is the Eleona Church on the Mount of Olives. Constantine, via Helena, constructed this edifice over a cave which, according to Bagatti, 'had seen cult in former times, beginning with Apostolic days'.[1] We shall consider here whether this statement is borne out by the surviving evidence, literary and archaeological.[2]

It was argued above that it is very unlikely that the tree at Mamre or the tomb and rock at Golgotha were subject to any Christian veneration before the fourth century. The cave at Bethlehem was visited by Christians in the latter part of the third century, but in fact its main identity was that of a cave of Tammuz-Adonis. It is not surprising that the place of Christ's crucifixion and burial left a distinct memory, but the Nativity did not and could not have done so, since it is very unlikely that the accounts of Christ's birth in Bethlehem are historical. It is well known that neither Mark nor John has a Nativity story, and those of Matthew and Luke are incompatibly different. John even reports that a reason people did not believe Jesus was the Messiah was that he did not come from Bethlehem (John 7: 42).

As with the location of Christ's birth, so with the Ascension; we need to assess the earliest date from which what was probably a legend can be affixed to a certain place. In other words, it is almost certain that the crucifixion of Jesus actually happened, and therefore it is not surprising that the community of Christians in Jerusalem passed on the memory of the placement of this critical event. However, the Ascension as an *historical* event raises problems. Matthew 28: 16–20 has Jesus appearing on a hill (Tabor?) in Galilee to give final instructions to the apostles; the

---

[1] (1971c), 134, see also Mancini (1984), 171–3; Bagatti (1971d), 61; Testa (1964a), 106–12.
[2] For a survey of Byzantine Jewish and Christian references to the Mount of Olives, see Limor (1978).

shorter recension of Mark ends with the young man's instructions to the women to tell the disciples to go to Galilee, where they would see Jesus (16: 5–7), while the longer recension has only, 'So then the Lord Jesus, after he had spoken to them, was taken up into Heaven, and sat down at the right hand of God' (16: 19); John (21: 1–23) tells of a final meeting between Jesus and the disciples on the shore of the Sea of Galilee; Luke 24: 50 contains a pericope which has Jesus parting from the disciples at Bethany, but not going up into heaven. Only in the Acts of the Apostles does Jesus *visibly* ascend into the sky from the Mount of Olives (1: 6–12).

The evidence given by Testa and Bagatti for early 'Jewish-Christian' veneration of the cave is entirely textual, since the area of the great church 'on Eleona' (cf. Egeria, *Itin*. xxx. 3; xxxi. 1; xxxiii. 1–2; xxxv. 1–2)[3] was thoroughly excavated by Vincent in 1910[4] and nothing found could be construed to be Jewish-Christian in character (see Figure 12A). The partially rebuilt cave, which acquired its sizeable dimensions in the fourth century, is associated with the present Church of the Pater Noster and Carmelite Convent. The cave is no longer extant in its Byzantine form but has been used as a basis for the present cave chapel. The *kokhim* tomb on the west side was not part of the original cave, but was broken into at the time of the Constantinian expansion of the grotto, and then resealed (see Figure 12B).

The principal piece of evidence given for an early veneration of the cave is the Gnostic *Acts of John*, probably written at the start of the third century. In this text, the beloved disciple John flees to a cave on the Mount of Olives during the course of the earthly Jesus' crucifixion. Here, the heavenly Jesus appears and illuminates the subterranean cavity with a spiritual light. He teaches John the meaning of salvation and is thereafter taken up (*Acts of John* xcvii).[5] The language is figurative. Jesus illuminates the dark grotto as the illuminating knowledge (*gnosis*) he imparts to John banishes the darkness of ignorance.

---

[3] 'Eleona' appears to have been the name of the Mount of Olives in the Jerusalem speech of the day, which attached the Aramaic/Syriac emphatic ending -*a* to the Greek word ἐλαιών 'olive garden'; see Vincent and Abel (1914*b*), 382.

[4] Vincent (1908), (1911); Vincent and Abel (1914*b*), 337–74; Loukianoff (1939); Crowfoot (1941), 30–4; Ovadiah (1970), 71–83; Abel (1918), 555–8; Wilkinson (1981), 49–50.

[5] In *NTA* ii. 232; *ANT* 254.

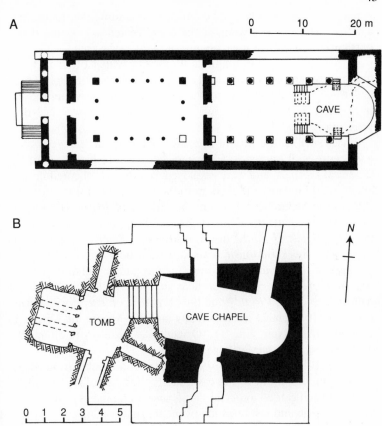

FIG. 12. A: The Constantinian basilica of Eleona with cave; B: Remains of Eleona cave with *kokhim* tomb

As in the case of Bethlehem and Golgotha, there is not a simple relationship between texts and sites which would require us to presume that the identification of these sites preceded such stories. In fact, the inverse is much more probable. From stories which describe certain events as taking place somewhere in general areas, later specific locations were identified in the land of Palestine. This was true for both biblical and apocryphal stories. It would be methodologically unsound to use such citations in apocryphal literature as proof of a site already having been venerated,[6] just as it would be unsound to assume that mention of a house where Jesus went in the New Testament means that a particular house must have been venerated at the time the Gospels were written. Popular religious literature, which often included fictional biographies of New Testament personalities, played an active role in contributing to the identification and veneration of holy sites. Such literature was not simply a passive record of veneration.

Places such as the Mount of Olives, Bethlehem, and Jerusalem itself were well known to Christians everywhere by means of the canonical Gospels, and were employed as settings in the multifarious apocryphal Gospels and Acts from the second and third centuries. It is on the Mount of Olives, in the *History of Joseph* (Proem, i), that Jesus recounts the death of Joseph. It appears as a location in the *Apocalypse of Paul*,[7] the *Apocalypse of Peter*,[8] a Manichaean fragment,[9] the *Wisdom of Jesus Christ*,[10] the *Pistis Sophia*,[11] the *Gospel of Bartholomew*,[12] and in the many versions of the *Assumption of Mary*,[13] as well as in the Greek version of the *Apocalypse of the Virgin*[14] and the *Discourse of Theodosius* (iii).[15] Justin Martyr places Jesus' agony on the Mount of Olives in general (*Dial*. xci; ciii. 1). Origen has Jesus foretelling the desertion of his disciples here (*Comm. in Matt*. xxvi. 20).

The fact that in the *Acts of John* there is a combination of the highly symbolic motif of the cave and the locality of the Mount of Olives, which gained a special significance to Gnostics as the site of the Ascension and last teaching by means of a conflation of Acts 1: 6–12 and Matthew 28: 16–20 (see below), should not lead us to suppose that an actual cave on the Mount of Olives was identified by Gnostics, let alone other Christians, as having particular importance from the very beginning. The tradition was the amalgamation of two common motifs. The topographical knowledge of the author of the *Acts of John* may have extended to the

---

[6] *Pace* Wilkinson (1976), 84: 'the Acts of John is probably reflecting (in a Gnostic way) a tradition of Christian belief about the cave on the Mount of Olives, which at the time it was written was already accepted by the Jerusalem church. The Gnostic author thus takes this cave as the scene for his particular version of a story of teaching and ascension, because it is already associated with teaching and ascension in the orthodox Christian tradition.'

[7] *NTA* ii. 757, 795–6.   [8] Ibid. 668.   [9] *NTA* i. 353.
[10] Ibid. 246–88.   [11] Ibid. 253–6.   [12] Ibid. 492 ff.
[13] *ANT* 218, 222.   [14] Ibid. 563.   [15] Ibid. 198.

fact that the Mount of Olives is pot-holed with caves, but it is hard to imagine that the Gnostics, who read the *Acts of John*, could themselves have taken an interest in identifying a *material* cave where their esoteric tale took place. Rather, it appears more likely that during the course of the third century, in response to the story and others like it, the site was identified by the local Christians and adopted for their needs.[16] While an interaction between Gnostic stories and those of the orthodox Church at the end of the third century may seem surprising, that this particular tradition first arose in a Gnostic context seems to be plain from the existing literature. This may imply that there was a less clearly defined dividing line between the two wings of the Church, at least among the mass of ordinary believers, than the chief theologians of the day would wish to concede. Eusebius himself, who admits to knowing the *Acts of John*, claims that it is, like other spurious works, irreconcilable with true orthodoxy (*Hist. Eccles.* iii. 25. 6), and yet it is Eusebius who appears to connect the legend of the *Acts of John* with an actual cave.[17]

In *Demonstratio Evangelica* (dated *c*.318) Eusebius writes that,

Those who believe in Christ from all over the world come and congregate [in Jerusalem], not as in the old days because of the splendour of Jerusalem, nor that they might assemble and worship in the old Temple at Jerusalem, but in order to learn together the interpretation, according to the prophets, of the capture and devastation of Jerusalem, and that they may worship at the Mount of Olives, opposite the city, where the glory of the Lord went when it left the former city. According to the common and received[18] account, the feet of our Lord and Saviour, himself the Word of God, truly stood . . . upon the Mount of Olives at the cave that is shown there. On the ridge of the Mount of Olives he prayed and handed on to his disciples the mysteries of the end, and after this he made his ascension

[16] The influence of apocryphal stories on the development of local traditions about sites is also suggested by Walker (1990: 207–8).

[17] Many have found Eusebius' description a problem. Grabar (1946: 248–9) suggests that Eusebius must have meant that the Ascension itself was located on the summit; cf. Walker (1990), 202–17. This certainly seems to be the case, see n. 19 below.

[18] The word ῥητήν is used by the Church Fathers to mean 'canonical' when referring to texts, and 'literal' when referring to meaning; cf. Eus. *Dem. Evang.* vii. 1; see Lampe (1961), 1217. It seems that Eusebius is referring to the Ascension as told in the Acts of the Apostles, which he goes on to quote, but the clause 'at the cave that is shown there' and what follows is dependent on another tradition.

into Heaven, as Luke teaches in the Acts of the Apostles. (*Dem. Evang.* vi. 18; cf. *Laud. Const.* ix. 16–17)

In the canonical Gospels Jesus does not pass on the 'mysteries of the end' immediately prior to the Ascension; these are passed on earlier (Matt. 24: 3–25: 46). There is no mention of a cave in the ridge at the top of the Mount of Olives. Despite Eusebius' condemnation of Gnostic texts, there appears to be some conflation of the Gnostic and canonical Gospel tradition. Eusebius himself associated only the teaching with the cave; he believed that the Ascension took place on top of the Mount (*Vita Const.* iii. 41) 'after this', not in the cave itself.[19]

In *Vita Constantini* Eusebius writes not of the canonical Gospel as the source of the tradition, but of 'a true account' (λόγος ἀληθής) which identified the cave with Jesus' secret teaching.

The emperor's mother also raised up a stately edifice on the Mount of Olives, in memory of the journey into Heaven of the Saviour of all. She put up a sacred church, a temple, on the ridge beside the summit of the whole Mount. Indeed, a true report holds the Saviour to have initiated his disciples into secret mysteries in this very cave. (*Vita Const.* iii. 43; cf. iii. 41)

In the *Acts of John*, the mysteries are passed on during the actual crucifixion, while for Eusebius these mysteries are probably passed on after, as in the apocryphal *Apocalypse of Peter*, which Eusebius also knew (*Hist. Eccles.* iii. 3. 2, 25. 4; vi. 14. 1). It was easy to conflate apocryphal stories. It is unlikely that Eusebius is here referring to the apocalyptic discourse of Matthew 24: 3–25: 46 because when Eusebius discusses this discourse elsewhere in his writings he never once makes mention of the cave as its location (cf. *Theoph.* iv. 35; *Comm. in Luc.* xxi. 25).[20]

While Eusebius is perhaps careful to avoid blatant Gnostic phrasing that would refer to 'illumination' and 'knowledge', the language of his accounts, and in particular, the final part (ἐν αυτῷ ἄντρῳ τοὺς αὐτοῦ θιασώτας; μυεῖν τὰς ἀπορρήτους τελετὰς τὸν τῶν ὅλων Σωτῆρα) is very strongly reminiscent of the vocabulary of mystery cults.

[19] See Walker (1990: 210–13), who convincingly uses Eusebius, *Vita Const.* iii. 41–3, to argue that Eusebius believed the Ascension took place from the summit of the Mount.

[20] *Pace* Walker (1990), 203–4.

The handing on of secret mysteries by the heavenly Christ upon the Mount of Olives was central to the teaching of many Gnostic groups. It is found not only in the above-mentioned *Acts of John*, but elsewhere in their literature, for example, in a text discovered in Nag Hammadi, Egypt: the *Letter of Peter to Philip* (cxxxiv. 10 ff.); and in the *Sophia Jesu Christi*, where the location is a mountain called 'the Mount of Olives' in *Galilee*;[21] the *Gospel of Bartholomew* (iv. 1–12);[22] the *Pistis Sophia*;[23] and the Ethiopic text of the *Apocalypse of Peter*.[24] In a Manichaean fragment there is a reference to a conversation between Simon Peter and the Risen Christ.[25] The Risen Christ appeared, according to the Sethians, to a few of the disciples who were capable of understanding the great mysteries which he would impart to them (Irenaeus, *Adv. Haer.* i. 30. 13). The same idea occurs in the *Apocryphon of James* (ii. 8 ff.) and the *Apocryphon of John* (i. 30 ff.) from the Nag Hammadi library. For some, the Risen Christ was a continuing presence, but groups such as the Ophites believed that the Risen Christ remained only eighteen months with the disciples (Irenaeus, *Adv. Haer.* i. 30. 14; cf. i. 3. 2), while in the *Pistis Sophia*, Christ remains twelve years. It was in some way to respond to these Gnostic speculations that the relatively orthodox apocryphal work *Epistula Apostolorum* was composed,[26] which purports to be a letter from Christ to the apostles.

Jerome would also employ the language of Gnosis in his comments on Matt. 24: 3:

He sat on the Mount of Olives where the true light of knowledge was born, and the disciples who desired to know the mysteries and the revelation of the future came to him secretly. They asked three things: what time Jerusalem would be destroyed, when the Christ would come, and when would be the consummation of the age.

The sixth-century Jerusalem monk Sophronius would be even more liberal in his 'Gnostic' phrasing.

---

[21] *NTA* i. 246.
[22] Ibid. 495–6; cf. *The Book of the Resurrection of Christ by Bartholomew the Apostle* in *ANT* 184–5.
[23] *NTA* i. 253.
[24] *NTA* ii. 668; *ANT*, 510.
[25] *NTA* i. 354.
[26] See ibid. 191–227.

Highly will I praise the endless depth of the divine Wisdom, by which he saved me. Swiftly will I pass thence to the place, where, to his venerable companions, he taught the divine mysteries, shedding light into secret depths; there, under that roof, may I be! (*Anacreonticon* 19. 5–12)[27]

It is interesting that despite the post-crucifixion language appropriate to instruction by the Risen Christ, Jerome has placed the time of this instruction before Christ's death, and clearly refers to Matt. 24: 3 ff. This reorientation of chronology, perhaps to detach the traditions of the cave from their Gnostic roots, is found very early on in the Byzantine period. Despite Eusebius' apparent testimony to the earlier tradition, innovations appear to have been encouraged soon after the erection of the Eleona Church. The Bordeaux Pilgrim refers to the cave as being the place where Jesus taught *before* his Passion (*Itin. Burd.* 595). Egeria says the same (xxx. 1–3; xxxix. 3; xliii. 6; cf. xxxv. 2–3), as does Peter the Deacon (*Lib.* I), probably reflecting her words, though he refers to the cave as a 'bright (*lucida*) grotto', which again probably echoes Egeria's terminology,[28] and recalls the original language of mysteries. The sixth-century pilgrim Theodosius (*De Situ* 17) writes of the cave as the *Matzi* (from οἱ μαθηταί, 'the disciples') where Jesus used to rest when he was preaching in Jerusalem, and yet the text of Theodosius contains an addition which has the beloved disciple lying on the Lord's breast at this place, which is perhaps a residual memory of the *Acts of John*.

Adomnan's description here is particularly important, for it shows that there was, in the seventh century, still some debate about what instruction in particular was given in this cave, and when. He writes: 'we must take care to ask what address this was, when it took place, and to which particular disciples the Lord was speaking' (*De Loc. Sanct.* i. 25. 2–3).[29] Even as late as the seventh century, then, the Gnostic and the orthodox legends were in simultaneous circulation. Adomnan duly recommends consultation of the Scriptures, and concludes that the Lord spoke the address in reply to Peter, James, John, and Andrew two days before Passover, that is, when he was still in his earthly incarnation. The passage from Scripture which Adomnan cites, Matt. 24: 1–26: 2 (cf. Mark 13. 3–37) is precisely that which the Bishop of Jerusalem

---

[27] Trans. by Wilkinson (1977), 92. [28] Wilkinson (1981), 184.
[29] Trans. by Wilkinson (1977), 102–3.

read out to catechumens in the cave itself (Egeria, *Itin*. xxxiii. 2). We know from this that the tendency to associate the instruction in the cave with a segment in the life of the earthly Jesus was probably encouraged by the leaders of the orthodox Jerusalem church via catechetical instruction.

Adomnan closes by carelessly mentioning that the church built by Constantine was still (i.e. *c*.670) held in reverence (cf. Ps.?- Eucherius, *Ep. Faust*. i. 10); but in fact the church was destroyed by the Persians in 614 (Eutychius of Alexandria, *Annales* i. 215) and not rebuilt. The lack of interest in reconstructing Constantine's great edifice on the Mount of Olives is testimony to the success of the orthodox programme to remove the taint of Gnosticism from the site. In terms of the maintenance of the church's importance, it was counter-productive to remove the earlier tradition, for what remained to commemorate after the subtractions hardly seemed to warrant a grand basilica. Having repositioned the time of instruction from after to before the crucifixion, they had to reposition the associated (Gnostic) Ascension.

Already, as to Eusebius, it must have seemed incomprehensible to the orthodox that the Ascension might have taken place from a cave. The Bordeaux Pilgrim (*Itin. Burd*. 595–6) understood a little rise or hill (*monticulus*) beyond Constantine's church to be the place where Jesus was *transfigured*[30] (cf. Matt. 17: 2), but fifty years later Egeria would attest the 'Imbomon' (ἐν βωμῷ, meaning 'on the platform' or 'on the high place'; cf. Hebrew *bamah*) to be the site of the *Ascension* (*Itin*. xliii. 5; cf. Jerome, *Ep*. cviii. 12), and it was this identification that was encouraged. It is not clear where Cyril locates the event, but he does not mention its being commemorated by the Constantinian basilica, or as taking place in a cave. The site of the Ascension is given by him as being, simply, the Mount of Olives (*Cat*. x. 19; xiii. 38), but he may well have thought that the summit where the Imbomon was to be located was the actual site.[31]

---

[30] The Transfiguration appears to have been fixed to Mount Tabor in Galilee by the time of Cyril (*Cat*. xii. 16); see Walker (1990), 145–55. Walker (pp. 213–14) suggests that the Bordeaux Pilgrim or his/her guide became confused, or else was influenced by the *Apocalypse of Peter* i and xv (*NTA* ii. 664), in which an event like the canonical Transfiguration precedes the final Ascension of Jesus. This is very possible.

[31] See Walker (1990), 214–17.

While Cyril refers to the Mount of Olives as 'the gate of the Ascension' (*Cat*. xiv. 23), one can trace in this only vague vestiges of Gnostic jargon. The round Imbomon or 'Holy Ascension' Church was constructed late in the fourth century by an imperial lady, Poemenia (Palladius, *Hist. Laus*. 35),[32] and, after the destructions wrought by the Persians in 614, it was immediately restored by Bishop Modestus. Arculf's plans show the layout of the building[33] after these restorations. The site of the present Mosque of the Ascension (dating from the seventeenth century) is located at the same spot, and preserves the 'footprints' of Jesus on a large stone.[34] These 'footprints' are first mentioned by Paulinus of Nola (*Ep*. xxxi. 4) and were probably therefore 'found' at the time of the church's construction late in the fourth century. Archaeological investigations in 1959 were successful in determining the extent of the Byzantine structure.[35]

Tradition altered. The supposed site of the earthly Jesus' teaching of his disciples became the place where Jesus taught the Lord's Prayer, and four centuries after Constantine's great basilica was destroyed the Crusaders built an oratory in the ruins to commemorate this event.

The history of this site therefore leads to many questions about the relationship between Gnosticism and orthodoxy at the beginning of the fourth century, but these are not relevant to the present study. It also shows how traditions changed, and could do so within a relatively short space of time. Perhaps the most important thing to note in all this discussion, however, is that Eusebius specifically states, in a piece written before Constantine's triumph, not only that Christians from all over the world congregated in Jerusalem to learn about the capture and devastation of the city, but that they worshipped on the Mount of Olives, where it was thought that the glory of the Lord went after it departed from the Jewish Temple. This may be understood at first sight to imply that Christians knew of holy places on the Mount of Olives before Constantine's innovations, but this is not quite what Eusebius says. In fact, Eusebius knows of no holy places in his writings prior to Constantine, only places that are visited by

[32] It is attested by Jerome, *in Zeph*. i. 15 f. (AD 392); *Arm. Lect*. 57, and by Peter the Iberian (ed. Raabe, p. 35).
[33] See Wilkinson (1977), 192, 194.
[34] See Canaan (1927), 79, 98, 293.   [35] Corbo (1960), (1965).

Christians interested in learning interpretations of their Christian past. Even in his writings about the Eleona cave, Christians are not described as venerating it. It is simply shown to the Christian visitors. The Mount of Olives as a whole, it would appear, was considered by certain Christians to be the seat of God's glory, or presence, which could no longer abide on Mount Moriah.

This notion is based on the words of the prophet Ezekiel, who predicted that after the promise of the new covenant the glory of the Lord would rise from the middle of Jerusalem and halt on the mountain to the east of the city (Ezek. 11: 23). Perhaps also for this reason, Zechariah announced that the Messiah would come via the Mount of Olives (14: 4). Strictly speaking, these references come from the time after the destruction of the First Temple. Curiously, the Babylonian Talmud asserts that the presence of God did not dwell in the Second Temple (*b. Yoma* 21b), but quite a different attitude is attested in earlier post-exilic writings (Joel 2: 27; 4: 17; Ps. 135: 21; *m.Sukkah* 5. 4).[36] Indeed, the first Christians appear to have believed that God's presence dwelt in the Second Temple, since there is the statement attributed to Jesus: 'He who swears by the Temple swears by it and by him who dwells in it' (Matt. 23: 21).[37] Josephus writes of the actual departure of God's presence from the Second Temple in his account of the final stages of the siege of Jerusalem (*BJ* vi. 299); upon entering the Sanctuary, priests heard a loud noise of movement and then a cry of voices saying, 'we are leaving this place'. The same incident is also reported by Tacitus (*Hist.* v. 13).

Where the presence of God went after its departure was a matter of debate amongst the rabbis. By the time of *Midrash Exodus Rabbah* (2. 2), there was a general view that the presence of God withdrew to heaven and was no longer to be found on earth, though Rabbi Eliezar believed it was still to be found at the surviving western wall of the Temple precincts. Clearly, Christians let go of the idea that the glory of God rested on the Mount of Olives after other holy places were developed. But the notion that

---

[36] See Clements (1965), 123–34.

[37] Many manuscripts of the New Testament have the aorist participle instead of the tricky present κατοικοῦντι here, but this is presumably due to subsequent Christian insistence that God no longer dwelt in the Jerusalem Temple. I am grateful to Prof. G. I. Davies for sending me a copy of his paper, 'The Presence of God in the Second Temple and Rabbinic Doctrine', read at the Annual Meeting of the BAJS, Cambridge, July 1989, in which he makes this point (n. 18).

Jesus would return via the Mount (cf. Zech. 14: 4) was retained (cf. Cyril, *Cat.* xii. 11).

It appears from what Eusebius writes that before 325 Christians in Jerusalem and visitors from elsewhere met on the Mount of Olives to worship God in the same way that they had met to worship in the Temple in New Testament times (cf. Acts 2: 46). Certainly, given the centuries of persecution, it may also have been a case of expediency. The Mount of Olives had many nooks and crannies that could be exploited for the purpose of clandestine Christian worship. Perhaps, by the end of the third century, the (Gnostic) cave identified as where Christ passed on teachings was one of them. Whatever the case, it was the Mount of Olives as a whole which was thought to be imbued with the glory of God. This makes it a kind of holy place, on the Jewish model of the Temple; but a specific holy place which was venerated because Jesus happened once to have been there is not attested. The cave was not holy because of Jesus having been there, but the Mount of Olives was holy because of the abiding dwelling of the presence of God. We have here two distinct types of holiness; one the heritage of paganism and one the heritage of Judaism. Only the latter is evidenced by Eusebius' words, but subsequent Christian holy places would be developed with the former idea as the paramount criterion for sanctity.

There was only one Temple, only one genuine 'holy place' in Judaism,[38] despite the popular veneration of the tombs of the righteous. Blessings made by those of a particularly pious bent at particular localities were incidental; one did not go to specific places in order to make blessings, nor would one go to a spot at which Aelia Capitolina was visible just to rend one's garments. A place was significant in sacred history without being intrinsically holy. Only the Temple had been a place of true, awesome holiness, and there was only one Temple. The presence of God

---

[38] As Martin Goodman has explored in a recent lecture for the Anglo-Israel Archaeological Society, London (summarized in *BAIAS* 10 (1990–1), 104–5), there are synagogue inscriptions, dating from the 3rd cent. onwards, which describe the synagogue as a 'holy place'. Goodman suggests that Jews were espousing Gentiles' views about synagogues for various reasons, including a hope that this would protect them from attack. If certain communities really did ascribe sanctity to synagogues, then in what sense we should understand it is unclear, but it was not of the same order as the sanctity of the former Temple. It seems likely, however, that the language was formulaic, written for the benefit of pagan passers-by. Synagogues were not always recognizable from the outside as places of worship.

could rest only at one place at one time. If the Mount of Olives was seen by Jerusalem Christians as the successor to the Temple as the place of the presence of God, then it would be logical to assume that they too had only this one place which could be accounted holy.

The question of whether Eusebius actually shared the view that the glory of God was resting on the Mount of Olives will be explored in the final chapter. Certainly, an idea that is so completely founded on the Prophets, an idea that is so essentially Jewish, would be most likely the property of a church that had strong Jewish foundations, like that of Jerusalem. The Caesarean church, influenced by the more esoteric notions of Origen, may have been more doubtful about the matter. Visitors may have gathered on the Mount of Olives as much for convenience as for anything. Furthermore, it provided a fitting location—looking down on the fallen Jerusalem, now pagan Aelia—for an exegesis of Scripture. The judgement upon Jerusalem as a result of its part in the death of the Saviour was clearly visible to all.

In conclusion, we cannot assume on the basis of apocryphal stories that an actual cave on the Mount of Olives was venerated from Apostolic times at a site adjacent to the place of the Ascension. The 'secret teaching' supposed to have been imparted there was not connected with Jewish-Christians, but with Gnostics who composed a symbolic legend featuring a cave on the Mount of Olives. This was later identified with an actual cave.

If the cave had long been important to orthodox Christians, for orthodox reasons, there would have been no reason for Eusebius and others to invent such a dangerously Gnostic history for the site, which later had to be expunged. Eusebius was anything but a Gnostic himself. He seems rather to have been preserving a popular belief about the cave which, soon after, was radically changed to align traditions with 'correct' theology.

If people came from outside Palestine to Jerusalem in order to learn about the place and its history, and to worship on the Mount of Olives, it may be that it was the Gnostics among them who identified the cave there where they believed Christ passed on special teaching to his disciples. It may have been utilized for the purpose of clandestine worship. This does not mean, however, that it was a holy place venerated by pilgrims; rather, the entire

Mount of Olives appears to have been considered sacred by certain Christians, since some held that God's glory rested there. It may be that this belief arose in the predominantly Jewish-Christian church of Jerusalem prior to the year 135, and that the idea continued there that the Mount of Olives was somehow a Christian replacement of the Jewish Temple. Whatever the case, we have very little evidence on the matter, and the belief does not seem to have survived the momentous changes to the Church wrought by Constantine.

8

Caves and Tombs

A DISCUSSION about a particular cave on the Mount of Olives glorified by the emperor Constantine leads on to consideration of the many caves which, according to the titles of one of Testa's articles upon the subject, are alleged to be 'grotte dei misteri' belonging to early Jewish-Christians.[1] The Bagatti–Testa school believes that Jewish-Christians utilized 'mystic grottos' or 'caves of light' in which they enacted sacred mysteries. Constantine's glorification of three caves was, then, somehow in keeping with the fact that Jewish-Christians had employed these; Eusebius' language, when speaking of these three 'mystic caves' (*Laud. Const.* ix. 16–17) is indebted to Jewish-Christian terminology. This argument can be countered by looking at the phenomenon of the Byzantine use of caves in general.

The previous chapter has shown how a legendary cave came to be identified with a particular place on the Mount of Olives towards the end of the third century. We have also seen how an artificial cave was created on the east side of the Rock of Calvary to correspond to pilgrim expectations engendered by apocryphal literature. One might suspect that the Christian employment of caves themselves had much to do with the expectations of pilgrims, rather than with a hypothetical group of Jewish-Christians. Indeed, there was a curious partiality to caves among Byzantine Christians. Not only was Jesus thought to have been born in one, but his mother, Mary, was supposed to have dwelt in a cave in Nazareth (Egeria, in Pet. Diac., *Lib.* T). Mary and Joseph apparently lived in a cave in Bethlehem for two years after the birth of Christ (Daniel the Abbot, *Zhitie* 48).[2] John the Baptist

---

[1] Testa (1964*a*).

[2] The position of this cave as described by Daniel, 'a bowshot to the south' outside the city wall (see Wilkinson (1988), 122, 144), corresponds roughly to the position of the Milk Grotto. For contemporary traditions about the Milk Grotto, see Canaan (1927), 60, 80, 98, 110.

was another troglodyte (Epiph. Mon., *Hag.* ix. 17 f.; xi. 19),
though perhaps more explicably so considering the penchant of
later ascetics to occupy caverns. Local Christians of today still
believe that Jesus spent his entire fast in a cave on Mount
Quarantine, near Jericho (Belard of Ascoli, iv).[3] As we shall see,
Byzantine Christians thought that Jesus was arrested in a cave
(Egeria, in Pet. Diac., *Lib.* I; Eusebius, *Onom.* 74. 16; Epiph.
Mon., *Hag.* viii. 10–14) where he ate a last meal with his disciples
(*Breviarius* A and B. 4).

The preference for identifying caves as localities in the life of
Jesus owes nothing to catholic theology and probably owes more
to pagan modes of thought than to Gnostic legend; very rarely can
the origins of holy caves be traced back to the symbolic stories of
the Gnostics and to other apocryphal texts. As was discussed in
Chapter 3, there was widespread pagan devotion to geological
protruberances, caves, woods, and springs. This appears to be
reflected in the choice of sites shown to the Bordeaux Pilgrim of
333. Christians who had recently converted from paganism, if not
most Christians living in a pagan environment, would have found
caves an appropriate place for prayer; though this is not to say that
they envisaged Christ as another chthonic god. The continuation
of the employment of the landscape's sacred places through into
Muslim folklore demonstrates just how natural this phenomenon
must have seemed. In Egeria's account, only the bishop is
permitted to enter the holy caves. Indeed, the sacred cave
replaced the pagan *adyton* as a zone of tremendous sacredness and
fear. This same fear is reflected in Palestinian Muslim attitudes to
certain caves, some of which are so feared that no Muslim would
enter them, while others are entered only during the day, because
their *wahrah* (condition of inspiring awe) is so strong.[4]

Paganism, in whatever form it took, appears to have made great
use of caves. Dionysus was worshipped underground, as was,
famously, Mithras. When Eusebius writes that Constantine's
Christian soldiers went to 'every gloomy cave, every hidden recess'
(*Vita Const.* iii. 57. 4) to stamp out paganism, he tells us much
about the profusion and extent of these places as well as the
comprehensive approach taken by Constantine's men. However,
as Robin Lane Fox has pointed out, Eusebius was overstating the

---

[3] Canaan (1927), 293.   [4] Ibid. 43.

case, for not even Constantine's whole army could hope to find each 'cave of Nymphs, the many caves which claimed Zeus's birthplace, the underground shrines of Mithras, the caves of Cybele and Attis or the many cavernous entries to Hades'.[5] It must have been clear to the Christians of the early Byzantine period that it would be useful to employ caves to commemorate important moments in the life of Jesus and his associates. Some of these were already in pagan use. Certainly, it must have been crucial to the Christian authorities that the Christian holy caves superseded those that went before, in order to stamp out the vestiges of paganism in what would become a holy land. The appropriation of the cave in Bethlehem may have had much to do with the attempt to destroy the worship of Tammuz-Adonis by encouraging the god's identification with Christ, and then using this as the justification for annihilating the pagan shrine.

According to Testa, the use of caves was polemical, for the light of Christ had penetrated the dark grottos to illuminate humankind: 'Le grotte mistiche dei Giudeo-Cristiani e delle Chiesa universale sono . . . la risposta polemica contro le iniziazioni dei misteri pagani.'[6] Indeed, it is probable that the Byzantine employment of grottos had the pagans in mind, simply because they appear to have had pagans in mind throughout the course of their building programme; Jerome (*Ep.* xlvi. 13. 4) wrote that churches had been erected like 'banners of the victories of the Lord'. Isidore of Pelusium (*Ep. Lib.* xxvii) found it amusing that a tomb had eclipsed the famous temples.

Cyril of Jerusalem

The most important piece of literary evidence given by the Bagatti–Testa school in support of supposed Jewish-Christian use of caves comes from the *Catechetical Lectures* given by Cyril of Jerusalem *c.*348.[7] In *Cat.* xviii. 26 Cyril states:

If at some time you are staying in a city, do not just ask, 'Where is the church [κυριακόν]?', for indeed the sects of the ungodly endeavour to call

---

[5] Lane Fox (1986), 673.   [6] Testa (1964*a*).
[7] Bagatti (1971*c*), 133.

their caves 'churches', nor just, 'Where is the assembly [ἐκκλησία]?'
but, 'Where is the catholic [καθολική] assembly?'

Standing on its own, and taken literally, this passage could be
understood as being evidence that certain Christian sects were
liable to worship in caves which they referred to as 'churches'. This
is the Bagatti–Testa interpretation. Moreover, the sects are
thought to have been Jewish-Christian. As a matter of good
methodology, however, it is important to check the context of the
passage under consideration. Cyril, in fact, makes it quite clear to
whom he is referring, and Jewish-Christians are not mentioned.

Cyril points out that the Church is 'catholic' because it is
universal and comprehensive (xviii. 23). It is an ἐκκλησία
because it calls everyone out (cf. ἐκκαλέω) and assembles them
together (xviii. 24). In former times there was an *ekklesia* of the
Jews (cf. Ps. 68: 26 LXX), but the Jews fell from favour and the
Saviour built a second holy church of Gentiles; the 'church' of
Judaea (Judaism, not Jewish-Christianity) was cast off and the
churches of Christ abounded (xviii. 25). Then Cyril turns his
attention to others who are outside the compass of the catholic
Church: the sectarians like 'Marcionites, Manichaeans, and the
rest' (xviii. 26). Avoiding the use of ἐκκλησία by using
συστήματα instead, he exhorts the catechumens to flee from such
polluted 'gatherings' and to remain within the catholic Church. It
is at this point that he asks them to take care when they journey to
other cities that they ask specifically for the *catholic* church.

Cyril refers to a *kuriakon*, 'the Lord's house', by which he
means a church building. The building in which Manichaeans,
Marcionites, and others met together may have been a house-
church, or a more sophisticated structure: but certainly it was one
which was not immediately distinguishable by the naïve newcomers
to the faith as being any different from those in which they were
accustomed to worship, or else Cyril would have pointed out its
architectural peculiarities. When he uses the word σπήλαιον,
'cave', it is extremely likely indeed that he is speaking metaphorically, in the same way that Jesus himself refers to the Temple as
being turned into a 'cave of robbers' (Matt. 21: 13; Mark 11: 17;
Luke 19: 46, from Jer. 7: 11); Jesus was not saying that an actual
cave was used in the Temple precincts. Perhaps not altogether
irrelevant, given Christian attitudes to the female body, is the fact

that σπήλαιον was used euphemistically as a replacement for αἰδοῖα, the female *pudenda* (cf. Hab. 2: 15 LXX).[8] It was a word with heavy negative connotations when used metaphorically. Caves were dark places which could be the dens of wild animals and hiding places for bandits. They were employed by pagans (i.e. occupied by demons, to the Christian mind) and, as we shall see, magicians used them for sorcery. The use of the cave in apocryphal Nativity stories leans heavily on its grim associations: the light bursts through in the subterranean darkness, good overcomes evil, truth defeats ignorance. Translators of the passage in Cyril have accordingly translated 'cave' here, as in the New Testament, with the English word 'den', that can carry a similar derogatory metaphorical meaning.[9]

Cyril is not necessarily telling us, then, that sectarians like the Marcionites, Manichaeans, and others actually met in caves in the hillside. The additional reference to *ekklesia* may also refer to Jews who, if using Greek, perhaps would still speak colloquially of an assembly at the synagogue as an *ekklesia* (in the Septuagint it translates *qahal*). The terms were not as exclusively used as they are today, and indeed Christians of the second century could sometimes refer to their meetings as 'synagogues' (Ignatius, *Ep. Polycarp* iv. 2; *Shepherd of Hermas* xlv. 9; Justin Martyr, *Dial.* lxiii. 5). Pagans would have spoken of assemblies of many different kinds as *ekklesiai*. Cyril was not the first to point out the ambiguity of the term. Origen made a play on the double meaning of *ekklesia* as both 'church' and 'assembly' in *Contra Celsum* (iii. 29–30):

He made the gospel of Jesus to be successful, and caused *churches* to exist in opposition to the *assemblies* of superstitious, licentious, and unrighteous men. For such is the character of the crowds who everywhere constitute the *assemblies* of the cities. And the *churches* of God which have been taught by Christ, when compared with the *assemblies* of the people where they live, are 'as lights in the world'. Who would not admit that even the less satisfactory members of the *Church* and those who are far inferior

---

[8] Beaulieu and Mouterde (1947–8).
[9] The translation of σπήλαιον as 'den' in *Cat.* xviii. 26 is, for example, given by Telfer (1955a), Gifford (1894), and Newman (1838).

when compared with the better members are far superior to the *assemblies* of the people?[10]

Cyril wanted orthodox Christians to go to the right 'church'.

Cyril's words appear to inform us that in his day there was the same theological diversity among the Christians in Palestine as we met early in the century in the writings of Eusebius. Epiphanius would later confirm that Marcionites were found in Palestine (*Pan.* xlii. 1. 1) at the end of the fourth century. Cyril speaks of these, of Manichaeans, and of other unspecified Christian sectarians, but not of *Jewish-Christian* sectarians. Even if the reference to caves is taken literally, which is extremely doubtful, then Cyril means to link the caves with Marcionites, Manichaeans, and all other heretics in general, not specifically 'Ebionites'. Cyril, then, provides us with no positive evidence for a Jewish-Christian use of caves.

Cyril employs the word 'cave' with an eye to negative connotations which cannot have been lost on his audience, but Christians were at this time, quite paradoxically, turning caves into holy places. Not all caves were bad, and certainly there was the neutral use of caves for cellars, stables, and olive-pressing works, which Christian cannot have felt any repugnance about. The good caves—the 'mystic caves' of Bethlehem, Eleona, and (the tomb at) Golgotha—were a curious and new phenomenon. The cave itself, in these sites, was redeemed, cleansed, and glorified: it was ablaze with the light of candles and decked with fabulous adornments. Burial caves and tombs too, which had universal negative associations, were, to the Christian mind, cleansed by the presence of a saint, so that these places exerted a powerful positive magnetism. Christians turned things around: the unclean became clean through the saving power of God.

Many caves were soon found worthy of Christian attention, and polemic against the pagans was only part of the reason that this phenomenon gained popularity. It has occasionally been suggested that Christians met in some of these places during persecution (as, just possibly, in the case of Eleona, see p. 154 above), but in fact

[10] Trans. by Chadwick (1953), 147, italics mine. After this rendering of Origen's Greek, Chadwick notes: 'throughout the passage the play on the double meaning of *ecclesia*, as the secular assembly and as the Church, cannot be reproduced in translation.'

no Church Father gives us any information to support this convenient hypothesis. It would appear, as we have seen, that the Byzantine employment of caves owes much more to the appropriation of the pagan use of caves, but there was a twist. The sanctification of caves had symbolic resonances. Caves were saved from pagan exploitation. Christians 'discovered' that they were in fact once used by saints, or in a significant biblical event, and that they therefore deserved redemption. As more and more pagans embraced Christianity, more and more caves were 'saved' and turned into Christian holy places.

Caves may have been attractive to the ascetics precisely because their faith could be well tested in these murky environments, but soon caves appear to have been seen as appropriate places for many biblical events, despite, or rather because of, their unsavoury former associations. The dark cave was the state of fallen humanity before Christ; but a cave could become holy, bearing the aura of the divine, given an association with the godly. The theme of the miraculous transformation of caves is the same as that which runs through their utilization in the apocryphal Gospels and Acts.

Ein Karim

Christians redeemed pagan caves, but they did so quietly. It need not seem strange to us that Christian historians are often mute about certain appropriations of pagan sacred sites. Archaeological remains show us that a church building programme of great magnitude swept through Palestine during the Byzantine period and deeply altered its character, but details of this phenomenon are lacking in Christian literary sources. In his *Vita Constantini*, Eusebius mentions that the sites of Golgotha and Mamre were 'defiled' by pagans, but he does not mention the very same 'defilement' of Bethlehem in the cave where Christ was reputedly born. Perhaps it was considered unwise to blame the pagans at every opportunity for defiling many later Christian holy places. Nevertheless, Christians appropriated pagan sites in the region with great impunity. We must also remember that once the accusation was established that pagans had used Christian holy places for their own foul deeds, then the way was clear to treat any pagan site as a potentially 'defiled' Christian holy place in need of purification, and this included their caves.

At Ein Karim, for example, a town located seven kilometres south-west of Jerusalem, a marble statue of the goddess Aphrodite was discovered in the area immediately west of the present Church of the St John the Baptist, along with a large quantity of column shafts and other smaller fragments of statues (one probably representing the leg of Adonis).[11] These finds confirm that a temple for the worship of the goddess Aphrodite was located on the site during the Roman period. In this region there was a cave, which is to be found within the present church. It would be very surprising indeed if this cave had not been put to pagan use, lying as it did within a pagan sanctuary. In the fifth century a Byzantine church was constructed here which obliterated the former structures, and incorporated the cave into its architecture. The first Christian identification of the cave was that it was where Elizabeth, the mother of John the Baptist, had her dwelling (so Theodosius, *De Situ* v). The church constructed over the cave was likewise in memory of Elizabeth, as the Jerusalem calendar records.[12] However, during the course of time the initial identification was modified, so that by the twelfth century, the cave was considered to be the birthplace of John the Baptist (Daniel the Abbot, *Zhitie* 59), an identification which remains to this day.

It should be noted that Bagatti believes that the grotto was venerated by Jewish-Christians, which in turn gave rise to a legend in the *Protevangelium of James* (xxii. 3), which describes how, in order to avoid Herod's programme of infanticide, Elizabeth fled to the hill country (from Luke 1: 39, 65), where a hill was split asunder to hide her. This is pushing the evidence to an astonishing degree. The area was contained within the precincts of a pagan sanctuary at the time Bagatti wished the cave to be venerated by Jewish-Christians. More importantly, if it is stated that a hill swallowed up the refugees, then pilgrims would have sought to identify a hill, and not a cave. Tawfiq Canaan tells a similar story current in Palestinian folklore which justifies the veneration of a particular rock:

It is said that while Mary was coming from Bethlehem to Jerusalem carrying her child, she passed Jews threshing beans on the rock east of

[11] See Saller (1946), 108–16.   [12] Goussen (1923), 30.

Tantūr. Christ cried for some, and she asked the people to give her a handful. They refused and said they were not beans but only stones. And forthwith they turned into small stones. The workers at once followed her and accused her of being a witch. She hastened to escape and when she was on the point of falling into their hands she asked a rock to hide her. At once the stone opened and sheltered her. In vain did her pursuers search for her. This stone carries the name of *srīr es-Saiydeh*.[13]

Bethesda

In Jerusalem, the grotto between the two pools of Bethesda, mentioned in Chapter 3 above as a site for the worship of Serapis, was identified early in the Byzantine era as being the location for Solomon's expulsion of demons (*Itin. Burd.* 589).[14] Prior to its pagan employment there was, according to the Gospel of John (5: 1 f.) a structure with five porches. The remains of this are archaeologically indistinguishable from the pagan remains, but the area was probably a Jewish site of folk medicine before it was pagan. There was a belief that when the water rippled, indicating the presence of an angel or spirit, the first person to step into the pool would be healed from disease or infirmity (John 5: 4). On account of this and the relationship between the site and a story about Jesus healing a paralytic (John 5: 1–9), a church was constructed directly over the cave between the two pools (cf. Cyril, *Hom. in Par.* ii). To ensure this location, the church had to be something of a feat of Byzantine engineering, with high arches built up from the bottom of each pool to support the structure on the northern and southern sides.[15] In this instance, the ecclesiastical authorities appear to

[13] Canaan (1927), 80. *Srīr es-Saiydeh* means 'the crib of Christ'.

[14] Solomon's reputation as an arch-magician began in Judaism (Jos. *Ant.* viii. 2. 5; *b.Gitt.* 68a), but it was adapted by Christians; see Duling (1983), 935–87. The motif of Solomon as the warrior spearing Lilith, found frequently on Jewish and Samaritan amulets, was taken over by Christians to use on their amulets. The motif was adapted so that Solomon became St Sisinnius, and Lilith more often a snake: the same iconography as that of the later St George and the dragon. For a discussion of the development of this form of amulet iconography and the related motif of the 'evil eye', see Bonner (1950), 208–21; Goodenough (1953–8), ii. 227–35. Goodenough mentions that there exists a Christian carved ivory depicting 'Solomon the Prophet', which shows 'the direct potency of the figure of Solomon' (p. 232). See too Naveh and Shaked (1985), 111–22.

[15] For a discussion of the archaeological excavations, see Vincent and Abel (1914b), 669–742; Jeremias (1966). Testa (1964b) asks whether the site was part of Jewish-Christian tradition.

have preserved an actual site visited by Jesus that was in fact converted to pagan use. However, it must have been a Jewish, and not a Christian, area prior to its conversion. Since the pools of Bethesda continued to be used as a healing sanctuary, it was not hard for the Church to keep the memory of the place.

Byzantine Christian Caves in Jewish Areas

We should not seek to find a pagan past behind every cave used by Byzantine Christians. A glance at B. Cohen's detailed index to Ginzberg's survey of Jewish legends[16] demonstrates that some Jews too found caves to be significant places in which to site important events in the lives of their religious figures; such popular folk beliefs probably also show pagan influence. Besides the many references to the Cave of Machpelah, there is the cave where Moses and Elijah dwelt,[17] the cave where the Book of Raziel was hidden,[18] the cave, which disappeared, where Aaron died,[19] the cave leading to Luz.[20] Certain caves were perceived as being hiding places for biblical personages: for the Ninevites,[21] of for Saul,[22] and there is also a reference to a monster living in a cave.[23] None of these caves was, however, holy. Whether Jews utilized local caves for any regional religious commemorations is not known, but it is likely that some of the actual caves of Palestine were identified as the location for legendary events, and had meaning for the area's Jewish communities. In the medieval cabalistic textbook known as the *Zohar*, the cave has a significance as a symbol for life in this world, but there are implications that actual rituals, like 'blessing the cup', actually took place in caves.[24] The evidence which Ernest Goodenough[25] cites for ceremonies in tombs may cover caves as well, given the ubiquitous use of caves as burial sites. Moreover, the Giv'at ha-Mivtar inscription specifically refers to a tomb as a 'cave'.[26]

There must remain doubt as to whether Christians appropriated caves which had significance in Jewish folklore, or whether they

[16] Ginzberg (1955), vii. 81–2.
[17] Ibid. i. 83; iii. 137.
[18] Ibid. i. 156.
[19] Ibid. iii. 324–6, 445.
[20] Ibid. iv. 30.
[21] Ibid. i. 407.
[22] Ibid. iv. 68.
[23] Ibid. ii. 160.
[24] Goodenough (1953–8), iv. 93–4; vi. 179: during the ritual, supernatural words were 'revealed to us while we are in the cave'.
[25] Ibid. i. 4.
[26] See E. S. Rosenthal (1973).

created sacredness *ex nihilo* in certain caves lying within Jewish areas of the land.

At the foot of Mount Tabor, there was a sizeable Jewish town named Dabeira (*Onom.* 78. 5–7). A large plastered cave (measuring 4.3 × 2.6 m. and 1.7 m. high) was found on its summit. In the plaster are the remains of an indecipherable Christian inscription surrounded by *chi-rho* monograms. Bagatti suggested that this was a sepulchre, though there is no evidence for this.[27] The cave may have started its Christian usage as a commemorative site for the Transfiguration (Matt. 17: 1–8; Mark 9: 2–10; Luke 9: 28–36; cf. 2 Pet. 1: 17–18; Cyril, *Cat.* xii. 16; Jerome, *Ep.* xlvi. 12; cviii. 13), but this must remain speculation. This region of Galilee appears to have been an entirely Jewish area prior to Christian developments there, and it is therefore unlikely that this particular cave was used by pagans. It could nevertheless have been developed out of a natural cave with no previous associations for the the Jews of the vicinity.

John 11: 38 states that the Tomb of Lazarus was a cave (σπήλαιον) with a stone lying against it. According to Eusebius (*Onom.* 58. 15–17; cf. *Theoph.* iv. 10) the 'place of Lazarus' was pointed out to visitors, but this may refer to the village of Bethany rather than to a cave or tomb. When the *Lazarium* church came to be built in the fourth century, the builders would not have needed to hunt long for a suitable grotto or tomb in the cavernous slopes around Bethany. It cannot now be determined whether the existing Tomb of Lazarus was ever a first-century Jewish tomb, or simply a natural cave.[28]

At et-Tabgha (ancient Heptapegon), on the western shore of the Sea of Galilee, a cave was found under the ruins of a fourth-century church which most likely commemorated the meeting of the Risen Jesus and the apostles by the shore of the lake (cf. John 21. 4 ff.). This would explain the altar and rock-cut steps leading up from the waterside (cf. Pet. Diac., *Lib.* V3), now adjacent to the Church of the Primacy of St Peter, which could be understood as the place where Jesus prepared bread and fish for the disciples.[29] This tradition was later adapted so that the place became known as the site of the multiplication of the loaves and fishes found in the

---

[27] Bagatti (1977*a*). [28] Wilkinson (1978), 110.
[29] So Kopp (1963), 224 ff.; Wilkinson (1981), 196–200.

Synoptic Gospels (Matt. 14: 13–21; Mark 6: 30–44; Luke 9: 10–17)).[30]

On a nearby mountain[31] there was a cave identified as the place where Jesus spoke the Beatitudes (Egeria, in Pet. Diac., *Lib.* V4)[32] which is perhaps the cave now known as *Mghāret Aiyūb*.[33] Around the cave are basalt slabs belonging to an enclosure wall. Numerous Byzantine sherds were collected from the locality. Bagatti's identification of the rock-hewn cistern under the nearby fifth-century monastery as the original cave of the Beatitudes seems unlikely. Even if a cave pre-dated the artificial cistern, which is by no means certain, the builders showed a disrespect which would not be in keeping with the proposed sanctity of the grotto by using it as a cistern.[34]

Byzantine Christian Caves in Pagan Areas

In most pagan areas we cannot know whether caves subsequently used by Byzantine Christians had had pagan religious functions earlier. They should, however, be noted.

The place where the angels told the shepherds the good news of the Messiah's birth was identified as a natural cave near the present village of Beit Sahour (cf. Pet. Diac. *Lib.* L1), outside Bethlehem. This was made into an underground chapel in the fourth century.[35]

At Kursi (Gergesa), a fourth-century chapel, which abutted the rocky slope, was discovered in recent archaeological excavations. It appears to have commemorated a cave where the madman of Mark 5: 1–20, Matthew 8: 28–34, and Luke 8: 26–39 was thought to have lived.[36]

---

[30] See Loffreda (1970b); Schneider (1937).

[31] Valerius (*Ep.* 396) says that Egeria called the mountain 'Eremus'.

[32] Wilkinson (1981), 200.

[33] It was called this since, according to Palestinian Muslim tradition, Job (Aiyūb) was healed after God told him to cover his body with earth from the cave and wash seven times in the spring (*Hammam Aiyūb*); see Bagatti (1971b), 89–91; Baldi (1955), 354.

[34] Bagatti (1937).

[35] Tzaferis (1975); Kopp (1963), 36–42; cf. Mancini (1984), 104a.

[36] Tzaferis (1983a), ch. 3 n. 176. For the site in general, see Tzaferis and Urman (1973).

While pagans of the second and third centuries used caves for religious purposes, and Christians adopted and adapted the idea, caves were, as stated above, employed for profane purposes as well: for stables, cisterns, shelters, store-rooms, or for other agricultural uses. In Eboda, caves were part of the architecture of the residential district, which consisted of 350–400 residential units of caves and houses arranged in terraces along the western slope of the hill.[37]

The Shephalah

Over 3,000 caves have been discovered in the region of Beth Guvrin, and some of these were later used by Christians. While the main reason for digging these cavities was to mine chalk, some of the caves were used as tombs, cisterns, and granaries.[38] Agricultural employment of the caves continued throughout the Roman and Byzantine periods, and sometimes into the early Arab period, as at Tel es-Safi[39] or into the Crusader period, as at Arak el-Kheil.[40] Bagatti believes that the presence of crosses inscribed in the bell-chamber of Khirbet el-Ain, located opposite Tel Goded (Judeideh), indicates that Jewish-Christians used the cave.[41] As we saw, Eleutheropolis (Beth Guvrin) was a town with a mixed population. Whether the Christians there used caves as hiding-places during the persecutions, as did Bar Kochba's supporters in the Shephalah 180 years before,[42] is unknown. We do know, however, that Byzantine Christians used the caves intensively for many different reasons. A Byzantine cemetery existed at Horvat Midras, two and a half kilometres north of Khirbet el-Ain.[43] A church commemorating the father of John the Baptist, Zechariah (Piacenza Pilgrim, *Itin.* xxxii), was located at Azekah (Bethzachar on the sixth-century Madaba mosaic map). Present day Tel Zakariya or Tel Azeqa lies seven kilometres north of Tel Goded. According to Sozomen (*Hist. Eccles.* ix. 17. 1), the body of Zechariah was discovered here in 415.[44] R. A. S. Macalister

---

[37] *EAEHL* ii. 353–4.   [38] Ben Arieh (1962).
[39] Bliss and Macalister (1902), 259.
[40] Ibid. 257.   [41] (1950), 121–2.
[42] See Kloner (1983); Kloner and Teper (1987).   [43] Kloner (1978).
[44] Wilkinson (1977: 154) argues that Tel Zakariya is not the site of ancient Caphar Zakariya, but that it is at Horvat Bet Dikrim, 8 km. south-west of the tel,

discovered numerous caves in this vicinity, one of which on the northern slope he believed to have been used for Christian assembly (no. XXXVII)[45] since it had two Latin crosses and other crosses on the side of a staircase[46] along with, curiously, a Kufic inscription. In the so-called 'great Souterrain' Macalister discovered a cave[47] with 'rude crosses and some lettering'; the latter consisted of the abbreviations *KC IC XC OΠ*(?) with the words *NONON NOCH*.[48] This is meaningless as it stands, but *Nóvov* may be the accusative of the name *Nóvoς*. This name is found throughout the Empire during the Byzantine period.[49]

At Khirbet Medawir, the hill opposite Tel Goded, there are several caves. In a pair of bell-chambers Macalister found sherds of Roman-Byzantine pottery, one of which was scratched with a cross with bifid arms.[50] At Tel Sandahanah (Mareshah) there is a chamber analogous to that of Khirbet el-Ain. Above the entrance is a cross in relief, and in the cave there are numerous crosses.[51] Elsewhere in this cave complex there is a graffito of a praying figure[52] and a plain Greek cross.[53] Praying figures were also found at Arak el-Ma at Beth Guvrin.[54] At Beit Leyi a rock-cut Christian

since the site of the Tomb of Zechariah was about 3 km. from Kefar Turban (John Rufus, *Assur*. 90, understood by Wilkinson to be Khirbet Attraba) and was visited by the Piacenza Pilgrim after Eleutheropolis on the way from Jerusalem to Ascalon. This latter point may be explained by the fact that the pilgrim says that from the main road from Jerusalem to Ascalon, they went off on a side road to Eleutheropolis. Perhaps they then returned to the main road, stopping off at the St Zechariah basilica on the way back. Eusebius located Azekah between Eleutheropolis and Jerusalem in *Onom*. 18. 10, and presumably this is the same place as later Bethzachar, but there is room for doubt. Wilkinson has presented some serious objections to the site's identification. As regards the argument presented here, since even Horvat Bet Dikrim lies in the general region, it is sufficient to prove that the vicinity was traversed by pilgrims.

[45] (1899), 27.

[46] Cf. Bliss and Macalister (1902), 222, fig. 83.

[47] no. 10 in Bliss and Macalister (1902), pl. 94.

[48] See Macalister (1900a), 48–50. Macalister read an *iota* before each of these words, but on the basis of his drawing of the graffiti, it would seem more likely that these are simply vertical scratchings of no importance.

[49] *Nóvvoς* or *Nóvoς*; see Preisigke (1922), col. 236; Foraboschi (1966), 209; Negev (1977), 15, 25–6. For the Nonnos Onesimus inscription at the Church of St Stephen, Jerusalem, see *DACL* xiii. col. 839; *RB* (1892), 576.

[50] Bliss and Macalister (1902), 223–4.

[51] Ibid. 248 ff. It is no. 34; cf. pl. 102.

[52] Ibid. 251, pl. 101.

[53] Ibid. 252.

[54] Ibid. 238; pl. 100; Warren and Conder (1884), 267.

chapel came to light.[55] The walls were inscribed with bifid-armed and crosslet-armed crosses, and there was a partially defaced picture which probably depicted a Virgin and Child. No date has been proffered for the employment of this chapel. Warren and Conder[56] described inscriptions (one of which is in Syriac) and a 'Byzantine cross' on rock and plaster in caves at Deir Dibrin. The crosses and inscriptions were incised in the course of excavations of the caves in the area.[57] In June 1982 and November 1983, A. Kloner excavated a Byzantine (sixth-century) cemetery consisting of seventy graves, east of the Roman town of Beth Guvrin.[58]

At Khirbet el-Ain the presence of crosses with typical Byzantine forms (bifid arms, for example) would fit the period of Christian occupation. The crosses fall into the general pattern of Byzantine remains in the region. Macalister believed that they were inscribed to exorcize pagan gods from a pagan place of assembly in the bell-chamber,[59] but his reasons for considering the vault pagan are rather nebulous: the chamber was large enough (12.19 m. in diameter at the bottom with a depth of 10 m.) to hold a crowd; he could not understand the curious swastika and another curved sign; and he interpreted a recess and raised passage as being used for 'the performance of some priestly fraud',[60] though why an ordinary passage should be regarded in this way is unclear. Furthermore, he seems to have been influenced by his knowledge that 'we know from other countries Early Christians often attempted to consecrate a place defiled by the rites of previous religions by affixing thereto the symbol of redemption'.[61] It may be better to consider the crosses on the walls of the bell-chamber to be the result of enthusiastic Christian quarriers. They are, after all, positioned 9 metres above the floor of the cavern, and must have been carved in the soft chalk during the course of quarrying. The two curvilinear graffiti would have been carved into the wall at the time the chamber was converted into a columbarium, during the early Arab period; the dating for this is provided by the fact that the crosses were cut into when the loculi were created. The spiral

---

[55] Macalister (1901), 226–9.
[56] (1884), 443.
[57] Ben Arieh (1962), 61; so too Oren (1965).
[58] See *Excavations and Surveys in Israel 1983* (Eng. edn. of *Hadashot Arkheologiyot* no. 82–3; Jerusalem, 1983), ii. 12.
[59] Bliss and Macalister (1902), 262.   [60] Ibid.   [61] Ibid.

design shows some similarity with that of the Muslim 'two snakes' shown by Tawfiq Canaan.[62]

Bethphage: A Tomb

Another employment of caves to be considered here is less well known. The identification of a cave at Bethesda as a place where Solomon worked beneficent magic reflects an understanding that magicians went to caves and, especially, tombs to work their spells. For example, in his account of the life of Joseph of Tiberias, Epiphanius (*Pan.* xxix. 7. 1–8) tells a story of how the young patriarch 'Judas' becomes enamoured of a Christian girl he sees in the hot baths at Emmatha, near Gadara. His aides decide to equip him with magical power to help his cause, and after sunset they take the lad 'to the tombs; it is thus in my country one calls artificial caves, full of bodies,[63] which are hewn out of rock' (*Pan.* xxix. 8. 2).[64] The aides recite various incantations and spells and do impious acts, but Joseph discovers what is taking place and hastens, with another elder, to where the group is making magic among the funerary monuments. After the group has gone, Joseph defiles the magical apparatus, which has, curiously, been left on the ground (8. 6). This act, and the fact that the girl is a Christian and therefore, by implication, immune to magic, ensures that the young patriarch is frustrated in his ambitions.

If, therefore, one finds mysterious signs on the walls of a tomb from the Roman period one might be advised to consider a magical interpretation. It would appear very possible, in fact, that some of the cryptic scratchings on the wall of a tomb (no. 21, see Figure 13) in the area of Bethphage, on the Mount of Olives, are magical signs of some kind, not, as the Franciscan excavators assume, 'Jewish-Christian' symbols indicating a millenarian theology.[65]

Before proceeding to attempt identification of the graffiti found within this tomb, it is important to fix the tomb within its

---

[62] (1927), 13, 32–3. [63] Literally, 'full of men'.

[64] Williams (1987: 125) translates this passage as: 'In my country there are places of assembly of this kind, called "caverns", made by hewing them out of cliffsides.' I do not understand how 'places of assembly' can be read here.

[65] Saller (1961), Testa (1961). These two articles have been printed together in Saller and Testa (1961), in which Testa's discussion of the graffiti is at pp. 84–120. The following references are given to this work only. See also Mancini (1984), 79–80.

A – B

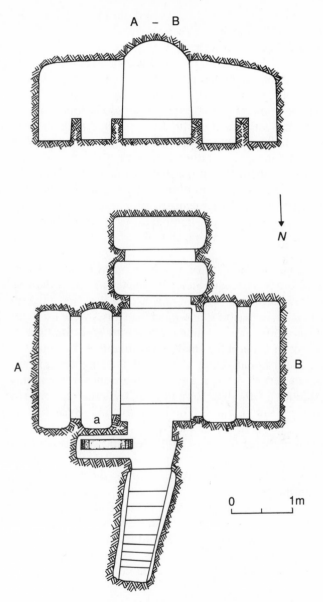

N

0   1m

FIG. 13. Tomb 21 at Bethphage

archaeological context. It is carved out of the hillside as part of a sequence of tombs (nos. 19–22) placed side by side,[66] so that one would expect them to have been constructed at more or less the same time. Tombs 19, 21, and 22 are all *arcosolia*-type tombs, and Tomb 20 was begun but never finished. Tomb 19 was sealed with a flat, rectangular blocking stone,[67] and Tomb 21 with a round blocking stone. The same type of *arcosolia* tomb (no. 3) is found 130 metres away near the present church. Another *arcosolia* tomb (no. 26) differs substantially from the rest in its layout and is entered from above rather than from the side. It shares similar features to three Byzantine shaft graves in the area.[68] Tomb 26 is also datable to the Byzantine era by crosses within circles carved into the wall and characteristic Byzantine sherds.[69] Apart from Tomb 21, none of the homogeneous *arcosolia* tombs have any markings. There were no datable artefacts found within any of these tombs.

The key to the date of Tomb 21 may be the employment of a round blocking stone. Saller believed this dated the tomb to the 'last Jewish period',[70] but Amos Kloner has shown that during the early Roman period round blocking stones were used only for the entrances of large, monumental tombs with multiple chambers, and not in general for small tombs like this. He found only three examples of small tombs with round blocking stones from the early Roman period.[71] The round blocking stones were employed more frequently in the late Roman and Byzantine periods (the rolling stone of the 'Garden Tomb' is a good Byzantine example). However, Tomb 19 has a typical rectangular stone which was commonly used for blocking the entrances of small tombs in the early Roman period.[72] A suggestion might be that the *arcosolia* tombs of Bethphage were cut during the late Roman or early Byzantine period.

If we now look at the graffiti inside Tomb 21 (see Figure 14), it should be noted at the outset that Testa is really discussing Gnostic speculations based on number and letter symbolism (cf. Irenaeus, *Adv. Haer.* i. 15–16). There is no real evidence that Jewish-Christians indulged in such speculations.

---

[66] See Saller and Testa (1961), 70–4.
[67] Ibid. 70.
[68] Ibid. 78–83.
[69] Ibid. 74–8.
[70] Ibid. 73, echoing Vincent.
[71] (1980), 215–16; (1985b), 62–3 nn. 24–7.
[72] Kloner (1980), 214.

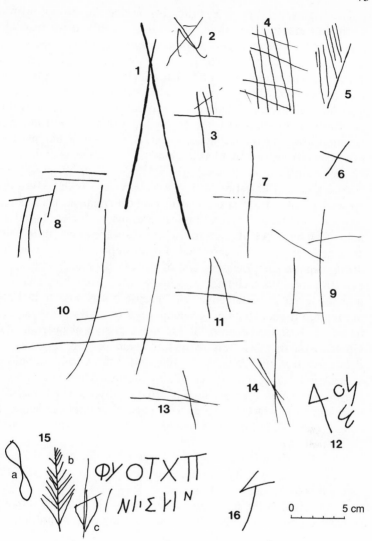

FIG. 14. Graffiti on walls of Tomb 21, Bethphage

The letters *Φ Y*(?) *O T X Π* (no. 15) on one line do not form a word, but may be the initial letters of a formula, if we read the second letter as a strangely slanted *upsilon*. However, they may well be musical notation. The peculiar slant of the *upsilon* is found in the vocal notation, as given by Curt Sachs,[73] where it represents the bass note D, while a regular *upsilon*, without the slant, is E♯ or G♯. All the characters fall very neatly into the repertoire of the vocalic bass notation as listed by Sachs, which put into modern notation would be the full notes: G, D, B, G, F, A. When played, this is a short melody that has a symmetry which seems unlikely to be the result of pure chance.

As a native of Palestine in the second century, Julius Africanus shows how important music was in magical rituals in his records concerning the craft.[74] Notation for different modes was based on the Greek alphabet, though the characters were often cut in half, upturned, or otherwise modified. For example, 'the signs of the *proslambanomene* [lowest notes] of the Lydian mode' were '*zeta* defective and *tau* reclining': the first written something like the number seven, 7 (a defective *zeta* because it was missing its base line), and the second a *tau* turned 45 degrees, as if it was lying on its side.[75] Perhaps because the harmonic system of instrumental Graeco-Roman music was extremely complex, it is less easy to determine that the signs of the line under the vocalic notation, which read *N I' Σ H* [N], are creditably musical. However, a good reason for seeing them as such is provided by the small mark ', after the *iota*, which in the ancient musical notation indicates a treble note.[76] The final letter could be a *zeta* 'reclining' or else a very small *nun*.

Preceding these letters is a roughly scratched depiction of a harp (Figure 14. 15*c*), which may be an indication that we are to read the characters as musical notation.

To the right of the harp are two symbols: one of which is like a number eight (15*a*). This is found on its side in Latin inscriptions

---

[73] (1944), 203–4.

[74] Thee (1984), 112, 114–15, 118, 120, 123, 125, 138, 190.

[75] Ibid. 112.

[76] Testa thinks that it is an abbreviation sign, so that the *N I'* might be a shortened form of νίκη, 'victory', though this would be semantically redundant given the employment of the palm branch. The small mark may also indicate a number.

as an abbreviation for 1,000,[77] but the closest parallel is a magical sign.[78]

The other symbol is a palm branch (15*b*; cf. 5), which is a sign found in pagan and Jewish contexts[79] as well as in many Christian inscriptions[80] and in Muslim shrines.[81] Universally, it is the symbol of life and victory, and sometimes of fertility.

Numerous light scratchings on the wall of the tomb, some of which are cross marks (1–3, 6–7, 9–11, 13–14), would fit in well with a magical interpretation, since crosses of various kinds are found in the magical papyri.[82] The specific motif of the cross mark inside a rectangle (2) is found on three occasions,[83] while the figure-of-eight sign (15*a*) appears once.[84] The large capital letters standing on their own, *II* (8) and, probably, *T* (16),[85] likewise appear in the papyri,[86] but it is not certain in either case whether these are intentional markings, or markings that simply appear like letters. The same can be said for some of the crosses. It is interesting that the cross markings appear only over one trough (Figure 13: *a*) and to the left of the entrance. Unlike Christian crosses, these 'crosses' are not purposefully drawn, and may be indicators rather than symbols: they are to draw the visitor's attention to a particular corpse. The mark on the outside of the tomb, which is a very roughly drawn X (Figure 14.1), would be a sign to the visitor that this is the special tomb. Why it should be special cannot now be known.

Certainly the most interesting graffiti are four letters (Figure 14. 12) scratched right of the rest and angled in such a manner as would suggest the writer was in some way leaning over from the standing area to make these markings. These are written in palaeo-Hebrew or Samaritan script. A comparison between the coin alphabet of the First and Second Revolts and the Samaritan alphabet used on the third–fourth century bilingual Emmaus inscription demonstrates a very close relationship between the two

[77] *TLL* viii. cols. 973–5. [78] *PGM* 276.
[79] Goodenough (1953–8), vii. 87–134, figs. 103–36; cf. Beaulieu and Mouterde (1947–8).
[80] *DACL* xiii. cols. 947–61, s.v. 'Palme, Palmier'.
[81] Canaan (1927), 12–13, 32–3.
[82] *PGM*, 71, 107, 129, 150, 195, 253, 276, 311.
[83] Ibid. 128, 150, 276. [84] Ibid. 276.
[85] I am not sure whether the small diagonal line at the top is part of the letter or a coincidental scratch.
[86] *PGM*, 107, 121, 143.

scripts,[87] so that in this case it is impossible to say if the inscription is one or the other.

Testa read the four letters as Aramaic *nun*, *waw* and *resh* on the first line, and *shin* on the second. The first letter is clearly a *nun*, but Testa's identification of the second as a *waw* is quite wrong. It never appears as a circle in the entire history of the script.[88] It was *ayin* that was written as a circle or a triangle. Testa has drawn this marking as having a light scratch in the middle, though this is not apparent on the photograph (Testa's fig. 5). If a line does exist, which is doubtful, then the second letter is likely to be a *tet*. The third letter is identified by Testa as *resh*. This was written similarly in coinage from the First and Second Revolts, but it is *dalet* which is most like the character here. On the Samaritan Emmaus inscription, however, *resh* appears as here, and also in a graffito on a Jerusalem ossuary.[89] If the third letter is *dalet* then the inscription may read *na'id*, 'we will testify' (Hiphil of the root *'wd*). No word spelt with the consonants *ntd* exists in Hebrew.

It seems most likely, however, that the first three letters should probably be read as *na'ar*. Testa may be correct to consider the inscription a name (or title) followed by the letter *shin*, which is lying rather on its side. This is unusual, but may possibly be explained as an error caused by the difficulty of scratching the inscription at an angle, which should be read as an abbreviated form of *shalom*, as in Jewish inscriptions (Frey, *CIJ*, nos. 904, 1090, 1392). If the reading is *na'ar shalom*, then it would mean 'a youth, peace' (cf. Frey, *CIJ*, no. 668). This is interesting, because *na'ar* was a title of the great angel or 'lesser Yao', Metatron, in the Hekhalot texts. In 3 Enoch 3: 2 *Na'ar* is the predicate by which Metatron is called by God.[90]

Whatever the meaning of these graffiti might be, it seems unlikely that we should accept that these are the scratchings either of a millenarian Jewish-Christian or Gnostic sect prior to the

---

[87] Diringer (1958), 88–94; (1968), i. 188–9, ii. pl. 14. 10–12; see also Naveh (1982*b*: 112–14) on the use of palaeo-Hebrew in the Second Temple period.

[88] See Diringer (1968), ii. 160–1.

[89] Rosenthaler (1975).

[90] Odeberg (1928). See 3 Enoch 2: 2; 3: 2 (and Odeberg's note to 3: 2 on p. 7); Scholem (1960), 43–55. In a passage in *Shiur Komah* the heavenly tabernacle of the High Priest is called 'tabernacle of the youth', Scholem (1960), 49, also 50. Interestingly, the epithet 'of the youth', which also means 'servant', is found in Christian Gnostic literature and Mandaean sources as a reference to the Logos/ Jesus; see Odeberg (1928), 68–9, 191.

Byzantine developments or of a primitive Christian holy place of any kind. Rather, this may be evidence of a Jewish or Samaritan group who wrote in a deliberate palaeo-Hebrew or Samaritan script for their own reasons. Since Jews were not permitted in the environs of Jerusalem from the middle of the second century, it is possible that the secretive quality of these graffiti derives from a necessity to be clandestine. There is, however, nothing that would stop this tomb being assigned to the early Byzantine period, when the ban on Jews was more laxly enforced. Whatever the case, the tomb was considered significant by certain persons, as shown by the indicator markings around the entrance and over the signified trough. It is very possible that the meaning of the graffiti is magical or mystical, but its character is more likely to be Jewish or Samaritan than Christian.

To conclude, caves of various types were used in Palestine by Byzantine Christians as holy places. Some of the caves had been significant in pagan, Jewish, and Samaritan tradition, and were provided with a Christian tradition that would supersede the former. Some of the caves had not been religiously significant before the Christians made use of them. At least one 'cave', the Bethphage tomb, that has been assigned to Jewish-Christians by the Bagatti–Testa school, is unlikely to have had any connection with Christianity in any form. Nothing would suggest that Jewish-Christians in general made special use of caves as 'grotte dei misteri'. Byzantine Christians most likely derived the idea of employing caves as zones of sacredness from pagans, but caves could have a symbolic value to the Christian mind that was new. These were dark, unsavoury places redeemed by their contact with Christ, or another saintly figure, just as fallen humanity would be redeemed. They became 'caves of light' rather than darkness, holy places rather than grottos inhabited by demons. Even caves which had formerly been used for nothing more than agricultural purposes could be utilized in the Byzantine period as holy places, because the idea of using caves in general as sites for numerous biblical events exerted such a powerful attraction.

9

The Bethany Cave, Gethsemane, and the Tomb of the Virgin

THREE places on the Mount of Olives apart from the Eleona cave require special attention. The first of these, the Bethany Cave, is a very recent rediscovery and is not yet developed into a tourist site. The latter two have never been forgotten; they are more or less part of the same complex, and are visited by a great many people every year. On the Mount of Olives, especially on the side facing Jerusalem, there are a number of different Christian holy sites. It is important not to see them as a package; if one site is genuine, then it does not mean that all are, and vice versa: if one site was invented out of nothing much, then this should not predispose us to think that all the sites must be Byzantine inventions. In the case of the Bethany Cave, it is important to establish just what it was in the Byzantine period, because its identification has been lost over the centuries. This is not necessary in the case of the Gethsemane Cave and the Tomb of the Virgin.

The Bethany Cave

On 28 March, 1950 a cave was discovered in the property of the Daughters of the Charity of St Vincent de Paul, Bethany. It measures 5.4 by 4 metres and on the walls are graffiti as well as a painting and inscription done in red paint (see Figures 15 and 16). The Franciscans were the first to publish news of the find in their popular journal *La Terra Santa*,[1] where the view was expressed that the graffiti on the walls of the cave showed that it was frequented and venerated at various periods. The article goes on to report that the monograms from the time of Constantine and other graffiti give the feeling of a Christian atmosphere; the

---

[1] *TS*, 25 May (1950), 148–9.

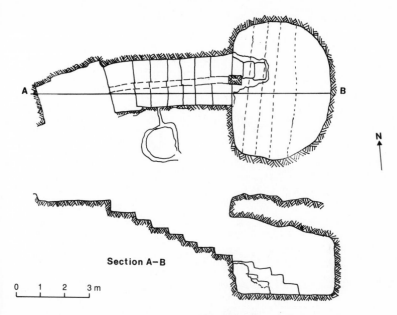

N

Section A-B

0   1   2   3 m

FIG. 15. The Bethany Cave

inscriptions and a study of the ceramics found on the site indicate a date in the Byzantine era;[2] and the locality indicates that some memory lived on here at Bethany, possibly of the Lord's Supper.

The Dominican Fathers of the École Biblique et Archéologique Française were invited by the Sisters to study the cave. P. Benoit and M. E. Boismard subsequently published a corpus of the graffiti and a detailed analysis of the site.[3] They successfully deciphered most of the scratchings and concurred with the anonymous writer of the article in *La Terra Santa* that this was a Christian holy place. In their opinion, the abundance of graffiti and emblems indicated that it was visited by pilgrims over a long period,[4] probably between the fourth and seventh centuries. It was not identified by Benoit and Boismard with any site mentioned in the written sources.

---

[2] '. . . la paleografia e la ceramica ritrovata ci manifestano il tempo bizantino', ibid. 149.
[3] Benoit and Boismard (1951).
[4] Ibid. 216–17.

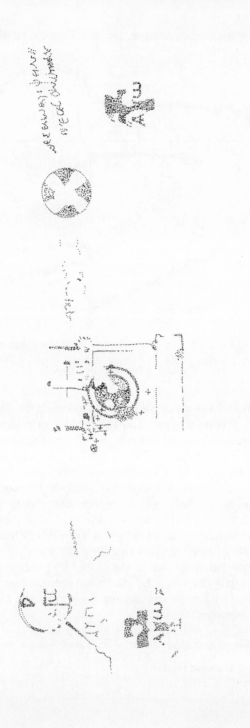

Fig. 16. Red paintings on the plastered walls of the Bethany Cave

Bagatti mentioned the cave in an article two years later, and suggested that the cave was one of three places where 'last suppers' were held by early Christians.[5] His sole source for this supposition is the sixth century (Ps.-?)Eutychius of Constantinople (*Serm. Pasch.* iii, *PG* 86, 2392) who wrote that *Christ* held three suppers with his disciples before his death: one at Gethsemane, one at Bethany, and one on Mount Zion.

S. Saller noted the existence of the cave in his study of Bethany;[6] however, apart from this, the cave was virtually forgotten until Testa developed Bagatti's ideas in his article on 'mystic grottos'.[7] In the absence of any clear identification of the site, he presented the argument that here a Jewish-Christian 'supper' rite was enacted, at which the participants received spiritual gifts.[8] Testa believes that the grotto was used for Christian worship before the Byzantine period. A date in the Roman period was proposed on the basis of Byzantine archaeological remains—two coins, fragments of glass and pottery—which Testa believed *post-dated* the cave's employment for Jewish-Christian worship.[9] This is extraordinary reasoning. As a rule, coins and identifiable pottery fragments are used by archaeologists to date the human use of a site to the period of these items. No objects prior to the fourth century were found in the cave. Moreover, Byzantine coins, pieces of glass, and pottery sherds are precisely what we would expect to find in a place venerated by Christian pilgrims. The pieces of glass would originate from receptacles used to carry holy oil home from sacred sites.[10] The pottery derived from lamps and small bowls containing offerings (cf. Piacenza Pilgrim, *Itin.* ii).

Using Bagatti's suggestion of the early Christian 'last suppers', Testa takes up the motif of the messianic banquet (cf. Prov. 9: 5; Isa. 25: 6; 55: 1–3; cf. Luke 14: 16–21) to argue that mystical suppers were taking place in Judaism. The suppers of the Essenes (cf. the Dead Sea Scroll texts *1QS* vi; 1QSa ii) and Therapeutae, as reported by Philo in his essay *De vita contemplativa* (v–xi), may appear to be of this nature. According to Testa, however, Jewish-Christians continued this tradition. He uses Jean Daniélou's observation[11] that Melchisedek's offering of bread and wine was

[5] (1953*a*), 131 n. 38.   [6] (1957), 354.   [7] (1964*a*), 128–31.
[8] Ibid. 130.   [9] Mancini (1984), 31.   [10] See Barag (1970–1).
[11] (1951), 196 f.

considered from a very early date to be a figure of the Eucharist, to argue that it was Jewish-Christians who believed this, when in fact it was widely known throughout the early Church (cf. Clement of Alexandria, *Strom.* iv. 25; Cyprian, *Ep.* lxiii. 4; Ambrose, *De Sacr.* v. 1). According to Testa, Eutychius is polemicizing against the Jewish-Christians, especially Ebionites, who spoke of three suppers of the Lord: one at Gethsemane, one at Bethany, and one at Zion.[12] The text of Eutychius provides no such corroborative evidence. He is simply reporting a sixth-century belief that Christ ate three suppers in these three separate places. The belief is at no time attached to 'Ebionites'.

The forms of names used in the graffiti argue strongly for the site being a pilgrimage centre rather than a sacred grotto for Jewish-Christian mysteries. Testa attempted to use the presence of a few Semitic-sounding names, Makai (Benoit and Boismard's no. 6), Abidella (no. 13), Barab (no. 32), Anamos (no. 43), and an unreadable inscription in Syriac (no. 70), to argue for the presence of Semites, viz. Jewish-Christians. It is an error, however, to assume that any Christian with a Semitic-sounding name was a Jewish-Christian. The northern church at Herodion, dating from the sixth century, has three inscriptions from a family with largely Semitic names,[13] but there is no evidence that they were Jewish-Christian. The Semitic names in the Bethany Cave, along with the Syriac dipinto, demonstrate that pilgrims from Syria and local regions came to the cave as well as those from further afield. The majority of names are Greek and can be found throughout the Mediterranean world during the Byzantine period. The language of the graffiti is also Greek apart from the one Syriac inscription and a cryptogram (no. 50), the language of which may be Syriac or Arabic.[14]

Testa's most intriguing argument for the cave's Jewish-Christian employment rested on his interpretation of the paintings done in red.[15] These form the central focus of the cave's decoration and depict four cross motifs around a large central object (see Figure 16). A very faded inscription is painted across the breadth of the field of decoration. The crosses are arranged two on each side of the

---

[12] (1964a), 124, 127.   [13] Birger and Netzer (1987).
[14] So Benoit and Boismard (1951), 230.
[15] Cf. the reconstructed drawing in Testa (1964a), 129, and Mancini (1984), 30; also the careful record of existing remains in Benoit and Boismard (1951), pl. IV.

central object, and one above the other. The lower pair are identical Latin crosses (each 45 cm. high) with *alpha* and *omega* on either side, and traces of circles around them; the upper pair are both within circles: the one on the left being a *chi-rho* cross monogram with *alpha* and *omega* under the horizontal bar, and the one on the right having equal arms which thicken as they meet the circumference of the circle. As one can see from the layers of plaster, the red drawings belong to the latest period of the cave's employment. The earliest graffiti were incised into a primary coat of plaster composed of lime and ash. Then, at some stage, the walls were coated again with limewash and the red decoration was painted.

The use of red pigment to decorate the plastered walls of tombs and holy places is found at a number of sites in Palestine. The Garden Tomb in Jerusalem has two large red crosses, on the north and east walls respectively, which also have the abbreviations of Jesus Christ, *IC XC*, and the Greek letters *alpha* and *omega*. These four components, *IC, XC, A, ω*, occupy each of the four spaces created by the arms of the cross, clockwise from the top left. The date of these crosses is fifth to sixth century.[16] At Ein Yalu an almost identical cross painted in red (30 cm. high) was found on one of the walls of a Roman bathhouse, which was employed during the Byzantine period.[17] Numerous dipinti in red paint were found in tombs in the Wadi er-Rababi (Valley of Hinnom) in Jerusalem.[18] A Byzantine tomb in Beth Guvrin discovered early this century has roosters, peacocks, flowers, a grape-vine, and crosses (14–17 cm. high) all painted in red.[19] A cave in Wadi Suwenit, belonging to the Laura of Firminus, has red crosses with Greek and Syriac inscriptions also in red.[20] Sixteen red crosses with Greek letters were found on the walls of the fifth-century burial cave at Horvat Midras, in the Shephalah.[21] In all cases the red-painted decorations are middle to late Byzantine, no earlier than the fifth century. Cross motifs themselves are probably all

---

[16] G. Barkay (1984).
[17] Shimon Gibson, personal communication. I am indebted to him for the following four references.
[18] Macalister (1900b).
[19] Moulton (1921–2), pls. 1–4 and frontispiece. Moulton notes that other tombs he has seen in this area also have red drawings (p. 101).
[20] Patrich (1986); Hirschfeld (1987), 114, illus. 81.
[21] Kloner (1978), 115–16.

Byzantine in Palestine; Vasilios Tzaferis has argued that crosses are not found in Palestine prior to the fourth century.[22]

Testa understood the central object depicted in the red decoration of the Bethany Cave to be a throne, which he proceeded to interpret as a pre-Byzantine Jewish-Christian motif. The 'empty throne' motif is, however, one of the standard images of Byzantine iconography.[23] In some instances the throne is shown in perspective, and sometimes not. Testa insists that the throne he sees here is in perspective, because otherwise the small vertical lines in the upper centre of the structure could not be accounted for. These would be the back of the throne, which would then be comparable to the representation in the Arian Baptistery, Ravenna (c.493–520).[24] This throne seen by Testa is, however, unique in having wings to the backrest, which cause it to be a kind of three-sided box. Elsewhere the backrest is depicted as a square. The area of the legs is also usually square or rectangular, equal in area to the upper part.[25] The backrest is sometimes curved,[26] and elsewhere is absent altogether.[27] The object depicted in the cave lacks any horizontal line half-way up to indicate the seat, or round shapes that could be construed to be arm-rests. The horizontal lines above the medallion (see below) are too high to represent the seat, unless one supposes that this is a throne without a backrest. In this case, however, one would need to explain the vertical protrusions in some other way. One can make a cross out of the intersecting mass of lines of the centre, but the vertical lines on either side cannot be accounted for. It should also be noted that there is no evidence of red markings which would connect these two protruding vertical lines, either to each other or to the smaller vertical lines, which undermines Testa's view that they constitute parts of the backrest. Further key iconographical features of the throne, which are missing in this image, are a footrest[28] and a cushion.[29]

---

[22] Tzaferis (1971).

[23] See Nordström (1953), 46–54, pls. 8, 9, 11–13, colour pl. II. To save space, references here will generally be to the plates of the items he has listed and not to the originals.   [24] Ibid. pl. 9.

[25] Ibid. pls. 12:f–j; 13:b, e (square); pls. 11:d; 12:b; 13:f (rectangular).

[26] Ibid. pls. 8; 12:d; 13:c.   [27] Ibid. pls. 12:a?, c, e; 13:a, d.

[28] Ibid. pls. 8; 9; 11:d; 12:a, b?, c; 13:a, b, c?, d. It is absent from the coin images only for lack of space.

[29] Ibid. pls. 8; 9; 11:d?; 12:a, b, c, d?, e; 13:a, c, d, e. This is also missing on the coins.

The intersecting lines, if interpreted as a cross, or cross *chi-rho*, can be paralleled in other images,[30] but they may also be interpreted as a book on a stand with the letters *alpha* and *omega*. Books or scrolls are found resting on thrones or footstools;[31] in the case of a sixth-century bronze relief in the Hagia Sophia, Istanbul,[32] the book is propped up so that the pages face outwards. In some cases a peacock is represented in a 'medallion' of its outstretched tail feathers,[33] otherwise without this.[34] Elsewhere a dove appears[35] or a lamb,[36] in one case in a medallion.[37] In many instances the throne is draped with a cloth.[38]

It is possible to make another suggestion concerning the object depicted here which may be more likely: that the image is of an altar, not of a throne. If the painting does depict an altar, then it would have provided a focal point for visitors, especially since it is found directly opposite the entrance. If it is a throne, of some unusual type, then it would bring the pilgrims to contemplation of the coming judgement. The throne image has been interpreted by Carl-Otto Nordström to correlate with the idea of ἑτοιμασία, 'preparation, readiness'[39] which Testa has, somewhat strangely, reinterpreted in order to associate it with Jewish-Christians who were preparing to receive charismatic gifts.

The form of the object depicted here would fit well with what we know about the shape of altars at this time. A bare altar is depicted in the ceiling mosaic of the Orthodox Baptistery, Ravenna (*c*.430–450).[40] It consists of four pillar-like legs which stand on a rectangular base. The drawing in the cave also clearly shows pilasters and a base. This kind of altar was typical of the early Byzantine period, and could sometimes be a single block sculpted to give an illusion of a table resting on four pilasters.[41] Fragments

---

[30] Ibid. pls. 8; 9; 11:d, c, e; 13:b, c.
[31] Ibid. pls. 11:d; 12:b, c, d, e; 13: a, b, d.
[32] Ibid. pls. 12:d.   [33] Ibid. pls. 12:g, h; 13:f.
[34] Ibid. pls. 12:f, j; 13:c.   [35] Ibid. pls. 12:b, d, e; 13:d.
[36] Ibid. pl. 12:a, c.   [37] Ibid. pl. 13:e.
[38] Ibid. pls. 8; 9; 12:b, d, e, f, g, h, i (over the backrest); 13:b, d, f.
[39] 'Dieser Begriffsinhalt von *etimasia* stimmt aber nicht ganz mit den Erkenntnissen der jüngeren Forschung überein. Der Thron ist nämlich oftmals gar nicht für den kommenden Christus bereitet, sondern Christus thront schon auf ihm, wenngleich in symbolischer Gestalt', ibid. 47.
[40] See Bovini (1978), pl. 9.
[41] Braun (1924), pls. 1, 6; and see for the various forms of Byzantine altars, *DACL* cols. 3155–89, s.v. 'Autel'.

of Byzantine altars have been found in many parts of Palestine: Nahariya,[42] Khirbet el-Kuneitrah,[43] Khirbet Siyar el-Ghanam near Beit Sahour,[44] the sixth-century monastery of Theoctistus in the Judaean Desert,[45] Ras et-Tawil, five kilometres north of Jerusalem,[46] et-Tabgha,[47] Shavei Zion,[48] and at Khirbet ed-Deir in the Judaean Desert.[49] The altars were frequently made out of marble. One can see in the red drawing an attempt to show the moulding of the stone, and the protrusion at the base of the right colonette. The protruding side of the table top is easily seen on the upper left side.

In the church of S. Maria della Caponapoli in Naples there is a block altar with, at the centre front, a medallion containing an image of the rock of Golgotha and the cross,[50] which brings us to a consideration of the central circular image in the Bethany Cave. It certainly appears to be a medallion of some kind. The artist may be attempting to show that it was on a cloth draped over the altar. A cloth probably covered the altar during the course of the celebration of the Eucharist, as is shown in the 'Sacrifice of Abel' (c.526–47) in the Baptistery of San Vitale, Ravenna.[51] In a similar mosaic in Sant'Apollinaire-in-Classe, where Abel presents a lamb to Melchisedek, the table is arrayed with bread and wine, while the cloth over the table is decorated with a rectangular pattern incorporating small crosses. In this instance, the structure of the altar is completely obscured by the covering, but here, in the Bethany Cave, if we are to imagine a cloth, the structure shows through. The medallion may have contained a pantocrator motif. If so, this would explain the smudges over the lower left perimeter of the circle and over the upper right area, which would correspond to the sweeping movements of a right arm intent on removing a human image. This iconoclasm would have occurred during the eighth century. In 745 all religious art was forbidden in

---

[42] Dauphin and Edelstein (1984), 28, figs. 11–13, pl. VIIIa.

[43] Hirschfeld (1985), fig. 8. In this case the base is 25 cm. high and 105 cm. broad, and is very like the heavy base of the drawing in the cave.

[44] Corbo (1956), 23, photos 13, 18.

[45] Patrich and di Segni (1987), 274.

[46] Gibson (1985–6), 71.

[47] Schneider (1937), 30–1. One can see the square sockets for the column bases around the sacred stone.

[48] Foundations of an altar: Prausnitz, Avi-Yonah, and Barag (1967), pl. XI.

[49] Hirschfeld (1987), 164, illus. 140.

[50] Braun (1924), pl. 50.   [51] Ibid. pl. 7.

the Eastern Church, and widespread iconoclasm occurred.[52] On the other hand, it must be said that the representation of small crosses, seemingly randomly placed around and inside a circle, bears a striking resemblance to a plan in the eighth-century *Book of Mulling*[53] of Tech Moling, Co. Carlow, in Ireland, the monastery of the seventh-century(?) Saint Moling (or Mullins?), which plots the whereabouts of certain named crosses, and it is therefore not impossible that this red 'medallion' is also a plan of some kind.

As for what is resting on the altar, it may be best to envisage various objects rather than any cohesive structure. In the aforementioned ceiling mosaic of the Orthodox Baptistery at Ravenna, an open book rests on top of the altar. If this is the case here, we can conjecture that there is a depiction of a crucifix, from the arms of which hang the letters *alpha* and *omega*: a common Byzantine type.[54] The usual materials for such crucifixes were gold, silver, iron, and other metals. At the top of the vertical bar of the crucifix is a curving line which may indicate the top of a *rho*, or a small horizontal bar and the extremity of the vertical. If we opt for the latter interpretation, this would mean there were small end-bars at the extremities of all the arms of the cross. Indeed, at the right of the horizontal arm there is an area of coloration which could be understood as another end-bar, but this would make the crucifix very squat. It seems more likely that the area of coloration belongs to something else: a cultic object or candlestick.

The bold vertical lines on either side of the crucifix are quite probably long lamp-stands, of which the Israel Museum possesses a good example in bronze, said to have come from the Hauran.[55]

If the artist wished to depict a cloth over the altar, it would explain why the altar itself is shown only in outline: it indicates a certain transparency in the material. The objects on top of the altar are in solid colour. Certain markings along the upper rim of the altar do not appear to have anything to do with the structure or

[52] See Gombrich (1966), 97–8; p. 98 has a rare photograph of an image showing a Byzantine iconoclast whitewashing an image of Christ, from the Chulder Psalter (9th cent.) in the Moscow Historical Museum.

[53] MS Trinity College, Dublin 60; see Thomas (1971), 39.

[54] See the painted cross in the Catacomb of Pontianus, Rome, in Weitzmann (1982), 99, illus. 4.

[55] For pictorial examples of the long lamp-stands used in Palestine during the 5th cent., see Foerster (1986), 419; and also *DACL* iii. 2, cols. 1613–22, s.v. 'Cierges'.

the utensils, and they are not smudged. They appear to be the remains of writing at the top of the table, as in Y. Hirschfeld's reconstructed piece.[56]

The altar may have been a substitute for a real one, drawn at a late date when Byzantine control over the holy places had been weakened by Muslim domination. In the eastern end of the mosaic of the second room of the Beth ha-Shitta monastery complex (possibly eighth century) was a representation of an apse in the form of an arch with a lamp beneath it, which Avi-Yonah suggests may have been such a substitute.[57]

The faded red inscription, composed in a loose cursive script, appears to run on either side of the central altar. Only a small section in the far right is even slightly legible. It may well have provided a positive identification for the cave's employment, but in the absence of infra-red illumination which may show up further traces of the red markings, personal observation leads me to agree only in part with Benoit and Boismard's reading of the letters on the far right side as: ΘЄ ЄΙωΘЄΙ. ΦЄΙΛ.. ΑΛΦ... / ΛΟΥЄϹΘЄΑ. ΟΥΠΟΔΥϹΟΥ.[58] Their reading of ΘЄ ЄΙωΘЄΙ. seems doubtful on the basis of what remains (see Figure 16). There is clearly a *xi* after the first *epsilon*, and the letter after the second is more likely to be a *nun* than an *iota*. Moreover their third *epsilon*, with *iota*, appears to be an *eta*. The initial Θ is also doubtful, and may be connected with red markings which precede it, which Benoit and Boismard ignore. In short, the word ἐξενώθη, 'he was lodged', 1 aorist passive of ξενόω, can be distinguished.

This reading would support an identification of the cave as the *hospitium*, 'guest-room', of Martha and Mary (cf. Matt. 21: 17; Mark 11: 11–12; Luke 10: 38; cf. Matt: 26. 6), which I have argued for elsewhere.[59] It was a pilgrim site known to Jerome (*Ep.* cviii. 12), which was located in between Bethphage and the Lazarium at Bethany. The fact that it is a cave and not a proper house, as Jerome's words might seem to imply, is no obstacle. Caves were frequently identified as dwelling-places without mention that they were grottos: for example, the Piacenza Pilgrim appears to refer to the Cave of the Annunciation as 'the house of St Mary' (*Itin.* v). Jerome fails to mention that there was a cave in the Bethlehem

---

[56] (1987), 164, illus. 140.
[57] (1957*a*), 122; (1957*b*), 260, fig. 6, and p. 270.
[58] (1951), 244   [59] Taylor (1987*a*).

sanctuary in his account of Paula's journey (*Ep.* cviii. 10), referring to it as an 'inn' (*diversorium*) and a 'stable' (*stabulum*). When Jerome refers to the cave in two other letters, he uses only the word *diversorium* (*Ep.* xlvi. 11; lxxvii. 2), and does not mention that it was a grotto.

It has been assumed by others that the sanctuary of the *hospitium* was attached to the Lazarium at Bethany,[60] but the seventh-century Jerusalem calendar has the feast of Martha and Mary celebrated on 4 June in a church 'on the mountain *above* Bethany'[61] which would accord very well with the location of the cave. Later tradition relocated the site. In the Middle Ages, the house of Simon, where Mary Magdalene washed the feet of Christ and was forgiven her sins, was located within the actual town.[62] This site appears to have been within the Church of Lazarus (cf. Saewulf, *Itin.* xxiii), as Theoderic (*Lib. de Loc. Sanct.* xxxv–xxxviii) refers to the 'double church': one part of which was for Lazarus' tomb and the other for Martha and Mary, 'and there our Lord and Saviour used often to be entertained'.[63] A later relocation of the holy site would fit with the evidence of abandonment of the veneration of the Bethany Cave at the end of the seventh century. If it was no longer visited after this time, and over the centuries forgotten, then it would have been necessary for the Crusaders to choose a fresh site for the house of Martha and Mary.

The early history of the cave is less difficult to ascertain. It was not part of a real dwelling, but was a cistern of a common type, known, for example, at Tel Zakariya, Gezer, Samaria, Ein Karim, Hebron, Jerusalem, and in other parts of Bethany, as Benoit and Boismard point out.[64] It appears to have been converted to holy use in the Byzantine period, which accounts for the lack of remains before this time.

In conclusion, the Cave of Bethany was in religious use from the fourth to the seventh century, when it was identified as the *hospitium* of Martha and Mary. Prior to this time it was employed as a cistern. There is no evidence that Jewish-Christians ever

---

[60] Wilkinson (1977), 151; Saller (1957), 364.

[61] Baldi (1955), no. 579.

[62] Saewulf, xxiii; *Gesta Francorum Expugnantium Hierusalem, Guide*, ii; *De Situ Urbis Jerusalem* 07; *Work on Geography* clv; *Seventh Guide* cv; John of Würzburg, vi.

[63] Wilkinson (1988), 303.

[64] (1951), 204.

venerated the site or ate a special meal here. The graffiti on the walls and the red drawing should not be given a Jewish-Christian interpretation; they can be understood better in the context of the established norms of Byzantine iconography and epigraphy.

Gethsemane

As we have just seen, Testa believes that Jewish-Christians ate a meal symbolizing the messianic banquet 'e la moltoplicarono nei vari luoghi ove si era svolta la vita del Cristo':[65] the various places being Bethany, Gethsemane, and Mount Zion, in accordance with his interpretation of (Ps.-?)Eutychius of Constantinople. It is to the second of these places that we shall now turn: the Cave of Gethsemane, known as 'the Grotto of the Betrayal'.

It may seem strange to many Christians today that the betrayal was thought to have taken place in a cave and not in a garden; the Garden of Gethsemane has been a long-established traditional feature of the Passion story in popular understanding. In fact, there is no such place as 'the Garden of Gethsemane' in the Gospels, and it does not look as though early Christian pilgrims imagined that they should find such a locality either. This no doubt explains why it was many centuries before a 'Garden of Gethsemane' is mentioned on the Mount of Olives.

The first attestation of a specific place somewhere on the Mount of Olives where Jesus was betrayed is found in the account given by the Bordeaux Pilgrim of 333, who writes that as one ascends the Mount of Olives from the valley 'which is called Jehoshaphat, to the left, where there are vineyards, is a mass of rock (*petra*) where Judas Iscariot betrayed Christ' (*Itin. Burd.* 594).[66] Testa erroneously translates the word *petra* as 'cave'. In doing so he is able to find a definite literary attestation of this locality as early as the first part of the fourth century.[67] However, the *petra* could correspond with the mass of rock, known as the 'rock of the Agony', 90 metres

---

[65] (1964a), 123.

[66] 'Item ad Hierusalem euntibus ad portam, quae est contra orientem, ut ascendatur in monte Oliveti, vallis, quae dicitur Iosafath, ad partem sinistram, ubi sunt vineae, est et petra ubi Iudas Scarioth Christum tradidit' (*CCSL* 175, 17).

[67] Testa (1964a), 125. Some explanation for this interpretation is given by Finegan (1969: 105), who writes: 'The "rock" is . . . probably the very mass of rock in which is found the so-called Grotto of the Betrayal.'

south of the cave and above it on the hill, which is now incorporated into the Church of All Nations. While the pilgrim may have been referring to the mass of rock in which the cave was located, we cannot assume this to be the case on his/her evidence alone.

The traditions concerning the precise location of the betrayal underwent slight modifications during the course of the fourth and fifth centuries, but the locality of Gethsemane itself appears to have been remembered, even if it was not at first associated with the betrayal so much as with Jesus' prayer. Origen believed that Jesus was betrayed somewhere in the Valley of Jehoshaphat (*Comm. in Joh.* xviii. 1–2; cf. *Comm. in Matt.* xxvi. 36), which may imply that he knew Gethsemane was located there.

Eusebius described the betrayal as taking place in the Kidron Valley itself (*Onom.* 174. 26–7), and he also could understand Gethsemane as being the specific locality for this event (*Dem. Evang.* x. 3. 12; *Comm. in Is.* xxviii. 1), so it is a simple syllogism to deduce that Gethsemane was understood by Eusebius to be in the Kidron Valley. In the *Onomasticon*, however, Eusebius describes Gethsemane [Γεθσεμανῆ] as being: 'a place [χωρίον] where Christ prayed before the passion. It lies adjacent to [πρός] the Mount of Olives, on which [ἐν ᾧ] even now the faithful earnestly offer prayers' (*Onom.* 74. 16–18). Eusebius' language here is vague. Because he is echoing the usage of the Gospels, where Gethsemane is described as a χωρίον (Matt. 26: 36; Mark 14: 32), he does not require us to think either of a cave or a mass of rock. Either χωρίον or τῷ ὄρει τῶν ἐλαιῶν may be referred to by the relative pronoun, but since it is found in the second sentence of the description it most naturally refers to the Mount of Olives. This recalls that Eusebius wrote in regard to the Mount (*Dem. Evang.* vi. 18) that Christians prayed on it because they believed the glory of the Lord resided there. It may be implied, nevertheless, that a reason the faithful offer prayers is because of Christ's prayer at Gethsemane, and one may wonder therefore if, at the very beginning of the fourth century, Gethsemane was in some way out of bounds for Christian prayer. If the rocky mass pointed out to the Bordeaux Pilgrim was indeed that in which the Gethsemane Cave was located, it is striking that s/he does not appear to go into the cave.

In fact, even by the time of the Bordeaux Pilgrim, we are not told that a cave or a mass of rock was actually utilized by Christians, and s/he does not go anywhere to pray in imitation of Christ. It was simply one of the geological features Christians had begun to identify as significant in the life of Christ. However, some fifty years later, Egeria provides information which demonstrates that great progress had taken place in the development of the area, especially as regards the rock of the Agony, to which the Bordeaux Pilgrim may also have referred.

Egeria mentions a graceful church ('ecclesia . . . elegans') located where the Lord prayed (*Itin.* xxxvi. 1). This is undoubtedly the same church as that referred to by Jerome under his entry for Gethsemane (*Lib. loc.* 75. 19). Their references are to the Byzantine church uncovered in 1919,[68] a little up the hill to the south of the Cave of Gethsemane. This church was 20 metres long and 16 metres wide, and incorporated the mass of rock so that it lay immediately in front of the central apse, before the altar, precisely where it is positioned in the present Church of All Nations, which has incorporated the remains of the Byzantine structure.

Vincent[69] is responsible for the prevalent idea[70] that this church was constructed during the reign of Theodosius I (379–95), which may well be the case, but the source he uses as evidence, Eutychius of Alexandria (*Annales* i. 536), refers not to the Byzantine Church of the Agony but to the Tomb of the Virgin at Gethsemane when he writes: 'King Theodosius built in Jerusalem the Gethsemane church in which there is the tomb of Saint Mary, which the Persians destroyed at the time they destroyed the churches of Jerusalem'[71] (see below). Despite Jerome's description of the church under his heading for Gethsemane, the rock of the Agony was not considered to be part of 'Gethsemane' until recent times. Egeria (*Itin.* xxxvi. 1–3), for example, refers to 'Gethsemane' as a place further down the 'very big' hill. Interestingly, Cyril distinguishes between Gethsemane 'where the betrayal took place' and somewhere else on the Mount of Olives 'where they who were

---

[68] See Meistermann (1920); Orfali (1924); Vincent and Abel (1914*b*), 301–37; Kopp (1963), 345; Ovadiah (1970), 84–5; see also Bagatti (1938).

[69] Vincent and Abel (1914*b*), 306 n. 1.

[70] Cf. Hunt (1984), 158; Wilkinson (1977), 157.

[71] 'Struxit etiam Theodosius rex Hierosolymis ecclesiam Jesmaniah in qua sepulcrum erat sanctae Mariae, quam diruerunt Persae quo tempore Hierosolyma usque profecti ecclesias Hierosolymitanas destruxerunt . . .' (*PG* 111, 1028).

with him that night were praying' (*Cat.* xiii. 38). Certainly, the betrayal was firmly located here by the time Cyril wrote (c.350), and despite Cyril's mention of the disciples praying elsewhere, it was Jesus' prayer that was in the main detached from this site.

When Jerome encountered Eusebius' mention of Gethsemane in his *Onomasticon* as being the place where Christ prayed before the Passion, he knew only that the nearby rock of the Agony was the place identified as the spot where Christ prayed. In attempting continuity with Eusebius' mention of prayer (since his aim was, after all, to translate and update Eusebius and not write an entirely new book), he referred to the church along with the site of Gethsemane, but whether he meant to imply that this church was built directly on top of the Gethsemane cave is debatable. Jerome writes: 'Gethsemani, the place where the Lord prayed before the Passion; but above [*desuper*], at the foot of the Mount of Olives, a church is now built' (*Lib. loc.* 75. 18–19).[72] *Desuper* may be understood as 'upon' (cf. Jerome's Vulgate, Matt. 21: 7), but its basic meaning in late Roman Latin is simply 'above'.[73] The Byzantine Church of the Agony was literally above the cave in its height on the hill, and pilgrims understood it to be so. Hesychius of Jerusalem (*fl. c.*440), for example, says that Gethsemane lies at the foot of the Mount of Olives and that from here Jesus withdrew a stone's throw *towards the top* of the Mount to pray, thereafter returning to Gethsemane where he was arrested (*Diff.* xxxvi).[74]

Subsequent Byzantine and medieval pilgrims always make a distinction between 'Gethsemane', understood to be the cave and its immediate vicinity—which would incorporate the later garden and the Tomb of the Virgin—and the place of Christ's solitary prayer, which was seen to be above the cave, further up the hill.[75]

---

[72] 'Gethsemani, locus ubi salvator ante passionem oravit, est autem ad radices montis oliveti nunc ecclesia desuper aedificata.'

[73] LS (1879), 561; in earlier times it carried a sense of motion: 'from above, from overhead'.

[74] Wilkinson (1977), 157–8. See also Walker (1990), 229–34, esp. 232.

[75] *Breviarius* A and B. 7; Piacenza Pilgrim, *Itin.* xvii; *Commemoratorium* x. See also the English translations of Wilkinson (1988): *First Guide* iii (p. 88); *Ottobonian Guide* iv (p. 92); Saewulf, xvii (p. 106); *Guide Perhaps by a German Author* i (p. 117); Daniel the Abbot, *Zhitie* xx (pp. 133–4); *Gesta Francorum Expugnantium Hierusalem, Guide*, xiv (p. 175); *De Situ Urbis Jerusalem* 07 (p. 179); Muhammad al-Idrisi, xxxiii (p. 225); Belard of Ascoli, i (pp. 228–9); *Seventh Guide* civ (p. 235); *Second Guide* cxxiv (pp. 240 f.); Theoderic, xxiii–xxiv (pp. 298–300); John Phocas, xv.1–8 (pp. 325–6). Only John of Würzburg, cxxxvii–cxxxviii (pp. 255 f.) is vague.

The twelfth-century *Qualiter* has a reference to the 'Garden of Gethsemane' where the Lord prayed *with* his disciples and where he was betrayed by Judas, which is not a reference to the place of the Agony, since the Gethsemane Cave itself was, at least after Cyril, generally understood to be where Jesus and his disciples foregathered for prayer (cf. John Phocas, xv. 1). The writer of the Latin *Gesta Francorum Expugnantium Hierusalem*, *Guide* (xiv), familiar only with the church at Mary's tomb as being 'at Gethsemane', simply assumes that Jerome is making a reference to this building, not to the Church of the Agony.

Peter the Deacon (*Lib.* I) mentions that there was a church 'above' (*supra*) a cave on the other side of the Kidron and, as with Jerome, he surely means 'on the hill above', and not 'directly over', the cave. This description by Peter must in fact come from Egeria, because the church had been destroyed (probably by an earthquake) by the end of the eighth century, 300 years before Peter wrote. The church is last attested in Hugeburc's *Life of Willibald* (xxi) written *c.*780 but reporting here the year 724. The cave seems to be identified by Peter the Deacon as the place where 'the Jews arrested the Saviour', just as it was identified by pilgrims after Egeria. In the present text of Egeria's account (*Itin.* xxxvi. 2–3), she writes that from the church commemorating where Christ prayed, where they had gone at dawn, the party of pilgrims celebrating Passion week slowly descend *in Gessamani*. Here the pilgrims are provided with hundreds of church candles 'so that they can all see'. At this place they have a prayer, a hymn, and a reading from the Gospel about the Lord's arrest. Although it is not specifically stated here that the pilgrims actually went into the cave, Egeria's description would cohere perfectly with its location and character. It could be that the mention of church candles may indicate only that it was still very dark outside, since Egeria goes on to say that the time when people could first recognize each other occurred as the group reached the gate of the city, after the service at Gethsemane (xxxvi. 3), but the group had already been walking around the Mount in darkness all through the night without the aid of candles. The provision of candles would certainly fit well with their arrival at the cave, where it was necessary for the service that everyone should see adequately. Most importantly, Egeria identifies 'Gethsemane' as being the place where Jesus was arrested.

Clearly, then, there are two distinct places in the region which, by the end of the fourth century, were venerated by Christians. One was the rock where Jesus was thought to have prayed and the other was 'Gethsemane' proper, a cave in which Jesus was thought to have been arrested in the company of his disciples.

As we have seen, about thirty years before Egeria, Cyril of Jerusalem attested that Gethsemane was the place where Jesus was arrested, and 'shows Judas still to the eyes of our imagination' (*Cat.* x. 19; cf. xiii. 38), but he too fails to mention that the locality was a cave. The *Breviarius* has a reference to the same place of arrest, and includes, for the first time in the tradition history, a mention of a final supper eaten by Jesus and his disciples at the place (*Breviarius* A and B. 4). Had there existed a pre-Byzantine custom of eating a supper at the cave in commemoration of one celebrated by Jesus and his disciples, it is surprising that it does not surface into the literary evidence until this stage, in the sixth century. From this point on, however, the supper forms a part of the mythology of the holy site. Now too we find the first attestations, apart from Peter the Deacon's later record of Egeria's observations, that 'Gethsemane' was in fact a cave.

Theodosius (*De Situ* x) writes of a cave in which there were four 'couches' for the twelve apostles. People came here to light lamps and eat food in the place where Christ washed the apostles' feet. The Piacenza Pilgrim of 570 (*Itin.* xvii) writes that there were three (an error?) 'couches' in the place where the Lord was betrayed, failing, as those before him, to mention that it was a cave. By the time of Arculf the four rock 'couches' were understood to be tables. One was just inside the entrance to the cave, and the others were further in. There were also two cisterns of great depth (Adomnan, *De Loc. Sanct.* i. 15. 1–3).[76] A further interpretation of the rock ledges is provided by Epiphanius the Monk (*Hag.* viii. 14– 20), who explains that they are thrones on which Christ and the twelve apostles will sit to judge the twelve tribes of Israel. He writes that at the head of one of these was a cavity in the floor occupied by 'spirits'; clearly a reference to a cistern. Bernard the Monk (*Itin.* xiii) reports that there were four round tables for the supper in the 'church'; he too fails to mention that it was a cave. It

[76] Wilkinson (1977: 99, 157) is probably right that Adomnan misunderstood Arculf when he reports that the rock where Jesus prayed was in the church of St Mary.

is most likely that the idea of placing the supper in the cave arose to explain the existence of these rock-cut ledges, which are no longer extant. In the Middle Ages, pilgrims understood these to be the beds where the disciples went to sleep (Saewulf, *Itin.* xvii; Theoderic, *Lib. de Loc. Sanct.* xxiv; *Second Guide* cxxiv).

Testa would see in the sixth-century practice of eating a meal in the Gethsemane Cave (Theodosius, *De Situ* x) a continuation of an ancient, albeit hypothetical, Jewish-Christian rite. This is very doubtful. The accounts by Byzantine pilgrims show that they shared the belief attested by (Ps.-?)Eutychius of Constantinople that Jesus ate a supper in this place with his disciples. The belief itself accounted for their habit of eating here. Whatever Jesus experienced at any given holy site, Byzantine pilgrims enacted an abbreviated version of the same, in order to enter into Christ's life more fully. They filled a waterpot at Cana (Piacenza Pilgrim, *Itin.* iv), or drank the water from the pot (Hugeburc, *Vita Will.* xxiii). They drank from the sponge allegedly used at the crucifixion (Piacenza Pilgrim, *Itin.* xx; cf. Matt. 27: 48), and bathed at the place of baptism at the Jordan (Hugeburc, *Vita. Will.* xvi). Most notably, they followed the course of Christ's Passion in a series of processions from the Mount of Olives to the Edicule at Golgotha: a practice which continues to this day.

Returning now to the identification of a cave as 'Gethsemane', it was noted above that Eusebius is echoing the Gospels in using the word χωρίον to refer to Gethsemane. It does not follow that he could not be referring to a cave, simply because he fails to mention it as such. Certainly, he located it in the same area as the cave is located. We know that by the end of the fourth century the cave was considered the location of the betrayal, and yet pilgrims are frequently silent about the fact that it was a cave. Of the nineteen medieval guides and pilgrim itineraries which mention the site of the betrayal, only six mention the fact that the place was a cave (Daniel the Abbot, *Zhitie* xx; *De Situ Urbis Jerusalem* 07; Belard of Ascoli, i; John of Würzburg, cxxxvii–cxxxviii; Theoderic, xxiv; John Phocas, xv. 4–5). Others refer to Gethsemane as a 'house', 'farm', or even 'village', depending on how they interpret Jerome's Vulgate translation of χωρίον as *villa* (Matt. 26: 36) and *praedium* (Mark 14: 32). Jerome clearly understood χωρίον to have some agricultural associations if he could translate it as either 'estate' or 'farm'; perhaps it meant an 'agricultural area or installation' in general. Unfortunately, *villa* was a sufficiently loose word in itself to account for numerous further interpretations. Origen's *Commentary on Matthew* 26: 36, which survives only in the Latin translation, has *praedium*,[77] from which we can infer that Origen used the Greek word χωρίον, in Matthew 26: 36 and Mark 14: 32.

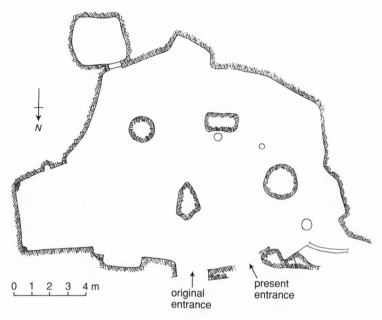

FIG. 17. The Gethsemane Cave

Archaeological evidence suggests that the Cave of Gethsemane was indeed used for agricultural purposes during the Roman period.[78] The cave has been greatly changed over the course of the centuries, but its dimensions appear to have remained much the same (see Figure 17). It is extremely large, measuring approximately 11 by 18 metres, and was supported by four rock-cut pilasters, of which three still exist in the present shrine. The remains of the original entrance can be seen on the north side. A roughly square artificial cave cut into the eastern side housed an olive-press. The evidence for this is a hole cut into the south wall of this recess,

[77] GCS 38, *Origenes Werke* XI, ed. E. Klostermann, p. 204.
[78] Corbo (1965), 1–57; Vincent and Abel (1914*b*), 335, fig. 147.

which was to hold the wooden horizontal bar of the press.[79] We can be sure that the press was for olives, and not for grapes, because wine-presses are never found underground. Caves were used for oil-presses on account of their warmth.[80] There are many examples of underground olive-presses in the region of Beth Guvrin.[81] A gutter to the right of the present entrance, along with a cistern, also suggests an agricultural use. Into the outside north wall was carved a drain which led to a small pool and then to the cistern. A hole was cut in the ceiling of the cave for light and ventilation, and below it was another cistern to collect rainwater. The rock-cut pilasters may also date from the time of the cave's earliest use. The four rock 'couches' attested by pilgrims may have been the remaining 'uprights' of screw operated presses.[82]

It is well known that the meaning of the Greek Γεθσημανί (Matt. 26: 36; Mark 14: 32) is 'oil-press', from conjectural Hebrew *gat-shemanim*. The word *gat*, in Hebrew, Aramaic, and Syriac, frequently means 'wine-press'; nevertheless, in rabbinic literature, *gat* is sometimes found as a place for the preparation of oil (*j.Peah* 7. 1; *t.Ter*. 3. 6). The broader meaning of the word is any cistern or pit excavated for a particular purpose (cf. *m.Zeb*. 14. 1). The word *shemanim*, in plural, is used for kinds of oil (*b.Sabb*. 2. 2), gifts of oil (*j.Bez*. 1. 9), and oil stores (*b.Midd*. 2. 5).[83] As we have seen, Matthew and Mark refer to this Gethsemane as being a 'place', χωρίον, and not a garden. Luke (22: 39–40) has it that Jesus went 'to the spot' (ἐπὶ τοῦ τόπου) on the Mount of Olives. Only in John (18: 1) is there any mention of a garden (κῆπος) on the other side of the Kidron Valley. It is from the conflation of the Johannine and the Synoptic traditions that we arrive at the concept of a 'Garden of Gethsemane'. But it is quite possible that John is referring to the whole cultivated area of the Mount of Olives itself, since κῆπος can mean any cultivated tract of land from a small herb garden to a plantation or an orchard, and John does not otherwise mention the Mount of Olives at all. Eusebius himself seems to do the same in his spiritual reading of Zech. 14: 4, where the Lord's olive garden (his Church) is identified with the *Mount*

---

[79] See for olive-presses in general Dalman (1935a), iv. 153–290; B. Frankel (1981); R. Frankel (1981); Heltzer and Eitam (1987); Kloner and Hirschfeld (1987); Peleg (1980); Shatel (1980); Yeivin (1966).

[80] Dalman (1935b), 322.

[81] Teper (1987); Kloner and Sagin (1987).

[82] See Gichon (1980).

[83] See Dalman (1935b), 322.

(*Dem. Evang.* vi. 18). Whatever the case, John, like Luke, refers to the actual spot where Jesus and his disciples were gathered as τὸν τόπον, ὅτι πολλάκις συνήχθη Ἰησοῦς ἐκεῖ μετὰ τῶν μαθητῶν αὐτοῦ (John 18: 2).

If the cave was used as a large oil-pressing works, which the meagre archaeological evidence would tend to suggest, and since the New Testament accounts write of Jesus and his disciples spending the night in a place called 'oil-press' on the Mount of Olives, there is good reason to put the two together. One can, of course, only stress probabilities. The cave is unusual because of its impressive size. As an important oil-pressing works, it would have been well known. If it continued to be used as an oil-pressing works for the olive groves of the Mount, and there is no evidence that it did not, then there is reason to suppose that the local population continued to call the place 'oil-press'. It should not seem at all strange if Jesus and his disciples decided to use this cave as a place to sleep. As anyone who has camped out in the Judaean hills knows, the dew is heavy, especially in spring, and the nights can be very cold (cf. John 18: 18). No one in their right mind would think of sleeping under the stars at this time of year. G. Dalman suggests that oil-presses were used only in the autumn,[84] so that by the Passover it would not have been utilized.

Whether the property was personal or communal is not known, but if by the time of Eusebius the public or private owner was not as sympathetic to the Jerusalem Christians as the first-century owner to Jesus and his followers, this would account for the faithful of the early fourth century not going to Gethsemane itself to pray. Shortly after Constantine had secured the East, though possibly not quite in time for the visit of the Bordeaux Pilgrim, the site was appropriated by the Church, along with an adjacent site, and these were determined to commemorate two important actions in the course of Jesus' Passion: the Cave of Gethsemane was understood to be where Jesus was arrested, and a nearby mass of rock was believed to be where he went to pray alone. The hypothesis that Jewish-Christians used the cave for their supposed suppers, however, is an idea unsupported by any evidence at all.

[84] Ibid.

The Tomb of the Virgin

The Tomb of the Virgin, which is located adjacent to the Cave of Gethsemane, is an extremely important holy place to the Orthodox Church. Three days before the Assumption of Mary, to mark the death of the *Theotokos* (God-bearer), thousands of Orthodox Christians go on a procession in which a wooden effigy of the Virgin on her deathbed is taken from the Old City to the tomb. During the eight days of the Assumption it remains there, and then the icon is taken out and walked back through the Old City accompanied by songs and dances.

In 1972, after the Church of the Tomb of the Virgin had been flooded, the Greek and Armenian monks in charge of the site decided to restore the structure, and invited Father Bagatti to make observations and take photographs in order to illuminate its history.[85] However, it was not on account of new archaeological information that he argued for an early veneration of the tomb, for Bagatti had already suggested this before the flood.[86] Despite the fact that there is good reason to suppose that a tomb (of what type is impossible to say, though Bagatti believed it to be first century[87]) was identified as that belonging to the Virgin Mary, and that it was carved away from the hillside in like manner to the supposed Tomb of Christ at Golgotha,[88] Bagatti stressed the importance of literary sources as evidence for the site's early history.

Bagatti concentrated on the range of apocryphal literature dealing with the death and Assumption of Mary.[89] While he noted that the texts show signs of modification over time to suit a 'liturgical reading', he asserted that there are many 'original parts'.[90] Bagatti believed he could distinguish pre-Nicene theological expressions in the story, and that these expressed the terminology

---

[85] His subsequent publications about the site include Bagatti (1972*b*), (1972*c*), (1973*a*), (1973*b*); Bagatti, Piccirillo, and Prodomo (1975).

[86] Bagatti (1963*b*), (1971*f*); cf. Hammerschmidt (1973).

[87] (1972*b*), 19–23, 57.   [88] Ibid. 48–9.

[89] For a sample of the many texts see *De Transitu Mariae Apocrypha Aethiopice*, ed. Arras; *Apocalypses Apocryphae*, ed. Tischendorf, pp. 112–36. See also translations by Heibach-Reinisch (1962); *ANT* 194–227; Wenger (1955).

[90] (1972*b*), 237; Bagatti, Piccirillo, and Prodomo (1975), 10.

of Jewish-Christians of the second to third centuries.[91] This theological terminology includes references to the 'Christus-angel', 'cosmic ladder', 'seven skies', and 'secrets' which one most naturally associates with Gnosticism, despite what Bagatti has argued in his studies on the matter.[92]

Bagatti's argument is that the references in the Ethiopic text of the *Transitus Mariae* attributed to Leucius[93] and in the manuscript Vat. 1982,[94] which describe the Tomb of Mary on the 'left side of the city' or in the Kidron Valley (Ethiopic text), are pre-Byzantine. If they are pre-Byzantine, then we must, according to Bagatti, see in these texts evidence of Jewish-Christian veneration of the tomb.[95] He believed the Jewish-Christians built no structure and were content to worship in the bare tomb.

The texts themselves have yet to be given a proper 'form-critical' study, which would illuminate the development of the traditions contained within them, but a few cursory remarks should be sufficient to cast doubt upon Bagatti's reasoning. In the first place, despite the Gnostic terminology, there is nothing to indicate that the texts are prior to the fourth century. In the second place, it should be noted that the Mount of Olives and the Kidron Valley were the traditional cemeteries of Jerusalem, so that, if the origins of these apocryphal texts are to be placed prior to the fourth century, one might at most suggest that the editors had some knowledge of this fact. Bagatti himself pointed out that only in the later Byzantine period is the tomb specifically located on or beside Gethsemane (the cave).[96] Again, it would seem probable that the popular literature which located the Tomb of Mary somewhere in the Kidron Valley influenced the later choice of site, which is specifically mentioned as being in the Valley of Jehoshaphat,[97] or Gethsemane,[98] in later editions of the legend.

There is no mention of a commemorative site for Mary in patristic literature or in pilgrim accounts until the sixth century, when Theodosius (*De Situ* x), the Piacenza Pilgrim (*Itin.* xvii), and the *Breviarius* (A and B. 7) mention the Church of St Mary; the latter specifically refers to her tomb there. From this time onwards

[91] Ibid. 14.   [92] (1970a), (1971e), (1971f), 42–8.
[93] *De Transitu Mariae Apocryphae Aethiopice*, ed. Arras, 72–105.
[94] Wenger (1955), 209–41.
[95] Bagatti, Piccirillo, and Prodomo (1975), 15; Bagatti (1972b), 240.
[96] Ibid. 238.   [97] See *ANT* 198, 199, 215, 217.
[98] Ibid. 208.

it became part of the Jerusalem pilgrimage circuit (cf. Adomnan, *De Loc. Sanct.* i. 12. 1–5; Bernard Mon., xiii; *Commemoratorium* x). St John Damascene (*Hom.* xxi. 18) uses a source which states that the church here existed during the days of the Bishop Juvenal (425–59). Eutychius of Alexandria (*Annales* i. 536) in the tenth century, wrote that the church at Gethsemane containing the Tomb of the Virgin was constructed during the reign of Theodosius I (379–95). The dates for Theodosius II (408–50) may be more suitable, since Egeria and Jerome both fail to mention the monument, and even the *Armenian Lectionary* of 417–39 omits any reference to it. A date of *c.*440 may be the earliest possible for the building's construction.

The only datable Byzantine remain in the present church on the site is a fifth-century funerary inscription for a woman named Euphemia.[99] In 1937 trenches were sunk in the Armenian area west of the Tomb of the Virgin. Mosaic floors were uncovered along with an inscription reading 'Tomb of Kasios and Adios', which is probably sixth century.[100] Walls in the north-west, north-east, and south-west, along with the rock-cut walls in the south-east around the tomb inform us that the lower church was cruciform[101] (see Figure 18). The Greek Orthodox Patriarchate has arranged digging in the region in recent years but their excavations have not been published. In the course of restoration work, however, the marble and plaster of the tomb has been stripped and the original rock ledge on which Mary was supposed to have been laid has been exposed. It is 45 centimetres high and 70 centimetres broad, and, like the ledge in the Tomb of Christ, it has been chipped away by pilgrims who wished to take a piece of the rock home.[102]

The original church around the tomb survived until the Persian conquest of 614 when, according to Eutychius of Alexandria (*Annales* i. 536, see above), it was destroyed.

---

[99] Saller (1965).

[100] See Johns (1939), 129 ff.

[101] See Bagatti, Picirillo, and Prodomo (1975), 49–57; Vincent and Abel (1914b), 805–31, pl. 81. See also Meistermann (1903), fig. 5. It should be noted that Vincent's plan of an octagonal upper church is purely hypothetical.

[102] Berder (1988), 29.

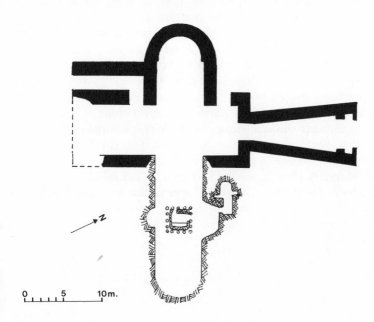

FIG 18. The earliest church of the Tomb of Mary at Gethsemane

Conclusion

Neither the Bethany Cave nor the Cave of Gethsemane can be understood as places venerated by Christians before the fourth century. The former was a cistern during the Roman period, and was adopted as the 'guest-room' of Martha and Mary early in the Byzantine period. The Gethsemane Cave was an olive-pressing works, which may well have been the actual place where Jesus and his disciples used to spend their nights. It has a good claim to authenticity. Its later identification by Byzantine Christians depended on the continuation of its name and its agricultural use, combined with the traditions of the Jerusalem community, but not, it would appear, on any continuous veneration from apostolic times.

The literary evidence which 'proves' the early veneration of a site where Mary was supposed to have been buried is of doubtful historical value. There is no archaeological material that would support the notion that Jewish-Christians venerated a tomb here. The shrine was constructed by isolating an early tomb from the rocky cliff in which it was found, in the same way that the Tomb of Christ was isolated. There were many tombs in this area that could have been chosen as the site of Mary's resting place. It seems probable that in order to satisfy the expectations of pilgrims who were familiar with the stories of the Virgin's burial in the Kidron Valley, some of which *may* have started to circulate before the Council of Nicaea, a particular tomb came to be identified as that of Mary. A church was built over it in the middle to late fifth century. Here again it would appear that popular apocryphal stories influenced the development of a particular Christian holy site in the Byzantine period, and its origins are not to be found in ancient veneration.

Zion

BETHANY and Gethsemane are two of three places to which (Ps. −?)Eutychius of Constantinople refers when he describes the pilgrim practice of eating meals at certain sites; Mount Zion is the third (*Serm. Pasch.* iii, *PG* 86, 2392). Pilgrims refer to a great Byzantine basilica on this hill named 'Holy Zion',[1] but the first evidence of pilgrims believing that a/the Last Supper was celebrated here comes from the fifth century[2] with (Ps.-?)Hesychius (*Comm. in Psalm.* l. 17; liv. 14; cix. 2; *Serm.* viii).[3] The basilica was not constructed to commemorate the last supper.

The Bagatti–Testa school does not linger long in consideration of (Ps.-?)Eutychius' text in regard to this site, but prefers to concentrate on other evidence which is claimed to demonstrate Jewish-Christian occupation.[4] As the Benedictine archaeologist Bargil Pixner has recently argued,[5] on Mount Zion we are to imagine the first Church of James, the central Jewish-Christian church. We will address here the question of whether the first Christians met on Mount Zion, and continued to meet here—despite the disturbances that befell Jerusalem—up until the Constantinian developments.

---

[1] Theodosius is first to call the Byzantine basilica *Sancta Sion*; cf. Eutychius of Alexandria, *CSCO* 193, 142; Piacenza Pilgrim, *Itin.* xxii; Epiphanius, *Hag.* ii–iii; see also Wilkinson (1978), 165. The name 'Holy Zion' is confirmed by the graffiti found in a Byzantine tomb in the Valley of Hinnom (Wādi er-Rababi) which apparently belonged to the monastery of 'Holy Zion', see Macalister (1900*b*), pls. I, III: *MNHMA TH C AΓIAC CIωN*). The Hebrew word *Tsion* was transliterated into Greek as Σιών with an initial *sigma*, but since the English form of the word today is Zion, with a *z*, this will be used here. Some writers prefer to use the word Sion, following the Greek and medieval usage.

[2] The late fourth-century *Didascalia Addai* appears to identify the upper room of the Last Supper with the upper room of Pentecost, but does not mention Mount Zion; cf. Vincent and Abel (1914*b*), 453, and the translation by Howard (1981).

[3] *PG* 93, pp. 1205, 1217, 1323, 1480. See also Sophronius, *Anacreon.* 55–62; Hippolytus of Thebes, i. 5; *Arm. Lect.* 39.

[4] Though see Testa (1965).

[5] Pixner (1990).

At the outset, it should be remembered that 'Mount Zion' of the Byzantines was not the *Tsion* of the Old Testament, which was originally the eastern hill of Jerusalem, now known as the City of David (2 Sam. 5: 7), located south of the Temple Mount. By the second century BC, Mount Zion came to refer to Mount Moriah, on which was the Temple (1 Macc. 4: 37, 60; 5: 54; 7: 33; cf. Is. 60: 1). In the first century AD people believed that the original Mount Zion was the highest hill of the Herodian city, the western hill where the Upper City was located. Josephus, for example, places Mount Zion here (*BJ* i. 39; v. 137, 143; cf. *Ant.* vii. 62–6). It was this identification that was followed by Byzantine Christians (Jerome, *Vita Paul.* xlvi. 5; *Comm. Esa.* i. 17 ff.). The displacement of Zion is, of course, one of the most notorious examples of a lack of continuity of geographical identifications in Jerusalem. The suggestion that the area was the Essene quarter, which then became Christian, has been made by Pixner.[6] However, Magen Broshi's archaeological excavations of 1971 brought to light frescos with representations of birds, trees, wreaths, and buildings, as well as mosaics; such decorative work is more consistent with the usual interpretation that this was an upper-class residential area, not a lower-class one.[7] The rather loose attitude to the prohibition on graven images shows that the attitude of the inhabitants was not religiously puritan. The identification of the Palace of Caiaphas here in the fourth century (*Itin. Burd.* 592; Cyril, *Cat.* xiii. 38) indicates that the Christians of that time recognized the ruins in this region as coming from grand structures. King David's palace was also pointed out here (*Itin. Burd.* 592), in the part of Mount Zion included within the city. This may actually have been a portion of the ruins of Herod's palace. Certainly, the socio-economic character of this part of Jerusalem would make it very unlikely that Christians had their main centre in this quarter. The early Christians were not an upper-class movement, and it would be very surprising indeed to find their principal base among the residences of the very chief priests, Herodians, and other privileged persons they most scorned; this was Jerusalem's Belgravia, not its Bethnal Green.

Eusebius writes that Mount Zion was 'a hill in Jerusalem' (*Onom.* 162. 12) and, as we have seen, 'near the northern parts of

---

[6] Pixner (1981), (1986).   [7] Broshi (1976*a*), (1976*b*).

Mount Zion' Golgotha was pointed out (*Onom*. 74. 19), as was Akeldama (*Onom*. 38. 20–1); but otherwise, especially in his later writings, Eusebius prefers to keep with the usage of the term as a reference to Mount Moriah, on which was the Temple (*Comm. Esa*. xxii. 1; *Comm. Psalm*. lxxiii. 2), or else to the whole of Jerusalem (*Comm. Psalm*. lxiv. 2; lxxv. 3).[8] Eusebius certainly knew that Mount Zion was part of the city of Jesus' time, since he writes that Jerusalem and Mount Zion (together) were places 'where our Lord and Saviour for the most part lived and taught' (*Dem. Evang*. i. 4. 8; cf. vi. 13. 4; ix. 14. 6). Since it is very difficult to determine in each instance of the word precisely which Zion is referred to by Eusebius, his words are more helpful for what they do not say than for what they do. Eusebius mentions Mount Zion repeatedly in *Demonstratio Evangelica* (cf. vi. 13), often making reference to the south-western hill, without once mentioning that it was the locality of the first church in Jerusalem: a glaring omission if this was believed at the time he wrote the work, *c*.318.

Did the Jerusalem church have a permanent centre outside Aelia on Mount Zion? Nowhere does Eusebius write that the Christian community, whether past or present, met in this area. His remarks on the chair of James might suggest that the object was in the keeping of successive members (leaders?) of the Jerusalem community, but that it had no definite home (*Hist. Eccles*. vii. 19): 'The throne of James has been kept until now and the brothers in this place look after it in turn . . .'.[9] Eusebius does not say it had been housed in some particular church in Jerusalem, but rather that it was looked after by certain members of the Christian community. This is quite understandable if one remembers the fear of persecution experienced by Christians prior to Constantine. A permanent base, where sacred texts and treasured objects were deposited, would have been an invitation to arsonists and vandals (as Christians discovered to their cost). In the light of the political and religious climate of the times prior to the Peace of the Church, one would need to question whether it is necessary to

---

[8] For Eusebius' use of the term 'Zion' see Walker (1990), 298–307. It appears that Eusebius used 'Zion' most frequently as a spiritual term for the heavenly kingdom, the Church of God on earth, the individual soul, or else the evangelical word.

[9] By the time of Egeria (*c*.383), the throne was housed in the basilica of Holy Zion (cf. Pet. Diac., *Lib*. E). On 25 December there was the annual celebration of St James; cf. *Arm. Lect*. 71.

envisage one particular location as being the site of church assemblies, from the earliest days onwards. Certainly, there would have been, at any one moment, a main meeting place, perhaps where the bishop lived. It may have been a simple house-church like that of Dura Europos (dated to 241–2). Adherents of pagan mystery cults met in private houses. The adherents of the Church did likewise, gathering in the houses of wealthier members of the community, from the first century until the fourth.[10] One must also remember that the earliest celebrations of the *agape* meal would have taken place in numerous abodes, since the membership of the church of Jerusalem was too large for all to be accommodated at one dinner. It is interesting that nowhere do we find any reference to where the Christians of Jerusalem were meeting at the actual time of Constantine's victory over Licinius in 324, let alone before this date.

In 333 the Bordeaux Pilgrim records that there had been seven synagogues which stood on Mount Zion, but only one remained. The rest had been 'ploughed and sown' (*Itin. Burd*. 592–3). The pilgrim's language echoes Micah (3: 12), 'Zion shall be ploughed like a field, and Jerusalem shall become a heap of ruins.' Eusebius knew the area as being ruined and quarried (*Dem. Evang*. vi. 13. 15–17; viii. 3. 1–15). Both writers suggest that Mount Zion was a region of ruins, and yet also one of agriculture. If this was so, even leaving aside the fact that Jews did not live in or around Jerusalem during this period, it is unlikely that the synagogue was used. After all, Eusebius explicitly states that synagogues had been established everywhere in Palestine *apart from* Jerusalem and Mount Zion (*Dem. Evang*. vi. 13).

It is Cyril of Jerusalem who mentions, for the first time, *c*.348, 'the upper church of the Apostles' (*Cat*. xvi. 4) on Zion. The language recalls the upper room where the disciples gathered when the Holy Spirit descended at Pentecost, even though Cyril does not specifically mention the event. We know from Cyril's attestation of the existence of a church on Mount Zion that it had been built by the year 348. We also know, from Optatus of Milevis, that by 370 the synagogue mentioned by the Bordeaux Pilgrim had disappeared (*Schism. Don*. iii. 2). In 392 Epiphanius (*De Mens. et Pond*. xiv) presented the same legend as that given to

[10] For a survey of Christian house-churches of the third century and an outline of how Christian architecture changed during the fourth, see White (1990).

the Bordeaux Pilgrim; he reports that there were seven synagogues on Mount Zion, one of which stood until the time of Bishop Maximus of Jerusalem (335–49) and the emperor Constantine (till 337). We know, then, that the church appeared between 333 and 348 and that, apparently, the synagogue disappeared by the year 337. It is logical therefore to propose that this synagogue was flattened by the erection of the basilica of Holy Zion about the year 336. There is no suggestion in the texts that this synagogue was a house-church or that part of it was the original 'upper room'. If anyone believed this, then someone would surely have mentioned it when writing of the synagogue. It may also be noted that Cyril's attestation of a church here must be seen in the light of his comments about Zion as being an area of cucumber fields. It seems likely that the Church of Holy Zion was a single building in a field, a large basilica in an agricultural district. Cyril would quote Isaiah 1: 8 to say Zion was 'a watchman's shelter in a vineyard; a shed in a field of cucumbers', and note that 'now the place is full of cucumber fields'[11] (*Cat.* xvi. 18; cf. Epiphanius, *De Mens. et Pond.* xiv; Optatus of Milevis, *Schism. Don.* iii. 2; Jerome, *Comm. in Ps.* lxxxvi. 2). The image used must have been considered appropriate to describe the appearance of the area, which still lay outside the precincts of Jerusalem proper.

Epiphanius alone records a quite separate tradition about a *church* on Mount Zion. According to him, when the emperor Hadrian entered the city after defeating Bar Kochba, he found Mount Zion in ruins, except for a few houses: 'The little house of the community of God alone remained, where the disciples went up to the upper room after their return from the Ascension of the Saviour from the Mount of Olives' (*De Mens. et Pond.* xiv). It should be remembered, however, that Epiphanius is writing almost fifty years *after* the Byzantine church on Mount Zion had been built and had accrued numerous legends to justify its existence there. It was already known as being on the site of the house with the 'upper room' of Acts 1: 13. A few years earlier, *c.*383, Egeria had described the church on Mount Zion as being at the place where Jesus appeared after the Resurrection (*Itin.* xxxix. 5; xl. 2–5) and at Pentecost (*Itin.* xliii. 3; cf. Eucherius, *Ep. Faust.* iv; Pet. Diac., *Lib.* E). Therefore, we know that the identification of

[11] Or 'field of melons'; see Walker (1990), 301.

the upper room as lying under the site of the Byzantine church had been made already, before Epiphanius wrote, so he tells us nothing new on this; what is interesting is Epiphanius' allegation that the house-church was standing when Hadrian entered the city. We have no way of assessing the historical reliability of this statement. All we do know is that there is no mention by anyone of the house-church standing two hundred years later.

The architectural differences between a synagogue and a house-church are significant as far as the internal arrangements went, but outwardly they may have been similar. It is just possible that the two structures were confused.[12] It is also just possible that the Byzantine Christian community in Jerusalem identified Mount Zion as being the region in which stood an early house-church because they had managed to preserve a recollection of this fact, but it is worth noting that Eusebius fails to mention this in any of his works. While Eusebius may have had theological reasons to downplay the importance of the Jerusalem church after the embarrassing events of 325 and the manœuvrings of its Bishop Macarius against him, as Peter Walker has argued,[13] his silence on the matter is striking in all his writings prior to 325, in which he otherwise shows a positive attitude to the Jerusalem church and an interest in its traditions.

Bagatti and Pixner have put the two traditions—the seven synagogues of which one remained and the house-church of the early disciples—together in a neat package that would require us to imagine that the extant synagogue and the house-church were one and the same.[14] Elsewhere, Bagatti has argued that the Byzantine basilica on Mount Zion was built in the years 397–417, during the bishopric of John II,[15] which would mean that Cyril (*Cat.* xvi. 4) is referring to Bagatti's proposed synagogue-church rather than the new basilica. Pixner presents a similar view, arguing that an octagonal church was built here in the reign of Theodosius I (379–95), while the Holy Zion basilica was built after 415.[16] Their arguments rest on those of Michel van Esbroeck, who believes that a first church on Mount Zion was built during the reign of Theodosius I, under the bishopric of John II (387–

[12] Walker (1990), 286, 290.
[13] Ibid. 282–308.
[14] Bagatti (1971c), 117–18; cf. Briand (1973), 35–62; Pixner (1990), 23–8.
[15] (1968a); (1981), 249.　　　　　　　　　　　　　　　　[16] (1990), 28–31.

419), on the basis of certain Georgian texts which date the basilica to the reign of Theodosius.[17] Other eastern lectionaries of the eighth century and after date the building to the time of John II. This evidence, however, is comparatively late and doubtful.

We have an excellent early source for the dating of the basilica in a letter of 415 by a presbyter named Lucianus (*Ep. Luciani*: *PL* 41, 807 ff.). He describes his recent discovery of the remains of St Stephen in the village of Caphar-Gamala. Lucianus lauds his bishop, John II, with praise, and stresses how the remains will be the glory of his episcopate. John promptly transfers the remains of the saint to the great basilica on Mount Zion, built on the alleged site of the church in which Stephen was believed to have been an archdeacon ('sanctam ecclesiam Sion, ubi et archdiaconus fuerat ordinatus', *Ep. Luciani* viii). Lucianus was an eyewitness who wrote at the very time that events took place. He tried his utmost to glorify John II, so it is important that he does not credit John with the building of the basilica. If it was known to Lucianus that John was the one who constructed the basilica, then he certainly would have said so. It would seem that the transfer of the saint's remains by John was so celebrated an event that it became the foundation for a later tradition that John actually built the church.[18] It should be remembered that today's tradition in the Palestinian churches would credit Helena with the foundation of most of the Byzantine churches in Palestine, a tradition first attested in an anonymous *Life of Constantine* of the eighth or ninth century.[19] Later foundation legends of churches need not bear any great resemblance to historical fact. It seems much more preferable to follow Vincent and Abel in dating the building from the time of Bishop Maximus, as Epiphanius' account implies.[20]

There is therefore no good reason to doubt that Cyril is referring to the great basilica which was constructed on Mount Zion. If we turn now to archaeological evidence, however, we get very little to clarify what we already can assume from the texts.

The so-called Tomb of David, with the Cenacle above it, is largely a Crusader structure. It has been known for over a century

[17] Tarschnichvili (1959), 80, no. 565; Van Esbroeck (1975), 314–15; (1984).

[18] Hunt (1984), 217–18.

[19] Trans. in Wilkinson (1977), 202–3, from the text published by M. Guidi, *Rendiconti della R. Accademia dei Lincei, Classe di scienze morali, storiche, e filologiche* 16.5 (Rome, 1908), 46–53.

[20] See Wilkinson (1977), 171; Vincent and Abel (1914b), 450; Kopp (1963), 325.

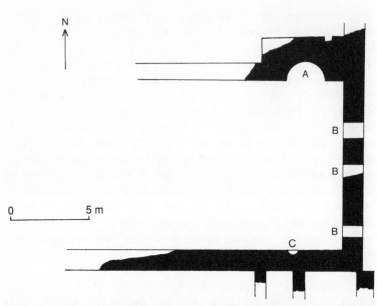

N
↑

0 ———— 5 m

A

B

B

B

C

FIG. 19. Byzantine remains in the present Tomb of David, Mount Zion

that some of the walls were earlier than medieval. In 1951 Jacob
Pinkerfeld removed the plaster from the interior and examined
these older walls. It was noted that there were remains of pre-
Crusader masonry preserved on the north, east, and south of the
eastern part of the building (see Figure 19). Pinkerfeld thought
that since the stones used were too large for a domestic building
(they measure between 49 and 110 cm. wide), the remains were
from a first-century synagogue which formed the structural basis of
the Crusader building. According to him, this synagogue measures
10.5 by 5.8 metres, and has a niche on the north wall, in the
direction of the Jewish Temple. The niche is 2.48 metres in
diameter, 1.2 deep, and 2.44 high. The bottom of this niche is 1.92
metres higher than the original floor, which is 70 centimetres
below the present floor. Pinkerfeld suggested that the niche was
meant for Torah scrolls, like the niches in the synagogues of
Naveh, Eshtemoa, and Arbel.[21] The finely executed masonry was
considered typical of the late Roman period.[22] The area around

[21] (1957), 128–30; (1960). See also Finegan (1969), 147–54.
[22] Hirshberg (1968), 56–9; (1976).

this building included outbuildings, the possible remains of which were discovered in 1859 by E. Pierotti.[23] Bagatti distinguished in Pinkerfeld's synagogue the house-church/synagogue he imagined to have existed from his amalgamation of traditions.

However, doubts have already been expressed about whether the structure was a synagogue.[24] Indeed, the niche is just a little too high and large for it to have been designed for Torah scrolls. The bottom of the niche is higher than the height of an average man today, let alone one from the first centuries AD. It would be more suitable as a niche for relics of some kind that were venerated but not touched. Its length would easily accommodate a sarcophagus.

Moreover, the niche is not in the centre of the preserved ancient wall. On the east it is 1.2 metres from the corner of the wall, but on the west side the wall continues for 2.6 metres without any indication of a corner of another wall having ever existed. If the niche is to be centred, using the known corner as a guide, then the 'synagogue' would have been only 4.88 metres wide, which is rather narrow for its length. The ancient walls on the south side also show no signs whatsoever of any corner where one might expect it. The wall continues westwards for over 17 metres without interruption.

The size of the blocks of stone used are inconsistent with the small size proposed for this synagogue. The blocks measure 90–108 centimetres on the south-east angle, and 96–110 in its third course, a size more appropriate for the walls of a far larger structure. The width of the walls also indicates that the structure was large. The wall into which the niche was built is approximately 2.65 metres wide, and narrows at the western side. The other walls are about 1.4 metres wide.

It seems highly likely that all the walls are Byzantine, the remains of the south-eastern corner of the basilical Church of Holy Zion, on the basis of the disproportionate niche. The wall in which the niche is found is probably a short projection which formed the exterior of an inscribed apse.[25] The suggestion that the masonry was Byzantine was made long ago by Vincent,[26] and despite the

---

[23] (1864), i. 210–18, esp. 214 f.   [24] Murphy-O'Connor (1986), 94.
[25] Wilkinson (1978), 168–70; cf. id. (1977), 171.
[26] Vincent and Abel (1914*b*), 421–81, esp. 431–40, fig. 168; cf. Dalman (1935*b*), 316–18.

discovery of the niche and speculations that its use was Jewish, or Jewish-Christian, there seems no very good reason to doubt that he was correct.

Pixner has rightly noted that the ashlars, though of first-century date, are reused. They show clear signs of having been dragged to their present positions. The corners were damaged during transportation. Furthermore, the irregular heights of the stones also point to secondary use. While Pixner then goes on to propose that the construction of the building was immediately after the destruction of Jerusalem in AD 70,[27] it seems much more likely that Byzantine Christians were the ones with the resources to utilize these massive building blocks and haul them into position. The poor group of first-century Christians remaining in the city would surely have been more inclined to use field stones for any little building they wished to construct.

Those who advocate the synagogue theory usually fail to mention that among the fragments of plaster scraped off the wall in the course of Pinkerfeld's excavations were pieces with Greek graffiti.[28] These are undoubtedly the work of Christian pilgrims. Bagatti, Testa, and Pixner believe that these are 'Jewish-Christian' items dating from the Roman period, but this is unlikely in view of the the fact that the language of the graffiti is Greek as opposed to Aramaic. The few letters and parts of words surviving seem entirely typical of the Byzantine pilgrim graffiti which we know from many parts of the Empire.

Pixner has argued that the original floor on which the plaster fragments were found must be prior to a Byzantine structure because it is 10 centimetres below a mosaic which probably comes from the fifth century.[29] It is far more likely that in this part of the basilica a fourth-century pavement made of smooth stones on plaster was given a mosaic pavement during reconstruction work later on. The practice of overlaying stone pavements with mosaics when funds permitted was common in Byzantine churches, and older mosaics would also be overlaid with new, finer ones, sometimes within a short space of time. Reconstruction work in the basilica of Holy Zion may well have taken place when the

[27] Pixner (1990), 25–6.
[28] Bagatti (1971c), fig. 25. Testa's reading of the pieces owes much to imagination. The only clear word is *autokratoros*.
[29] (1990), 23.

bones of St Stephen were transferred here in 415. Indeed, the niche would have made a good initial resting place for the remains of the saint.

The evidence that the existing walls are blackened by fire around the niche also accords with the fact that the Church of Holy Zion was burnt by the Persians in 615 (Antiochus Mon., *Ep. Eust.* *PG* 89, 1427; Strategius, *Capt.* xiii. 15). It was all but destroyed again in 965 (Yahya ibn Said of Antioch, *Annals*, *PO* 18, 183), and was in ruins when the Crusaders arrived. During their rebuilding, it was understandable that they would make use of parts of the basilica still standing. Those who support the synagogue or synagogue/house-church theories must imagine that, despite the evidence to the contrary, there were no Byzantine remains whatsoever in this area, and that the Crusaders built directly on top of remarkably well-preserved late Roman walls. This does not seem very likely.

The only other Byzantine remains that have been uncovered are aligned perfectly with the ancient walls of the Tomb of David.[30] In 1899, H. Renard discovered a section of wall with a doorway which he dated to the Byzantine period.[31] His area was re-excavated in 1983 by E. Eisenberg,[32] who was able to confirm Renard's dating. Two column drums were also found, which came from the atrium of the basilica. Eisenberg also discovered north of the Dormition Abbey the north-west corner of the Crusader Church of St Mary, which also aligns with the walls of the Cenacle and Tomb of David, and corresponds with the orientation of the Crusader walls uncovered by Renard.[33] M. Gisler excavated a small garden opposite the Dormition Abbey in 1935, where massive foundations (4 metres broad) and walls were discovered and found to be on the same axis as those found by Renard.[34] It would seem very likely in view of the relationship between the Crusader and Byzantine masonry that the Crusader church was built on what could be salvaged of the Byzantine foundations and substructural walls.

While it may be initially tempting to see the surviving synagogue

[30] See Wilkinson (1978), fig. 115.
[31] (1900), 18–19; Vincent and Abel (1914b), fig. 168, and pp. 431–40.
[32] Eisenberg (1984).
[33] For a plan of this, with the remains, see Pixner (1990), 31.
[34] Gisler (1935), 6–9.

described by the Pilgrim of Bordeaux and Epiphanius as being that which Pinkerfeld has identified, his identification does not, in the end, stand up against an argument that the ancient walls of the area of the Tomb of David are Byzantine. The synagogue of the literary sources was presumably obliterated when the great basilica was constructed. Renard estimated that this basilica was 60 metres in length and 40 metres wide: a sizeable building. In the Madaba Mosaic it is depicted as the largest church in the city. The wide walls with huge stones found in the Tomb of David would be appropriate to a building of this grand scale. There was certainly no reason for the Byzantine architects to wish a synagogue ruin to be preserved within it. If the synagogue is not to be equated with the ancient walls of the eastern part of the Tomb of David, there is also no reason to imagine that the synagogue was considered by the Byzantines to be the first house-church, where the disciples of Jesus met together. Whatever traditions were in existence concerning the early community and Mount Zion, they were not attached to any particular ruin.

One might argue nevertheless that the great basilica of Holy Zion stood on the site of the first church of the apostles, even though no material remains survive, and even though its location in the heart of Jerusalem's affluent quarter seems unlikely. One could propose that the first church in Jerusalem, while composed of people from the lower classes, met in the house of someone quite affluent, who happened to live close to the palaces of the priests and Herodians. But one might also suggest that the choice of Mount Zion as the location for the Byzantine basilica owed much to expediency. As noted above, Mount Zion was an area which largely lay outside the city. This part was full of ruins and fields, and was, accordingly, ripe for development. Without the constrictions of space imposed on structures within the city, the Church of Holy Zion could be as large as the planners wanted. It would serve as a fitting base for the Jerusalem church, which prided itself on being the 'mother of all the churches' (Theodoret, *Hist. Eccles*. v. 9. 17).

It seems very possible that the Church of Holy Zion was constructed partly in order to allow pilgrims to gather there to recall the events of Pentecost. The Martyrium at Golgotha, and the associated Tomb, had allowed pilgrims to follow through the events of Christ's death, burial, and resurrection in a suitably awesome architectural environment. Constantine's Eleona basilica on the Mount of Olives had allowed pilgrims to recall the Ascension in a similar context. But clearly the important intermediate events of Christ's appearance(s) before the Ascension had no 'home' in the form of a fitting building where pilgrims could worship.

The basilica soon began to accrue further traditions and relics that enhanced its prestige. As we have seen, by the fifth century pilgrims came to believe that not only Pentecost but also the Last Supper occurred here. Later pilgrims would eat the commemorative meal mentioned above to recall this event. The supposed pillar to which Jesus was tied to be flogged was also shown here; this had already been shown to the Bordeaux Pilgrim among the ruins of Mount Zion (*Itin. Burd.* 592.4 ff.). The episcopal chair of the Jerusalem church, attested by Eusebius (see above) was installed here (Pet. Diac. *Lib.* E). By the sixth century, from the evidence of the Piacenza Pilgrim (*Itin.* xxii), we know that the alleged stones used to execute St Stephen were displayed in the church.

It was suggested that the niche in the wall of the Tomb of David would have made a good place for the remains of St Stephen. In fact, these remains did not stay long in Holy Zion. The bones were so highly regarded that their position in the basilica was soon perceived as being too marginal, and indeed the niche was on one side of the church, not its central focus. The saint's remains were removed to a new Church of St Stephen, built outside the city's northern gate on the spot where it was believed that Stephen met his death. This church was dedicated by the empress Eudocia on 15 May 439.

This examination therefore finds no evidence that would prove that a Jewish-Christian community existed on Mount Zion at any time. If Christians met on Mount Zion during the first century, this would have been inconsistent with what we know about their socio-economic characteristics, as it was a wealthy part of the city. A synagogue may have existed on Mount Zion prior to Byzantine developments, but this was a Jewish structure and not a Christian house-church. The traditions about a church being located here before the construction of the great basilica of Holy Zion all come from after the basilica's construction (*c*.336). What made the Christians of Jerusalem build their church here in the fourth century may just owe something to tradition, but it may also have been expediency. The area had not been built upon for at least a hundred and fifty years, and was an attractive building site. Many of the ruins of the first century on Mount Zion outside the city, including any synagogue, were presumably obliterated when the basilica was constructed.

The remains that have been identified as coming from the Jewish(-Christian) synagogue(-church) are most probably part of the Byzantine basilica, possibly the part which housed the alleged remains of St Stephen from 415 until 439.

Nazareth

WITH Capernaum, Nazareth is one of the most extensive sites in which the Bagatti–Testa hypothesis has been used to interpret the archaeological evidence. According to Bagatti and Testa, Nazareth was a Jewish-Christian town until well into the fifth century. The Byzantine holy places of Nazareth were just a continuation of those venerated by Jewish-Christians, in particular a Jewish-Christian synagogue-church. This theory has been devised by putting together various pieces of literary and archaeological data. It is necessary to address its numerous components separately, in order to determine if there is evidence that might show that any site in Nazareth was venerated by Christians before the fourth century.

In accordance with Bagatti's order in his publication of the excavations,[1] the literature will be examined first, followed by the archaeological material.

Literature

Bagatti concluded, from a review of texts relating to Nazareth, that Jewish-Christians occupied the town. He wrote: 'the literary texts . . . are the basis for an understanding of the monuments.'[2] Bagatti therefore analysed the archaeological evidence with firm ideas derived from his study of the literature. There is nothing necessarily wrong with this approach, if the study of the literature is itself undertaken with care. Bagatti, however, used a deductive method which first determines an hypothesis, and then looks for proof of this hypothesis in the literature. Again, if rigorous analysis is undertaken, this can provide valuable insights, but if it leads scholars to build one hypothesis upon another, and find

---

[1] Bagatti (1969).   [2] Ibid. 9.

proof of a theory on tenuous evidence, it can also be misleading. The question to be asked in a re-examination of this literature is whether there is anything that has to be read as providing solid evidence of any Christians in the town venerating places in the first three centuries of our era.

The Gospels

From the evidence of the different nativity accounts in Matthew and Luke, Bagatti concluded that there were two separate edifices in Nazareth known to the evangelists: the 'house of Mary' (cf. Luke 1: 26–38, 56) and the 'house of Joseph' (cf. Matt. 1: 18–25). Bagatti's notion that the existence of first-century memorial shrines gave rise to the discrepancies in this part of the nativity stories is a new one. Most commentators would accept that the accounts arose from two different churches with very different traditions concerning the birth of Jesus. If one community chose to emphasize Joseph's house, and another Mary's, this should not lead us a priori to conclude that there existed two venerated holy places in the first century.

Bagatti pointed out that Matthew speaks of the synagogue in Nazareth as 'their synagogue' (Matt. 13: 54, cf. 'the synagogue' in Mark 6: 2, Luke 4: 16). According to Bagatti, the pronoun 'their' in reference to Jews means that there was another synagogue that could be referred to by the pronoun 'our', i.e. a Jewish-Christian synagogue as opposed to one belonging to the Jews.[3] This is rather much to infer from one little pronoun. Moreover, the precedent for referring to 'their' synagogues in general is set by Mark. It is from here that Matthew derives his use of the pronoun. At the end of a pericope in which Jesus heals the sick (Mark 1: 32–4), Jesus goes to a lonely place to pray, where Simon and others find him. Jesus then says: 'Let us go to the next towns that I may preach there also' (Mark 1: 38), and Mark duly reports: 'And he went preaching in their synagogues, in the whole of Galilee' (Mark 1: 39). One must assume that 'their' refers to the towns of Galilee. Luke (4: 44) modifies Mark by putting, 'And he was preaching in the synagogues of Judaea (or: of the Jews/of Galilee)' at this point, placing 'And he taught in their synagogues' earlier in his narrative

[3] Bagatti (1969), 10.

(Luke 4: 15). Matthew is more or less faithful to Mark's text: 'And he went about the whole of Galilee, teaching in their synagogues' (Matt. 4: 23), but he detaches this sentence from what preceded it in Mark, so that it is not clear to what 'their' refers. Matthew later repeats the formula (9: 35), this time making clear that the reference is to the towns: 'And Jesus went about all the cities and villages, teaching in their synagogues.' In the story of Jesus teaching in the synagogue of Nazareth, Matthew (13: 54) adds the pronoun αὐτῶν to Mark's account (Mark 6: 1–6a), although again it is not clear to whom he is referring. It appears to be those of the same verse who are astonished at his knowledge, but the people who heard him are mentioned specifically only in Mark (6: 2). It looks as though Matthew has not transferred the subject of 'their' from his source. At any rate, it seems clear that Matthew refers to the people of Nazareth in general rather than to a group of Jews in the town over against an enclave of Jewish-Christians.

Apocryphal Texts

Bagatti believed that the *Protevangelium of James*, composed in the third century, was written 'to promote the fortunes of Christian Judaism in Palestine',[4] in contrast to the usual view that the text shows such a nescience of Palestinian geography and Jewish customs that it can only have derived from a non-Jew who had never been to the country.[5] It is unclear what conclusions Bagatti wished to draw from this work. The author places the Annunciation in Judaea, beside a well where Mary is drawing water. Bagatti considered this a Jewish-Christian tradition which was transferred (returned?) to Nazareth at a later date.

Bagatti then discussed the fourth-century *History of Joseph* in which the death of Joseph is recounted. The complete edition is found in Arabic, derived from a Coptic text, the original of which is said by Bagatti to be 'probably Jewish'.[6] Like the *Protevangelium*, the *History of Joseph* demonstrates an ignorance of Palestinian geography; it places Nazareth in Judaea, for example, within walking distance of the Temple. What Bagatti found significant is that it has Joseph's corpse placed in a cave, closed by a door, in

---

[4] Ibid. 11.　　　　　　　　　　　[5] Oscar Cullman, in *NTA* i. 372.
[6] (1969), 12. Bagatti (p. 11 n. 6) mistakenly reports that a Latin translation from *Hebrew* was seen in the 16th cent.; in fact this was from Arabic (*ANT* 84).

which were also the bodies of his ancestors ('Extulerunt eum ad locum ubi sita erat spelunca et aperuerunt ianuam, et condiderunt corpus eius inter corpora patrum eius'[7]). Bagatti extrapolated from this that it was a 'family tomb, cut in the rock and closed by a stone door', namely, 'a burial chamber very like those we find in use in the 1st century'.[8] A description of a family burial cave, closed by some kind of door, is not quite specific enough for us to make any such conclusion. M. R. James has pointed out that far from being Jewish, this book is Egyptian; fragments exist in Bohairic and Sahidic as well as the Arabic translation. Moreover, it has 'highly Egyptian descriptions of death'.[9] Cave burial was quite common in Egypt. Bagatti, however, concluded that the evidence of the *History of Joseph* demonstrates that Jewish-Christian veneration of the actual tomb of Joseph in Nazareth was possible. He pointed to the use of the 'cosmic ladder' idea in the *History of Joseph*, to support his understanding that this was a Jewish-Christian work,[10] but Bagatti himself has outlined how the ladder to heaven was a motif used widely in the early Church, both in literature and art;[11] it cannot therefore be used to argue for the text being specifically Jewish-Christian.

Relatives of Jesus

Bagatti believed that relatives of Jesus lived in Nazareth from the first century onwards, and that these were all Jewish-Christians. He mentioned, from the New Testament writings, not only Mary but the four brothers—James, Joseph, Simeon, and Jude—and sisters (Matt. 13: 55–6; cf. 12: 46) along with others like James and Joseph, sons of Mary (Matt. 27: 56),[12] Cleophas (John 19: 25), and James 'of Alphaeus' (Matt. 10: 3). Some of these were opposed to Jesus (cf. Matt: 12: 46; Mark 3: 31–5; Luke 8: 19–21; John 7: 5), but Paul notes that certain 'brothers of the Lord' were working for the Gospel (1 Cor. 9: 5; cf. Acts 1: 14).[13] Bagatti concluded that the relatives of Jesus enjoyed a privileged position in the early Church (cf. Eusebius, *Hist. Eccles.* iii. 36. 3), and it was for this reason that James became leader of the Jerusalem community (cf.

[7] Quoted by Bagatti (1969), 12.   [8] Ibid.   [9] *ANT* 84.
[10] So too Testa (1962*a*), 576.   [11] (1971*c*), 209–12.
[12] This may be a reference to Jesus' brothers James and Joseph.
[13] Cf. Bagatti (1969), 10.

Acts 15: 13–22; 21: 18–26; 1 Cor. 15: 7; Gal. 2: 9, 12), and thereafter Simeon, Jesus' cousin, was given this role. This may well be true, but it is another thing again to assume that all Jesus' relatives believed in his messianic status.

Bagatti laid great emphasis on the letter to Aristides from Julius Africanus, quoted by Eusebius (*Hist. Eccles.* i. 7), in which it is stated that the relatives of Jesus went around the country expounding their genealogy. As I have argued in Chapter 2, Jesus' relatives in Nazareth and Kochaba were by no means necessarily Christians. Quite the opposite: they seem to have been Jews intent on proving their connection with the royal line of David. Furthermore, the literary evidence suggests that Nazareth was a Jewish town well into the Byzantine period, and that it was also occupied by people from the caste of priests (see p. 36).

We have also seen that the Hebrew term *minim* did not necessarily refer to Jewish-Christians (*pace* Bagatti) and that central Galilee was almost entirely Jewish in character in the second and third centuries, apart from a pagan presence in Sepphoris/Diocaesarea and Tiberias (pp. 48–56). The story of the grandsons of Jude (Eusebius, *Hist. Eccles.* iii. 20. 1–5) suggests that there may have been some Jewish-Christians living in Nazareth at the end of the first century. The rabbinic evidence of a man named Jacob of Kfar Sikhnin/Samma seems to present us with a Christian Jew at the beginning of the second century.[14] It is quite possible Jewish-Christians lived in Galilee during the late Roman period, and there may even have been Gentile Christians in Diocaesarea and Tiberias, but the literary evidence does not specifically refer to them. There is a lacuna in historical information regarding the fate of the early communities of Jewish-Christians in Galilee reported in Acts. Perhaps, with the shift of the centre of Jewish religious life from the environs of Jerusalem and the coastal plain to Galilee after the Bar Kochba War, those who wished to be part of the Church gradually emigrated from the Jewish heartland, and went to Caesarea or other cities in Palestine where there was an ethnic and religious mix.

Bagatti considered the silence of Christian sources concerning Jewish-Christians in Galilee as speaking volumes. The reason why the hypothetical shrines of Nazareth were not mentioned by

[14] See Ch. 2 for a discussion about the lack of positive evidence for Jewish-Christians in Palestine from the middle of the 2nd cent. onwards esp. pp. 25–36.

Christians until the sixth century, he said, was because they were in the hands of Jewish-Christians[15] whom everyone wished to ignore. Not only is this statement inaccurate, for Nazareth is mentioned as having a Christian shrine as early as the fourth century (see below), but also Bagatti failed to notice that the early Church writers did not in general exhibit a tendency to remain silent about groups that offended them; quite the opposite.

Byzantine Nazareth in Literary Sources

Eusebius mentions Nazareth in his *Onomasticon* (138. 24–140. 2) but notes nothing of interest about the place, only that Christ was given the name 'Nazarene' because of his coming from here, and that members of the Church were 'once Nazarenes but now Christians'. Bagatti's conclusion that this implies a distinction between the Jewish-Christian 'Nazarenes' (or 'Nazoraeans') and the Nazarenes of the ancient Church is strained. The Bordeaux Pilgrim bypassed Nazareth, which certainly does suggest that there was nothing to be visited in the town. Unlike the Christian visitors who had preceded them, pilgrims were not scholarly tourists undertaking travel for the purposes of historic interest; Christian pilgrims went to specific places in order to recollect a meaningful event which apparently took place there and to pray. If there was nowhere for them to pray, and no specific place identified as the site of a biblical event worthy of contemplation or affording inspiration, then there was not a strong incentive for them to visit the town. In 373 Melania the Elder hastened to bring alms to Christians who had been exiled from Egypt to Sepphoris, but she did not visit Nazareth, which tends to suggest there were few Christians there to sustain.[16]

The first person to mention that a Christian shrine existed in Nazareth was Egeria, *c*.383. Her words, recorded in the text of Peter the Deacon, describe a garden, a cave, and an altar: 'In Nazareth is a garden in which the Lord used to be after his return from Egypt' (Pet. Diac. *Lib*. P4), and 'there is a big and very splendid cave in which she (that is, Holy Mary) lived. An altar has been placed there' (Pet. Diac. *Lib*. T).[17] One may wonder, at this stage, if there was not some small structure connected with the

[15] (1969), 18.   [16] Kopp (1963), 59.
[17] Quoted from Wilkinson (1981), 193.

cave; a consideration that should be borne in mind when looking at the archaeological evidence. Who might have constructed this Christian shrine?

As we have already seen, Epiphanius' *Panarion*, written *c*.375–7, gives us an account of the labours of the *comes* Joseph of Tiberias, a Jew who converted to Christianity, in which it is stated that he received permission from the emperor Constantine to build churches in Jewish strongholds such as Nazareth (*Pan.* xxx. 11. 10). Epiphanius proceeds to describe his efforts in Tiberias, where he succeeded in building a little church in part of the (ruined?) Hadrianeum (*Pan.* xxx. 12). Moreover, 'in Diocaesarea and also in each of the others he completed buildings' (*Pan.* xxx. 12. 9).[18] Joseph succeeded, therefore, in building a structure in Nazareth. Indeed, it would be hard to imagine why Epiphanius would have specifically mentioned the town if Joseph had not built something there. The date of his receiving permission from Constantine must of course have been before 22 May 337, when the emperor died. Epiphanius associates Joseph with two patriarchs named Hillel and Judah. It would appear that Epiphanius got the names of the patriarchs right, but confused their identities in the story; most likely, Joseph was at the deathbed of Judah III (*c*.320), and involved with the young Hillel II until the early days of his taking office (cf. *Pan.* xxx. 10. 9 ff.); he was Patriarch from *c*.330 to 365.[19] Joseph was sent by Hillel to Cilicia, where he converted to Christianity, and thereafter visited the emperor's court. On the basis of this literary evidence, one might therefore suggest *c*.335 as the date of church construction in Nazareth. This allows Joseph time in Cilicia before his conversion and further time at the court of Constantine. It is also after the date of the Bordeaux Pilgrim's visit.

In his revision of Eusebius' *Onomasticon*, Jerome does not write of what existed in Nazareth (cf. *Lib. loc.* 143; *Com. Matt.* ii. 23), but since he records that Paula visited the town during her pilgrimage, he provides us with some evidence that there was a place, however insubstantial the shrine, where Paula could pray (*Ep.* cviii. 13. 5). Theodosius, at the beginning of the sixth century, mentions Nazareth in a list of distances useful for pilgrims (*De Situ* iv). All this shows that Nazareth was visited by pilgrims

[18] τίσι here seems to have the sense of 'each'.
[19] Goranson (1990), 59–62.

from the late fourth century onwards, even if what was there was not deemed particularly worthy of comment.

However, one might ask why it was that the Jewish population of Nazareth did not tear down the Christian shrine the moment Joseph left the town. It would appear from Epiphanius that he went in and built it without any loud missionary proclamations, despite his apparent idea that building churches in Jewish areas would effect conversions. Perhaps a low-key approach was the very reason why he was successful in his building operations. With some kind of small shrine or church in Nazareth, with perhaps a few caretakers in residence, the Jewish authorities would have felt no serious threat, despite Joseph's probable ambition that Christian pilgrims would influence some Jews to convert.

For the main part, when Christian pilgrims, like Egeria and Paula, started to come to the town, they would have brought with them revenue, which may have been more important to the town than any possible religious danger. The pilgrims' yearning for relics and mementoes could be readily exploited for commercial gain, and, of course, pilgrims needed to eat and buy the necessities of life as well.[20] Pilgrims could be pandered to for the sake of their appreciative 'tourist dollar' and enticed in many ways to part with cash. This situation is made amply clear as regards Nazareth by the report given by the gullible Piacenza Pilgrim of 570:

We travelled on to the city of Nazareth, where many miracles take place. In the synagogue there is kept the book in which the Lord wrote his ABC, and in this synagogue there is the bench on which he sat with the other children. Christians can lift the bench and move it about, but the Jews are completely unable to move it, and cannot drag it outside. The house of St Mary is now a basilica, and her clothes are the cause of frequent miracles.

The Jewesses of that city are better-looking than any other Jewesses in the whole country. They declare that this is St Mary's gift to them, for they also say that she was a relation of theirs. Though there is no love lost between Jews and Christians, these women are full of kindness. (Piacenza Pilgrim, *Itin.* v)[21]

One can well imagine the mirth of the Jews who yet again demonstrated to the visiting Christians that they could not lift the

---

[20] Hunt (1984), 135–47.   [21] Trans. in Wilkinson (1977), 79–80.

bench in their synagogue.[22] One can also imagine a bevy of the most beautiful girls in the village idling outside the basilica in order to do kind things for the visitors. 'The donation of funds for pious ends', as David Hunt puts it,[23] was a source of revenue and could be encouraged.

The Piacenza Pilgrim's account seems to imply strongly that the town's population was still Jewish in the sixth century. From him, we also learn that the small structure built by Joseph of Tiberias had been superseded by a basilica. In 614, however, the Persians invaded Palestine from the north. The Jews of Nazareth apparently joined Chosroes II in destroying churches and murdering Christians in Jerusalem.[24] In revenge, the emperor Heraclius reluctantly singled out Nazareth for special punishment.[25] The fact that the men of Nazareth went to fight with the Persians shows that there was no significant Christian presence in the town which they needed to worry about in regard to the safety of their wives and children.[26]

At the end of the century, Arculf, whose impressions were recorded by Adomnan, speaks of two large churches; there is no mention of a Jewish population or a synagogue (*De Loc. Sanct.* ii. 26). Peter the Deacon (*Lib.* T) and the thirteenth-century pilgrim Burchard[27] mention that the synagogue was converted into a church. Again these pieces of literary evidence should be borne in mind when we come to look at the archaeology of Roman and Byzantine Nazareth.

To conclude this survey of literary material, it suffices to say that there is nothing that can be found which definitively points to Jewish-Christian presence in the town much past the first century, or Christian veneration of the place before the fourth. The town was clearly Jewish until the seventh century; whether some of these Jews became Christians after Christian pilgrimage began is not recorded. The sixth-century women of Nazareth certainly played on the pilgrims' expectations that they may have had a family connection with Jesus, as a way of procuring appreciative gifts of money, but there is no reason to think that they were Christian. There is no literary material which would require us to approach the archaeology with any expectation of uncovering

---

[22] So Kopp (1963), 55.
[24] Eutychius, *Annales* 22, *PG* 111, 1083.
[26] Kopp (1963), 56.

[23] (1984), 137.
[25] Ibid. 245, *PG* 111, 1090.
[27] See Wilkinson (1981), 193.

Jewish-Christian remains in Nazareth or evidence of pilgrimage to the town prior to the fourth century.

Archaeology[28]

In 1892 Benedict Vlaminck, a Franciscan monk, discovered Byzantine remains in the Franciscan property in Nazareth.[29] The remains were studied by Prosper Viaud, who undertook further excavations.[30] After the demolition of the eighteenth-century church which commemorated the Annunciation, the Franciscans began renewed excavations, which were undertaken under the supervision of Bagatti in 1955.[31] Further sporadic excavations continued until 1966, during which time a new church, the Basilica of the Annunciation, was built over most of the archaeological remains, partially incorporating and partially obliterating them. The basilica was dedicated in 1968 and is a major tourist attraction. Near by is the Church of St Joseph, also belonging to the Franciscans, under which archaeological investigations were conducted during the 1930s by Father Viaud.

Bagatti began his examination of the archaeology of the region around the so-called Shrine, or Grotto, of the Annunciation by examining the rock-cut features which stretch over an area measuring 75 by 85 metres, and possibly beyond (see Figure 20 and Plate 3). These are: Middle Bronze Age tombs,[32] silos from the Iron Age[33] onwards, a wine-press installation,[34] an olive-pressing installation,[35] holes for holding storage jars, and bell-shaped cisterns. There are also uniform depressions which indicate where the foundations of walls were laid. One can add that under the site now occupied by the Sisters of Nazareth, 100 metres west of the present Basilica of the Annunciation, and under the Church of St Joseph, to the north, there are caves containing cisterns from the Roman period.[36] The remains indicate that the entire area was used for agricultural processing activity. Domestic buildings may

---

[28] In order to maintain consistency, the numeration of my Figures is based on Bagatti's.
[29] Vlaminck (1900). This report is only five pages long and contains three plans.
[30] Viaud (1910).
[31] See Bagatti (1969), 2.   [32] Ibid. 27, 32, 35, 37, 245.
[33] Ibid. 27, 29.   [34] Ibid. 52–6.   [35] Ibid. 58–9.
[36] See Livio (1967).

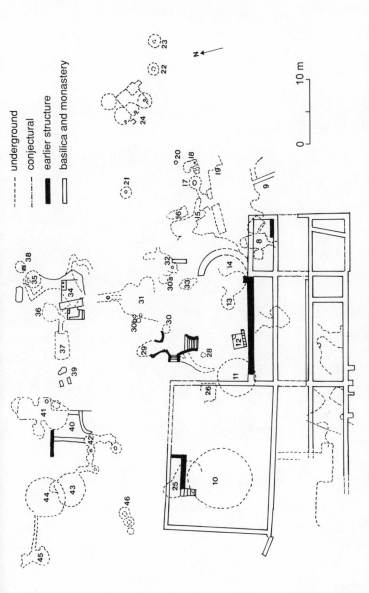

underground

conjectural

earlier structure

basilica and monastery

0   10 m

Fig. 20. Agricultural installations in the region of the present Basilica of the Annunciation, Nazareth, with Byzantine walls

PLATE 3. Nazareth: view of agricultural installations looking from east

have been constructed over the complexes. The remains bring to mind the words of the Piacenza Pilgrim, who stated that Nazareth's grain, wine, oil, and apples were of superior quality (*Itin.* v).

A large number of Roman and Byzantine tombs found mainly on the hill west of the basilica, and some on the hill to the east, have been examined by C. Kopp.[37] Further tombs have been found in Nazareth Illit (map ref. 181233),[38] Ya'ad (17352533),[39] and in the property of the Sisters of Nazareth.[40] Nearly all of the Roman and Byzantine tombs appear to be Jewish, along with a first-century Aramaic funerary inscription.[41] A Roman period sarcophagus was discovered east of the basilica,[42] but no ossuaries have been found. Bagatti considered that Tomb 79,[43] which contains many indecipherable graffiti and scratched figurative drawings, was utilized by Jewish-Christians on the basis of his reading of a few Greek letters as misspelt φῶς, 'light', since he associates the word solely with Jewish-Christians. Bagatti's *phi*, however, is clearly an unintentional scratch through the mouth of a representation of a human head (see Figure 21). There are two such heads reproduced by Bagatti.[44] On the face of the first he reads an *upsilon*, when it seems plain from the photograph that the lines represent tears. The second head, on which Bagatti saw *ΦΟΣ*, has the letters: *ΛΔΟΞ*. It would appear that Bagatti misread the final letter as the old form of *sigma*, *Σ*. The *delta* is upside down, which may indicate that it is musical notation. Further reason to suppose this is suggested by the form of the heads, which are depicted as having open mouths as if to show people singing or wailing. There is no reason to consider these as being scratched by Jewish-Christians, rather, there may be a magical significance in the employment of these designs.

A Greek funerary inscription was dated by Bagatti on palaeo-graphical grounds to the third century, although his palaeographical assumptions, that an enlarged *M* and round *O* must require this, were not quite correct. In the first place, the *M* is not enlarged. It is more significant that it is curvilinear, of a form which is

---

[37] Kopp (1938). [38] Comm. by N. Feig, *IEJ* 33 (1983), 116–17.
[39] Comm. by N. Feig, *IEJ* 38 (1988), 76–8. [40] Livio (1967), 30.
[41] *CIJ* ii. no. 988, p. 173. [42] Bagatti (1969), 246.
[43] No. 15 in Kopp (1938), 202. [44] (1969), 245, figs. 197–8.

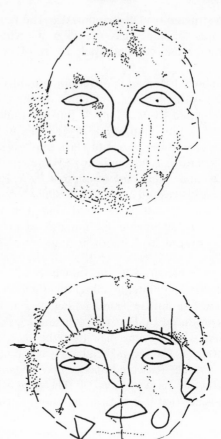

FIG. 21. Graffiti of faces incised on the walls of a tomb in Nazareth

characteristic of the letter in the fifth century.[45] In the second place, a round, as opposed to an oval, *O* is not a feature that provides a precise date in epigraphy. It is found in inscriptions from Gerasa from the first to the third centuries, and from the fifth to the sixth.[46]

The Grotto of the Annunciation (Figure 20, no. 31) was

[45] Cf. the inscription of Euphemia found in the Tomb of the Virgin, dated to the 5th cent., in Corbo (1965), 78, fig. 65.

[46] Kraeling (1938), 357–66.

originally part of the wine-press complex (no. 34: the 'Kitchen of the Virgin'), to which it was connected by a tunnel.[47] The matter to be determined is when this cave was singled out and converted into a Christian holy place: before or after Constantine, or, more specifically, Joseph of Tiberias. Bagatti believed that in the third century, at the initiative of Jewish-Christians, a synagogue-church was constructed over and around the cave. The grotto itself, he thought, was venerated from the very beginning, which would suggest that it really was the actual place where the Annunciation took place.

Bagatti was able to establish that a basilical Byzantine church with a nave and two aisles, an atrium, along with an attached monastery, existed adjacent to the Shrine of the Annunciation (see Figure 20). A number of walls remain, and some fine mosaics. The northern aisle was cut into by steps leading down to a cave complex constituted by the Chapel of the Angel, the small cave no. 29 (now known as the Martyrium), and the Shrine of the Annunciation. The nave was lower than the southern aisle and the monastery floors. In the walls of the church are blocks of stone in secondary use. The complex of buildings measured 48 metres in length and 27 metres in width, and was oriented to the east.[48]

It is important to establish the dating of this church with some accuracy, because under the mosaic of the central nave, in a rock-cut basin, and under the floor of the monastery, fragments of an earlier Christian building came to light; it is this that Bagatti claimed was a Jewish-Christian synagogue-church.

As was shown in the examination of literary material, the first evidence for the existence of a basilica comes from the Piacenza Pilgrim in 570; but how long before this date was the basilica in existence? The following examination will proceed to analyse all the pertinent archaeological evidence, in order to reach a conclusion. The nature of the earlier building will also be discussed so that it can be established whether or not it was used by Jewish-Christians.

Mosaics

Nine mosaics have been discovered to have decorated the Byzantine basilica, cave complex, and monastery (see Figure 22).

---

[47] Bagatti (1969), 51, 53–6, 176.   [48] Ibid. 80–97.

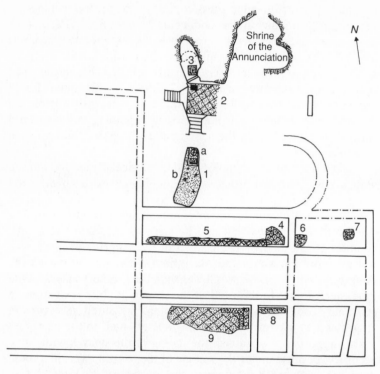

FIG. 22. Byzantine church and monastery at Nazareth, with mosaics

The mosaics of the Chapel of the Angel (the 'Conon mosaic', no. 2; see Plate 4), of the monastery, and the southern aisle (nos. 4–9) would stylistically all correspond to a fifth- to seventh-century date. However, the mosaics of cave no. 29 and the central nave appear to be more ancient.

The mosaic located in the nave (no. 1 see Plate 5) is oriented to the north towards the steps leading into the cave complex, but the basilica is, like other Byzantine churches, oriented to the east. The main decoration of the mosaic (labelled 1*a* in Figure 22) is contained within a border of black tesserae three pieces wide. The northern part of this band is lost, so that we do not know how closely it approached the beginning of the steps. The preserved part of the band was 89 centimetres broad and 1.69 metres long; this has been extended slightly by restoration. Inside it are three

PLATE 4. Nazareth:
the Conon mosaic
(mosaic no. 2)

separate areas of design. In its northernmost region there was a
pattern only partly preserved at the time of its discovery.[49] In the
restored mosaic now on show in the Basilica of the Annunciation,
no attempt has been made to reconstruct this pattern; the missing
portions have been filled in with plain white tesserae, so that it
appears to the modern visitor a rather strange shape.[50] Since the
mosaic is roughly geometrical and over a quarter of the pattern has
been preserved, it can be reconstructed to some extent by means
of mirror-imaging the existing motif. As a result of this, an oval
table can be distinguished. Inside this table, the remaining black

[49] Viaud (1910), 89–92, fig. 44. In case anyone be initially perplexed that the
picture published by Viaud is significantly different from the mosaic seen today, it
should be noted that Viaud's photograph was not of the actual mosaic: 'Nous en
donnons ici une photographie d'après des estampages pris un peu à la hâte, mais,
croyons-nous, suffisamment exacts' (p. 90); cf. Bagatti (1969), 95, fig. 51, p. VI;
Testa (1969), 126; Viaud's fig. 46 of the mosaic in cave no. 29 is also an
approximation.
[50] For an illustration, see Briand (1982), 41–2.

PLATE 5. Nazareth:
mosaic 1*a*

tesserae may be part of a Greek letter *mu*, the first letter of the word *Maria*, indicating the mother of Jesus (see Figure 23).

Flanking the table motif and continuing south, there is a rectangular frame of solid black triangles and a single line of black tesserae, which enclose a monogram of a Greek cross and *rho* within a wreath composed of red and black tesserae on a white background; around this are four *chi* crosses. Next, there is another simple frame containing two small crosses with connective lines of black tesserae and small oblong shapes.[51] Beyond this main design (1*a*) within the bold border, is a region of white

---

[51] Bagatti (1969: 99) sees in the latter a *delta* and a *chi*, which he relates to Jewish-Christians by means of Pythagoreanism and Gnosticism; cf. Testa (1962*b*), 83; (1969), 125–9.

Fɪɢ. 23. Nazareth: reconstruction of northern part of mosaic 1*a*

tesserae with randomly spaced crosses and diamond shapes, which stretches for a further 4 metres In this area the tesserae are larger than in the main design: 6 per 10 centimetres as opposed to 7.6 per 10 centimetres. It is well known, as a broad generalization, that mosaic tesserae increased in size during the course of the Byzantine period—apart, that is, from the tesserae used in high-quality mosaics, such as the nilotic mosaic of et-Tabgha or the upper mosaic (no. 5) of the southern aisle here, where the cubes are much the smallest in the church (12 per 10 centimetres).[52] Bagatti is therefore justified in wondering if this portion of the mosaic was added after the main design[53] even though no clear demarcation line is found. After all, a clever mosaicist would have ensured that a new portion would blend in with the old without an ugly line. There is no definitive boundary to this mosaic area. In its final form, it may have covered a large part of the western side of the central nave. Its orientation to the north is curious, as Bagatti rightly noted,[54] and would make better sense in a structure oriented towards the grotto.

The date of this mosaic is difficult to determine. The use of crosses on floor mosaics is uncommon, but not exceptional. An edict of Theodosius II (*Cod. Just.* i. 8. 1) dated 427 forbade the use of the cross motif in floor mosaics. One could at first sight assume, therefore, that both the mosaic and its extension were created before this date. However, crosses in floor mosaics have been found in various places in Palestine, and not all of these are to be dated before the edict (see below).

---

[52] Bagatti (1969), 100.   [53] Ibid. 99.   [54] Ibid. 100.

The mosaic (no. 3) in the small cave (no. 29), adjacent to the Chapel of the Angel, is very similar in style to mosaic no. 1. There is a black border three tesserae wide, measuring 1.07 metres square (though it is slightly irregular). It too contains the same cross-*rho* monogram. It has a square 'chessboard' design at the centre, with two diamonds on either side, and the same connective lines, but it is done with blue tesserae on a white background. The tesserae measure 7.3 per 10 centimetres.[55] The mosaic is oriented north, towards what may have been an altar or tomb (for which, see below).[56]

The Chapel of the Angel is paved with the so-called 'Conon mosaic' (mosaic no. 2, Plate 4), which has crosses within squares and a geometric design incoporating lozenges in squared areas. It contains an inscription which reads 'From[57] Conon, Deacon of Jerusalem'. While it also has crosses, the tesserae are larger than those of mosaics 1*a* and 3, measuring 6.5 per 10 centimetres. Stylistically, the Conon mosaic does not appear to derive from the same mosaicist. It uses three colours: blue, red, and white, and has a similarity to the fifth-century 'loaves and fishes' mosaic at et-Tabgha (which has lozenges within squares and crossed lines as well as small crosses on the loaves), also to mosaics nos. 6 and 7 in the sacristy of the Nazareth basilica and to the north-east nave mosaic at Shavei Zion.[58] A mosaic border of three tesserae in width runs along the base of the western walls of the Chapel of the Angel, which are not natural rock but built of hewn stones. This border and the walls themselves are older than the Conon mosaic.[59] No prior mosaic pavement was discovered underneath when the Conon mosaic was temporarily removed, so it seems that originally this was an unadorned vestibule between cave no. 29 and the venerated grotto no. 31, which was paved over only later, when the basilica was constructed.

So, to the question of dating on the basis of crosses in the pavements. Other cross designs are found on mosaic floors

[55] Bagatti has 9 per 10 cm., but my own average measurements indicate larger tesserae.

[56] For a 'Jewish-Christian' interpretation of the mosaic, see Testa (1969), 129–32.

[57] The *pi-rho* abbreviation here usually stands for πρός, 'from'; see Thompson (1912), 81. I am therefore not sure that Bagatti's translation of 'gift', προσφορά, is the correct one.

[58] Prausnitz, Avi-Yonah, and Barag (1967), 47, pl. XXXa.

[59] Viaud (1910), 88; Bagatti (1969), 32.

throughout Palestine. At Beit Sahour, in the rock-cut chapel at Shepherds' Field, there is a fourth-century mosaic with red crosses on a white background.[60] In Evron, near Nahariya, in the original basilical church dated to 415 by an inscription containing a wreathed cross-*rho*, there are cross-*rho* monograms at the entrance to the nave, in the eastern aisle of the atrium, and in two rooms north of the apse. Crosses are used in the pavement seven times in all.[61] Near there, at Shavei Zion, there are several mosaic crosses, including a wreathed cross, in the first church. The building is late fourth to early fifth century,[62] and Avi-Yonah thought the mosaics come from the beginning of the fifth century.[63] At Khirbet el-Bidat, in a church probably dated to the fifth century, is a mosaic with the motif of a medallion decorated with a cross placed at the centre of the choir.[64] At Beth ha-Shitta, west of Beth Shean, in a small Byzantine monastery farm, there are two small rooms paved in mosaics of three colours. In the first room is a red cross in a circle, with four small crosses in the corners; in the second room is a pavement with a field of seventy squares filled with geometric designs, fruit, and Greek letters. Avi-Yonah considered that the style of the mosaic is degenerate and the mosaic rough, which he thinks points to a late date, possibly even to the eighth century when the Byzantine edicts were no longer operative in Palestine,[65] but Y. Aharoni, who excavated the complex, dated it to the fifth or sixth centuries.[66] A cross-*rho* monogram was found in a mosaic floor of Beth Hanan, south of Jaffa, in an inscription which dated it to the thirty-first year of the 'emperor', which refers either to Justinian I,[67] or, as Bagatti has suggested, to Theodosius II,[68] who reigned 38 and 42 years respectively. In the former case the monogram should be dated to 558, and in the latter to 439. Both dates are *after* the edict of Theodosius. A Latin cross, among others, found in the mosaic of the fifth-century Church of St Kyriakos, excavated in Kibbutz Magen in the Negev, demonstrates that the use of the cross in floor mosaics continued right up until the date of

---

[60] Personal observation.

[61] See Avi-Yonah (1957a), 118–19; Tzaferis (1987); Jacques (1987).

[62] See Ovadiah (1970), 162.

[63] Prausnitz, Avi-Yonah, and Barag (1967), 49–55.

[64] R. Maoz (1990), 59. [65] (1957a), 122.

[66] Aharoni (1954). Bagatti suggested that the pavement is the work of Jewish-Christians; see (1971c), 281–5.

[67] Avi-Yonah (1934), 50. [68] (1969), 99 n. 8.

the edict, and possibly a little past it.[69] A Latin cross existed in Nazareth's mosaic no. 4, located in the south aisle.[70] At Kursi, two levels of mosaics were found in the chapel, *each* with several crosses. The second mosaic would have been laid very close to the time of Theodosius' edict, and possibly after; the monastery itself dates from the fifth century.[71] In Gerasa, the sixth-century Church of Procopius has a cross in the middle of a mosaic[72] and in the Church of St John the Baptist, also from the sixth century, crosses are found in the border.[73]

Bagatti himself noted that in Syria the monogram cross is found on mosaics until the sixth century, while in Rome his study of the dated mosaics shows it to have been used only until 425.[74] This is an interesting case to consider in any discussion about the efficacy of imperial edicts. Archaeological material tends to show that crosses on mosaic floors in Syria and Palestine cannot be dated before 427 simply because the edict was issued in this year. The evidence suggests that some crosses were clearly much *later* than this date, others were very close to it, and some were probably long before. Dating of floor mosaics with crosses must rest on other criteria.

From a preliminary examination, however, there appear to be three stages of mosaic decoration in the church at Nazareth. First, the cross-*rho* mosaics (nos. 1*a* and 3) were created. It is tempting to suggest that there may have been a third similar mosaic in the Grotto of the Annunication itself. There is no mosaic in this cave because part of the floor was lowered in 1730 when a new church was constructed on the site.[75] Vlaminck discovered mosaic tesserae at the Gabriel Altar in the shrine[76] and in the apse on its east side,[77] but these have disappeared.[78] Secondly, the mosaics of the basilica, the monastery, and the Chapel of the Angel (the Conon mosaic) were created. All these have tesserae of about the same size and show a stylistic similarity. Thirdly, a high-quality mosaic (no. 5) was laid over mosaic no. 4.

Bagatti's statement that there is 'nothing to prevent' the second phase of mosaics going back to a period prior to 427 is

[69] Cf. R. D. Kaplan (1979), 20, 22. [70] Bagatti (1969), 103.
[71] Tzaferis (1983*a*), 24, 27. [72] Kraeling (1938), pl. 83a, b.
[73] Ibid. pl. 69b. Both these instances are noted by Bagatti (1969), 107 n. 15.
[74] Ibid. 99 n. 8. [75] Ibid. 174–6.
[76] Vlaminck (1900), 3. [77] Ibid. 6. [78] See also Kopp (1963), 63.

insubstantial in the light of the evidence. There is nothing to prevent the mosaics from dating considerably after 427. Since the other wreathed cross-*rho* design in Galilee, at Evron, is dated to 415, one may on the basis of this parallel date the earliest Nazareth mosaic pavements (nos. 1*a* and 3) to the beginning of the fifth century. If we are to assign them to an earlier period, then other evidence must be brought to bear upon the matter.

Excursus: The Mosaic of Conon

The Conon mosaic (no. 2) is linked by Bagatti to a legendary martyr named Conon (who apparently came from Nazareth and was a relative of Christ[79]) because of the inscription naming a deacon of the same name from Jerusalem. The legendary Conon is attested in tenth-century sources as having been killed during the reign of Decius (249–51) at Magydos in Pamphylia.[80] Bagatti thinks that the deacon Conon wished to adorn the shrine out of love for his namesake.[81] There is no way of proving this one way or another, but one might wonder whether in this instance the pilgrimage site really did contribute to the formation of later legend. The tradition of the relatives of Jesus living in Nazareth (Africanus), the story of the grand-nephews of Christ renowned as witnesses, μάρτυρες, under Domitian (Hegesippus), and the inscription of the mosaic of Conon, may have all amalgamated into a legend. Late Byzantine pilgrims from Asia Minor might have used the three components and arrived at a legend of a relative of Jesus, Conon, who was martyred under Decius in Pamphylia.

Walls

From a close study of the masonry, Bagatti was able to determine that the stylobate between the nave and the southern aisle of the basilica belonged to an older building,[82] along with a stone indicating a corner just before the apse (Figure 20). A piece of wall

---

[79] Ibid. 54; Bagatti, (1969), p. 16.

[80] Archimandrite Hyppolitos, *Nea Sion* 15 (1923), 56; Hanozin (1935), 134–8; *Analecta Bollandiana* xviii, 180; Garitte (1958), 173; *PO* 21, 112–13. See also Meimaris (1986), 173.

[81] (1969), 198–9. It should be remembered of course that the name Κόνων was quite common and is found in other Palestinian inscriptions; see Meimaris (1986), 173: nos. 875. I, II; 231: no. 1144.

[82] (1969), 84–5, 115.

under mosaic no. 7 in the sacristy is aligned with these walls and would appear to be part of the same structure.[83] Corbo, who has recently re-examined the remains of the so-called synagogue-church in Nazareth, ignores this wall, but includes as part of the early structure a wall on the exterior of the Grotto of the Annunciation,[84] the walls which form the sides of the Chapel of the Angel, and the rock-cut steps to its south and west.[85] A number of stones in secondary use were found in the walls of the basilica and underneath the mosaics. Some of these had coats of white or coloured plaster, on a few of which there were graffiti which will be discussed below.

The Basin Under the Nave

When mosaic 1 was lifted, it was discovered that it rested on rock in its northern part, but that part of its southern section (1*b*) covered a rock-cut basin (Figure 20, no. 12) which aligns neither with the basilica, nor with the previous building, nor with the way into the cave complex dictated by the north-facing mosaic design 1*a*. Bagatti believed on the basis of Testa's interpretation of graffiti scratched on to the plaster of this basin,[86] that it was used for 'Jewish-Christian' initiation baths. Bagatti compared it with a similar basin found in the Church of St Joseph, which was interpreted as a baptismal pool.[87] These two basins will be considered together in order to establish whether they were used in any previous Jewish-Christian cult places.

The basin (see Figure 24) under mosaic 1*b* measures 1.95 by 2 metres, and is entered by a flight of five rock-cut steps on the southern side. The basin (2 m. deep) and the steps are coated with lime plaster. In the north-east corner there is a further basin (70 x 60 cm.) with a smaller one inside,[88] and on the northern wall there is a recess (*d*) measuring 63 by 61 centimetres. On the north and west walls graffiti have been incised into the plaster whilst it was still wet.[89] The fill of this basin will be discussed below; however, it should be noted that an oxidized curved knife of a type used for

[83] Bagatti (1969), 116–17, figs. 8:8h, 69.
[84] Cf. ibid. 181.   [85] Corbo (1987), 335, fig. 1.
[86] Cf. Testa (1962*b*), 78–94; cf. Bagatti (1969), 122–3.
[87] Ibid. 228–32.   [88] Ibid. fig. 70:b, c.
[89] Ibid. pls. VII and VIII; see p. 112 for a description.

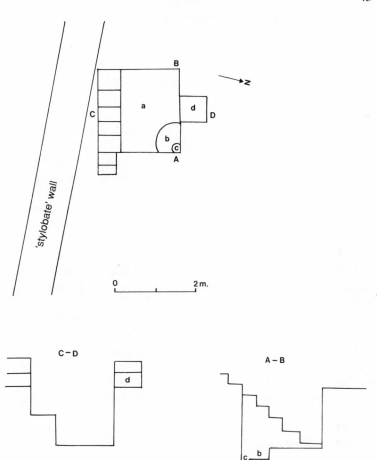

FIG. 24. Nazareth: basin under mosaic 1*b*

grape harvesting, as Bagatti himself noted,[90] was discovered in the recess.

From personal observation of the graffiti on the walls of the basin, I determined that the scratchings were all at the height of a small child, less than one metre from the floor. Testa identified roughly drawn boats, crosses, a 'cosmic ladder', plants, and letters which he connected with Jewish-Christians, mainly by recourse to

[90] Ibid. 120 n. 36.

Gnostic texts. Those of us familiar with the artistic work of small children might readily arrive at quite another interpretation (see Figure 25)! There are no Christian signs or Greek letters that are remotely definite. None of the supposed boats is drawn with the care typical of other such representations in Palestine (cf. those in Beth Shearim[91]), but rather with a technique that one can only describe as extremely loose; in fact, it is not at all certain whether these are boats at all. The networks of very roughly drawn criss-crossing lines may indicate fishing nets, and it is just possible to imagine a scene of fishing boats and drying nets near trees, but this does require some effort. It simply does not seem possible that these scratchings are intended as symbols of any kind. Moreover, if the basin was to be filled with water this would have obscured the graffiti; it is hard to understand why anyone would draw these to adorn an unseen place. Bagatti thought that the workman himself made the scratchings, but a skilled workman who has put considerable time and energy into smoothing over the plaster coating the walls would hardly go down on his knees to make these scribblings with such a wild hand.

The rock-cut and partly built basin underneath the Church of St Joseph (Figure 26: A; Plate 6) measures 2.05 by 2.20 metres, and is 2 metres deep. It is entered by a flight of seven steps. Both the floor, the steps, and part of the surrounding area were covered with mosaic, of which most still remains. The mosaic has a design of black rectangles on a white background. The sides of the basin are plastered. Sherds fixed into this plaster were identified by Bagatti as Byzantine,[92] but he also noted that they could just as easily be late Roman.[93] There is a small basin in the north-west corner, a narrow channel between the steps and the main part of the floor and a basalt block inserted into the floor east of the basin.[94] Testa has interpreted the seven steps as being representative of the ascending and descending of Jesus to and from heaven, the channel as the River Jordan, the basalt stone as Christ, and the mosaic rectangles as angels.[95]

[91] Mazar (1973), pls. XX.2, XXIII.1, 2; for Jason's Tomb in Jerusalem, see Rahmani (1967), 70–1, figs. 5a, b; for the (original) 'Jerusalem Ship' in the Church of the Holy Sepulchre, see Bennett and Humphreys (1974), fig. 2.

[92] (1969), 231.   [93] Ibid. 232.

[94] Ibid. 228–31; Viaud (1910), 142–4.

[95] Testa (1962a); (1969), 42–4.

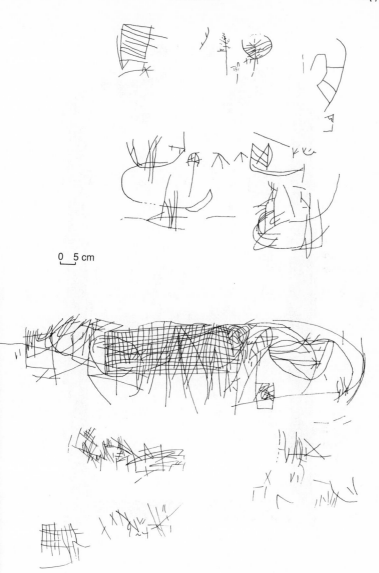

0 5 cm

FIG. 25. Nazareth: graffiti on plastered walls of basin under mosaic 1*b*

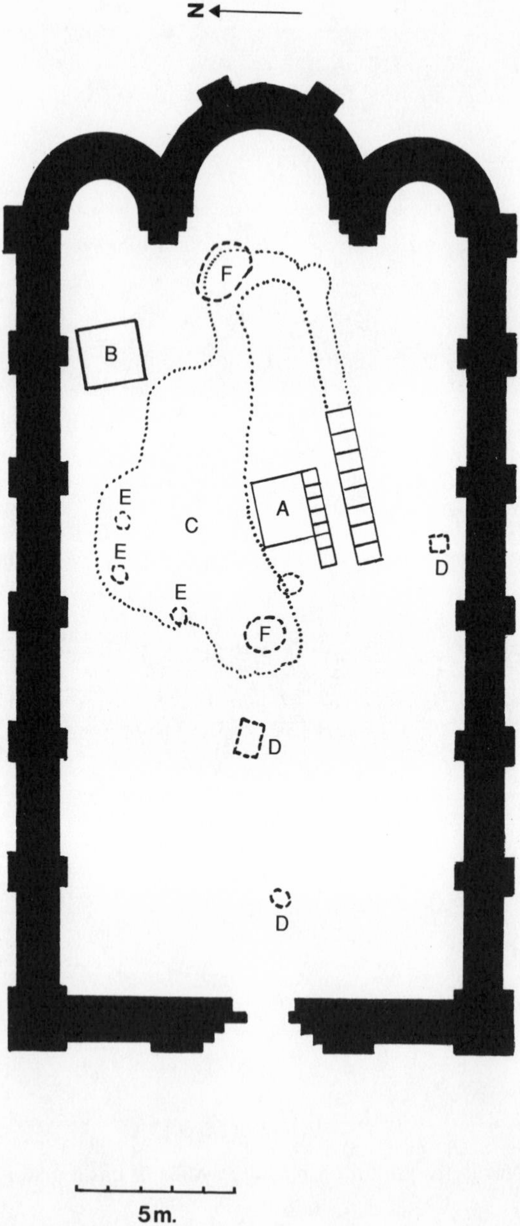

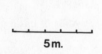

Z ←

B

F

E
E
E
C
A
E
F
D

D

D

5 m.

FIG. 26. Evidence of ancient agricultural activity found under the Church of St Joseph, Nazareth

PLATE 6. Nazareth: basin paved with mosaic in the Church of St Joseph

Jewish-Christians were undoubtedly baptized, just as other Christians, though one might expect them to have retained the same attitude to their baptismal baths as they had to the Jewish purificatory baths, or *mikvehs*. Jews never paved *mikvehs* with mosaics, since the cracks in between the tesserae might have harboured impurities.[96] However, it was quite common for the collecting vats used in wine-making to be provided with mosaic floors. The basin seems to be associated with other agricultural installations—cisterns, silos, another basin, and a large cave— found under the Church of St Joseph (see Figure 26), which makes it very likely indeed that it was used as part of such operations and not for Jewish-Christian initiation ceremonies.

[96] R. Reich, personal communication.

Wine-pressing complexes in Palestine consisted of a treading area, which was a square or rectangular slightly sloping floor, and a collecting vat connected to it either by an open channel or a closed pipe. In between, there was often a settling vat or a straining depression.[97] In Galilee the intermediary pit was small. The two Nazareth basins under consideration here have certain features typical of collecting vats, most especially the steps and depression in the corners. The plastered space (*d*) in the basin no. 12 under mosaic 1*b* (see Figure 24) is typical of the straining depressions in Galilean wine-presses. The basalt stone fitted into the mosaic in the basin in the Church of St Joseph (Plate 6) was to break the flow of juice so that it would not damage the mosaic.[98]

The entire area was, during the Roman period, a hive of agricultural activity; this makes it extremely improbable that any cultic use was made of its caves or basins. Only 20 metres away from basin no. 12 (Figure 20) there is a wine-pressing zone with a small sloping treading area (no. 34: in the 'Kitchen of the Virgin'),[99] about 3 metres square and 40 centimetres deep, and an underground fermenting vat (no. 35) to which the juice ran through a hole. As was stated above, this complex was connected to the Grotto of the Annunciation (no. 31) by a tunnel (*e*), so that it is safe to assume that the cave formed part of the complex. Bagatti has noted that on the west side of the cave, near the entrance, there was a rock-cut hole 10 centimetres wide and 10 centimetres deep which would have been used for holding a pointed storage jar or amphora,[100] and further north there are two depressions 58 centimetres in diameter, which may be the remains of basins[101] (these may also have been for large storage jars). In cave no. 29 there is a small basin,[102] the use of which has not been determined, but it is possible that this part of the cave complex was also used in wine production; the walls which separate it from the large cave no. 31 are artificial and formerly it would have been a kind of alcove. Furthermore, if the recess (Figure 24: *d*) in basin no. 12 under the nave was a straining depression, then on the basis of the usual plan of wine-pressing installations one would expect

---

[97] R. Frankel (1981), 200, illus. 6.1 and 9.6.2.
[98] I am indebted to Dr Frankel for these observations (letter of July 1986).
[99] Bagatti (1969), 53–5, figs. 20–1.
[100] Ibid. 176.   [101] Ibid. 175, 182, fig. 137:g, h.
[102] Ibid. fig. 137:p; Vlaminck (1900: 4) thought this was created by the Crusaders; cf. Bagatti (1969), 185.

the treading area to be located immediately north, underneath most of mosaic 1 and right in front of the cave complex. This treading area would then become a bridge between the collecting vat (basin no. 12) and the rest of the system. The rock between the top of the steps into the cave complex and the basin is flat, cut to create a level surface for the mosaic at the time the area was converted to a Christian use. The natural ground level can be seen south of the basin; it slopes down.[103] Therefore, one can presume that this slope continued upwards north of the basin before the mosaic came to be laid, and that the area was then an ideal site for a treading area.

The knife used for grape-cutting would have been dropped into basin no. 12 at the time of its original employment. One would expect other artefacts in the fill to have derived from the period of the basin's absorption into the first building here. Since the basin does not align with any features of this building (the 'stylobate' wall in fact passes within a few centimetres of the basin's south-west corner), it is highly unlikely that it was utilized. It must have been filled in when the building came to be constructed. If mosaic 1*b* dates to the time of the construction of the basilica, then it is probable that further debris was deposited in the basin prior to its being covered over. This is confirmed by the evidence of the fill. At the topmost level, close to the stylobate wall of the basilica,[104] there was a heap of plaster fragments which appear to have derived from the first building. These fell on top of pre-existing fill while the second building, the basilica, was being constructed and may come from the 'stylobate' wall of the first building. Many of these pieces were inscribed with graffiti. One other later piece is a fragment of Roman redware with a distinctive marking of small lines arranged to form a circle.[105] Hayes has classified the circle design as occurring *c*.350–80.[106] The rosette on the same piece, composed of incised wedges, is mainly found from 330 to 360.[107] This determines the date of the making, but not the date of the breaking, of the vessel. Since it is imported, this object would probably date from the latter part of the fourth century at the earliest. Loffreda has found the same kind of pattern in Capernaum

[103] Ibid. fig. 50.
[104] Ibid. 120.   [105] Ibid. 134, fig. 79, no. 28; pl. V.2.
[106] (1972), 235: fig. 40, style A, no. 24.   [107] Ibid. 239.

on fourth-century redware.[108] Largely, however, the basin was full of field stones, a few *nari* blocks, earth, and various bits of pottery dating from the late Roman period.[109] This is what we would expect of a fill which dates from the time of the earliest building, if we were to date this building to the first part of the fourth century.

The presence of coloured plaster pieces is consistent with the evidence of the reused blocks from the first building found in the walls of the basilica, which have coloured and white plaster coating. The earlier building must then have been coated with decorative plaster. The graffiti on the plaster pieces found in the basin are mainly in Greek, though three are Syriac.[110] There are parts of names as well as a cross with dots in the spaces between the arms.[111] Only one clear Greek name can be distinguished, that of Sisinios.[112] According to Preisigke,[113] Σισίνιος is a name first found in fifth-century papyri; spelt as Σισίννιος the name belonged to the Patriarch of Constantinople, who died in the year 427.[114] Foraboschi places the name in the sixth to eighth centuries.[115] Y. E. Meimaris has noted that the name appears on a bronze cross from Khirbet el-Mird,[116] probably to be dated to the sixth century. The Syriac graffiti seem to contain the names *Yohanan*, found from the first century onwards in Greek (Ἰοάννης), and (possibly) *Amoun*, which is found in Greek transliteration (Ἀμοῦν) in papyri from the third to the seventh centuries.[117] Since the languages of the graffiti do not include Hebrew or Palestinian Jewish Aramaic, they demonstrate that visitors to this place came from outside Jewish Nazareth; they were pilgrims rather than local residents and, moreover, Christians, as the cross demonstrates. We are then justified in referring to the building which existed prior to the basilica as a church of some kind.

Excavations under the Mosaics of the Basilica and Monastery

Mosaic no. 5 of the southern aisle (see Figure 22) rested on a layer of lime in which were small pieces of white marble, fragments of

---

[108] (1974), 81, photo 18, nos. 11, 15.
[109] Bagatti (1969), fig. 79, nos. 21–9.
[110] Ibid. 127–9.   [111] Ibid. fig. 76, no. 26; fig. 77, no. 7.
[112] Ibid. 127, fig. 77, no. 33, and pl. III.3.
[113] Preisigke (1922), col. 386.   [114] Bury (1899), 350.
[115] (1966), 294.   [116] (1986), 171, inscription no. 867.
[117] Preisigke (1922), col. 27; Foraboschi (1966), 31.

pottery, and a very small coin. Under this was the earlier mosaic no. 4, which rested on a bed of lime, earth, and stones, then another layer of lime.[118] In order to build up a solid foundation to the height of the nave, a large quantity of fill was deposited on the sloping bedrock. In this fill was pottery[119] including many Roman lamp fragments,[120] a glass hanging lamp of a type used in Byzantine churches,[121] pieces of the earlier church building, and tiles[122] to which mortar was attached.

The presence of a very small coin need not throw back the dating of the upper mosaic. Bagatti thought that the coin was pre-Byzantine because of its size,[123] but it was not until 498, under Anastasius I, that there was a currency reform in which a large bronze *follis* of 40 *nummi* was introduced to replace smaller denominations of 20, 10, and 5. The *nummus*, prior to the reform, measured 9 millimetres in diameter.[124] The old *nummus* would not have gone out of circulation immediately. Small oxidized *nummi* of the low denominations are extremely common in Byzantine sites of the fifth to seventh centuries.

Excavation of the monastery uncovered a floor in which were more of the small coins. Under this were part of an altar colonnette, fragments of tiles, pieces of white marble,[125] pottery, glass, painted plaster, and about seventy pieces of the earlier building.[126] Some of the pieces from the previous building have recently been redrawn by E. Alliata and republished by Corbo.[127]

A Reconstruction of the Early Church

Taking all the fragments of the previous building together, it can be concluded that the building was constructed of *nari* stone, and provided with a tiled roof supported by wooden beams. It was decorated with painted plaster and small pieces of white marble (possibly from a floor). Two of the blocks have cavities in which to rest wooden beams[128] and two of the bases have slots along their length.[129] The various parts of the building (which include five

---

[118] Bagatti (1969), 131.
[120] Ibid. fig. 81.
[122] Ibid. fig. 81, no. 18–20.
[124] Worth (1908), p. xiii, 35: no. 13.
[126] Ibid. 140–1, fig. 84.
[128] Bagatti (1969), 145.

[119] Ibid. 132–4, fig. 79, nos. 1–16.
[121] Ibid. 138, fig. 81, no. 17.
[123] Ibid. 131.
[125] Bagatti (1969), 139.
[127] (1987), 344–8.
[129] Ibid. figs. 84:4c, 87.

column bases, upon some of which are pilgrim graffiti;[130] three
plastered imposts of a double arch; two capitals; several cornices
with different mouldings and proportions and the remains of
plaster; various doorposts with remains of plaster and graffiti, as
well as other blocks with plaster and graffiti) have been used by
Corbo in a convincing reconstruction of the earlier building.
Corbo concludes that, in the construction of the early church
(which he calls a 'chiesa-sinagoga'), the cave area was cut away
from the surrounding rocky outcrop, and the rock, which declined
to the south was, as we have seen, levelled. The Chapel of the
Angel was expanded and walls were built within the cave complex,
along with the two flights of steps. Corbo has the ingenious idea
that a line of columns resting on a low wall constituted a transenna
in front of the cave complex,[131] from the steps leading to the
Chapel of the Angel for 8 metres to the west wall. Not only does
this make sense of some of the architectural elements, but in
suggesting that the column bases rested on a low wall, Corbo is
able to explain why pilgrims were disposed to scratch on these
which, if they had rested on the ground, would have been rather
low. This transenna of columns also solves the problem of how the
builders constructed the roof over the cave complex;[132] it formed a
central support. It also explains why pilgrims would have entered
the cave complex by the steps to the Chapel of the Angel, instead
of walking through to the Grotto of the Annunciation directly;
with the transenna in front of it there would have been no access.

The Grotto of the Annunciation is much changed from its
Byzantine form but, to recapitulate what has already been said, it
is clear that there was an apse, upon which Vlaminck saw pieces of
mosaic[133] in the east. The present floor is lower than the Byzantine
level, so that whatever mosaic it once had has been destroyed. The
cave measures 5.5 by 6.14 metres, but in the Byzantine period it
extended southwards for a further few metres. The rocky bank
appears to have been cut back by the Crusaders.[134] Sherds found
in rock fissures within the grotto date from Hellenistic to
Byzantine times.[135] There are a few fragments of plaster on the
wall, but only four Greek letters upon these have survived the
passage of time. All that can be known about its form in the early

[130] Ibid. fig. 84:4b; cf. fig. 108.1.
[131] (1987), figs. 1 and 2.   [132] Ibid. 338–9.
[133] Bagatti (1969), 177.   [134] Ibid. 174.   [135] Ibid. 185.

church is that it had an east-facing apse. The apse would not have been carved out of the wall during the time of the later basilica, because the basilica's apse superseded the one cut into the wall of the cave. It would appear that this was where the altar was placed in the earliest period of the cave's Christian use. This coheres with Egeria's remarks that an altar was placed in a cave.

The small cave no. 29, 2 metres wide, was discovered by Vlaminck[136] and studied by Viaud.[137] It was considered by Bagatti to have been a memorial to the legendary martyr Conon[138] (see above) whom he deemed a Jewish-Christian. The walls built on either side of the entrance and those forming the Chapel of the Angel derive from the time of the construction of the early church and are covered with plaster. Mosaic no. 3 (see Figure 22) was cut through in its southern part, probably when the same was done to the floor of the venerated grotto in the eighteenth century. On the north side is a rocky ledge, and on the east wall six layers of plaster have been preserved[139] with a profuse amount of graffiti. The earliest plaster layer was decorated with a mass of flowers on leafy stalks (Plate 7) and a wreath. Again, there is no definite evidence that would determine when the cave came to be venerated except the graffiti, which are all Greek, thus demonstrating that the cave was first visited when Greek-speaking pilgrims came to Palestine, some time in the fourth century. A coin identified by Bagatti as having been minted in Antioch during the reign of Constans— though he surely means Constantius II instead, who reigned in the East from 337 to 351 and over the entire Empire till 361—was found in layer c of the plaster. This indicates a *terminus ante quem* for coat c, but not a *terminus post quem*, as Bagatti appears to have thought.[140] Despite Bagatti's suggestion, there is also no clue as to what the cave was used for in the Byzantine period. Daniel the Abbot reports that the small cave was the tomb of Joseph (*Zhitie* 90).[141]

Corbo also notes that since the rock falls away to the south and a level was built up only when the monastery was constructed, then the early church structure was probably entered from the west.

---

[136] (1910), 3–5. [137] (1900), 85–95.
[138] Bagatti (1969), 218. [139] Ibid. 185. [140] Ibid. 210.
[141] Kopp (1963: 64–5) suggested that it was a tomb of Mary which was replaced by that in the Valley of Jehoshaphat.

PLATE 7. Nazareth: earliest plaster decoration in cave 29

The transenna of columns divided the structure into two parts;[142] on the north was the cave complex and in the south an open space. The entire building including the cave complex measured only 16 by 20 metres. It can be added that pilgrims coming in from the west would have walked over to the north-facing mosaic (no. 1), which led them in the direction of the entrance to the cave complex. They would then go eastward to pray before the altar, of which a fragment of a colonnette remains,[143] placed in front of the rock-cut apse in the Grotto of the Annunciation.

Bagatti has identified this structure as a Jewish-Christian synagogue-church solely on the basis of the form of the few architectural elements that have been preserved. He writes that these 'manifest a style well known from the synagogues of Galilee, whose mouldings are very similar'.[144] Bagatti failed to remember that synagogues and churches shared architectural features during the Byzantine period. They were distinguished not by the forms of column bases and capitals but by details (such as a hollow space

---

[142] Corbo (1987), 340.

[143] See above, and Bagatti (1969), 95, fig. 84, no. 21.

[144] Ibid. 140, 145–6; cf. Kohl and Watzinger (1919), figs. 244–6, 249.

below the apse for Torah scrolls or the community chest in the case of a synagogue), symbolic motifs, and, as C. Kraeling notes, orientation: synagogues were oriented toward Jerusalem and churches to the east.[145] The early structure in Nazareth has an *east*-facing apse. Because of the slope of the rock, the building would not have been entered from the south. Although mosaic 1a is oriented north, its orientation directs pilgrims to the steps leading to the cave area and does not dictate the axis of the early church. Moreover, if this structure was oriented north, this would make it face away from Jerusalem; a northern orientation is unlikely as much for a synagogue as for a church. Irenaeus states that the 'Ebionites' adored Jerusalem as if it were the House of God (*Adv. Haer.* i. 26. 2); why would they then turn away from it? The form of the building, from the available remains and from Corbo's reconstruction, bears no resemblance whatsoever to a synagogue. It is an unconventional structure designed to encompass the cave complex in a practicable manner.

To support his thesis further, Bagatti included two marble columns taken from relatively modern masonry near the Byzantine convent, as part of the architectural pieces of the early structure. These pieces have the symbols of a pomegranate, a crown, two concentric circles, and a flower. That they reveal 'well accented Judaeo-Christian characteristics'[146] is a matter he did not explain. Since the early Christian structure was not built with any marble, it is very unlikely that they should be considered part of it. Testa has interpreted inscribed markings on the piece of marble found in the Crusader church as being Aramaic of the first to second centuries and, moreover, a passage out of the Targum of Isaiah.[147] Even if this were so, it does not connect the piece with the hypothetical synagogue-church.

Bagatti noted that there is evidence of weathering on some of the pieces of the earlier structure, which indicates that the place was long in use.[148] The type of stone used was not of optimum quality and would not have weathered as well as marble. A century would have been sufficient time for the weathering to take place.

---

[145] Kraeling (1938), 239.   [146] Bagatti (1969), 169.
[147] Ibid. 170–1; Testa (1967); (1969), 79–86.
[148] Bagatti (1969), 140; cf. 146.

The Graffiti

A detailed analysis of each graffito found in the excavations of the Byzantine basilica is not required here. A few matters will be mentioned in order to refute Bagatti's and Testa's theory that the graffiti demonstrate the existence of Jewish-Christians. We will also discuss the relevance of the graffiti for dating.

To begin with, it should be noted that certain graffiti (Bagatti's nos. 1, 8, and 17) are written in *Armenian*. There is no doubt that Armenian pilgrims came to Palestine already in the fourth century[149] and continued to visit throughout the Byzantine period,[150] but they did not write in Armenian. The Armenian alphabet is generally held to have been invented by Mesrop-Mashtotz around the year 404.[151] The inscription of the earliest Armenian mosaic in Palestine, dated to the fifth century, is in Greek,[152] while mosaic pavements with the Armenian script date from the sixth and seventh centuries,[153] which shows that it took some time for literacy in the Armenian alphabet to become widespread. In the middle of the fifth century, the Armenians founded a scriptorium in Jerusalem, which undoubtedly helped spread Armenian literacy amongst the community there.[154] The graffiti cannot therefore pre-date the fifth century, and it is safer to date them later rather than earlier in this period, probably even to the sixth. Armenian was scratched on the rock faces of the Wadi Haggag by pilgrims on their way to Jebel Musa, but again these cannot be dated before the late fifth century.[155]

Given the very close relations that existed between the Armenian church and the church of Jerusalem, it would be most unlikely that Armenian pilgrims would go to a site venerated by a supposed heretical sect. It was not until the Council of Chalcedon in 451, when the Armenian church rejected the decisions there and identified themselves with monophysite theology, that they broke with orthodoxy,[156] but the rift did not become critical until the time of Justinian. Even so, that a group of fifth-century Armenians

---

[149] Hintlian (1976), 1, 38.
[150] See Stone (1986).
[151] Hintlian (1976), 14. Prof. C. Dowsett. personal communication.
[152] Vincent and Abel (1914b), 391; Hintlian (1976), 14.
[153] Arakelian (1978); Evans (1982); Narkiss (1979).
[154] Sanjian (1979).
[155] See Negev (1977), 77; Stone (1982).
[156] Burney and Marshall (1971), 224.

should have visited a place identified by Bagatti as a heterodox Jewish-Christian shrine would have been very strange indeed. Despite their monophysite beliefs, they were part of the mainstream of monasticism and pilgrimage in Palestine; all Christians visiting the country remained under the authority of the Bishop of Jerusalem and shared in common worship at the holy places.[157]

It seems to be clear from graffiti nos. 5 and 10 that the pilgrims came to Nazareth to venerate Mary. Graffito no. 5 reads (somewhat ungrammatically) in part: *(Y)ΠΟ ΑΓΙω ΤΟΠΟ Μ*, 'under the holy place (of?) M(ary)'.[158] Graffito no. 10 reads *XE MAPIA*: a pointed reference to the Christian belief that it was here that the angel Gabriel announced to Mary that she would bear the future Messiah (cf. Luke 1: 28).

It is an underlying purpose in the Bagatti–Testa school's discussion of Nazareth to show that the veneration of Mary was extremely ancient (even Jewish-Christian),[159] that with the discoveries in Nazareth 'this was the Marian devotion of the very early church coming to light', as J. Briand writes in the English version of the popular guidebook to Nazareth.[160] Briand goes on to tell his readers that palaeographic study of graffito no. 5 dates it to the second or third century,[161] an attribution which derives from Testa's conclusions[162] based on Bagatti's cursory palaeographic observations,[163] which are almost entirely derived from a knowledge of ossuary inscriptions that are, in this case, irrelevant to the item under consideration. The fact that the internal lines of the *M* do not join up is the result of the exigencies of the media (sharp object/knife on plaster/stone) rather than intent.

Furthermore, it is very unlikely indeed that any Jewish-Christians venerated the Virgin Mary. One of the principal matters for which the Church Fathers condemned 'Ebionites' was their refusal to accept the Virgin Birth of Jesus and their continued belief that Jesus was the physical, ordinary son of Joseph and

---

[157] Sanjian (1979), 11.

[158] For a doubtful reconstruction of the rest of the graffito, see Bagatti (1969), 151; Briand (1982), 23; Testa (1969), 70.

[159] Bagatti (1969), 152, 155.

[160] (1982), 26. In Bagatti's original Italian text, this graffito was misprinted as *KE MAPIA*; cf. Bagatti (1969), 156.

[161] (1982), 26.

[162] (1969), 75–6.

[163] (1969), 158.

Mary.[164] Eusebius actually distinguishes a second group of Ebionites who do accept the Virgin Birth but, as Klijn and Reinink have convincingly argued, this is a result of Eusebius' misinterpretation of Irenaeus.[165] It would seem more probable that these graffiti showing a great respect for Mary were inscribed close to the time of the third ecumenical council at Ephesus (431), which gave impetus to Marian devotion by upholding her title of 'Theotokos' after attacks against it by Nestorians.

On the eastern wall of cave no. 29, on the earliest painted plaster, there is an inscription painted in red, punctuated by the floral motifs.[166] This inscription has been provided with a Jewish-Christian interpretation by Bagatti and Testa, who have also supplied a number of missing and doubtful letters. It will therefore be examined anew here.

The reading of the inscription (Figure 27; Plate 8) is by no means clear. The first readable word is *TON*, an accusative masculine form of the definite article, which suggests that something came before it. The word following is unclear, but seems to contain the letters *CE*. Under *TON* are the letters *PEA*, which may be the end of the word δωρεά, 'gift', though this is conjecture. There is a Greek cross with the letters *alpha* and *omega* in the spaces, of a common Byzantine type, and under this are the abbreviations of 'Lord Jesus': *KY XP* followed by *CωCON*, 'save', and then what appears to be a name in larger letters reading . . . *NAO* . . . *N*. On the next line there is *COYOYΛEPIANTHN*. *EΠΙΑΣΘ* . . . *O*. The σοῦ should be placed with the preceding name to read 'your (name)', rather than with the possible name Ouleria that follows. Οὐλερία is a name not found in the papyri, but Οὐαλερία is common, found from the second to the fourth centuries.[167] The omission of an expected καί between the names is not unusual in Byzantine inscriptions. The remainder of the line does not read clearly. The mark shaped like a Latin *S* may be an

[164] Cerinthus: Irenaeus, *Adv. Haer.* i. 26. 1; Ps.-Tertullian, *Adv omn. haer.* 3; Epiphanius, *Pan.* xxviii. 1. 2; xxx. 14. 2; Ebionites: Irenaeus, *Adv. Haer.* v. 1. 3; iii. 21. 1; Hippolytus, *Ref.* vii. 34; Eusebius, *Hist. Eccles.* iii. 27. 3; Epiphanius, *Pan.* xxx. 2. 2; Jerome, *De Vir. Ill.* ix; Nazoraeans: Jerome, *In Esa.* ii. 2.

[165] (1973), 26. Jesus' descent from Joseph appears to have been quite the usual belief of Christians of the first century.

[166] Bagatti (1969), 191–9.

[167] Preisigke (1922), col. 246; Foraboschi (1966), 217.

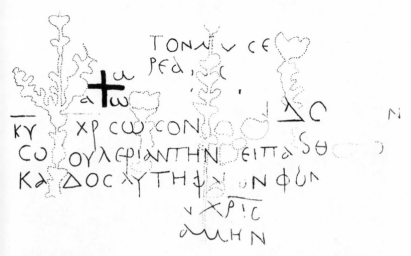

FIG. 27. Nazareth: the painted inscription on the earliest plaster of cave 29

abbreviation for αὐτός (etc.)[168] preceded by εἶπα, 'I said'. Underneath this line is *KAIΔOCAYTH*, καὶ δός αὐτῃ, 'and give to her', but the following letters are unclear. There may be *ΦNω*, after which is *NΦO*. The inscription finishes with . . .*N XPIC*, ἐν Χριστῷ Ἰησοῦ (cf. 1 Cor. 16: 24). To sum up, the lower portion of the inscription may read: 'Lord Jesus, save your (name) (and) Ouleria who(?) I myself said . . . and give her . . . in Christ Jesus. Amen.'

Given this, the reading and reconstruction of the inscription by Bagatti and Testa appears somewhat free. They translated it as: 'The memory . . . I made for the light . . . Christ Lord, save your servant Valeria. Here we praise the death of (name) and give to suffering the palm which (it is customary to give) to one who died for Christ. Amen.'[169] This version attempts to draw a relationship between the inscription and the supposed use of cave no. 29 as a martyrium for Conon, but this is based on extensive restoration and recourse to abbreviations. Many of the letters read by Testa

---

[168] Thompson (1912), 81.
[169] Bagatti (1969), 196–9; Testa (1969), 64–70.

PLATE 8. Nazareth: painted inscription in earliest plaster of cave 29

and Bagatti as sure readings are unclear or even, its seems, absent altogether.

In a second painted inscription done in red, Bagatti saw a *kappa*, which he suggests may be the first letter of the name Conon. Since almost nothing remains of this letter, this is impossible to verify.[170] Other graffiti of the earliest level of plaster possibly contain the names Genos, Elpisos, Achilles, Elpidius, Paulus Antonis,[171] and Julia or Julius.[172] Bagatti's date, 'no later than the third century',[173] for the transformation of this cave into a holy place is, on the basis of these graffiti, unjustified. As with the graffiti found in basin no. 12, these should be dated to the period when Christian pilgrims first came to Palestine from outside, some time in the fourth century.

None of the other graffiti understood by Bagatti and Testa to be indicative of a Jewish-Christian mentality is clearly convincing. Their *pièce de résistance*,[174] a figure holding an object upon which

---

[170] Bagatti (1969), 199–200, fig. 156:a.
[171] Ibid. 201–4.
[172] Ibid. 205, 209.
[173] Ibid. 215.
[174] It is used for the cover illustration of the paperback edition of Testa (1969).

PLATE 9.
Nazareth: graffito
of soldier with
ensign and shield

is a cross (Plate 9), identified by Bagatti as John the Baptist with a Jewish head covering,[175] is more likely a depiction of a helmeted soldier with an ensign and a shield, in a stance much found on early Byzantine coins.[176]

The interpretations given by Bagatti and Testa to letters, crosses, and other motifs are generally Gnostic rather than Jewish-Christian. Bagatti and Testa show a tendency to understand unintentional scratches as the Hebrew letter *waw* (written in the Jewish script),[177] which is then given a mystical meaning. The onomasticon of the graffiti scratched on the parts of the early church building possibly has the names Ananias (no. 1), Naukida

[175] no. 28. Bagatti (1964*c*); (1969), 164.
[176] Taylor (1987*b*).   [177] Cf. Bagatti (1969), 158, 162.

(no. 2), Zeninoi (no. 11), Ruth (no. 12), and Leones (no. 13).[178] There is nothing written in Hebrew or Aramaic. The Hebrew names, Ruth and Ananias, are biblical, and were therefore prone to be adopted by Christians.

Other Remains in Nazareth

As we saw in the discussion of literature pertaining to Nazareth, Bagatti believed that there were two Jewish-Christian edifices: one the House of Mary and the other the House of Joseph. It so happens that the Franciscans own the present Church of St Joseph, under which they would like to site this second very ancient, if entirely hypothetical, shrine. According to Bagatti, this is the church mentioned for the first time by Adomnan as standing on two vaults on the site where once there was the house in which Jesus was nurtured (*De Loc. Sanct.* ii. 26. 1–4). Adomnan writes that between the vaults there were arches and a clear spring, used by the entire population, from which water was brought up to the church above by a winch. Moreover, Bagatti thought this was the synagogue referred to by Peter the Deacon as being turned into a church[179] because Peter mentions a place where Mary drew water as being a cave. Peter, in fact, is confusing the Grotto of the Annunciation described by Egeria with contemporary accounts of the cave in which is the spring of St Gabriel (cf. John Phocas, x. 4–5).

The subterranean remains under the present Church of St Joseph (see Figure 26) have been discussed by Viaud.[180] There are a number of silos and the aforementioned basin in a cave now known as 'the Grotto of the Holy Family'.[181] The cave appears to have been converted into a sacred place by the Crusaders; before then it appears to have been a Roman-Byzantine agricultural area. There is nothing here that identifies the area as a Jewish-Christian baptistery (*pace* Testa). It is first identified as the workshop of Joseph in the seventeenth century, by Quaresimus, as Kopp has already pointed out.[182] The discussion by Kopp is sufficient to

[178] Ἀνανίας is a name found in the papyri from the second to the eighth centuries: Preisigke (1922), col. 29; Foraboschi (1966), 32. The other names are not found in the papyri, apart from Ῥούθ, found in the eighth century: Preisigke (1922), col. 354. Λέονης is itself not found, though Λέων and Λεωνίδης are common: Preisigke (1922), col. 195; Foraboschi (1966), 179.

[179] (1969), 23–5.

[180] (1910), 142–4.

[181] Bagatti (1969), 219–33.

[182] (1963), 82–6.

refute any assertion that this was an ancient venerated place or the second church identified by Adomnan, and need not be repeated here.

Whether Adomnan is referring to the spring under the Church of St Gabriel or under the property of the Sisters of Nazareth can remain a contentious point, though a good case for seeing the latter as the place has been made by J.-B. Livio.[183]

The synagogue need not be connected with Jewish-Christians; the Jews appear to have taken Christian pilgrims to their own synagogue rather than to a Christian structure called such.[184] It was converted into a church only after the Jews were expelled from the town (see above). Four column bases of white calcite coming from the synagogue have been discovered.[185] These have masons' marks of *lamed*, *dalet*, final *mem*, and a type of *tet* curiously more similar to Nabataean than the usual Jewish script. The Greek Orthodox consider their church as being on the site of the synagogue, though Dalman thought it was located on the site of the United Greek property[186] and reports that four rectangular blocks with Hebrew letters were discovered near by.[187]

It is now possible to conclude that there existed in Nazareth, from the first part of the fourth century, a small and unconventional church which encompassed a cave complex. Cave no. 31, which Egeria refers to as 'big and very splendid',[188] was understood to be where Mary received the message that she would bear a child (Luke 1: 26–38) and also where she lived (cf. Pet. Diac., *Lib*. T). If it was considered her abode, then it is possible that the structure itself came to be called the House of Mary, after the name of the

---

[183] Livio (1967: 29–31, 35) notes that Byzantine remains were discovered on the property, including granite columns, carved stones, marble columns and fragments, mosaic tesserae, and Byzantine money as well as undergound Byzantine (?) arches. Pottery fragments in the rock-cut cistern have been dated to the 5th to 9th cents. According to Livio, who has interpreted the unpublished material collected by Father Henry Senès, the property is situated on what was a little river which flowed down from the Nebi Sain. Livio also identifies two holes in the rock which, he says, was where the ropes of the winch mentioned by Arculf were affixed. One might add that the marble fragments from this church give a strong clue as to where the marble capitals thought by Bagatti to come from the 'Jewish-Christian synagogue-church' really belong.

[184] *Pace* Wilkinson (1977), 165.

[185] Bagatti (1969), 233–4.   [186] (1935), 68.   [187] Ibid.

[188] The word used, *lucidissima*, is understood by Bagatti and Testa to have a specifically Jewish-Christian meaning: Bagatti (1969), 23; Testa (1969), 74–6.

cave. This would explain why the Piacenza Pilgrim (*Itin.* v) wrote that 'the House of St Mary is now a basilica', rather than 'a basilica has been built over the House of St Mary.'

This early church was visited by numerous pilgrims, but the structure was modest. It did not attract as many visitors as the great holy places of Jerusalem. It was located in a Jewish town, and visitors may have had to encamp in the actual church or go on to Diocaesarea for lodgings. The main road from Ptolemais to Tiberias bypassed Nazareth seven kilometres to the north, so that Nazareth was a detour (cf. Epiphanius Mon., *Hag.* x. 1. 3–19). Egeria came to Nazareth from the south, from Neapolis, but later Samaritans were hostile to Christian pilgrims, and travellers such as Epiphanius the Monk avoided it.[189]

The church called the House of Mary was demolished in order that a basilica could be constructed. From the archaeological evidence, it would appear that this probably took place at the very end of the fifth century or the beginning of the sixth. The early church may have been damaged by an earthquake[190] or else there may have been an increase in pilgrim traffic which warranted a larger structure. There is no evidence that the basilica was structurally damaged by the people of Nazareth, even if they did fight against Heraclius.[191] One of the two big churches in Nazareth seen by Arculf is clearly the basilica (Adomnan, *De Loc. Sanct.* ii.

---

[189] Wilkinson (1977), 25 n. 73. According to the Piacenza Pilgrim (*Itin.* viii), the Samaritans burned away the footprints of Christian pilgrims with straw, detested Christians touching anything they did not buy (for it rendered the object unclean), considered them to be contaminated so that even money from Christians had to be dipped in water before they would touch it, and cursed Christians when they arrived. This generally created an unwelcoming atmosphere that would have put pilgrims off entering the region.

[190] Taylor (1987*b*), 147. There was a significant earthquake on 22 August 502 and another on 9 July 551. The latter caused a great deal of destruction in Palestine, see Russell (1985), 43–6. There were no known significant earthquakes in the mid- to late 5th cent. that would account for the destruction of the early church in Nazareth.

[191] See Avi-Yonah (1976*b*), 262–6. The Jews of Galilee joined with the Persians as they marched through the area in 614, and helped them take Jerusalem where, after the Persians had given the Jews jurisdiction, they joined the Persians in destroying churches and killing Christians. It would appear that the charge that the Nazareth Jews killed Christians and destroyed churches was born of the fact that they were known as being among those who did these things in Jerusalem. The archaeological and literary evidence shows that while the Jews may well have looted the basilica in Nazareth, they left it standing. There is no evidence of burning, and the mosaics are intact.

26. 1–5). Forty years later, Willibald found this church alone. It was under the jurisdiction of the Muslim authorities who had wanted to demolish it; they demanded from the Christians a ransom to ensure its preservation (Hugeburc, *Vita Will.* xiii). The *Commemoratorium* (xli) mentions twelve monks in Nazareth. The anonymous *Life of Constantine* (ix) from the ninth century[192] refers to the sanctuary of the Theotokos, so we can assume that the basilica was still standing. It may have been in a state of some disrepair by this time; a situation which was not helped by Muslim attacks. Saewulf (*Itin.* xxvii) says that Nazareth was in ruins, apart from the 'very famous monastery'.

The basilica, then, survived six centuries, while the earlier church probably stood less than two. Given the remains and the dating, it is very likely that the early church, the 'House of Mary', was constructed by the convert Joseph of Tiberias.[193] There is nothing to suggest that the church was a 'synagogue-church' built by Jewish-Christians. No evidence provides any justification for our supposing that Jewish-Christians occupied the town in the second and third centuries or that any site was venerated by Christians. The site of the Shrine of the Annunciation, once part of a wine-pressing complex, was converted to Christian use, probably to encourage pilgrimage, *c*.335.

---

[192] Wilkinson (1977), 202–4.
[193] So I have long believed, and argued in Taylor (1987*b*). Corbo appears to have reached the same conclusion independently; see Corbo, (1987).

Capernaum

THE site of ancient Capernaum is located on the north side of the Sea of Galilee. The western part of the site is owned by the Franciscans. It is here that there is the famous synagogue, the dating of which has been so fiercely debated, and the remains of a Byzantine octagonal church on the alleged site of the house of St Peter. The eastern part of ancient Capernaum is owned by the Greek Orthodox Church. Excavations here have as yet uncovered less sensational structures.

In this chapter, the focus will be the Franciscan side of the town (Plate 10), particularly the so-called 'House of Peter', and the claims made by the excavators that the octagonal church was built upon a Jewish-Christian house-church. It will also be necessary to consider the limestone synagogue, and what it might tell us about Capernaum in the early Byzantine period.

The 'House of Peter' and the Octagonal Church

Part of a basalt octagonal structure (Plate 11) south of the synagogue ruins was first uncovered by a Franciscan, Wendelin Hinterkeuser, prior to the First World War. In May 1921 excavations continued under the direction of Father Gaudence Orfali. He brought to light the rest of the building and the remains of mosaic pavements with a central motif of a peacock, as well as the walls of more ancient houses.[1] As a result of his excavations, it was determined that the main structure consisted of three concentric octagons, 8, 16.5 and 23 metres wide respectively.

In April 1968 V. C. Corbo and S. Loffreda renewed excavations at the site and proceeded to dig over a large area of the Franciscan property. The excavations continue until this day, although the

---

[1] Orfali (1922), 103–9.

PLATE 10. Capernaum: aerial view of the Franciscan site

region around the octagonal structure is now being enclosed within a large modern church.[2] Corbo identified two strata below the area of the octagonal structure: first, a house-church of the fourth century and, secondly, domestic buildings constructed late in the Hellenistic period which underwent subsequent modifications (see Figure 28). These three levels will be looked at individually in order to check the dating and to examine conclusions that have been drawn concerning the Jewish-Christians.

A fifth-century dating of the octagonal structure[3] seems reasonably sure on the basis of coins from the first two decades of the fifth century found beneath the mosaic pavements[4] and from pottery. It is possible that it should be dated later rather than earlier in this

---

[2] The four volumes discussing the excavation of the octagonal structure are: Corbo (1975); Loffreda (1974*a*); Spijkerman (1975); Testa (1972). A discussion also appears in Corbo (1969). See also more popular publications: Corbo and Loffreda (1969); Bagatti (1970*b*); Loffreda (1974*b*), (1978), (1985*a*).

[3] Corbo (1975), 56.

[4] Ibid. 54.

PLATE 11. Capernaum: the octagonal structure

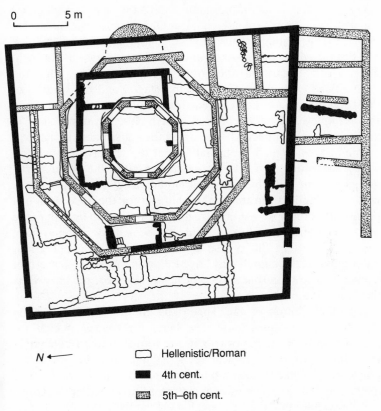

0   5 m

N ←

☐ Hellenistic/Roman

■ 4th cent.

▒ 5th–6th cent.

Fig. 28. Capernaum: plan of the octagonal structure and previous walls

century.[5] As Gideon Foerster points out, the structure is very similar in plan to the Church of the Theotokos on Mount Gerizim built by the emperor Zeno after the Samaritan revolt of 484.[6] The Church of the Theotokos was a larger and far more impressive construction, and it would seem that the builder of the little

---

[5] Foerster (1971a: 210) prefers a date in the early 6th cent. Strange (1977: 68), on the other hand, considers it to have been begun in the late 4th cent. and finished in the 5th, but he considers the date of the coins to be the date of the demolition and rebuilding, and this may be incorrect. The coins give only the earliest possible dates, not *the* dates *per se*, and other factors must be brought to bear upon the matter to establish a correct dating.

[6] Cf. Procopius of Caesarea, *Aedif.* v. 7. For the structure itself, see Schneider (1951); Ovadiah (1970), 140–2, Fig. 143; Magen (1990a).

octagonal church at Capernaum borrowed the architectural concept from Zeno's splendid edifice. Of course, the architects for both churches could have used the same model. An octagonal plan had been used for a Christian building already in 326, in Antioch, when work began on the great Golden Church.[7] But the similarities between the Capernaum octagon and the Church of the Theotokos, with their concentric octagons, are significant, and the example of Zeno's octagonal church close by may well have influenced the architect who designed the Capernaum structure.

The apse and small baptismal font at the Capernaum octagon were, according to Corbo, constructed after the main part,[8] because a lime floor between the middle octagon and the eastern wall was found to run under the platform for the apse. It is just possible that the apse was constructed not very much later than the rest of the building: mistakes could have been made and may have been corrected in the course of the same building operation. Alternatively, the church may have followed the Syrian pattern of having a square internal apse, which was changed, perhaps when the peacock mosaic was laid.

Like the Church of the Theotokos on Mount Gerizim, the church in Capernaum may have been constructed mainly for pilgrims.[9] The focus for prayer in the former was a fragment of rock taken from 'Holy Calvary'.[10] What was the focus for prayer in the octagonal church of Capernaum is unknown, but it is interesting that Egeria mentions, in regard to an earlier structure, that it was here that the Lord healed the paralytic (Mark 2: 1–12); some relic of this event may therefore have been displayed.

The only pilgrim to mention a church in Capernaum which just might correspond to the octagonal structure calls it, somewhat strangely, a 'basilica' (Piacenza Pilgrim, *Itin* vii), but of course it was nothing like a basilica, which was typically rectangular, not octagonal. This sixth-century pilgrim does say it was where the House of Peter used to be located, which corresponds with Egeria's testimony to the existence of such a place almost 200

---

[7] Downey (1961), 342–6. The octagonal model was used for many centuries, two of the most famous examples being SS Sergius and Bacchus, Istanbul, and S. Vitale, Ravenna; both date from the 6th cent.

[8] (1975), Figs. 2, 3, photo 13, Pl. VI:A; (1969), 11–12, 25–7.

[9] Strange (1977), 67.

[10] Cf. *SEG* 8:134, ΛΙΘΟϹ ΕΚ ΤΟΥ ΑΓΙΟΥ ΚΡΑΝΙΟΥ.

years earlier (for which, see below). Later sources, however, do
not confirm the existence of a House of Peter. They speak rather of a
'house of Saint John the Theologian' (Epiphanius Mon., *Hag.* x.1;
S. Hel. et Const. Vit. vii), or 'a house and a great wall . . . where
Zebedee used to live, and his sons John and James' (Hugeburc,
Vita Will. xiv). Gold tesserae found in the Greek Orthodox
excavations may derive from this structure. This would mean that
there was some kind of basilical church in the eastern side of the
town by the time the relevant part of Epiphanius the Monk's
account was written,[11] probably between the eighth and ninth
centuries. There is a possibility that the Piacenza Pilgrim was
misinformed, and was shown a new basilical church that, perhaps,
became known as the 'House of John' (theologian or apostle). If
this is so, then the octagonal church may have been in ruins by 570,
when the pilgrim wrote. However, a 'basilica' to the pilgrim was a
loose term, as we have just seen in regard to the pilgrim's
comments about Nazareth (*Itin.* v); the House of Mary was not a
regular basilica either, though somewhat more like one than the
Capernaum octagon.

At the second level, the remains of the so-called house-church,
the archaeological evidence has permitted a reconstruction of an
area bordered by an enclosure wall measuring 27 metres on the
north, west, and south sides, and 30 metres in the east (Figure 28).
The enclosed area was entered by a door on the south side, near
the corner with the west wall. Another wall ran from this entrance
for 16 metres northwards, 6 metres distant from the west wall.
Another door was situated opposite the first in the north wall. It is
difficult to know how many of the domestic buildings of the area
were preserved as part of the fourth-century complex within the
enclosure wall, but there was a central structure which appears to
have been utilized as a Christian church. The rooms of a previous
dwelling were made into a large room measuring 5.8 by 6.4 metres
This was provided with an arch which subdivided the space into an
eastern and western part. Three other rooms were included in the
central complex, which in total measured approximately 10 by
11 metres. Certain walls were rebuilt. A roof of strong mortar
replaced a previous roof of branches, earth, and straw. The walls
were plastered and painted with vegetal and geometric motifs, and

---

[11] This is an addition to the original; see Wilkinson (1977), 120, 200–1.

upon the plaster Christian pilgrims scratched their characteristic graffiti (see, for examples, Plates 12 and 13). Additional rooms were constructed to the east and to the north.[12]

At the very outset, it is important to note that the employment of the term 'house-church' for the fourth-century structure may be misleading. A house-church is generally thought to be an owner-occupied home in which a room or rooms have been converted for Christian assemblies. A house-church served as a meeting place for an established Christian community.[13] From the very beginning, Christians assembled in private houses (Acts 1: 13; 2: 46; 9: 37; 20: 9; 1 Cor. 16: 19; Col. 4: 15; Philemon 2; Ps.-Clem., *Rec*. x. 71). At Dura Europos, however, the entire house seems to have been made over for Christian use, incorporating an impressive baptistery and a bema for the cathedra.[14] The same is true for the house-church of Kirk-Bizzeh in Syria (*c*.300–30); it was almost entirely converted,[15] with an eastern sanctuary and a horseshoe-shaped ambo with cathedra. The private owners had in both cases given over the house to the community. The presence of architectural features which reflect the employment of the buildings for active Christian ritual and practice (baptistery, ambo, cathedra) shows that these buildings were used by active Christian communities. By contrast, the house-church at Capernaum seems bare and artificial. There are no vestiges of anything that might have been employed in the course of Christian instruction, initiation, or worship. The language of the graffiti, mainly Greek, demonstrates that it was a place visited by those from afar, rather than a meeting place for local Aramaic-speaking Christians (see below for a discussion of the alleged Aramaic graffiti). Instead of being employed within the church area, much of the large space bordered by the enclosure wall was left open. The reason for this was surely to accommodate the horses and donkeys of travellers, and indeed the travellers themselves. The structure in Capernaum is formed out of the component parts of previous dwellings, but calling it a 'house-church' may predispose us to assume too much. The presence of a church does not necessarily imply the presence of a Christian community *in situ* which actively used it for worship and

---

[12] See Corbo (1975), 59–74.   [13] See Davies (1968), 5–8.
[14] Rostovtsev (1938), 129–34; Welles (1967), 108–11.
[15] Davies (1968), 8.

PLATE 12.
Capernaum: example
of Syriac graffiti
incised in the plaster
walls of the House of
Peter

PLATE 13.
Capernaum: example
of Greek graffiti
incised in the plaster
walls of the House of
Peter

instruction. There may have been only a few Christian guardians of the site, and numerous visitors.

At this stage it is useful to consider what Egeria reports about the church she saw at Capernaum. She writes that the 'house of the prince of the apostles[16] has been made into a church, with its original walls still standing' (Pet. Diac., *Lib.* V2).[17] This corresponds exactly with the archaeological evidence of the fourth-century 'house-church'. A dwelling used throughout the Roman period had been utilized as the structural foundation for a church. This church, however, was unusual. It had no external apse, though it may have had some kind of relic as a focus for prayer. It was small for a church, even if large for a room. Around it was a spacious courtyard with, perhaps, some of the old buildings still standing to provide shelter for visitors.

What, then, can be made of the suggestions by the excavators that a pre-existing house-church served the Jewish-Christian community of Capernaum, before the fourth-century renovations? As was argued above in Chapter 2, the *minim* in Capernaum mentioned in *Qohelet Rabba* (1. 8) are by no means necessarily Jewish-Christians. The excavators assume that the reference to *minim* is a reference to Jewish-Christians.[18] Corbo's suggestion that Joseph of Tiberias built the fourth-century structure in Capernaum does not alter his identification of the place as fundamentally Jewish-Christian since, according to him, Joseph was himself a Jewish-Christian.[19] A Jew who became an orthodox Christian was not, however, a Jewish-Christian by definition. Joseph was no sectarian. As James Strange notes in his review of the Capernaum publications, Corbo considers it self-evident that Jewish-Christians are the builders of the house-church, without providing any argument for this supposition and without defining what he means by 'Jewish-Christianity'.[20] Corbo and Loffreda appear to be heavily influenced by the hypotheses of Bagatti and Testa and seem to have relied upon them to supply the correct interpretation of the evidence relating to the ethnic and religious

---

[16] This term is probably Peter the Deacon's; Egeria herself would probably have said 'Peter the apostle', so Wilkinson (1981), 194 n. 7.

[17] Trans. by Wilkinson, *Egeria*, p. 194. Paula visited Capernaum but Jerome gives no details as to what was there; cf. Jerome, *Ep.* cviii. 13. 5.

[18] Testa (1972), 98–9, 148, 183; Loffreda (1985a), 29–30; cf. Mancini (1984), 100 f., 127–8; Bagatti (1971c), 21, 128–32.

[19] Corbo (1975), 71–2.

[20] Strange (1977), 68.

characteristics of the population. Neither Loffreda, as an expert on pottery, nor Corbo, an archaeologist, was equipped as an *historian* to interpret the literary data or the graffiti. The interpretation of the graffiti was left to Testa, who applied his hypothesis about Jewish-Christianity in Palestine to their reading at every turn.

A detailed examination of each graffito is not required here, and for the moment it is necessary to complete the examination of the strata in the area of the octagonal church by turning to the remains of the domestic buildings constructed late in the Hellenistic period[21] (Figure 28). The houses of this part of Capernaum were constructed very roughly out of basalt field stones bound with smaller stones and earth.[22] The roofs were, as has been said, built of branches, earth, and straw, and the floors were made of field stones with earth in the interstices.[23] These poor dwellings stand in marked contrast to the buildings excavated in the Greek Orthodox part of the site. There, up against the present dividing wall between the two sectors and partly underneath it, a bathhouse dating from the Roman period marks the dividing line between the area of poor settlements in the western part of town and better housing to the east. In this eastern part, covered water courses provided a fresh supply of water from a spring further inland (now dry and as yet unlocated); a paved street running north–south contrasts with the rather irregular dirt roads in the western part of the town; a public-building complex is constructed with fine masonry. Houses are well built and have lime floors.[24]

The poorly constructed settlement to the west stretches all over the excavated part of the Franciscan side in a total of eight known housing compounds or *insulae*, as the excavators call them. The compound in which the octagonal church came to be built is known as '*insula* 1' or the '*insula sacra*' by the excavators.[25]

It is clear from the remains that the lower classes lived in the west and the more affluent in the east. As such, the archaeological evidence adds weight to the suggestion that it was in the western

---

[21] Corbo (1975), 75–106.   [22] Ibid. 76; (1969), 37.   [23] Ibid. 39.

[24] This area of Capernaum was excavated by Vasilios Tzaferis, along with Michal Peleg, Joseph Blenkinsopp, James Russell, John Laughlan, and George Knight. I am grateful to them for permitting me to participate briefly in the 1986 excavation in Capernaum and for discussing the site with me. See also Tzaferis *et al.* (1989); Tzaferis, Meidonis, and Kessin (1979); Tzaferis (1983*b*).

[25] See Loffreda (1985*a*), 8–9.

part of town that Simon Peter's house was actually located. It should, however, be noted that the two fish-hooks found in the excavations were located in the destruction level of the fourth-century structure, and not in the floor of the earliest domestic building.[26] They may then have been placed in the room by pilgrims wishing to recall the activity of Peter. The presence of agricultural equipment such as grinding-stones for wheat, stone bowls and craters, presses, and handmills in this quarter all show that the people here engaged in agricultural activity, and some may have been tenant farmers. This is precisely the area in which we would expect Jesus to have lived and worked, and it is here we would also expect his first group of disciples to have met together. Would they, all the same, have left any traces?

Corbo believes so. What was left, according to him, was a series of beaten lime floors in room 1, dating back to the first century. No other lime floors were discovered in any other part of the poor western sector of Capernaum; he therefore believes that the floors have a special significance. The fact that it was this room that was made into a central feature of the fourth-century house-church, and later formed the centre of the octagonal church, convinced Corbo that Jewish-Christians met in this room and somehow venerated it. In short, the fact that there was a series of beaten lime floors in the so-called *sala venerata* (room 1) was considered proof that this was indeed Peter's house.[27]

The stratigraphy of room 1 is discussed in detail by Corbo,[28] but despite the claims made, the evidence is not chronologically conclusive for the lime floors. Four trenches were sunk in the northern part of room 1 to explore the area under the mosaic pavement; from the west: trenches *d*, *a*, *b*, and *c* (see Figure 29). Summarizing the results, from the mosaic pavement to the virgin soil, the levels were as follows (Figure 30): (1) the mosaic pavement of the octagonal church; (2) a fill of red earth; (2a) the destruction level of the 'house-church', which included the fragments of painted plaster from the walls; (3) a polychrome floor of beaten lime; (A1) remains of another pavement with fragments of plaster painted red on a bed of stones; (A2) a bed of large stones. From this point onwards, the strata are not consistent over

---

[26] Cf. Corbo (1975), 97; Loffreda (1974a), 114.

[27] Corbo (1975), 97–8.

[28] Ibid. 79–98; cf. Loffreda (1974a), 113–7.

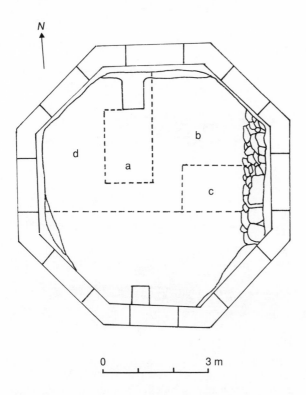

N

0   3 m

FIG. 29. Capernaum: inner octagon with excavation areas

the excavated region. There is a difference between what was found in the western third of the excavated space and the eastern two-thirds, suggesting that there was a dividing line, perhaps a wall, between these two areas which was removed in later rebuilding. In the western trench *d*, beds of basalt stones (B and C) with associated floors of beaten earth follow in close succession to the initial level of fill. Trench *a* has the same series of basalt beds in the west, but B does not continue underneath the fourth-century northern pilaster.[29] In the east of trench *a* there was a stratum of dark brown earth, under level A2. This stratum of earth is found on the eastern two-thirds of the space, appearing also in

[29] Corbo (1975), 80.

Section N – S

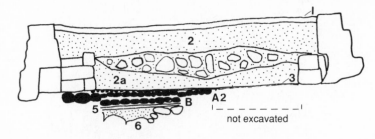

Section W – E

FIG. 30. Capernaum: sections of inner octagon excavation

trenches *b* and *c*. Under it, in trenches *b* and *c* is a stratum of very black earth and then three successive beaten lime pavements (4), each on a thin bed of black earth, followed by a bed of basalt stones corresponding to B, which does not continue toward the north. Adjacent to the east side of the northern fourth-century pilaster, excavation below the level of B uncovered four floors of black beaten earth (5) before striking the initial level of fill (6). In trench *c* there was only fill below the floors of beaten lime.

From this it can be seen that the region of three beaten lime pavements is found between the level of the beds of basalt stones B and A2.[30]

---

[30] So Loffreda (1974*a*), 116: 'Fra la massiciata A e la massiciata B compare una serie di pavimenti in battuto di calce.'

In dating the stratigraphy of room 1, it must be remembered that Loffreda's study of the pottery and, more importantly, his dating, forms the basis for a chronology of the strata of the area. If Loffreda's conclusions about the pottery dating are at any time found to be in need of correction, the chronology of the area will have to be revised. We shall begin from the bottom, from the earliest level of fill which formed the foundation for the first pavement of the room. In this level (6), pottery from the second to first centuries BC[31] was discovered. The next level is determined by the bed of basalt stones C in the west and a succession of beaten earth pavements in the east, close to the north pilaster. On the former, was a Hellenistic lamp and fragments of pottery dating from the first century BC, as well as Herodian lamps and other pieces[32] which bring the occupation period of this level to the first century AD and possibly to the first part of the second; in the case of the latter, the beaten earth pavements, fragments of pottery used from the first century BC to the middle of the second century AD[33] provide evidence of the same general chronology. On the bed of large stones B, there was pottery dated by Loffreda to a range between the first and third centuries. Given also what lies below it, this probably means that bed B was laid in the middle of the first century or at the beginning of the second and continued to be used as the western floor until at least the third century. Then comes the succession of lime pavements but, curiously, embedded into them were very minute fragments of lamps identified by Loffreda as being Herodian.[34] These lime pavements are followed by bed A2. On the bed of small stones (A1) and pavement was a coin of Constans II (341–6), clearly carried to the place by a Western pilgrim,[35] and another of the 'Late Roman' type,[36] along with pottery dating in a range between the late fourth and early fifth century.[37] There was no occupation level on the polychrome pavement (3), but in the destruction level above it was pottery mainly dating to the fifth century, as well as a coin from the time of

---

[31] Corbo (1975), 80.
[32] See Loffreda (1974a), 117.
[33] Corbo (1975), 97.
[34] (1974a), 116; (1985a), 57. No description or drawings are offered by either Corbo or Loffreda. Two Herodian lamps found between basalt blocks in the eastern wall do not provide any means of dating the floor.
[35] Spijkerman (1975), 26, no. 142.
[36] Ibid. 59, no. 552.   [37] Loffreda (1974a), 114.

Valentinian II (364–75), another of 346–61 and a third of the late fourth century.[38]

Of course, it should be remembered that the presence of a coin of a particular date does not date the pavement to the actual years of the coin's issue. While a coin may come from the reign of Constans II, this does not determine the date of the floor, since we do not know how long coins were in circulation. It is possible to conclude that the coin of Constans II on the pavement A1 means that the polychrome pavement (3) must have been constructed after the date of the first appearance of this coin in the Western Empire, in order to account for it being sandwiched below, but the polychrome pavement could have been constructed fifty or even a hundred years after the date of the coin's issue, if the coin was in circulation for that long. Likewise, the pavement below may have been built at any time before the date of the coin's issue but it could also have been built at any time before the coin went out of circulation.

Much the same goes for pottery. The Herodian lamps found on the bed of stones C and under bed B are therefore much more significant for dating than the tiny fragments of Herodian lamps (if properly identified) found in the lime mixture of the successive pavements (4). The latter could have been embedded in the mix if it was made in a refuse dump outside the city (a probable place for lime-burning), but the lamps sealed under the bed of stones B mean that B must have been laid either during or after the Herodian period, to account for their being sealed below. The identification by Corbo of the lime floors coming from a Jewish-Christian veneration of the domestic building of the first century AD[39] on the basis of the minute lamp fragments[40] seems therefore highly contentious.

In summary, it seems quite clear that the western floor C and the succession of beaten earth floors (5) were constructed in the first century BC on fill. The floor was re-laid on a fresh bed of stones (B) at the end of the first century AD, or the beginning of the second. The use of this continued at least as late as the third century until, at some point, the room was expanded, and beaten lime floors (4) were laid, culminating in a final bed of stones (A2). On this a pavement on a bed of small stones (A1) was laid in the mid- to late

[38] Spijkerman (1975), 13, 15, nos. 3, 4, 18.
[39] (1975), 98.   [40] Corbo (1969), 40.

fourth century, or even early fifth, over which was laid a polychrome pavement in the fifth century. It is unclear when precisely the intermediate beaten lime floors were laid; they may have been put down as late as the middle of the fourth century, or as early as the beginning of the third. There is insufficient evidence to be conclusive. They did not, however, come from the *first* century. It should be noted that in Corbo's Tavola III (cf. Figure 30), the north–south section of room 1 and its adjoining rooms has the level A2 labelled as lying under the north, fourth-century, pilaster, implying that the pilaster post-dates the laying of the bed A2, and certainly B; but the stones under the pilaster are much larger than those of bed A2 and lie below the level of A2. It seems much more probable that these form part of the foundation for the pilaster.

While it is impossible to conclude that the succession of beaten lime floors (4) on the eastern side of room 1 come from the middle of the fourth century, it is equally impossible to prove that they did *not* derive from this century. The assertion that the plaster of the wall of the room pre-dated the polychrome floor[41] seems only to apply to the final layer of plaster decoration and there were two to three layers before this.[42] For example, the pieces of red plaster on the pavement A1 must derive from a previous plastering of the walls. Corbo assigns A1 to the fourth century also,[43] though what lies below he considers more ancient. If the polychrome floor 3 was laid as late as the mid-fifth century, and A1 at the beginning of that century, then the lime pavements need not be prior to the fourth century. Rooms 2, 4, and 5 also had floors of beaten lime.[44] Certainly, the location of the lime floors on only two-thirds of the room could suggest that they pre-date the time of the renovation, which created a larger space supported by an arch. On the other hand, they may also indicate that the eastern part of the room was the more important, and that the builder intended to preserve the memory of the extent of the previous room; the arches themselves divided the space into an eastern and western sector. Given the known plan of the 'house-church', pilgrims may have entered the room somewhere on the west and perhaps stood only on the part that was not laid with beaten lime. The clergy, who probably occupied the adjoining rooms (2 and 4) would have been able to

[41] Ibid. 61, 66–7. [42] Testa (1972), 40.
[43] Corbo (1975), 98. [44] Corbo (1969), 58–61.

enter the room from a door leading from room 4 and would have been the only ones to walk on the beaten lime floor.[45]

Nevertheless, it seems more likely that too much is made of these lime floors as evidence of veneration by Christians. It may well be worth considering whether, even if the beaten lime floors are to be dated prior to the fourth-century developments, this is really so significant. In the Greek Orthodox side of the town, where lime floors have been uncovered in private homes, their existence is testimony only to the higher standard of living in that quarter. In the complete absence of other significant finds, the very most that could be concluded from the presence of third-century lime pavements is that the family who occupied this house were slightly more wealthy than the rest. This is the explanation that seems most convincing. At any rate, there are no grounds for Corbo's view that the lime floors are evidence of Jewish-Christian veneration of the building from the first century onwards.

The Graffiti of the 'Domus-Ecclesia'

Despite the extensive discussion of the graffiti by Testa, it is not necessary for each piece to be examined here. Testa considers the graffiti to be largely the work of pilgrims, but somehow considers the pilgrims themselves to be 'Jewish-Christians'.[46] The graffiti found on the plaster of the walls of the '*domus-ecclesia*' are mainly written in Greek (151 examples), with thirteen Syriac examples, and possibly two in Latin.[47] There are ten alleged Aramaic graffiti that may be used uncritically to confirm that writers of a Jewish Palestinian Aramaic (*viz.* Jews) visited the Christian shrine (*ergo*: they were Jewish-Christians), and therefore these will be examined here. Unfortunately, while there are photographs of some of the graffiti fragments, and while some are on display in the museum of

---

[45] Corbo (1969: 57) identifies room 2 as an atrium, but without reason.

[46] Testa (1972: 183) writes: 'Già prendendoli in blocco, i graffiti ci testimoniano la presenza di fedeli di lingua greca . . ., di lingua aramaica, di lingua estrangela e di lingua latina. La miaggior parte costoro devono esser stati pellegrini, arrivati sia dal famoso "quadrilatero" difeso dai Minim (Seforis . . ., Nazaret . . ., Tiberias . . .) sia da regioni piu lontane.' However, 'Tuttavia, pensiamo che la maggior parte fossero giudeo-cristiani, o viventi sotto l'influsso religioso di costoro.' Therefore, according to Testa, there was some kind of Jewish-Christian pilgrimage movement.

[47] Ibid.

the Studium Biblicum Franciscanum to be checked, some are presented only as figures drawn by Testa from the originals and, since every drawing of this nature may incorporate unconscious interpretations, these must remain a little doubtful. For my own drawings of the graffiti, see Figure 31.

1.[48] Testa identified an Aramaic *lamed* on top and a *gimel* underneath. The *lamed* may just as easily be Nabataean.[49] This may mean that the shrine was visited by a converted Nabataean, but it would be rash to conclude anything on the basis of such a scratch. The lines interpreted by Testa as a *gimel* recall the cryptogram found in the Bethany cave.

2.[50] Identified by Testa as Aramaic *qoph*, this letter is as likely to be the remains of a Greek letter *rho*.

3.[51] The letters are read by Testa as *shin*, *zayin*, and *yod*. However, the letters can more easily be read as the remains of a Greek *psi* followed by *omega*.

4.[52] The letters on this piece are identified by Testa as *ayin*, *zayin*, and final *mem*. They would seem to be more probably Greek: *omicron*, *iota*, and *chi*. It seems likely, moreover, that the letters should be read the other way up to Testa's reading, given the slip of the diagonal of the *chi*, so that the sequence would read *XIO* (as shown in Figure 31.4). The square form of the *omicron* was easier to scratch than a round form, and is found at Nazareth, as Testa himself has recorded,[53] as well as elsewhere in Capernaum.[54]

5.[55] Testa sees *qoph* followed by *mem*. The shape with bifid arms may be part of the same cryptogram found in the first example. The letter above could be part of an Estrangela *semkat*. This letter transliterated the Greek *sigma* in names ending in *-os* borrowed from Greek by Syriac speakers.

6.[56] This fragment has been split into two and is extremely unclear. Testa reads *tsade*, *pe*, *resh*, *yod*, and *tet*. Turning the piece upside down, one may just distinguish the Greek letters *ΛΘΕΤΟ* (as shown in Figure 31.6), though many scratches mark the piece

[48] Ibid. 93, no.95; cf. pl. XXIII.
[49] See Diringer (1968), ii. Fig. 15: 21.
[50] Testa (1972), 93, no. 96, pl. XXIII.
[51] Ibid. 93, no. 97, pl. XXIII.
[52] Ibid. 94, no. 98, pl. XXIII, Fig. 12.   [53] Ibid. pl. XXII.
[54] See Testa's no. 117, which reads *BOHΘHO* or *BOHΘHC*. Testa reads *POHΘHO(C)* (1972: 161, pl. XXXII, Fig. 16).
[55] Ibid. 95, no. 99, pl. XXIII.   [56] Ibid. 96–7, no. 100, pl. XXIII.

Fig. 31. Capernaum: graffiti on the plastered walls of the House of Peter

and it is difficult to see which are significant. At any rate, there seems no good reason to see the graffito as being written in Aramaic rather than Greek.

7.[57] This is clearly Greek read by Testa the wrong way up. The first line reads: *HIE* and the second: *ΛΝΚΑ*. Testa's drawing of the piece is inaccurate, and his reading of *shin*, *ḥet*, *he*, *qoph*, and *yod* cannot be sustained.

8.[58] Again, this appears to be upside-down Greek. The letters are *OϹ I*, but the *iota* has met with a long random scratch above it. Testa read *semkat*, *kaph*, and *nun*.

9.[59] This is very indistinct, but even without inverting the piece, the letters appear to be Greek. On the top line a *tau* or *iota* is followed by *omega* and *chi*. On the bottom line there is probably an *epsilon* followed by a *delta*. Testa saw Aramaic *gimel*, *shin*, *he* followed by *aleph*, *mem*, *shin*, and *kaph*.

10.[60] On this piece, Testa distinguished three lines of Aramaic letters: (1) *ybm yhp*, (2) *by*, (3) *ywḥšw yyʿp bšw*. However, the graffito is exceedingly unclear, and it may be possible to read it as a number of different scripts, especially if random scratches are read as being intentional. Greek seems the most likely, since on the bottom line there appear to be *mu*, *omega*, *psi* (made into an Aramaic *waw* by Testa), and *upsilon*.

In conclusion, most of the alleged Aramaic graffiti are quite clearly Greek, and among those that are doubtful, it would be presumptuous to suggest that they are Aramaic purely because of their obscurity. It should also be noted that a sherd found under the pavement of the courtyard west of the *sala venerata* was said by Corbo to be inscribed with three lines of 'Hebrew' of a Jewish-Christian cultic nature.[61] He read, 'Purify (the pitcher) of wine, (your) blood, O Yahweh,' from letters understood to be: (1) (. . .)*zq* (*ʾt*. . .), (2) (*yy*)*n dmh* (. . .), (3) *yhy*. But the inscription may be better read as, '(Name) the winemaker; wine which he squeezed. May it be for good', if the letters are understood to be: (1) (. . .) *zq(qʾ)*, (2) (*yy*)*n dsh(t)*, (3) *yhy* (*ltb*), as Strange has pointed out.[62] The letter read by Corbo as *mem* in the second line would

[57] Ibid. 97–9, no. 101, pl. XXIII, Fig. 12.
[58] Ibid. 99–100, no. 102, pl. XXIV, Fig. 12.
[59] Ibid. 100–3, no. 103, pl. XXIV.
[60] Ibid. 104, no. 104, pl. XXIV.
[61] See Corbo (1969), 107–11.   [62] (1977), 69.

certainly seem much more like a *semkat*, and therefore the reading by Strange is preferable.

Joseph of Tiberias

Nothing in the literary sources would require us to imagine that Capernaum was, prior to the fourth century, anything but an entirely Jewish town. In the excavations on both sides of the dividing wall, no artefacts of a pagan or of a definite Christian nature coming from before the fourth century have been discovered. The archaeological remains are therefore consistent with the notion that the town was Jewish. Epiphanius includes Capernaum in his list of Jewish strongholds in which Joseph of Tiberias wished to construct churches (*Pan.* xxx. 11. 10).

It seems very likely that Joseph constructed the 'house-church' in Capernaum. Not only does the date of this structure parallel the date of Joseph's building programme (*c.*330–7), but the building materials themselves provide added confirmation. This structure was built with a lime pavement, the walls were covered with lime plaster, lime mortar was used to bond the basalt blocks of the new walls, and the same lime mortar was employed in the roof.[63] If there is one thing we know from Epiphanius about Joseph's building technique it is that he employed a great deal of lime. Epiphanius tells the story that outside Tiberias Joseph constructed about seven kilns for burning lime. The Jews put a spell on the kilns so that they would not burn properly, thereby halting his work. Joseph rushed to the kilns with a pitcher of water, on which he traced the sign of the cross, and invoked Jesus' name to cause the water to counteract the sorcery. After this, he sprinkled the water on the kilns and the fire blazed up (*Pan.* xxx. 12. 4–8). Lime was clearly essential for his building.

Furthermore, the very idea of building not just a church pure and simple but a 'House of Peter' may have been Joseph's. We have already seen how the early church at Nazareth was probably called the 'House of Mary'. The language used by the Piacenza Pilgrim in regard to the church in Capernaum is very like that used to describe the changes at Nazareth: 'Also we came to Capernaum, and went into the house of Blessed Peter, which is now a basilica'

---

[63] See Corbo (1969), 58–9.

(*Itin*. v). Even if the reference is to the wrong building (the later basilica and not the octagon), the pilgrim gives us the name of the octagonal church.

One might ask: if Joseph called the churches he built at Nazareth and Capernaum the 'houses' of Mary and Peter respectively, did he also call the other churches he constructed, at Sepphoris and Tiberias, 'houses' and, if so, why? Interestingly, Egeria reports that at Tiberias there was a church on the site of the house of James and John (Pet. Diac., *Lib*. V2). She does not say it was the actual house, but 'on the spot where once stood the house of the apostles James and John'. This would therefore not contradict Epiphanius' account that Joseph built his church in Tiberias in a corner of the old Hadrianeum (*Pan*. xxx. 12. 1–2); the presence of a pagan temple did nothing to dissuade Christians from believing a Christian site lay buried beneath it, and, after the examples of Mamre, Bethlehem, and Golgotha, may even have encouraged the belief. As in so many instances of early Byzantine churches, the reference by Egeria is the only one we have for this 'house'. Pilgrims certainly visited Tiberias during the Byzantine period (Theodosius, *De Situ* ii; Piacenza Pilgrim, *Itin*. vii; Adomnan, *De Loc. Sit*. 25. 1), but none mentions what church there was at which to pray. Hugeburc writes that there were a large number of synagogues and churches at Tiberias (*Vita Will*. xv), but does not describe them.

Even more discouraging, in Sepphoris/Diocaesarea there is no specific reference in the literature to a 'house' of any kind, only to the relics of the flagon and bread-basket of Mary (Piacenza Pilgrim, *Itin*. iv). However, in Theodosius' account (*De Situ* iv) he mentions that Simon Magus came from Diocaesarea. This may not at first seem significant, but it is in fact quite curious. It is a well-attested tradition in patristic literature that Simon Magus came from Geth or Gitta in Samaria (Justin, *Apol*. xxvi. 6; Eusebius, *Hist. Eccles*. iii. 26. 3). Theodosius' belief, as a pilgrim, could very well have derived from the fact that he saw a 'House of Simon Magus' in Sepphoris. If there was such a place, it would have been perfectly in keeping with the interests of Joseph that he should have constructed a 'house' of the arch-magician (cf. Acts 8: 9–24); Joseph was interested in magic and a practitioner of its (pseudo-) Christian version (see the 'lime-kiln' story above, and *Pan*. xxx. 7. 1–8, 10; 10. 3–8). Later on in Sepphoris there was a church associated with a monastery,[64] but small, quirky, plastered churches covered in pilgrim graffiti have yet to be found in Sepphoris or Tiberias. If ever they are found in these two places, there would be quite good grounds for assigning them to the initiative of Joseph.

Had Joseph chosen to deem his churches to be commemorative of the houses of famous New Testament personages, it would explain too why Joseph was successful in building these shrines. The names would indicate the purpose: he built the churches as pilgrimage centres, 'tourist attractions', although he hoped that the visitors would effect some conversions among the Jewish populations. In calling a church the 'House of Mary' in Nazareth, he must have known that pilgrims would be attracted to the shrine. Furthermore, he would have succeeded in building the churches not simply because he had Constantine's blessing, but because the churches did not seriously threaten the existing Jewish community (despite Joseph's hidden agenda) and, moreover, could be seen as encouraging the influx of wealth. There must have been some reason why the Jewish communities in which he built the churches failed to muster any significant opposition. An economic reason could provide the key.

It is at this stage that the question of the magnificent white limestone synagogue of Capernaum, which stands barely 30 metres away from the 'House of Peter' and towers over it, must be considered.

The Question of the Synagogue[65]

The synagogue ruins of Capernaum were first surveyed by E. Robinson in 1857 and partly uncovered by C. Wilson in 1866.[66] After the site became the property of the Franciscans in 1894, Kohl and Watzinger cleared more of the structure[67] and Orfali continued this work.[68] With Corbo and Loffreda in 1969, modern excavations began and are continuing.

---

[64] Ovadiah (1970), 181–2.

[65] For a good discussion of the architecture see Chiat (1982), 89–97; Shanks (1979), 56–77; Sukenik (1934), 7–21, 52–3.

[66] Wilson (1869).

[67] Kohl and Watzinger (1919), 14–21.   [68] Orfali (1970), 21–101.

The synagogue consists of four elements: a prayer hall (23 x 17.28 m.), a courtyard to the east (23 x 10.8–12.6 m.), a southern porch, and a side-room near the north-west corner of the prayer hall. The façade faces south, towards Jerusalem.

The dating of the synagogue has been a source of some controversy. Corbo and Loffreda have held that the Capernaum synagogue should be dated to the fifth century, with the building begun in the late fourth century and finished in the mid-fifth.[69] The eastern courtyard has been shown to come from the late fifth century on the basis of fifth-century pottery and coins dated up to the reign of Leo I (*c*.474) found below its pavement.[70] Israeli archaeologists supported an earlier dating, based on the proposal by Kohl and Watzinger, who suggested that the white synagogue was built *c*.200 and destroyed in the fourth century.[71] B. Meistermann[72] and Orfali[73] attempted to argue that it could be dated to the Herodian period, but no one has recently followed such an early dating. Instead, the Israeli view was that the structure should be placed in the third century, before the triumph of Christianity in the region.[74] Doubts about the integrity of levels excavated under the pavement of the synagogue have been answered by Strange,[75] who notes that the presence of coins and pottery dating from the end of the fourth century and the beginning of the fifth[76] cannot be countered by an argument that this indicates later reconstruction, as the layer of mortar on which the pavement was set was not secondary.[77]

The reasons put forward for an earlier date for the synagogue owe much to stylistic considerations,[78] but the refusal to believe that the white synagogue could have been constructed in the fifth century also owes much to historical preconceptions. How could a synagogue tower over a small Christian building like this? As Michael Avi-Yonah wrote, 'Such a state of affairs might be conceivable in our ecumenical age, but it seems impossible to

---

[69] Corbo, Loffreda, and Spijkerman (1970); Corbo (1970), (1972), (1975), pt. II; Loffreda (1970*a*), (1972), (1973), (1981); Spijkerman (1970).
[70] Loffreda (1979).   [71] (1919), 4–40, 219.
[72] (1921), 163.   [73] (1922), 67.
[74] Sapir and Ne'eman (1967); Foerster (1971*a*), 207–9; (1972), ch. 3; Avi-Yonah (1973); Fischer (1986). One exception to the usual Israeli view is that of Z. U. Maoz (1981*b*), who believes that the synagogue itself was built by Christians.
[75] (1977), 69–71.   [76] Corbo (1975), 121.
[77] Strange (1977), 70.   [78] Cf. Foerster (1971*a*), 208–9.

imagine that it would have been allowed by the Byzantine authorities of the fourth century.'[79] The same concern is echoed by Hershel Shanks: the Byzantine ecclesiastical authorities would not have allowed the synagogue to be more magnificent than the church.[80] This begs the question: how do we know for sure that the Byzantine authorities had absolute power over the Jewish towns of Galilee in the fifth century? In the middle of the fourth century, the programme of Christianization begun by Constantine was interrupted by the reactionary reign of Julian, who supported the Jews. Jews had already revolted against Gallus Caesar in 351,[81] the result of which ensured Jewish national authority in Galilee.[82] Despite the promulgation of anti-Jewish laws,[83] attacks on synagogues, and the eventual destruction of the patriarchate, it would appear that Jews continued to exercise authority over their areas[84] and built synagogues (in Beth Alfa, Hammath Gader, Hammath Tiberias, Husifa, Jericho, Naaran, Maon, Ascalon, Gaza, Azotus, for example).[85] The Byzantine economic situation in Palestine was good[86] and the early fifth century saw something of a boom. Economic circumstances would have been particularly good in areas such as Capernaum in which there was a constant stream of Christian pilgrims bringing in valuable revenue. One might, then, suggest that this combination of material prosperity and threat from the Christian legislation may have been a prime reason why the Jews of Capernaum built one of the most beautiful synagogues in Palestine. It should not cause scepticism that they embarked on a project to make their synagogue far outshine[87] the Christian structure (at this stage only the little '*domus-ecclesia*').

Already, Christians had expressed interest in visiting the synagogue that existed prior to the white synagogue's construction, because of its connection with Jesus' ministry (cf. Mark 1: 23). Egeria wrote that in Capernaum, 'There is also the synagogue where the Lord cured a man possessed by the devil. The way in is up many stairs, and it is made of dressed stone' (Pet. Diac., *Lib.* V2). This earlier, black basalt synagogue probably occupied the same

---

[79] (1973), 45.
[80] (1979), 72.   [81] See Avi-Yonah (1976*b*), 176–81.
[82] Ibid. 181.   [83] Ibid. 208–29.   [84] Ibid. 237–8.
[85] Ibid. 238–9.   [86] Ibid. 221–3, 239–40; id. (1958).
[87] It is literally a case of black and white; the contrast between the imported white limestone of the synagogue and the black basalt of the rest of the town is powerful.

spot, and was constructed during the first century.[88] The new synagogue would have served as a source of pride and esteem in a community now under threat from the Christians, who held authority in the province as a whole. It may well be that the octagonal church was constructed as some recompense, so that the Christians also had a new building.

The contemporaneity of the two buildings is only a problem if we insist that the Christian authorities exercised an effective absolute rule over Capernaum. There is no real evidence to show that they did. The situation may well have been quite the reverse; only this would account for the archaeological evidence. The Jewish authorities of Capernaum permitted the construction of a small Christian pilgrimage site. With the new wealth they received from the influx of Christian tourists, and with a desire to promote Jewish religion and culture in an age in which it was threatened, they undertook, by means of contributions from the community, the construction of an elegant limestone synagogue that would indeed tower over the Christian structure.

Therefore, it is probable that Joseph of Tiberias bought the compound *insula* I sometime before the death of Constantine in 337, when he began building small Christian churches in four Jewish towns, in the hope that he could make converts by encouraging Christian pilgrims to visit certain places. He managed to convince the Jewish authorities that his proposition would be little threat, perhaps even that it would be politic given the religious persuasion of the emperor Constantine and his sons, and that it would provide extra income for the town. The old dwellings of the compound were renovated to accommodate Christian visitors and to provide a focus for prayer, even though it would have been an unusual, small, and unassuming church where perhaps only a few clergy ministered to its upkeep. As with Nazareth, Christians were guided to the Jewish synagogue as well.

From this survey of the archaeological evidence of Capernaum, it seems very unlikely that early Jewish-Christians venerated a room or house that was the genuine site of Simon Peter's dwelling. If there was some memory of the site of the actual house, then it may have been part of the folk traditions of the town rather than

[88] Loffreda (1985*a*), 43–9; Corbo (1982).

because an active group of Jewish-Christians lived there. Certainly, the church known as the House of Peter was located in the right general area of Capernaum, in the part where poorer people lived, and it was clearly in this quarter of the town that Jesus lived and taught. If Jewish-Christians continued to dwell in Capernaum past the first century, they have left no traces. Veneration of the place known as the House of Peter appears to have begun in the fourth century.

The Evolution of Christian
Holy Places

IN Chapter 3, we reviewed the religious demography of Palestine from the end of the Bar Kochba Revolt to the date that Constantine won the East in 324. We saw that pagans, Jews, and Samaritans lived in their own general regions where their own customs could be preserved, though there was some intermixture of populations in the large cities like Caesarea and Gaza. The archaeological and literary evidence would suggest that villages tended to be one thing or another: Jewish, Samaritan, pagan, even Christian. But as yet there is no instance of a rural community in which the religious pluralism of the cities can be ascertained. Christians were clearly a small part of the population and were found predominantly in cities.

Fifty years later, in the middle of the fourth century, the situation was quite different. Aelia Capitolina had been given its ancient name 'Jerusalem'. Splendid Christian basilicas stood in place of pagan temples. Churches were under construction everywhere. Jewish and Samaritan sites were visited by Christians from abroad who prayed at zones they considered to have been sanctified by God. Literally, heaven appeared to have descended to earth. From being a small, clandestine community focused on the life to come, who lived in constant fear of physical torture and death, the Church was now comfortable in its worldly existence. It was confident, propertied, and powerful. It administered sacred zones and relics of saintly bodies to which Christian pilgrims flocked in their thousands to pray.

From our archaeological and historical examination of the important Christian holy places, from Mamre to Capernaum, we have seen that there is no evidence at all that Jewish-Christians, or any other kind of Christians, venerated sites as sacred before the beginning of the fourth century. Restoration language used by the Church Fathers did not mean that a site was venerated prior to its

appropriation by the Church. It is far from the case that second-
and third-century apocryphal stories show evidence of veneration
of certain sites. Rather, these stories played an active part in
influencing the development of Byzantine sites, but are not proof
of sites being venerated prior to Constantine. Christians took over
places such as Mamre, Bethlehem, and 'Golgotha' from the
pagans, although the latter had been close to the place of Jesus'
death and burial. They sanctified caves that had been pagan, but
they sanctified many caves with no previous 'demonic' associations.
Some, such as the Bethany Cave, were created out of nothing
more interesting than a cistern. It is probable that some Christians
thought of the Mount of Olives as being, in some way, a sacred
mountain, in accordance with theologizing which was entirely
indebted to Judaism in its exegesis of the Prophets and its belief in
the abiding glory of God on the Mount; but the idea of any holy
place as being inherently sacred and therefore vouchsafed to
God's elect, the Christians, is not found in the early literature
connected with later holy places.

There had been Christian travellers around Palestine (for
example, Melito of Sardis and Origen), and we shall consider
below whether or not these visitors should be considered 'pilgrims'
as such. Certainly, however, they must have explored Palestine
with a different agenda from the pilgrims proper of the fourth
century onwards, for the development of sites as centres visited
because of their *intrinsic* holiness appears to begin with the
innovations of the emperor Constantine. It is to him that we need
to look now in order to understand the processes at work.

Constantine

If the accounts of Constantine's conversion[1] bear some resemblance
to reality, we can conclude that the primary reason for Constantine's
new belief in the power of the Christian God was that this God
provided him with military victory, in particular victory over his
Western rival Maxentius in the battle for Milvian Bridge, outside
Rome, on 24 October 312. According to Eusebius, Constantine

[1] Alistair Kee (1982: 13–14) has pointed out the inadequacy of this term,
because in many ways Constantine was simply exchanging divine patronage from
the sun-god to the god of the Christians.

saw a vision of a sign of the cross inscribed with the words, 'By this, conquer' (*Vita. Const.* i. 28), and this is precisely what Constantine did. The 'sign' is identified by Lactantius as the 'sign of Christ' (*De Mortibus* 45). Eusebius informs us that Constantine saw it drawn in the sky in light, whereupon 'the Christ of God' appeared with the same sign (*Vita Const.* i. 28–9). Despite the possible contradictions between the two accounts, there can be no real doubt that the sign was, as Eusebius tells us, some form of cross.[2] Constantine then had the Christian symbol incorporated into his standard, the *labarum*, with the *chi-rho* abbreviation used by scribes to mean 'good.'[3] For the emperor, and perhaps others before him, the *chi-rho* also stood for Χριστός, since the letters *chi* and *rho* were the first two letters of the name. The *labarum* became a symbol of the alliance between God and Constantine.[4] It effected a kind of magical power over the battlefield.

Constantine may not have been quite the Christian that modern Christians would have liked. He murdered his son, Crispus, and his wife, Fausta, and he appears not to have felt extreme discomfort in maintaining the ancient pagan rituals of Rome. There is nevertheless a danger in using sophisticated theological and ethical criteria to assess the commitment felt by this emperor towards his God. The commitment itself owed much to pagan devotion to a chosen deity, but there was nothing irresolute about it; the result of this commitment was a radically changed world.

Emperors in the third century had pointed to the existence of Christians as the prime reason for the Empire's pitiful state. As is well known, the Christians had become the scapegoats blamed for the third century's economic instability, civil unrest, war, rebellion, moral decline, and shortages. The logic was simple: the gods despised the Christians, who would not sacrifice, and since worldly harmony could result only when the gods were content with the way in which human beings worshipped them, peace would not be attained until Christians paid homage to the gods in the correct manner; if they refused outright, then it was necessary for them to die in order that the gods, in their indignation, would cease from

[2] Lactantius may have been referring to a sign of a cross with a loop on top, known to have replaced the word *stauros* in Gospel papyri of the third century, but this sign was not the same as the *chi-rho* found on Constantine's military shield. See Lane Fox (1986), 614–17.

[3] Ibid. 616.

[4] Kee (1982), 22.

causing further calamities on earth.[5] Constantine, pondering on this rationale, noted that many of the emperors who had lavished great persecutions upon the Christians had died premature deaths (*Vita Const*. i. 28), meaning that whatever deity was paramount in heaven did not approve of their efforts to eradicate Christianity; it was, therefore, the Christian God who should be worshipped. He promptly decided to side with the very people the Empire had blamed for its troubles for generations. After heralding his new allegiance in the battlefield, Constantine won victory. He was convinced.

While T. D. Barnes considered that Christianity was no 'small and insignificant sect' but 'powerful and respectable long before it acquired an imperial champion',[6] the evidence in support of such an assertion is wanting. As was shown above, the evidence of Christian presence in Palestine does not require us to envisage a very sizeable, widespread, or potent community. Most scholars would disagree with Barnes's supposition. Bury estimated that at the beginning of the fourth century four-fifths of the Empire was pagan, and dubbed Constantine's policy of religious change 'the most audacious act ever committed by an autocrat in disregard of the vast majority of his subjects'.[7] Constantine's religious policy was 'one of history's great surprises', as Robin Lane Fox puts it;[8] he considers that the Christians constituted only four or five per cent of the Empire's population.[9] Even this may be a generous figure. The army, the intelligentsia, the aristocracy, and, most importantly, the innumerable peasants were almost entirely pagan. Christianity was found mainly among the humbler urban free classes, although some Christian villages are also attested in the literature. The Christians lived largely in the big cities of the

[5] See Eusebius, *Hist. Eccles*. ix. 7. 8–9. The rescript of Maximinus (6 April 312) points to the Christians as inciting the wrath of the gods, who then caused crop failures, war, storms at sea, hurricanes, and earthquakes to express their fury. The Latin rescript was sent to many places in substantially the same form, a factor which emphasizes its importance; see Mitchell (1988) on part of the inscription found in the Pisidian city of Colbasa, Turkey.

[6] (1981), 191.

[7] (1899), 366.

[8] (1986), 609, and see 269–73 for evidence showing how Christians were few in number. Christians appear to have been widespread over the Empire and beyond, but thin on the ground.

[9] Ibid. 592.

Empire—Rome, Carthage, Alexandria, Ephesus, and Antioch, for example—and sometimes in smaller towns.[10]

Despite speculations based on the fact that Constantine's sister was named Anastasia, Constantine's faith was neither part of a trend, nor was it born of family preference, as Joseph Vogt has shown.[11] It was a personal decision, the source of which returns to the theology of Milvian Bridge: the Christian God won him battles. The form of prayer he gave to his soldiers aptly sums up the nature of his own beliefs (Eusebius, *Vita Const.* iv. 20):

We acknowledge you, the only God. We own you as our king and implore your aid. By your favour we have gained the victory. Through you we are mightier than our enemies. We give you thanks for your past benefits and trust you for future blessings. Together we pray to you and ask you long to preserve for us, safe and triumphant, the emperor Constantine and his pious sons.

This prayer was said on Sundays by all his troops, even if they were pagan. The language is therefore characteristically obscure, but the theology is not. Constantine believed that by honouring the Christian God, he was both invincible on the battlefield and guaranteed longevity. Christianity would henceforth be the religion of Roman emperors (excepting Julian). Constantine thereby elevated a faith found primarily among the urban lower free class to the status of the Empire's most favoured religion. Truly, the last became first. Even though this Cinderella did not defeat her stepsisters overnight, Constantine's policy toward other religions both illuminates the strength of his own commitment to the Christian God, and points to a primary reason for the establishment of Christian 'holy places'.

The history of the destruction of paganism by Christianity is by no means a simple story.[12] The legislation on this subject is repetitive. Constantine acted to restrict pagan rites (*Cod. Theod.* xvi. 10. 1–6). The suppression of pagan cult sites was gradually

---

[10] R. Browning (1975), 165. For Christian villages and the question of Christian presence in the countryside, see Lane Fox (1986), 287–93; for the social composition of the Church, see ibid. 293–312.

[11] Vogt (1963).

[12] See Boissier (1898); Chastel (1850); Hillgarth, (1986*b*); MacMullen (1984); see also Lane Fox (1986), 609–63; Bury (1899), 365–77; A. H. M. Jones (1964), 938–41.

intensified and edicts were reiterated, though the process was interrupted by the apostate reign of Julian. Eventually, on 14 November 435, the emperors Theodosius II and Valentinian III would interdict 'all persons of criminal pagan mind from the accursed immolation of victims, from damnable sacrifices, and from all other such practices that are prohibited by the authority of the more ancient sanctions' (*Cod. Theod.* xvi. 10. 25). Temples and shrines that, against all odds, had survived were then to be destroyed and cult sites to be purified by the erection of the sign of the 'venerable Christian religion': the cross. The punishment for the infringement of the law was death.[13]

There has been a tendency among scholars to show some surprise that paganism persisted, but at the same time to suggest that the edicts were sound and fury signifying little, as if paganism was, at the beginning of the fourth century, ready to lie down and die without much encouragement. A. H. M. Jones, for example, thinks that the profusion of edicts against the pagans shows that they were laxly enforced,[14] but this does not follow. The proliferation of legislation against paganism indicates rather that paganism was a multiplication of varied and flexible belief systems with stubborn roots that could not be pulled out with one tug. The task facing Constantine and his successors was great. To overturn paganism was, it must have seemed, nearly impossible; practicable only because God would grant the impossible to his faithful servants. As Lane Fox has argued, paganism was still as strong as it had ever been. Personal devotion to one or more gods was customary. The Roman aristocracy, who sustained an ossified religion closely associated with the glorious history of Rome (cf. Symmachus, *Rel.* iii), and who gave their children a sound classical education, did not dictate the essential character of paganism at this time. Nor was this to be found among the urban affluent or the army, who participated in the esoterica of mystery cults. The fundamental basis of the power of paganism was to be found amid the masses: the workers of the land, the lower classes who constituted the bulk of the Empire's population.

Of course, use of the word 'paganism' is not meant to imply that there was a coherent or self-conscious pagan religion as such, but, as G. Fowden puts it, '"Paganism" was just a collection of ethnic

[13] Pharr (1952), 476.   [14] (1964), 938.

polytheisms.'[15] The term was an invention of the Christian apologists who needed some way of grouping together all non-Christian and non-Jewish/Samaritan belief systems into a convenient package. The word 'pagan' was a pejorative term that meant, in substance, 'peasant'; a 'pagan' was an inhabitant of a rural district or *pagus*, and then any country bumpkin.[16] It came to refer to one who, to the Christian mind, thought like a simple peasant, one who believed in the old gods, though educated pagans called themselves, if anything, 'Hellenes', tracing their cultural roots to the glorious past of Greece. The peasants themselves seem not to have used any form of self-reference to categorize their religious devotions, which were based on beliefs which stretched back millennia. The Graeco-Roman pantheon had been in many places an overlay which rested on entrenched local traditions and ancient deities. These traditions and deities were closely connected with agriculture, so that in undermining the religious life of the rural population the Christian authorities had to sweep away the fabric into which the life of the countryside was woven, or else Christianize it. The peasants believed that honouring the agrarian gods ensured good harvests and fertile animals: in short, survival. The sophisticated among the urban populations of the Empire may have been inclined to find the issue of life after death critical. Their swap from the mysteries of Isis or Mithras to the mysteries of the Christian faith cannot have been too traumatic; the goals of salvation and spiritual longevity were more or less the same. For the peasants, however, it was life in this world that was of ultimate concern, and their gods were integrally connected with earthly regeneration, fertility, and bounty. Thus, when the Christians, especially the later monks, began destroying country shrines, Libanius protested that these were 'the soul of the countryside' that gave farm labourers hope (Lib., *Orat.* xxx. 9–10. 19).

It is not, then, at all surprising that paganism persisted, and we do not have to suppose that this was the result of official apathy. In Gaul, numerous pagan sanctuaries continued to be centres of popular religious devotion. Only under the reign of Gratian (367–83) did Martin of Tours succeed in Christianizing the countryside there with any degree of success; the great forest sanctuaries were gradually replaced by Christian churches.[17] In the last decade of

[15] (1988), 179. [16] LS, s.v. *paganus*; Ferguson (1970), 65.
[17] Hillgarth (1986*a*), 54 ff.

the century John Chrysostom urged Christian landowners in Antioch to try to convert their peasants by building churches and appointing priests on their land.[18] Even within important cities paganism continued; Augustine records the destruction of temples in the city of Carthage as late as 399 (*Civ. Dei* xviii. 54). This is far from being an isolated instance. To take Palestinian examples alone, we have a sixth-century reference to polytheists in the city of Caesarea (Procopius of Caesarea, *Secret History* xi. 26); Marinus, the Neoplatonist who succeeded Proclus as the head of the Platonic Academy in Athens, was a Palestinian from Neapolis, which shows that paganism existed there at the end of the fifth century; Gaza and Raphia were well known as pagan strongholds. At the end of the fourth century Gazan pagans were 'discouraged' from their beliefs by means of armed force, torture, mass executions, and the destruction of the temple of Marnas (Marc. Diac., *Vita Porph.* 35–51, 63–75, 99, 103).[19]

The fact that paganism persisted and that legislation at the end of the fourth century would punish those who sacrificed as if they had committed treason (*Cod. Theod.* xvi. 10. 11–12) might serve to cast Constantine in a liberal light. Some scholars have seen Constantine as a perfunctory Christian not completely convinced of his faith. For Jacob Burckhardt, the emperor was essentially areligious, an ambitious politician.[20] To A. Piganiol he was a syncretistic philosophical monotheist.[21] A. H. M. Jones thought him prone to accept the opinions of advisers.[22] More recently, Alistair Kee has argued that Constantine used Christianity as part of a grand strategy, but was not a Christian himself.[23] Indeed, the emperor did retain solar symbolism as part of his personal iconography but, as N. H. Baynes has shown, this is not at all inconsistent with his being a Christian at heart.[24] Constantine accepted the title of Pontifex Maximus, one which was not spurned until Gratian, who withdrew public money from the Senate House,[25] but Gratian acted with the solid support of those in high places. Had Constantine attempted to quash paganism thoroughly and absolutely at the beginning of the fourth century, he would have incited civil war, especially in the West. He was too much the

[18] R. Browning (1975), 160.
[19] See Macmullen (1984), 86–9.
[20] Burckhardt (1880).
[21] Piganiol (1932).
[22] A. H. M. Jones (1949).
[23] Kee (1982).
[24] Baynes (1930).
[25] Bury (1899), 368.

military stategist to ignore this. As it was, he did an extraordinary amount to abolish pagan belief, but he set 'safe' limits. In the West, especially in Italy, where pagan belief appears to have been firmer among those that counted than in the East, he made no serious attempt to introduce the prohibition he had made on sacrifices in the East (Eusebius, *Triac. Or.* vii. 1 ff.). Firmicus Maternus exhorted Constans, Constantine's son, to stop them in 343 (*De Err. Prof. Rel.* xvi. 4; xxviii. 1 ff.). Constans had extended Constantine's prohibition to Italy two years previously (*Cod. Theod.* xvi. 10. 2), but, like his father, he trod a fine line between religious aims and political prudence.

It may be perfectly true that Constantine's faith was not all that it could have been by modern standards, but if he blurred the distinction between Sol/Apollo and Christ at times, whether out of personal conviction or political acumen, it does not appear to have affected his commitment to the Church or to have inhibited his understanding of himself as God's latest apostle. Constantine believed that his particular mission was to make his subjects virtuous,[26] and one could not be virtuous and pagan. After defeating Licinius, Constantine expressed the view that God had searched for him and chosen him to carry out a divine purpose:

I myself, then, was the instrument whose services he chose and esteemed suited for the accomplishment of his will. Accordingly, beginning at the remote Britannic ocean . . . through the aid of divine power I banished and utterly removed every form of evil which prevailed, in the hope that the human race, enlightened through my instrumentality, might be recalled to a due observance of the holy laws of God, and at the same time our most blessed faith might prosper under the guidance of his almighty hand. (Eusebius, *Vita Const.* ii. 28)[27]

He wrote a letter in his own hand on the errors of paganism (*Vita Const.* iv. 8). He believed that he was elected to serve God and bring 'healing' to his pagan subjects (*Vita Const.* ii. 55). The terms he uses to grant pagans freedom of conscience are, as Paul Keresztes has observed, 'grudging';[28] temples are 'shrines of falsehood' and pagans are 'those who delight in error' (*Vita Const.* ii. 56).

[26] Baynes (1930), 9 ff.　　[27] Trans. by McGiffert (1890), 507.
[28] Keresztes (1985).

To understand the extent of Constantine's success in his policy towards religions other than his own, it is more illuminating to concentrate on the positive results of his policies rather than on the fact that paganism managed to survive. It is significant that, by the middle of the fourth century, prior to Julian's reactionary reign, pagan defiance of Christian religious policy required *courage*. Eunapius (*Vita Soph*. 491) reports how a praetorian prefect visited Athens in 358 and 'boldly' sacrificed and made a round of the shrines. This was understood to be both unusual and daring. Pagans who wished to preserve their sacred shrines pretended on occasion to be Christians. A sun-worshipper named Pegasius, for example, became a Christian bishop in order to protect the temple at Ilion. This bishop showed the young Julian the shrine of Hector, the temple of Athena of Troy, and the tomb of Achilles, but did not dare say outright that he was a worshipper of Graeco-Roman deities. Julian was left to note that the bishop failed to cross himself or whistle through his teeth to ward off evil spirits.[29] If a man like Pegasius was forced to take such extreme action to protect sacred sites, to be a dissident afraid of admitting his true belief, only thirty years after Constantine defeated Licinius, it shows that imperial policies toward paganism had been more draconian than lax, at least in the East. This situation could not have come about unless Constantine himself, followed by his sons—especially Constantius II—had enforced his religious policy with some stringency.

We may yet have to recognize to what extent Julian's short reign as Augustus (360–3) revived pagan confidence and impeded the progress of Christianizing measures; the tradition of belittling Julian's successes is a long one. The reign of Valens (364–78) was surprisingly tolerant, which perhaps shows that he felt a need to tread warily after the pagan renaissance. Only under Gratian was the Constantinian religious policy continued and reinforced, certainly in Rome, with greater severity. Had there been no apostate interruption in this policy, Constantine might well have appeared much less the liberal. Constantine struck the Goliath of paganism with a mighty blow, but he did not try, for political and religious reasons, to exterminate it. The probable political reason, that he did not wish to incite rebellion, has already been

---

[29] Julian, *Ep*. lxxviii.

mentioned. Constantine's religious reason was that although paganism was plainly false, pagans had to undertake the 'contest for immortality' voluntarily, not from fear of punishment (*Vita Const*. ii. 55; 57–8, 60). The destruction of pagan shrines was, then, seen by Constantine as *persuasion* rather than coercion.

All the same, it would be naïve to accept Constantine's benign view of his actions without reservation. Eusebius' account does not give us any indications that the emperor's persuasive methods were gentle. Entrances to temples in several cities were left stripped of their doors and exposed to the weather; the tiling of others was removed and roofs destroyed. Bronze statues were paraded contemptuously through public places. Gold and silver statues were confiscated. Emissaries from Constantine went throughout the Empire ordering pagan priests to bring their idols from temples. The statues were stripped of ornaments and exhibited; any precious metals were scraped off, melted down, and taken away by the emissaries (*Vita Const*. iii. 54). Constantine made a special onslaught on the grove and temple of Astarte at Aphaca on Mount Lebanon, destroying the building there with military force (*Vita Const*. iii. 55–6). The temple of Asclepius at Aegae, Cilicia, where thousands flocked continually to be healed, was razed to the ground by Constantine's soldiers.[30] Undoubtedly with Constantine's approval, Christians tortured the prophets of Apollo at Didyma and Antioch, whose oracles had contibuted to their former persecution (*Dem. Evang*. iv. 135c–136a).

The pagans, faced with the ruin and desecration of their temples everywhere, immediately agreed, according to Eusebius, that the worship of idols was pure folly. To what extent 'persuasion' played a role in extracting this admission from a proportion of the pagan population is, however, unknown. The demoralizing effect of the destruction of shrines and sanctuaries upon pagans should not be underestimated. Contrary to their expectations, their gods did not seem to put up much of a struggle against the iconoclasts; spectacular miracles did not occur to deter them. There were no thunderbolts from Zeus to stop the Christians; the gods themselves appeared to surrender unconditionally to one that was mightier. Libanius admits that the destruction of temples in Syria had made converts (*Orat*. xxx. 28). In *The Life of Porphyry* (Marc. Diac.,

---

[30] Eusebius, *Vita Const*. iii. 56.

Vita Porph. 41, Georgian text), the emperor reasons that when the pagans of Gaza saw their temple treated with contempt they would abandon their errors and embrace Christianity. The emissaries of Constantine may well have met with considerable success. Eusebius says that 'every gloomy cave, every hidden recess, afforded the emperor's emissaries easy access: the inaccessible and secret chambers, the innermost shrines of the temples, were trampled by the feet of soldiers' (*Vita Const.* iii. 57). Nevertheless, pagan caves, trees, springs, and hills were everywhere, and it is inconceivable that every cave and every recess was visited by Constantine's men. We know that paganism persisted, and people continued to visit shrines.[31] Pan's caves in Attica drew pilgrims throughout the first part of the fourth century.[32] This practice of pilgrimage was a deeply embedded part of pagan piety, a part which Constantine cannot have failed to notice.

Palestine and Pilgrimage

When Constantine, then emperor of the West, defeated his rival Licinius on 18 September 324, he took over the rule of the East, which included Palestine, and immediately set about a programme of Christianization. Throughout the Empire, the Edict of Milan (313), had already halted the persecution of Christians begun by Diocletian in 303, but positive steps in favour of Christians had not been taken by Licinius in the East. With Constantine, there was a purge of prominent pagans (*Vita Const.* ii. 18). He forbade officials to sacrifice, as was the custom, before official business; in fact, all sacrifice was banned, despite protests and infringements of the law (*Vita Const.* ii. 44–5). Governors and financial officials were to co-operate with bishops in providing funds for churches. No cult statues were to be erected, nor were pagan oracles to be consulted. Treasures were confiscated from pagan temples and shrines, and cult centres were suppressed (Eusebius, *Triac. Or.* viii.1 ff.).[33]

---

[31] Lane Fox (1986), 673. Newly discovered sermons written by Augustine about the persistence of pagan religion in North Africa will no doubt provide further proof of this.

[32] Ibid. 131.

[33] See also Barnes (1981), 210–11; (1985), 130–1.

Constantine began construction in Palestine of four magnificent buildings which would become awe-inspiring pilgrim attractions. These would commemorate four events connected with Christ: his pre-incarnation appearance to Abraham at the terebinth of Mamre, the Nativity at Bethlehem, his death and resurrection on Golgotha, and the Ascension on the Mount of Olives. The latter three were closely connected with the creeds central to the Christian faith.[34] We do not know the order in which these buildings were constructed. Eusebius, in *Vita Constantini*, seems to list them in order of importance: Golgotha, Eleona, Bethlehem, and Mamre. It has been necessary in this study to discuss them in a different order, for the sake of the argument.

Constantine's mother, Helena, took an active role in identifying the 'right places' for the edifices. She chose sites in Bethlehem and on the Mount of Olives, while the emperor's mother-in-law, Eutropia, chose Mamre/Terebinthus as a fitting place for a church. There is no reason to believe, despite the legends that grew up about Helena during subsequent centuries, that these women were more than pawns in Constantine's grand plan, even though Eusebius credits Helena with building churches at Bethlehem and Eleona in his biography of Constantine (*Vita Const.* iii. 41–3, 46).[35] It would be greatly exaggerating the importance of women at this time to imagine that Constantine obediently followed the whims of his female relatives. The correspondence recorded by Eusebius on the subject of Mamre (see above, Chapter 4) indicates rather that the emperor was in charge, and indeed manipulated Helena and Eutropia for his own ends.

The pious, though limited, pilgrimages of Helena and Eutropia were the prototypes for all Christian pilgrimage that would follow. Christians who had visited Palestine prior to the imperial ladies did not go to places they believed were imbued with sanctity from ancient times in order to pray and recollect the divine events that had occurred at these places in a suitably Christian atmosphere. This complete lack of interest in such a display of devotion is

[34] Wilkinson (1977), 35; Vincent and Abel (1914*b*), 360.
[35] *Pace* Walker (1990), 186. Walker (188 ff.) believes it was *Eusebius* who advised Constantine to build three basilicas over the caves. As we saw above in Ch. 6, however, the 'finding of the cross' legend appears to have been based on actual historical events: Constantine believed this artefact had been uncovered at Golgotha. Eusebius, on the other hand, appears not to have endorsed the relic as genuine.

reflected in what exegetes prior to the fourth century do *not* say concerning Septuagint Psalm 131: 7 (132: 7): 'let us worship in the place where his feet stood'. Clement of Alexandria (*Paed*. ii. 8. 62. 1) believed this verse made a reference to the feet of the apostles in the universal Church (cf. Victorinus, *Comm. in Apoc*. 1. 15a). It was only after Christian pilgrimage and Christian holy places were established in the fourth century that the verse was interpreted in the light of Helena's pilgrimage to places where Christ had once stood (*Vita Const*. iii. 42).

Constantine brought to Christianity a pagan notion of the sanctity of things and places. We have already noted that in Constantine's sight Golgotha was 'holy from the beginning' (*Vita Const*. iii. 30) and that Mamre was imbued with 'ancient holiness' (*Vita Const*. iii. 53). According to fifth-century Church historians, it was Constantine who above all promoted the belief in the spiritual efficacy of bits of wood said to come from Christ's cross by placing pieces in his bridle and helmet (Socrates, *Hist. Eccles*. i. 17; Sozomen, *Hist. Eccles*. ii. 1).[36] He himself had hoped to visit Palestine on a pilgrimage (*Vita Const*. ii. 72. 2) and even wished to be baptized in the Jordan River (*Vita Const*. iv. 62. 2).

Nevertheless, the reasons for Constantine's building programme may not all have been born of an excess of pagan-cum-Christian piety. It would seem that when the emperor turned his eye to Palestine, he saw the opportunity of creating a focal point for the Christians of the Empire. If pilgrimage was characteristic of popular pagan religion, it would be characteristic also of the new Christianity which Constantine hoped would supersede the former erroneous ways. Devotees of pagan gods made trips to certain sacred shrines, which were places connected with the deity's mythology, sites revealed as particularly special to a god, or simply temples.[37] Many of these were the caves, groves, springs, and hills upon which Constantine's soldiers wished to trample. The majority had been recognized as being numinous for hundreds, if not thousands, of years. It was common to have festivals associated with these sites, which were attended by vast multitudes of pilgrims. People went to pray at healing sanctuaries or sacrifice on altars adjacent to the sites. Many caves claimed their status from the fact that the infant Zeus apparently sheltered in them: Ida in

[36] See also Walker (1990), 111; Telfer (1955*b*).
[37] Lane Fox (1986), 41.

Crete, for example, or the cave near the temple of Zeus in Aezanae, Phrygia. At Thibilis, North Africa, the magistrates processed for ten miles outside the town and climbed to a cave of the god Bacax. Temples were also visited: the shrine of Hera on Samos, Asclepius on Cos, or Plutonium by the caves outside Nyssa.[38]

Constantine clearly wanted to create new shrines in Palestine that would invalidate such powerful places. Later pilgrims would recognize implicitly that a contest was being waged, as Jerome's emotive prose in regard to Bethlehem shows:

With what words, with what voice, can we describe the Saviour's cave? And that manger where the Babe cried is to be honoured more by deep silence than by feeble speech. Behold, in this small hole in the earth the Founder of the heavens was born, here he was wrapped in swaddling clothes, here seen by the shepherds, here shown by the star, here worshipped by the wise men, and this place, I think, is holier than the Tarpeian rock, where traces of its having been frequently struck by lightning show that it displeases the Lord.[39]

In constructing temples to his God, Constantine was simply being traditional. Generals of the past had paid homage to their deities by building temples and instigating cults in Rome.[40] Constantine naturally began in this city, and endowments were provided for St John the Lateran and the Sessorian basilica (via Helena), but his architectural 'deluge of Christian publicity', as Lane Fox puts it,[41] was to surpass anything ever seen. Certainly, patronage of public and religious buildings was a noble virtue proper to great princes, as it had been since Alexander, and no pagan could have found it sinister at first that Constantine should continue the norm, but he went beyond all standards. No other Roman emperor sent his soldiers through the Eastern Empire stripping pagan religious shrines of their precious metals, and had he not done so it is difficult to see from where his bottomless supply of personal funds could have come. Spending on public buildings could, moreover, cover a multitude of sins. In 326

[38] Ibid.
[39] Jerome, *Ep.* cxlvii. 4, trans. here from Dalman (1935*b*), 43; cf. Jerome, *Ep.* cviii. 2–7.
[40] Lane Fox (1986), 622.
[41] Ibid. 623.

Constantine executed his son, Crispus, and wife, Fausta (Eutropius, *Brev*. x. 6. 3; Jerome, *De Vir. Ill.* 80; Zosimus, *Hist. Nova* ii. 29. 2). His zeal for building grand churches may have helped to quash significant Christian criticism of his actions.

Fausta's mother, Eutropia, must have journeyed to Palestine before the death of her daughter, after which her own position would have been insecure, at best. Given the formidable logistics involved in organising an imperial tour, it seems probable that Eutropia was part of Helena's entourage visiting the East (*Vita Const.* iii. 49). Certainly they must have made their trips at about the same time. Helena's journey to the eastern provinces appears to have been undertaken partly to inspire allegiance to Constantine's policies amongst the troops there, by giving gifts to the soldiers, and partly to reassure the populace, by dispensing charity in general (*Vita Const.* iii. 42, 44). This must have occurred shortly after Constantine defeated Licinius. The pilgrimage Helena made to 'holy places' to pray was then part of a tour which had various purposes, but it was the pilgrimage aspect of the tour which captured the imagination of Constantine's subjects.

Some years later, much encouraged by the example of these women, especially Helena, it became fashionable among those who had sufficient means for such a venture, to travel to the land where Jesus lived in order to visit holy sites. It was quite natural for those recently converted from paganism to think along such lines.

As mentioned above, Palestine had already been visited by Christians, but it is doubtful whether one can call these visits 'pilgrimages' as such. The Christian visitors prior to the fourth century were educated men, often scholars, who came out of scholarly interest. At the end of the second century, for example, Melito of Sardis wrote that he had visited the East and arrived at 'the place where the messages of the Bible were preached and done' (Eusebius, *Hist. Eccles.* iv. 26. 14), Palestine, where he managed to acquire a list of Old Testament books. It appears that Melito's purposes in going to Palestine did not include veneration of specific sites. In Aelia the place where Jesus was believed to have been crucified was pointed out to him, but it does not seem to have been his goal to pray there or to venerate it.

Christian pilgrimage is more than mere Christian travel or scholarly investigation. A pilgrim goes to a specific 'holy' site in order to recall events that took place there and pray.[42] The experience is much more emotional than intellectual, and lays great store on the site's imbued aura of sanctity and importance. But Melito himself said that the earthly Jerusalem had no esteem at all, since it was here that God was slain (*Pasch. Hom.* lxx). He was a learned Christian who had come to Palestine out of an historical interest in the land in general. It must be stressed that learned Christians of the second and third centuries were interested in the cities of Palestine in the same way that classical scholars, ever since Herodotus, had been interested in the classical cities:[43] visiting the place helped one interpret and understand the literature. Origen calls his movements around Palestine an ἱστορία, an investigation, a technical term which implies that he knew he stood in a fine old tradition. An *historia* was a sort of learned tourism, a grand 'study tour'; the word crops up frequently in the writings of Eusebius when he mentions Christian visitors prior to the Constantinian developments (e.g. to Eleona: *Dem. Evang.* vi. 18; to Bethlehem: vii. 2. 14). Origen went on 'an investigation of the traces' (*Comm. in Joh.* i. 28) in order to better understand the Bible, and there were undoubtedly many others who did likewise. An *historia* was not a pilgrimage. Jerome elucidates the motives for such a trip thus:

In the same way that they who have seen Athens understand the Greek histories better, and they who have sailed from Troy through Leucaten, and from Acroceraunia to Sicily, and from there to the mouth of the Tiber understand the third book of Virgil, so he who has contemplated Judaea with his own eyes and knows the sites of the ancient cities, and knows the names of the places, whether the same or changed, will regard scripture more lucidly. (*Praef. in Lib. Paralip.*)

By Jerome's day, of course, this scholarly interest had become amalgamated with the general idea of what it meant to be a pilgrim, but prior to the fourth century an interest in history and literature appears to have been the only real motive for Christians visiting Palestine. Eusebius' repeated mention of places being pointed out to visiting Christians means that there was an interest in identifying locations, but nothing is ever said in the *Onomasticon* of any Christians venerating such places as being inherently holy.

[42] See Wilkinson (1977), 33.   [43] Hunt (1984), 77–8, 94.

Jerome does mention that a third-century Cappadocian bishop, Firmilianus, came 'for the sake of the holy places' (*De Vir. Ill.* 54), but his language is undoubtedly anachronistic, a contracted way of referring to a group of sites of interest to Christian visitors.

Another third-century visitor named Alexander wished, according to Eusebius (*Hist. Eccles.* vi. 11. 2), to 'examine the historic sites', but Eusebius also adds that he prayed (εὐχῆς καὶ τῶν τόπων ἱστορίας ἕνεκεν). At first sight this may imply that some kinds of 'holy places' existed to which Alexander could go to pray, but in fact Eusebius makes it clear elsewhere that there was only one: the Mount of Olives (*Dem. Evang.* vi. 18. 23; *Onom.* 74. 16–18). For certain Christians, this hill had something of the holiness of the former Jewish Temple; it must have been seen as a kind of geological tabernacle in which God's glory was abiding. Nevertheless, the divine was not intermixed with the material in any inherent or inseparable way. The Mount was not holy simply because it had been touched by Jesus as if by a magical wand. Of course, Christians did not just pray here, but could pray anywhere, at any time, and certainly must have done so. What is missing in these early accounts of Christian visitors is any sense that biblical sites were seen as appropriate places for prayer because of their special, intrinsic holiness.

On the Mount of Olives people who had come to Jerusalem in order to understand more about the meaning of its destruction (and appropriation by pagans) would gather and pray. We can see here the scene being set for Helena. There may have been an increase in the numbers of Christian visitors during the third century, which would parallel the rise of Christianity through the Roman Empire's social classes at this time, so that more and more educated persons were embracing the faith.[44] It would not be hard for educated Christians who had become accustomed to the idea of going to Palestine in order to learn, who would perhaps gather for prayer looking over the sorry sight of Aelia Capitolina from a hill that some believed closeted the refugee glory of God, to accept the idea that Christians could go on pilgrimages proper to many sacred sites in order to pray and recollect events that had taken place. It is

---

[44] It is clear from surviving Christian literature that, during the course of the 2nd and 3rd cents., Christianity became increasingly popular among those who had had the benefit of a classical education. See Lane Fox (1986), 293–312, esp. 306–8.

a fine distinction that needs to be drawn here, but there is nevertheless a marked difference between those who visited Palestine prior to Helena and those who came after.

There was also a difference in the sex of many of the visitors. We know of no women who visited Palestine prior to the fourth century; the Christians who travelled to Palestine for learned investigations were, it would seem, predominantly men. This is not surprising, when one considers that it was affluent men who had the means for both an advanced education and travel. But neither Helena nor Eutropia was a scholar, and the two pilgrim accounts of the fourth century—that of the Bordeaux Pilgrim (who may well have been a woman) and the nun Egeria—reflect minds which have had only a modicum of learning; enough to write and reflect with wonder on biblical events. Their prose, especially Egeria's, shows an excitement about what they saw and a complete willingness to believe what they were told about the places. They make no effort to elucidate points of Scripture, but only refer to biblical personalities and events uncritically. The Bordeaux Pilgrim also mentions places useful for women: a spring near Caesarea where women wash who wish to become pregnant (*Itin. Burd.* 585.7), and the spring of Elisha near Jericho where women drink for the same reason (*Itin. Burd.* 596); the former of these appears to have no Christian associations at all. Affluent women, particularly older women, with a certain degree of education appear to have been a key component in fourth-century pilgrimage, and indeed seem to have given their stamp to the way in which Christian pilgrimage would develop—from Helena to Jerome's companions at the end of the century, Paula and Eustochium.

By contrast, in the account of the martyrdom of Origen's contemporary Pionius, the writer indicates that Pionius' interest in Palestine was broad, and not focused on specific places or the wonder of biblical events: 'I saw the land which until now has borne witness to the wrath of God' (*Mart. Pionii* iv. 18). Prior to the fourth century, learned Christians visited in order to see how Palestine had been brought low; this must have been a component of the interpretation of the places. After Constantine, Christian pilgrims came to see the land's glory. Before Constantine the earthly Jerusalem, Aelia, was unimportant in comparison with the heavenly Jerusalem which was the reward of God's children (cf.

Origen, *Contra Celsum* vii. 28–9).[45] Christ's kingdom was not of this world (John 18: 36). Even as late as 309, Egyptian Christians visiting Caesarea claimed, when interrogated by the governor of Palestine, that they were citizens of (the celestial) Jerusalem (cf. Gal. 6: 26),[46] but they were clearly uninterested in trekking to Aelia Capitolina for any purpose. Suddenly, with Constantine, the Church began to focus on the earth; the divine substance intermixed with certain material sites and resided in things which could be carried about.

To put it bluntly, the Church prior to the fourth century was concerned with the heavenly Jerusalem only (cf. John 4: 21–4); the earthly Jerusalem existed only as a witness to God's fury at the execution of his Son and the unbelief of those who murdered him. There is a complete absence of texts prior to the later works of Eusebius which might show interest in considering land sacred or a site being intrinsically holy because of Christ having once been there; even the Bordeaux Pilgrim does not refer to places as being holy.

Eusebius himself is an interesting case. His life and work began well before Constantine, but he had to accommodate the momentous changes wrought by the emperor. At the end of his life he would admit to there being the three 'holy places' of Golgotha, Bethlehem, and Eleona (cf. *Vita Const.* iii. 25–8), but his vindication of others is wanting. Even this acknowledgement of Christian sacred zones was a significant about-turn. The younger Eusebius was firmly of the 'old school', which rejected the materiality of the pagan idea of holy places, and which even doubted the sanctity of the Jewish and Samaritan temples (John 4: 23; cf. Eusebius, *Theoph.* iv. 23). Eusebius had written that worship in 'specific places' was incompatible with Christian 'spiritual worship' (*Dem. Evang.* i. 6. 40), and here we can even detect scepticism about the idea that the presence of God was abiding within the Mount of Olives; this may well have been a Jerusalem tradition, based on exegesis of the Prophets alone, about which the Caesarean church was doubtful. Eusebius paraphrased Jesus' teaching as: 'Since I give liberty to all, I teach people to look for God not in a corner of the earth, or on hills, or in temples made with human hands, but that each person should worship and adore

---

[45] See Wilken (1985), 446.   [46] Eusebius, *Mart. Pal.* ix. 6–14.

him *at home*' (*Dem. Evang.* i. 6. 65, italics mine). Certainly, Eusebius had to move a long way to arrive at the point where he could pay lip-service at least to the emperor Constantine's actions. One might wonder that there was so little Christian opposition to the changes wrought by the emperor, but if Eusebius, of all people, would make allowances for the emperor's decisions, the rest of the Christian world would have been more enthusiastic. The recent examination of Eusebius' writings by Peter Walker has shown how Eusebius was dragging his heels on the question.[47] He stands in marked contrast to someone like Cyril of Jerusalem, who was completely convinced of the efficacy of visits to holy sites and never doubted that this was completely consistent with the Christian faith as it had always been.

Cyril believed in the intrinsic sanctity of material parts of Palestine, the 'holy places' (*Cat.* i. 1; iv. 10; v. 10; x. 19; xiii. 22, 38–9). These were witnesses which proved the truth of the Gospel (*Cat.* x. 19; xiii. 38–9; xiv. 22–3).[48] A pilgrim could see and touch places once seen and touched by Christ, and thereby step closer to the divine (cf. *Cat.* xiii. 22).

The evidence of Cyril shows just how quickly Christians adopted these new notions. By the death of Constantine's son, Constantius II, in 361, Jerusalem had been refurbished as a holy city. It was probably no more than forty years between Eusebius' wholesale denial that Christians should worship anywhere but at home[49] and Cyril's catechetical lectures, in which numerous Christian holy sites are referred to and pilgrimage is accepted as a fitting expression of Christian piety. The evidence of Cyril shows how Constantius must have consolidated the revolutionary changes wrought by his father, and proceeded further along the same course.

The veneration of the tombs of the saints was a fundamentally different matter from the phenomenon of pilgrimage to Christian holy places, and derived from the Jewish veneration of the tombs

[47] See Walker (1990), 93–130.
[48] Ibid. 37–8. See also Cardman (1982), (1984).
[49] Since Christians gathered for the celebration of the Eucharist and other sacraments in house-churches, either these must have been included as being 'at home', or else private worship was counted as being separate from group worship; cf. Matt. 6: 6: 'But when you pray, go to your private room, shut yourself in, and so pray to your Father who is in that secret place, and your Father who sees all that is done in secret will reward you.'

of the righteous (for which, see below). Prior to the fourth
century, it was only the pagans (and Samaritans who had been
strongly influenced by them) who believed that a divine epiphany
or manifestation at a certain site would mark it as sacred.[50]
Christians of the fourth century adopted this notion, with certain
modifications.[51] The language used by Eusebius to endorse (at
last) Constantine's view of 'holy places' clearly reflects Eusebius'
understanding that their conceptual source was in paganism.
Eusebius attempts to pay homage to Constantine, but his language
gives away his former, if not his true, feelings. He writes of the
three 'mystic grottos' glorified by Constantine by referring to them
as ἄντρα. The word ἄντρον for 'cave' is unusual, the normal
term was σπήλαιον. Elsewhere, Eusebius uses the word ἄντρον
(especially with the word μυχός, 'the innermost place') in a
pejorative way to refer to pagan venerated grottos.[52]

The older cult of the saints would also provide new holy sites,
for these saints were soon understood to 'manifest' themselves in
their relics and residues.[53] Christians had greatly valued martyrs'
remains from at least the middle of the second century. Around
the year 150, the Jews of Smyrna apparently took away the corpse
of Polycarp so that the Christians would not start a cult of it. By
the middle of the third century, parts of the bodies of saints were
used for healing.[54] As a component of his anti-Christian measures,
Maximinus banned Christians from assembling in cemeteries
(Eusebius, *Hist. Eccles.* ix. 2. 1; cf. vii. 9. 2), which may imply
that, at the beginning of the fourth century, it was notorious that
Christians had a practice of meeting in cemeteries in order to
venerate tombs. The cult of the martyrs was promoted by
Constantine, who assigned all tombs of martyrs to the churches as
their property, regardless of where they lay (*Vita Const.* ii. 40). He
ordered the construction of a huge basilica over the supposed

---

[50] Lane Fox (1986), 98–167.
[51] Ibid. 674.
[52] *Dem. Evang.* v. 29; *Theoph.* ii. 11; iv. 6; *Vita Const.* iii. 26. 3, 54. 6; see
Walker (1990), 191 n. 63. Eusebius seems determined to pander to Constantine in
Vita Constantini. Walker may be right that Eusebius' usage of the term could reflect
Constantine's (using the Latin *antrum*; cf. *Vita Const.* ii. 50), but it is curious that
he fails to apologize for its heavy pagan associations. It seems that Eusebius knew
of them and used the word with full knowledge of the implications.
[53] Lane Fox (1986), 678.   [54] Ibid. 446.

Tomb of Peter in Rome.[55] The veneration of saintly bones would soon form such a critical component of churches that the emperor Julian would flippantly refer to church buildings as 'charnel houses' and fume to the Christians: 'You continue to add multitudes of recently deceased bodies to the corpses of long ago. You have filled the whole world with tombs and sepulchres' (*Contra Galilaios* 335c).

To sum up: it would appear that Byzantine holy places in Palestine were created out of diverse elements with the right potential, in particular biblical sites that scholarly Christians had identified as suitable locátions for the interpretation of Scripture, and tombs at which a saint or martyr was buried. Up until the time Constantine won the East, evidence of Christian veneration of sites cannot be found in surviving literature or archaeology; Christian visitors to Palestine were not 'pilgrims' strictly speaking. Constantine created in Palestine a focus for Christian reverence by identifying for the first time *Christian* holy sites, based on the established model of pagan shrines. Two imperial matrons were provided as prototypes for a new breed of pilgrim: Christians.

In choosing the right locations for his shrines, Constantine did not utilize dreams and auguries, as a pagan emperor might have done. The manifestation of Christ would, in each place, have its fundamental foundation in the Scriptures, the 'divine oracles', as Eusebius repeatedly calls them; but three of the four were also designed to supersede pagan cult places. Identifications by scholarly Christians and local churches could be swept aside if inconvenient, as the case of 'Golgotha' shows. Scripture is vague on locations, and if a pagan site could be made redundant by a new Christian one, so much the better. As we have seen, Palestine was, before the fourth century, littered with pagan sites. Constantine would have grasped that building spectacular Christian edifices at certain Christian 'holy places' would attract a flood of pilgrims, convert some of the locals, and lure Christian settlers. He could thereby discourage the worship of false gods in the land of the Bible. It is important to recognize just how quickly and comprehensively Palestine became a 'holy land'. We should also understand

[55] For a discussion of the early history of the Tomb of Peter, see Guarducci (1960). For other discussions, see de Marco (1964), a representative and annotated bibliography of the excavations. Constantine's basilica stood until the 16th cent. on the site of the present St Peter's in Rome.

the means employed by the Church in order to effect the Christianization of the region and the removal of paganism. Some examination of the whole process, of which there is considerable evidence in Palestine, will help to place the formation of early Christian holy sites in context.

The Christian Appropriation of Sites

Constantine's destruction of the temple of Venus in Aelia and his accusation that Hadrian had smothered the holy ground of Golgotha underneath it permeated the Christians' attitude to pagan sites throughout the country and beyond. It was considered unarguable that Constantine had every right to demolish the temple because the pagans had taken the site from the Christians, incarcerated the wood of Christ's cross and the tomb in which he had been laid, and profaned them with the most heinous idolatrous practices (e.g. *Vita Const.* iii. 27; Jerome, *Ep.* lviii. 3; Socrates, *Hist. Eccles.* i. 17). The same was true for Mamre. Sozomen makes it sound as if pagans conspired against Christianity's sacred shrines from the very beginning: they 'heaped up mounds of earth upon the holy places' and, as far as Golgotha was concerned, cunningly concealed the site with a temple. Incidentally, as we have seen, he provides us with a good inverted indication of *Christian* self-justification regarding the appropriation of sites sacred to other religions when he writes that the *pagans* hoped that in covering Golgotha with a temple for Venus those who came there would seem to worship the goddess, and the true cause of worship in the place would soon be forgotten (*Hist. Eccles.* ii. 1). In many a pagan holy site, a new Christian edifice built on or near the spot would have attracted the same pagans, who knew only of the intrinsic sacredness of the vicinity. Pagans were used to the idea that one god could live comfortably with another, and if Christ dying-and-rising was now to be honoured above all in Jerusalem, then initially it was probably no more devastating to many of them than the idea that dying-and-rising Adonis was to be emphasized above his lover in this particular location. A true conversion of the pagan heart may have taken somewhat longer to effect.

Indeed, Christians were keen to convert pagans, but their

actions were also motivated by sheer revenge. Pagans had to be punished. The propaganda put about by the Church was that the pagans had covered up Christian holy places at Mamre, Bethlehem, and Golgotha through malicious intent. Such acts justified fierce reprisals. Sozomen finishes his account by saying that everywhere people overturned temples and statues and erected 'houses of prayer' in their place (*Hist. Eccles.* ii. 5). Sometimes this meant that a new Christian shrine was built deliberately close to a former pagan sanctuary. St Cyrus and St John's church on the Egyptian coast replaced the old shrine of Isis. St Therapon replaced a shrine of Asclepius in Mytilene. Near the old shrine of Asclepius at Aegae, Christians had similar dreams and visions to their pagan predecessors, but this time they were inspired by St Thecla in her church on the nearby hillside (Egeria, *Itin.* xxiii. 1–6).[56]

We can also see from literary and archaeological sources that temples were sometimes used as churches. A chapel built in the fourth century over a corner of the abandoned temple of Artemis at Sardis is testimony to a lack of squeamishness on the part of Christians when faced with the opportunity to appropriate a pagan building. The temple of Apollo at Daphne, a suburb of Antioch, was subverted rather than converted (*c*.358) by means of the erection of a church built immediately in front of it by Julian's half-brother Gallus. Later in the fourth century the Bishop of Alexandria expressed the desire to make the temple of Dionysus into a church and asked the emperor Theodosius to assign it to him. Pagans learnt of this and protested by occupying the Serapeum. This demonstration eventually led the emperor to condemn all the temples in Alexandria to be destroyed as punishment (Rufinus, *Hist. Eccles.* ii. 22 ff.; Sozomen, *Hist. Eccles.* vii. 15).[57] Early in the fifth century, it was necessary only to

---

[56] Lane Fox (1986), 676.

[57] Hanson (1978) has argued that pagan temples themselves were not appropriated as Christian churches until the middle of the 5th cent. because they were looked upon with such horror that they had to be utterly destroyed before the site was used. He uses as an example Constantine's basilica in Jerusalem which was constructed only after the Hadrianic temple of Venus had been dismantled down to its foundations (Eusebius, *Vita Const.* iii. 26–9). However, as we have seen, Constantine appears to have had other reasons for dismantling the Hadrianic structures. The utter annihilation of the Venus temple was, in this case, a polemical statement. It enabled him also to appear to find the wood of Christ's cross buried below. Moreover, he was perfectly content to fit a little church into the sacred enclosure at Mamre, and otherwise leave the place intact.

use the sign of the cross to purify a pagan cult place before it was used as a church (*Cod. Theod.* xvi. 10. 25), and many temples, such as the temple of Apollo at Didyma and the temple of Aphrodite at Aphrodisias, were converted.

It is important here to stress that in the polemic issued by the Church Fathers the pagans stood accused of *stealing* certain sites, which seems to be based on their supposed behaviour in regard to Golgotha, Bethlehem, and Mamre. It gave the Christians the justification for claiming numerous sites as theirs; it was not a question of appropriation, but of *restoration*. Christians did not steal, but rather they rightfully reclaimed their property. Wherever there was a pagan cult place, Christians could have a revelation that a biblical site—or a site important to a saint or martyr—lay covered. In looking at the origins of Christian holy places in Palestine, this must always be borne in mind. As we saw in the case of Mamre, however, restoration language used by the Church Fathers does not mean that Christians ever owned or venerated a site prior to its appropriation by the Church in the fourth century.

The archaeological remains in and around Palestine confirm those found in the wider Empire, which attest widespread destruction of temples in the fourth century, and sometimes their employment as Christian edifices. The cathedral of Gerasa, constructed north of the south Decumanus, absorbed a temple on the second terrace. On this same terrace a Christian festival was held on the anniversary of the marriage of Cana (John 2: 1 ff.), but inscriptions indicate that this feast began in the cult of Dionysus/ Dushara.[58] Pagan traditions became incorporated into Christian life in Palestine as elsewhere.

A temple at Pella was used intact as a Christian church.[59] In Eboda, two churches, a north and a south, were built on the acropolis, superseding the former temples.[60] The Marneion in Gaza was destroyed and the Eudoxiana church was completed on the same site in 408.[61] The pagan sanctuary of Emmatha (Hammat Gader) was also converted into a Christian site, the Baths of Elijah, by the time of the Piacenza Pilgrim, in the late sixth century.[62] The great temple of Zeus in Damascus was converted into the cathedral of St John the Baptist during the reign of

[58] *EAEHL* ii. 426–8.   [59] *EAEHL* iv. 939.
[60] *EAEHL* ii. 345–54.   [61] See above, Ch. 3, on Gaza as a pagan city.
[62] Piacenza Pilgrim, *Itin.* vii.

Theodosius I. The twelve stones of the 'mortals'[63] in Gilgal (cf. Eusebius, *Onom.* 66. 5) were either taken by Christians or superseded by other 'Christian' stones.[64] Joseph of Tiberias built a church in Tiberias by converting part of the Hadrianeum there (Epiphanius, *Pan.* xxx. 12. 1–9). Even the pyramids of Egypt were conceptually appropriated; they were understood to be the granaries built by Joseph to store corn during the famine (so Egeria, Pet. Diac., *Lib.* Y1). The nearby temple of Apis in Memphis was converted into a church.[65]

Christians appear to have had a real interest in 'redeeming' sites previously utilized by pagans. A basilica of the first part of the fourth century in Dora was erected over the remains of a Hellenistic temple that had lain in ruins for several hundred years. What was probably continuing, and what needed to be suppressed by the Church, was a cult associated with a cave there. This cave had been incorporated into the temple as a subterranean *adyton*, a 'holy of holies'—a fact suggested by the alignment of the cistern wall north of it with a wall beyond the external northern aisle, as Claudine Dauphin has pointed out.[66] The Christians 'desanctified' the cave by turning it into a cistern.

Sites special to Jews and Samaritans fared as badly as did the shrines of the pagans. The Christians were as interested in Old Testament events as the New. It is well known that the art of the Christian catacombs in Rome demonstrates a concern with the stories and personalities of the Hebrew Scriptures, which were given a particular Christian interpretation by means of typology.

Jews and Samaritans honoured tombs of the notable personalities of Scripture long before the Christians. The first material evidence we have for Christian veneration of tombs concerns not the vacant Tomb of Christ but the sepulchre containing the remains of Peter in Rome, visited at least from late in the second century.[67] It is quite possible that early (predominantly Jewish-)Christians venerated it

---

[63] 'Mortals' probably refers to pagans.

[64] Jerome translates the reference in Eusebius as 'ab illius regionis mortalibus' (*Lib. loc.* 67. 5); cf. Piacenza Pilgrim, *Itin.* xiii; Adomnan, *De Loc. Sanct.* xiv; Hugeburc, *Vita Will.* xcvii. 1. The stones were also known to the rabbis, who observed and commented on their size but record no hint that they were venerated by Jews (*t.Sotah* 8. 6).

[65] Piacenza Pilgrim, *Itin.* xliii; Epiph. Mon., *Hag.* vi. 14–19; Dicuil, *De Mens.* 24–5.

[66] Comm. by C. M. Dauphin, 'Notes and News', *IEJ* 35: 271.

[67] Guarducci (1960), 87.

from the time of Peter's death, in the same way that other Jews venerated the tombs where the remains of the righteous dead were interred. Jews and Samaritans together venerated the Tombs of the Patriarchs in the Cave of Machpelah in Hebron. Samaritans venerated, among other places, the Tomb of Aaron on Mount Hor in Petra and the Tomb of Joseph in Sychar.[68] Jews had the Tombs of the Prophets (cf. Matt. 23: 28–30; Luke 11: 47–8) and many other burial places for the respected dead, including the Tombs of David and Solomon in Jerusalem (Josephus, *Ant.* xvi. 179–82; cf. Acts 2: 29; Cassius Dio, *Hist. Rom.* lxix. 14. 2).

The veneration of such graves appears to have been maintained mainly at a popular level, but it is difficult to determine what the early beliefs and practices concerning Jewish and Samaritan venerated tombs may have been, since most of the literary material about them comes from the fourth century and after, and may then show evidence of Christian influence. For example, certain rabbinic texts indicate that certain Jews believed that the righteous ones were present on earth in some way in their tombs. Speaking about the Tombs of the Patriarchs in Hebron, the fourth-century rabbi Pinhas ben Hama sums up the Jewish tradition of venerated tombs and those interred within them:

If the fathers of the world (the patriarchs) had wished that their resting place should be in the Above, they would have been able to have it there: but it is when they died and the rock closed on their tombs here below that they deserved to be called 'saints'.[69]

According to this view, the Jewish tombs were 'holy' because they made available to the faithful on earth a measure of the power of mercy in which they might have rested in heaven.[70] In the Babylonian Talmud, Abraham calls Rabbi Bana'a into his tomb (*b.Baba Bathra* 58a), so he was somehow there to do the calling. At the tomb of King Hezekiah, the fifth-century *Lamentations Rabbah* (25) tells us that Rabbi Yehuda addressed the king saying,

---

[68] Jeremias (1958), 40; Pummer (1987*b*), 10–12.

[69] *Mid. Psalm. Rab.* 16. 2, trans. by P. R. L. Brown (1983), 3; for a slightly different translation, see Braude (1959), 197. The *Midrash on the Psalms* was possibly composed as late as the 9th cent., though it reports the traditional sayings of much earlier rabbis. There is a chance that Christian ideas and practices influenced the final redaction.

[70] P. R. L. Brown (1983), 3.

'Teach us'; it must have been understood that he was present to hear this plea. While it is perfectly possible that Christians adopted this idea from Jews, the Jewish idea may have been taken and adapted from developing Christian beliefs in the abiding presence of the saint; if we wish to argue that the Christian idea of a saint's presence was taken from a Jewish model, we must have very early sources.

The Jewish text known as *The Lives of the Prophets*, which was written in the first century, would have been very valuable in illuminating our knowledge of the early veneration of the tombs, except that the surviving texts contain a lot of Christian material,[71] and it is difficult to extricate this to arrive at the original form of the document. There is also a likelihood that the popular practices of Jews in the second and third centuries were influenced by the practices of pagans, and therefore underwent changes. Some Jews collected soil from around the Tomb of Jeremiah to heal asp bites: a magical procedure.[72] The role of the tombs in popular magic and healing has yet to be investigated, and in this field more than any other the boundaries of what was pagan, Jewish, Samaritan, or Christian are notoriously difficult to determine. The Jewish veneration of tombs may have borrowed from forms of pagan worship at their holy shrines in many ways and over a long period, and the separation of this type of devotion into pagan or Jewish elements may also be an impossible task.

Whatever the case, the Jewish righteous or 'saints' were not given the same kind of attention that the Christian saints were given.[73] It was left to the Christians to expand and develop the whole theology of saintly intercession, and to come to believe in the healing property of mortal remains. The question of whether the Jewish righteous ones interceded for Israel is, as is the case in this whole sphere, complex. A variety of opinions are found in the sources. The Christian belief in saintly intercession is found already in the first century (Rev. 5: 9; 6: 9; 11: 17; 15: 2; 19: 6), and certainly it derived from some strand of Jewish thought (as found in 1 Enoch 39: 5; cf. 2 Macc. 15: 14; Philo, *De exsecr.* 165 f.; *b. Taan.* 16a), but quite the opposite view is also attested in Jewish

---

[71] See Schürer (1986), 784.   [72] Jeremias (1958), 137.

[73] P. R. L. Brown (1983: 9) writes: '. . . the leaders of Jewish learning and spirituality did not choose to lean upon tombs, as Christian bishops did, with the result that these maintained a low profile.'

material (2 Bar. 85: 12; Ps.-Philo, xxxiii. 5). The belief in the idea
of the interceding martyr was born in the days of the Maccabean
Revolt against Antiochus IV (173–164 BC). The dead heroes of
this revolt were believed to have become martyrs present in
heaven (not on earth?) before God's throne (4 Macc. 17: 8; cf.
2 Macc. 7: 9 ff.). As is stated in 4 Maccabees (16: 25), dating
from the first century, 'Those who die for God, live unto God'.[74]

To the Christian mind, the saints were both present with God, in
spirit, and present on earth, in their physical remains. Martyrdom
permitted the saint to enter heaven immediately, where s/he could
hear the prayers of the faithful. The assembly of saints were a
heavenly lobby, an extra way for those left below to contact God.
According to Origen, for example, there were numerous interces-
sors: angels, the apostles, the patriarchs, and the martyrs.[75] These
saints were not only useful in heaven, but their remains could
effect miraculous cures on earth.

Despite the veneration of tombs by Jews, the sepulchres were
considered ritually unclean, which tended to stop people from
interfering with the actual bones. The wall built by Herod around
the area of uncleanness on top of the Cave of Machpelah in
Hebron was to keep people out; there was no door until late in the
fourth century, when Christians built a church within the precincts.[76]
By the end of the sixth century Jews would come into these
precincts (Piacenza Pilgrim, *Itin.* xxx), which is a good example of
how Christian practice influenced Jewish customs. This modification
of the Jewish position, which entailed the exemption of the
righteous from corpse uncleanness, is reflected in several later
sources (*b.Baba Bathra* 17a; *Mid. Lam. Rabbah* 25; *Mid. Eccles.
Rabbah* 11. 2; *Mid. Psalms Rabbah* 16. 10, 11). Christians
understood the body of a Christian to be someone who had 'fallen
asleep', waiting to rise again, and saw a corpse as no more unclean
than a living person (see *Didasc. Apost.* xix). This was a novel
idea. Just as a living saint could possess powers of healing and

[74] For the differences between Jewish and Christian attitudes to martyrdom, see
Lane Fox (1986), 436–8; for Christian martyrdom and the cult of saints in general,
see ibid. 434–50; also P. R. L. Brown (1983).

[75] Origen, *Comm. in Cant.* iii; *in Lev. Hom.* iv. 4; *Exhort. Mart.* xxx. See Lane
Fox (1986), 445.

[76] Jeremias (1958), 93; Egeria, in Pet. Diac., *Lib.* N1; Jerome, *Lib. loc.* 7. 20. I
am grateful to Canon John Wilkinson for letting me see a draft paper in which he
noted this.

exorcism, so too the saint's remains, they believed, also possessed these powers. Death did nothing to stop the process. Items touched by the saint could also be imbued with this power. Items touched by Christ were, of course, prized above all: hence the huge demand for bits of wood from the cross. Egeria reports that a pilgrim kissing this relic in the Martyrium surreptitiously bit off a piece to take home (Egeria, *Itin.* xxxvii. 2). We do not find anything quite like this happening in connection with Jewish or Samaritan tombs or objects associated with their righteous dead.[77]

The patriarchs, and other Old Testament figures, were post-humously accorded all the attributes and powers that the Christians believed their saints and martyrs to possess. Therefore, finding in the countryside of Palestine the traditional Jewish tombs of the prophets, patriarchs, and matriarchs, the Byzantine Christians systematically took them for themselves. They were incorporated into the corpus of sacred places available for Christian prayer, for here, too, pious pleas would be relayed to God via the intermediary saint: St Rachel, St Abraham, and so on. The earliest Christian pilgrims visited Jewish tombs attested by Josephus in the first century: for example, the tombs of Rachel (Jos., *Ant.* i. 343; *Itin. Burd.* 599. 5), Eleazar (Jos., *Ant.* v. 119; Egeria, in Pet. Diac., *Lib.* L2),[78] and Joshua (Jos., *Ant.* v. 119; *Itin. Burd.* 587. 5). They also went to the graves of Isaiah (*Itin. Burd.* 595. 3), Amos (Egeria, in Pet. Diac., *Lib.* L2), Elisha (Egeria, in Pet. Diac., *Lib.* V6), and others. All through the fourth and fifth centuries, Jewish 'saintly' tombs were being discovered and appropriated by the Church. For example, the remains of Job were found some time before 383 in Carneas by a monk of the Hauran (Egeria, *Itin.* xvi. 5). Between 379 and 395 the remains of Habakkuk and Micah were found in Ceila and Morasthi respectively by a Bishop Zebennus of Eleutheropolis (Sozomen, *Hist. Eccles.* vii. 29; cf. Pet. Diac., *Lib.* V8). In 412 the prophet Zechariah's bones were found near Eleutheropolis by a peasant named Calemerus, and a church was built over the tomb (Sozomen, *Hist. Eccles.* ix. 16). In 415, in Kefar Gamala, the bones of Paul's teacher Gamaliel and his sons

---

[77] See Lane Fox (1986: 447–8) for a brief discussion on the different attitudes of Jews and Christians to saintly remains.

[78] In the 5th cent., there were two Tombs of Eleazar: one derived from Samaritan tradition at Awarta, and another from Jewish tradition a Jibiya; see Jeremias (1958), 48 n. 15.

were found along with the bones of St Stephen (Sozomen, *Hist. Eccles.* ix. 16).[79]

The venerated Jewish tombs had never been holy in the way that they soon became holy to Christians. Jews differed from pagans in admitting only one God, and accepting no other Temple than the one on Mount Moriah, Jerusalem. The presence of the one God could rest at only one place at one time. As both the Gospel narratives and Josephus attest, pilgrimage to the Temple, especially at Passover, had been a feature of Jewish religious life up until AD 70.[80] After the destruction of the Temple, Judaism was without a holy place that could be compared to the pagan model. With the departure of the presence of God from the Temple, Jewish pilgrimage had ceased. Though lamented over (cf. *Itin. Burd.* 591), neither the ruins of the Temple nor Mount Moriah itself were intrinsically holy.

Nevertheless, Jews had places, like the tombs of the righteous, which were of spiritual importance. The tractate *Berakot* in the Babylonian Talmud (54a) preserves provisions for blessings to be recited by a Jew who sees the crossings of the Jordan, the stones in the descent of Beth Horon, the stone which Og, king of Bashan, intended to throw against Israel, the stone on which Moses sat while Joshua was fighting Amalek, Lot's wife, and the wall of Jericho which was swallowed up on the spot. These six places may have been very important, but they were by no means the only sites. Mamre/Terebinthus appears to have been visited by some Jews as well as pagans. Already in the Mishnah, *Berakot* (9. 1) advises that 'if a man saw a place where miracles had been wrought for Israel, he should say, "Blessed is he that wrought miracles for our fathers in this place".'[81] The Madaba mosaic map, completed c.560–5, demonstrates how Christians used the knowledge of the Jewish inhabitants of Palestine to identify sites for pilgrimage: Elisha's fountain, for example, or 'Mount Gerizim', which they placed near Jericho (cf. *Gen. Rab.* 32. 16; Epiphanius, *Pan.* ix. 2. 4).[82] It is likely that Jews identified many places where 'miracles had been wrought for Israel', but the blessings which were made upon seeing these places were part of a whole gamut of blessings that

[79] See Wilkinson (1981), 281–3; Avi-Yonah (1976b), 221.

[80] For a discussion of the Passover festival and the pilgrimages associated with it, see J. B. Segal (1963).

[81] Trans. in Danby (1933), 9.   [82] Avi-Yonah (1954), 32–3.

were made by a religious Jew at many points during the course of life, in response to a recognition of God's mercy. Jews did not go to these places with the specific intention of saying a blessing, but would say such a blessing if they happened to be passing by.

Jews appear to have been wholly unprepared for what took place in the fourth century in regard to tombs and sites which had spiritual significance. A singularly unprophetic saying[83] by the early fourth-century Rabbi Judah ben Simeon ben Pazzi (*Gen. Rab.* 79. 7) expresses the view that the Cave of Machpelah in Hebron, the Jerusalem Temple Mount, and the (Samaritan) Tomb of Joseph, near Neapolis, were, on account of their being purchased and paid for in ancient times, 'the three places which the Gentiles cannot take away from Israel by saying: "You have obtained them by robbery".' What this tells us is that the Christians were appropriating sites belonging to Jews and Samaritans by claiming that the Jews and Samaritans stole them at some stage in the past. This is precisely the same accusation as was levelled at the pagans, and springs from the same basic understanding; sites which Byzantine Christians deemed to be holy were holy from the beginning and therefore had to be in the pure hands of the Church in order that their spiritual cleanliness could be vouchsafed. In other hands, the sites were stolen and, certainly in the case of pagan ownership, defiled.

As for the Jewish reaction to the loss of their venerated tombs, a certain amount of pragmatism appears to have prevailed. As we saw, the earliest pilgrims to provide us with an account of their travels, the Bordeaux Pilgrim and Egeria, had much success in finding Old Testament localities and tombs, from which we can infer that local Jews were reasonably helpful in pointing them in the right direction. The Bordeaux Pilgrim visited New Testament sites as well, but these were often curious features of the countryside. Apart from the Constantinian basilicas, the pilgrim mentions a spring or pool in Caesarea, known as the 'Bath of Cornelius' (*Itin. Burd.* 585. 7); the Well of Jacob at Sychar, actually a Samaritan holy place (588; cf. John 4: 5–6); the

[83] Of the three places he mentions, only the Temple Mount was left untouched by the Church, and only because the sight of Jews coming to lament over the ruins there served as more excellent propaganda than would any new edifice; cf. *Itin. Burd.* 591. 4; Cyril of Jerusalem, *Cat.* x. 11; xv. 15; Jerome, *Comm. Soph.* i. 15; Eusebius, *Hist. Eccles.* i. 1. 2.

Bethesda/Bethzatha pool, recently converted from being a sanctuary of Serapis (589–90); Siloam, Hadrian's *tetranymphon* (592); some architectural ruins known as the Houses of Caiaphas and Pontius Pilate (593); a rock in the Kidron Valley, where Judas betrayed Jesus (594); a palm tree, believed to be the tree from which people took branches during Jesus' entry into Jerusalem (594; cf. Cyril, *Cat*. x. 19); a little hill on the Mount of Olives, where Jesus was transfigured (595); a burial cave in Bethany known as the Tomb of Lazarus (596); a sycamore tree near Jericho which was climbed by Zacchaeus (596); the spot in the Jordan River where Jesus was baptized (598); and a spring at Bethsur where Philip baptized the eunuch. Such sites reflect a pagan propensity to sanctify springs, pools, rocks, caves, hills, and trees, but one can only speculate that some of these might have been pagan holy sites before a Christian reclassification. Certainly, the Jewish and Samaritan sites were as high on the Bordeaux Pilgrim's agenda as these geographical features, especially sites which had to do with Elijah.[84]

The Jews' willingness to co-operate can be understood if we remember that most of the early pilgrims to Palestine were affluent.[85] It is no wonder that we hear of Jews going to great lengths to pander to the visitors. As we saw in Nazareth, for example, the Piacenza Pilgrim (AD 570) was shown by the local Jews how Christians were able to lift a bench in the synagogue (where, they said, Jesus learnt his ABC), while the Jews pretended to be unable to move it or drag it outside.[86] It was an astoundingly simple trick, but one which the pilgrim fell for with much wonder. We are not told, but it is likely that the gullible visitors freely parted with a few *nummi* for the upkeep of the synagogue after such a miracle. Jews and Samaritans were much used as guides.[87] The finding of the Virgin's clothing in the keeping of a Jewish woman in Jerusalem may indicate that a family theft had taken place,[88] since these clothes had previously been used to

---

[84] For example: Sarepta, where Elijah asked a widow for food (583); Mount Carmel, where Elijah sacrificed (584); the city of Jezreel, where Elijah prophesied (585); the spring of Elisha near Jericho (596); the hill where Elijah was taken up to heaven near the Jordan (598).

[85] T. B. Jones (1978), 21.   [86] Piacenza Pilgrim, *Itin.* v.

[87] Jerome mentions that it was a Jew who showed him the birthplace of Nahum the Elkosite, *Prol. in Naum*, *PL* 25, 1232; see Avi-Yonah (1976*b*), 221.

[88] Leo Grammaticus, *Chron.*, p. 114; George Cedrenus, *Comp. Hist.*, p. 614.

effect miracles in Jewish Nazareth (Piacenza Pilgrim, *Itin*. v). The economics of early Byzantine pilgrimage, relics, and sites have yet to be examined in depth, but if the medieval model is revealing for the early Byzantine world, there was clearly much money to be made in the exploitation of pilgrims. Those who catered to the Church's demand for relics must have been rewarded.

The Samaritans fared less well than the Jews, partly on account of their tendency to revolt during this period. Whatever remained of their temple on Mount Gerizim was destroyed in the middle of the fifth century and replaced by the Church of the Theotokos, built by the emperor Zeno. The Well of Jacob at Sychar became Christian in the fourth century. Jerome records that Paula visited there (in 404).[89] The Tomb of Joseph (cf. Acts 7: 16) was also claimed by the Christians in the middle of the fourth century. The Samaritan Chronicles (*Abul Fath* 169) preserve a story that the Christians were frustrated in their attempts to appropriate the site, but this appears to be a polemical modification of history. A church, or martyrium, existed there at the time of Egeria (Pet. Diac., *Lib*. R). On the former Samaritan site of Mount Nebo, a Christian monastery existed prior to Egeria's visit (Egeria, *Itin*. xxii. 1).

Pagan sacred places, Jewish and Samaritan sites, and venerated tombs rapidly passed over to Christian hands. Constantine wanted churches built fast. In a letter to multiple addressees including the Metropolitan of Caesarea, Eusebius, Constantine called for the restoration of 'ruined churches'. The bishops were asked to 'repair or enlarge those [churches] which at present exist, or, in necessary cases, erect new ones' (*Vita Const*. ii. 46). Funding for these operations could be demanded from as high an officer as the Praetorian Prefect. Constantine also granted lands to the churches (*Vita Const*. iv. 28). Some of these lands were probably confiscated from pagan areas.

Byzantine Christians appear to have embarked on a campaign to mark Palestine as a land with a Christian character.[90] Before Constantine, Palestine was not a Christian 'holy land', though in an attempt to discourage emigration, certain rabbis had sought to inspire Jews with the idea that the Promised Land was sanctified by God in some vague way (cf. *b.Ket*. 110b–111a; *m.Kel*. 1. 6).[91] It

[89] *Ep*. cviii.   [90] Avi-Yonah (1976*b*), 221.
[91] See also the issues explored by Wilken (1985).

may well have been Constantine who first recognized that Palestine could be transformed into an entire region of holiness.[92] Again, the concept is rooted in the ideology of pagan epiphany which was adapted to fit Christian circumstances. Since the earthly Jesus walked over a great part of the province, and God participated in history in this specific area, the entire region was, in a sense, a place of epiphany. It was therefore pervaded with the aura of the sacred shrine. In the concept of a holy land, pagan thought and Christian belief merged. The idea would not become firmly established until the fifth century, in the heyday of Palestinian monasticism, when Jerusalem had become a Christian capital.[93] Monks and nuns living in Palestinian deserts then spoke of themselves as 'inhabitants of this holy land'.[94] This sense of the land being in some way holy is, of course, with us to this day, and has complicated the delicate politics of the region ever since its inception.

Constantine's contribution to the eventual creation of the Holy Land was to begin the process of sanctification and appropriation of sites, and to provide, with his mother and mother-in-law, the models for pious Christian pilgrimage. He set precedents for what would follow. His reasons were partly political, partly religious, and, it would seem, partly motivated by gut feeling: he believed that the sites were holy. There is no doubt that his innovations greatly aided the fortunes of Christianity in the region, if not the Empire as a whole. Going on pilgrimages to sacred places was something that pagans had liked to do, and liked to continue to do upon conversion to Christianity.

This is not to say that Christian pilgrimage was just a continuation of pagan pilgrimage with a twist; far from it. Christian pilgrimage soon exploded into a phenonemon that pagan pilgrimage could never have been. Pagan pilgrimages to sacred shrines had been predominantly local, and were frequently connected with festivals that occurred at specific times. This is in keeping with the fact that 'paganism' is a loose term to refer to a vast variety of different polytheisms connected with different areas and ethnic groups. All these had in common some type of veneration of shrines, and the visiting of such shrines, but a Syrian would rarely have been particularly moved to travel a long

---

[92] See Telfer (1955*b*).   [93] John Cassian, *Collationes* xiv. 8.
[94] Cyril of Scythopolis, *Vita Sabas* lvii.

distance to visit an Egyptian shrine, and vice versa. A visitor who happened to be passing through a foreign city might, out of curiosity, good manners, and prudence, visit the city's main temple, or another that seemed attractive, or participate in a festival; but gods of a different country, even though syncretized, could not attract a multitude of visitors from distant lands. People had their own deities and shrines at home which generally seemed to them much more meaningful than those abroad.

Christianity was an altogether different religion, transcending ethnicity, local culture, and customs, and uniting Christians in a universal and common worship of one God, who participated in history at one general location. Christianity's sacred shrines were therefore concentrated in one part of the world, apart from those which were built to house the remains of martyrs. The growing number of Christian holy places in Palestine drew pilgrims from the far reaches of the Empire. To go on a pilgrimage to Christianity's sacred shrines, one had to be prepared to embark on an expensive and gruelling long-distance journey.

Christian pilgrimage to holy places was a radical innovation, a combination of an ancient story set in one particular landscape and the newly Christianized veneration of sites and things. It fused together diverse elements found in Jewish and Samaritan tradition with pagan piety, and became something more significant than the mere sum of its parts. The fervour of Christian pilgrims, who would endure all kinds of travellers' hardships in order to pray at the holy places of Palestine, whose wonder was boundless, and sheer energy astonishing, provided Christian pilgrimage with a dynamism that was significantly greater than anything that had gone before.

This study of the important Christian holy sites of Byzantine Palestine has shown that nothing supports the notion that Christians venerated these before Constantine: the idea of a place sacred to Christians because of its inherent holiness appears to have been his invention, and is essentially a pagan concept grafted on to Christianity. Christians transferred new concepts of holiness on to the existing cult of the matryrs and their relics, which had its roots in Jewish thought and practice. In due course, Christians appropriated very many Jewish and Samaritan tombs and other sites, and elevated their sacredness in a peculiarly Christian way, influencing too the attitudes of Jews and Samaritans to these places. In particular, the Christian sanctification of places helped the process of the destruction of paganism in Palestine. Pagan sites were taken over by the Church and reclassified as Christian holy places. Christian pilgrimage superseded local pagan pilgrimages and became a vastly more important phenomenon. The Holy Land became a zone of varying degrees of intrinsic sanctities and biblical resonances. No other region had this heady mix of the divine and the material; consequently, no other country was more worth fighting for than Palestine.

Conclusion

THE Bagatti–Testa school believes that Jewish-Christians kept the memory of numerous sacred places before their appropriation by the Byzantine church. It has defined a hypothetical group of Jewish-Christians as Christians of Jewish race living in Palestine who embraced a heterodox theology. These people apparently celebrated baptismal mysteries in sacred grottos, devised a system of cryptic signs and symbols, and venerated certain sites special to Christians, like the place where Christ was born in Bethlehem, the Virgin Mary's House in Nazareth, and so on. The Bagatti–Testa school uses a deductive approach which first asserts a theory and then fits available data into it; but already there have been cases in which the school has been known to be in error. The Dominus Flevit ossuaries, for example, are simply Jewish, and the Khirbet Kilkish funerary *stelai* are forgeries, even though much of the Bagatti–Testa school's understanding of the theology of Jewish-Christianity in Palestine was based on an interpretation of the markings on these spurious *stelai*.

The Bagatti–Testa hypothesis is an argument for the authenticity of present Christian holy sites in Palestine. In positing the existence of groups of Jewish-Christians who descended from Christ's first followers and continued to live in Palestine, Bagatti and Testa are able to fill the gap between mention of certain places in the New Testament and their identification and development in the Byzantine period.

It was considered important at the outset to establish a precise definition of who the historical Jewish-Christians really were, and we began with an examination of this question. Jewish-Christians, it was argued, were practising Jews who believed in Jesus as Messiah. These Jewish-Christians observed Jewish customs and festivals, circumcised their sons, kept the food laws, honoured the Sabbath day, and so on. The definitive part of being a Jewish-Christian was the upholding of Jewish praxis, not simply ethnicity or theology.

By the middle of the second century, most ethnic Jews within the Church had abandoned Jewish praxis and saw themselves as being released from the Mosaic law, in accordance with Pauline teaching. Certain groups, a minority, maintained Jewish praxis. These groups were often called 'Ebionites' by Church Fathers who sought to classify them under this term as an heretical sect. At the beginning, the term may have been used by one particular group who formed the antithesis of the Marcionite sect, but it soon came to refer to all Christians who followed Jewish customs. Some of these later groups, and perhaps the original Ebionites, may not have been ethnically Jewish, but rather 'Judaizing' in seeking to introduce the maintenance of Jewish customs in churches which had long abandoned these, or had never observed them in the first place. A precise Jewish-Christian theology is impossible to trace in the groups classified as Ebionite (or sometimes as Nazoraean) by the Church Fathers. It may be possible to distinguish elements of the theology of groups following Peter or James in the New Testament writings, but the first-century conflicts of theological outlook appear not to have continued into the second century in any significant way; at least, not so that we can distinguish 'Jewish' and 'Gentile' streams of theology which flow from the earliest communities in a continuous unbroken current. It is very likely indeed that Jewish-Christian groups embraced a wide-ranging spectrum of theological beliefs.

In identifying archaeological material as Jewish-Christian on the basis of a definition of Jewish-Christianity which stresses race and theology above praxis, the Bagatti–Testa school has wrongly attributed this material. Furthermore, in seeking to argue for the earliest possible veneration of many Christian holy places, the school has used literary and archaeological material carelessly.

In re-examining the evidence interpreted to provide proof of Jewish-Christianity in the heartland of Roman Palestine, it was concluded that nothing indicates that Jewish-Christians lived there from the middle of the second century onwards. The Palestinian *minim* mentioned in rabbinic sources are rarely to be identified as Jewish-Christians, and in the few cases where they are likely to be such, the material seems to refer to a period before the Bar Kochba Rebellion. The relatives of Jesus in Nazareth and Kochaba, referred to in patristic sources, were probably not Christians; their interest was in claiming descent from David rather than in spreading the Gospel message. Literary and archaeological evidence may suggest that some Jewish-Christians lived in the Bashan through to the fourth century, but clearly they had no interest in maintaining sacred caves or holy sites in this region. If the Bagatti–Testa school wishes to continue to argue that Jewish-Christians maintained holy sites in the heartland of Palestine, the evidence must be such that no other interpretation is possible. From literary material, however, it would seem very likely that Jewish-Christians moved away from Jewish areas by the middle of the second century, possibly because their position there was increasingly uncomfortable, and went to the cosmopolitan cities like Caesarea, Gaza, or Scythopolis, where they soon largely abandoned Jewish praxis. The same fate may have befallen the Jerusalem church, which prior to the Bar Kochba Revolt was predominantly Jewish-Christian. However, it is possible that some members of the church abandoned Jewish praxis at this time and continued to live in the transformed city, Aelia Capitolina.

As regards the demography of Palestine from 135 until 324, it would appear that Jews were concentrated in Galilee, Samaritans in a 'strip' around Mount Gerizim, and Christians in the cosmopolitan cities and a few southern villages. The largest population group appears to have been pagan. The pagans lived throughout the country, and along its border regions: in the Negev, Nabataea, east of the Jordan River, the Hauran, the Bashan, and Hermon areas. Pagan influence was strong in northern Galilee, Idumaea, and along the coast. Populations mixed in many of the large cities.

Archaeological and literary evidence taken together bears out the impression that Byzantine Christian holy sites were not venerated by Christians prior to the fourth century.

Mamre had been a sacred site to pagans and Jews for a long time, and it was given over to the Church only after the visit of the emperor Constantine's mother-in-law, Eutropia. Christians may have visited the site before this time, but the restoration language used by the Church Fathers in regard to the place does not mean that it was ever venerated or owned by Christians prior to Eutropia's visit. Constantine clearly saw Mamre as being intrinsically holy and therefore the property of the Church, who alone could vouchsafe its spiritual cleanliness. Since it should have been in the hands of God's true servants, the Christians, long before, the pagans who had continued to possess the site were accused of stealing and defiling it.

The Bagatti–Testa school claims that the other three Constantinian sites of Bethlehem, Golgotha, and the Eleona Cave commemorating the Ascension on the Mount of Olives were all venerated by Jewish-Christians prior to the fourth century. In Bethlehem, the available archaeological evidence tells us little, but the literary sources appear to indicate that a pagan grove and cave of Tammuz-Adonis were established prior to the site's Christian use. A highly symbolic Christian story arose, by the middle of the second century, which located the birth of Christ in a cave in the desert outside Bethlehem. This strongly influenced the imaginations of Christians when they tried to envisage the birth of Christ. By the end of the third century, the pagan cave was identified as the birthplace of Christ by Christians visiting the area, possibly influenced by the local inhabitants who may themselves have encouraged this identification. It was then an easy target for appropriation at the beginning of the fourth century.

In the case of Golgotha, the site was probably remembered by the Jerusalem community as lying under the region of the western forum of Aelia Capitolina, possibly near the colonnaded Decumanus or Cardo Maximus roads close to the northernmost slope of Mount Zion. With Constantine, this location was shifted north to lie under the Hadrianic temple of Venus, which was subsequently torn down. A basilica in honour of the cross was built in its stead. An outcrop of rock on which had been erected a statue of Venus was reused as a podium for a crucifix, and over the years came to be identified as the specific site of Jesus' death. A cave cut into the rock's eastern side, identified by the Bagatti–Testa school as being Jewish-Christian, was actually created in the seventh century, and owed its being to speculation on stories about the Tomb of Adam being located under the cross on which Christ died. The sepulchre which was identified as the Tomb of Jesus is very unlikely to be authentic.

The Eleona Cave on the Mount of Olives was identified as important under the influence of an apocryphal story, this time of a Gnostic nature, which described Christ passing on secret teaching to his disciples before the Ascension. The church of Jerusalem sought to negate this identification by placing the site of the Ascension further up the hill, and ensuring that the cave became the site of Christ's teaching *before* his death. The Mount of Olives as a whole appears to have been considered holy by some Christians, who maintained that God's presence rested there after it left the Jewish Temple.

The Bagatti–Testa hypothesis makes much of the idea of the 'mystic grotto', which it suggests was a Jewish-Christian concept. Many caves later used by Christians as holy places are considered by the school to have been once Jewish-Christian. Our examination has shown this to be unlikely. Caves were used by pagans, for mysteries, and also by Jews, for magic, but there is no evidence that Christians of any kind employed caves in Palestine as meeting places. Caves were very often used for agricultural purposes. This was the case for the Bethany Cave and the Cave of Gethsemane. The former was a cistern until its creation as a holy place (the guest-room of Martha and Mary) in the fourth century. The latter was an olive-processing works until it was appropriated by the Church. In the case of Gethsemane, it is very likely indeed that this was where Jesus and his disciples actually took shelter but, as with the case of Golgotha, there is nothing to suggest that Christians considered it hallowed ground before Constantine, even though the name of the locality was preserved and the site was correctly identified. The Tomb of Mary was built in the fifth century, and had no Jewish-Christian origins. It appears to have been created to satisfy the expectations of pilgrims familiar with apocryphal stories about the death of Mary.

Mount Zion was an area of ruins at the beginning of the fourth century. The Jerusalem community built for itself the magnificent Church of Holy Zion on a site which they claimed was that of the first apostolic church of Jerusalem. However, despite these claims, archaeological excavations in the region cannot confirm these suggestions as being historically accurate. The area was the most affluent in first-century Jerusalem, which would make it unlikely that the primitive community met here. Walls and a niche considered by the Bagatti–Testa school to come from a Jewish-Christian synagogue-church in fact derive from the Byzantine structure, and may have been where the bones of St Stephen were deposited in the fifth century.

The two most extensively excavated Franciscan sites in Galilee, Nazareth and Capernaum, have also been found to have no early signs of Christian veneration. Both towns were Jewish in the

Roman and early Byzantine periods. They were probably each provided with a small pilgrim church in the fourth century by Joseph of Tiberias, who, though a Jew who converted to Christianity, was not a sectarian Jewish-Christian, but almost an envoy of Constantine. He wished to encourage Christian belief in the Jewish heartland, and appears to have convinced the Jews of Nazareth and Capernaum that it would be prudent to allow Christians to visit.

In the case of Nazareth, the so-called Jewish-Christian synagogue-church seems to be the structure built by Joseph (*c*.335), and nothing would suggest that the area was venerated prior to this time. Graffiti on the walls of this church indicate that there were Christian visitors from throughout the Empire. The same is true for the graffiti of Capernaum. The alleged Jewish-Christian house-church there is probably also the work of Joseph of Tiberias. Lime floors which may date from the third century, found on part of a room in this structure, are most likely indicative of affluence and not of veneration.

In both Nazareth and Capernaum, the Jewish community permitted an influx of Christian pilgrims, and pandered to them, for the sake of revenue. Perhaps some proof of the economic boom afforded by these circumstances is shown in the splendid limestone synagogue that the Jewish community was able to build in Capernaum in the fifth century.

There is an important difference between being interested in a site as an educated visitor or tourist (undertaking an *historia*), and venerating a piece of sanctified ground by praying there as a pilgrim. Christians appear to have had no interest in the sanctification of the material land of Palestine, or any part of it, before Constantine. The historical and archaeological evidence clearly points to the beginning of the fourth century as the time at which pilgrimage to certain Christian holy sites began and the sites themselves were developed.

With the changes wrought by the first Christian emperor came the origins of Christian sacred places and the beginnings of Christian pilgrimage. Jews had once had a holy place *par excellence* in the Temple on Mount Moriah, and Samaritans their temple on Mount Gerizim. Both groups had places of significance and veneration in the form of tombs and geographical features at which a particularly devout person might say a blessing if he or she happened to pass by. In the main, however, it was the pagans whose many religious acts required pilgrimage to sacred places and the veneration of such sites as holy in themselves. The entire Roman Empire, including the land of Palestine, was peppered with sacred zones and had been for centuries. Some Jews and Samaritans themselves may have participated in cult festivals at such holy sites, probably despite 'official' disapproval; this was the case at Mamre. Festivals around sacred places were a powerful force in the preservation of pagan cult.

Constantine waged a war against paganism. He destroyed a great many pagan sanctuaries and temples, and reversed laws that had previously attacked the Church. He set about a programme of Christianization, and sought to stamp out paganism in Palestine. He wished to create *Christian* holy sites which would supersede pagan shrines. While educated Christians had visited Palestine before to learn more about the history of the place, Christian pilgrimage as such began with the visits of the emperor's mother, Helena, and mother-in-law, Eutropia. Three Christian holy places were promptly redeemed from pagan desecration, and one from Gnostic speculation. Soon Christians claimed many sites which had previously been important only to pagans, Jews, or Samaritans. Anything that had a biblical association could be 'restored' to the hands of God's elect in order to have a church built on the place which could attract a new generation of now *Christian* pilgrims. The beginnings of Christian holy sites and the beginnings of Christian pilgrimage go hand in hand. Pilgrims went to holy sites in order to pray and recollect the events that purportedly took place there. The increase in the amount of holy sites in Byzantine Palestine probably parallels the increase in the numbers of pilgrims coming there during this time.

Christian holy places in the Byzantine period were different from the tombs of the saints which Christians had honoured before. The Jews had given Christians the practice of venerating, to a degree, the graves of the righteous dead. The tombs were honoured because of the holiness of the people whose remains were interred. For the Jews, however, the site of the Temple on Mount Moriah had been the only real holy place, and since the departure of God's presence from this location in AD 70, its holiness had ceased, and pilgrimage to the ruins did not continue. Jews kept a distinction between the material and the spiritual; a site was not intrinsically holy because of some past event, but to the Byzantine Christians a site was holy because God had participated in history at a particular location. The early Christians had rejected the materiality of this fundamentally pagan idea of the holy place, and had even cast doubt on the special holiness of the Jewish and Samaritan temples, concentrating instead on the heavenly Jerusalem and the world to come.

After Constantine's innovations, all this began to change, though not in a uniform way. Christian holy places had various beginnings. Many had been pagan, Jewish, or Samaritan sites; these and others were identified as being where biblical events took place or where a biblical figure lay buried. Some of these sites were probably genuine locations mentioned in the New Testament: the pool of Bethesda and Gethsemane, for example, the identifications of which had probably been preserved by the population of Aelia as a whole, and the Jerusalem church among it. Some of the sites had been identified in the third century after popular apocryphal stories took hold of the imaginations of local Christians and visitors: the Eleona Cave, for example, or the Bethlehem Cave, but identification did not mean sanctification. The site of Golgotha had been remembered, but it was moved north by Constantine. Apocryphal stories continued to exert an active influence in the formation of later holy sites, like the Tomb of Mary or the Cave of Adam in the Rock of Calvary. Many sites were pagan, Jewish, or Samaritan and were appropriated when the Church was given new powers. Some sites were created as holy places out of nothing very much, like the Bethany Cave; since it lay on the probable route to the Lazarium at Bethany, it must have been considered a good place for a shrine. Expediency was a good reason for the identification of certain sites: the Church of Holy Zion, for example, was probably built on its site because it was simply a fine place for a large church. Traditions soon accrued which justified the existence of these structures.

In Galilee, the instrument of the establishment of holy places was Joseph of Tiberias, who acted with the blessing of Constantine. He provided churches for pilgrims to visit in Nazareth, Capernaum, Tiberias, and Sepphoris, though only his structures in the former two towns have been excavated.

The idea of the Christian holy place therefore began in the fourth century with the innovations of the emperor Constantine. It is his figure that looms large over the course of events which led to the establishment of hundreds of holy sites and churches in Palestine throughout the Byzantine period. Christian pilgrimage began in the wake of his innovations, and not before, though Christians had visited the land prior to this time. The concept of the intrinsically holy place was basically pagan, and was not in essence a Christian idea. Nevertheless, by the sixth century Palestine as a whole was considered to be imbued with the aura of the divine; it became the Holy Land, vouchsafed to the care of God's chosen—the Christians—for ever. Such property rights were worth fighting for, and would lead the way to the door of the Middle Ages and the Crusades, and even to modern times. Indeed, the concept has found its way to the contemporary Christian and Muslim consciousness, and influenced Jewish thought. The idea of sanctified places, to which pilgrims might come to pray, cannot, however, be found in Christian teaching prior to Constantine, and certainly not in any Jewish-Christian 'theology' that might be traced back to the very origins of the Church. It would appear rather that the idea of the holy place is dangerously close to idolatry. The intermixture of the physical and the divine is a powerful one which lies at the heart of strong passions about the ownership of the region to this day.

References

Principal Ancient Sources

ADOMNAN, *De Locis Sanctis*, ed. L. Bieler (*CCSL* 175; 1965).

Armenian Lectionary, *Le Codex Arménien Jérusalem 121*, ed. A. Renoux (*PO* 35–6; 1969–71).

Apocalypses Apocryphae, ed. C. Tischendorf (Leipzig, 1866).

BASIL OF CAESAREA, *Epistulae*, ed. J. Garnier and P. Maran (*PG* 32).

BERNARD THE MONK, *Itinerarium*, ed. T. Tobler and A. Molinier, in *Itinera Hierosolymitana et Descriptiones Terrae Sanctae* (St Gallen and Paris, 1879).

BORDEAUX PILGRIM, *Itinerarium Burdigalense*, ed. P. Geyer and O. Cuntz (*CCSL* 175; 1965).

Breviarius de Hierosolyma, ed. R. Weber (*CCSL* 175; 1965).

CASSIUS DIO, *Historia Romana*, ed. U. P. Boissevain (Berlin, 1901).

Chronicon Paschale, ed. L. Dindorf, 2 vols. (CSHB 7–8; 1832 = *PG* 92).

PS.-CLEMENT, *Homilies and Recognitions*, ed. B. Rehm and F. Paschke: *Homiliae* (*GCS* 42; 1953); *Recognitiones* (*GCS* 51; 1965).

Commemoratorium, ed. T. Tobler and A. Molinier in *Itinera Hierosolymitana et Descriptiones Terrae Sanctae* (St Gallen and Paris, 1879).

CYRIL OF JERUSALEM, *Catecheses*, ed. A. A. Touttée and P. Maran (*PG* 33); also ed. A. Rousséau (*SC* 100; 1965).

CYRIL OF SCYTHOPOLIS, *Vita Sabas*, ed. E. Schwartz (*TU* 49; 1939).

DANIEL THE ABBOT, *Zhitie i knozhenie Danila rus'kyya zemli igumena 1106–1108*, ed. M. A. Venevitinov (Palestinskiy pravoslavnyy sbornik 3, 9; St Petersburg, 1883–5).

DICUIL, *De Mensura Orbis Terrae*, ed. G. Parthey (*Dicuili liber de Mensura Orbis Terrae* (Berlin, 1875)).

Didache, ed. W. Rordorf and A. Tuilier (*SC* 248; 1978).

Didascalia Addai, ed. P. de Lagarde (Leipzig, 1854).

Didascalia Apostolorum, ed. H. Achelis and J. Flemming, in *Die syrische Didaskalia* (*TU* 10.2; 1904); also Latin reconstruction: *Didascalia et Constitutiones Apostolorum* ed. F. X. Funk, 2 vols. (Paderborn, 1905; repr. 1960).

Disputation of Sergius the Stylite against a Jew, ed. A. P. Hayman (*CSCO* 338–9; 1973).

EGERIA, *Itinerarium*, ed. A. Franceschini and R. Weber (*CCSL* 175; 1965).

Epistle of Barnabas, ed. P. Prigent and R. A. Kraft (*SC* 172; 1971).

EPIPHANIUS OF SALAMIS, *Panarion*, ed. K. Holl (*GCS* I.1/2/3; 1915, 1922, 1933).

—— *De Mensuris et Ponderibus*, ed. J. E. Dean (*Epiphanius' Treatise on Weights and Measures: The Syriac Version* (Chicago, 1935)).

EPIPHANIUS THE MONK, *Hagiopolita*, 'Die Palästinabeschreibung des Epiphanius Monachus *Hagiopolita*', ed. H. Donner, *ZDPV* 87 (1971: 66–82.

(Ps.-?) EUCHERIUS, *De situ Hierosolimae Epistula ad Faustum Presbyterium*, ed. I. Fraipont (*CCSL* 175; 1965).

EUSEBIUS, *Chronicon*, ed. R. Helm (*GCS* 45: *Eusebius Werke* VII.1/2; 1956).

—— *Oratio Constantini*, ed. I. A. Heikel (*GCS* 7: *Eusebius Werke* 1902), 149–92.

—— *Demonstratio Evangelica*, ed. I. A. Heikel (*GCS* 23: *Eusebius Werke* VI; 1913).

—— *De Laudibus Constantini*, ed. I. A. Heikel (*GCS* 7: *Eusebius Werke* I; 1902).

—— *Historia Ecclesiastica*, ed. E. Schwartz (*GCS* 9.1–3: *Eusebius Werke* II.1–3; 1903–9).

—— *Martyrs of Palestine*, ed. E. Schwartz (*GCS* 9: *Eusebius Werke* II: 1908: Greek, short form); ed. W. Cureton (London and Edinburgh, 1861: Syriac, long form).

—— *Praeparatio Evangelica*, ed. K. Mras (*GCS* 43:1–2: *Eusebius Werke* VIII.1–2; 1954, 1956).

—— *Onomasticon*, ed. E. Klostermann (*GCS* 11: *Eusebius Werke* III.1; 1904).

—— *Theophania*, ed. H. Gressmann (*GCS* 11: *Eusebius Werke* III.2; 1904).

—— *Tricennial Oration* (*Triakontaethrikos*), ed. I. A. Heikel (*GCS* 7: *Eusebius Werke* I; 1902), 193–259.

—— *De Vita Constantini*, ed. F. Winkelmann (*GCS* 7: *Eusebius Werke* I.2; 1975).

EUTYCHIUS OF ALEXANDRIA, *Annales*, ed. I. Selden *et al.* (PG 111; Latin trans.); also ed. L. Cheikho (*CSCO* 50/Ar.6; Arabic, Ibn al Batriq).

GEORGE CEDRENUS, *Compendium historiarum*, ed. E. Bekker (CSHB 4–5; 1838).

GEORGE HAMARTOLOS, *Short Chronicle*, ed. E. de Muralt (*PG* 110).

GEORGE SYNCELLUS, *Chronographia*, ed. G. Dindorf (Bonn, 1829).

The Georgian Lectionary, ed. M. Tarchnischvili (*Le Grand Lectionnaire de l'Église de Jérusalem* (*CSCO* 188–9; 1959)).

HIPPOLYTUS, *Refutatio omnium Haeresium*, ed. P. Wendiand (*GCS* 26; 1916).

HUGEBURC, *Vita Willibaldi*, ed. O. Holder-Egger (*Monumenta Germaniae Historica* 15.1; Hanover, 1919).

IGNATIUS, *Epistulae*, ed. Th. Camelot (*SC* 10; 1969).

IRENAEUS, *Adversus Haereses*, ed. A. Rousseau and L. Doutreleau (*SC* 263–4; 1979).

JEROME, *Commentarium in Jeremiam*, ed. S. Reiter (CSEL 59; 1913).

—— *De Viris Illustribus*, ed. E. C. Richardson (*TU* 14; 1896).

—— *Epistulae*, ed. I. A. Hilberg (*CSEL* 54–6; 1910–18).

—— *Liber locorum*, ed. E. Klostermann (*GCS* 11: *Eusebius Werke* III.1; 1904).

JOHN CHRYSOSTOM, *Homilies and Commentaries*, ed. B. de Montfaucon (*PG* 48–9).

JOHN MALALAS, *Chronographia*, ed. L. Dindorf (Bonn, 1931).

JOSEPHUS, *Bellum Judaicarum*, ed. H. St J. Thackeray (Loeb, vols. ii–iii; London and Cambridge, Mass., 1927–8).

—— *Antiquities of the Jews*, ed. H. St J. Thackeray (Loeb, vols. iv–ix; London and Cambridge, Mass., 1930–63).

JUSTIN MARTYR, *Dialogue with Trypho*, ed. P. Maran (*PG* 6).

—— *Apologies*, ed. A. Wartelle (Paris, 1987).

LEO GRAMMATICUS, *Chronografia*, ed. E. Bekker (CSHB; 1842).

MARK THE DEACON, *Vita Porphyrii*, ed. H. Grégoire and M.-A. Kugener (*Marc le Diacre, Vie de Porphyre* (Paris, 1930)).

MELITO OF SARDIS, *Paschal Homily*, ed. B. Lohse (*Die Passa-Homilie des Bischofs Meliton von Sardes* (Leiden, 1958)).

PS.-MELITON, *Oration of Meliton the Philosopher*, ed. W. Cureton, in *Spicilegium Syriacum* (Leiden, 1855, 22–35).

Odes of Solomon, ed. J. Charlesworth (Oxford, 1973).

ORIGEN, *Contra Celsum*, ed. M. Borret (*SC* 132–6; 1967–76).

—— *De Principiis*, ed. P. Koetschau (*GCS* 22: *Origenes Werke* V; 1913).

Patrum Nicaenorum Nomina, ed. H. Geltzer, H. Hilgenfeld, and O. Cuntz (Leipzig, 1898).

PAULINUS OF NOLA, *Carmina et Epistulae*, ed. G. de Hartel (*CSEL* 29–30; 1894).

PETER THE DEACON, *Petrus Diaconus: Liber de Locis Sanctis*, ed. R. Weber (*CCSL* 175; 1965).

PETER THE IBERIAN, *Vita*, ed. R. Raabe (*Petrus der Iberer* (Leipzig, 1895)).

PHILOSTORGIUS, *Historia Ecclesiastica*, ed. J. Bidez, rev. F. Winkelmann (*GCS* 21; 1981).

PHOTIUS, *Myrobiblion*, ed. E. Bekker and A. Schott (*PG* 103–4).

PIACENZA PILGRIM, *Antoninus Placentinus: Itinerarium*, ed. P. Geyer (*CCSL* 175; 1965).

PROCOPIUS OF CAESAREA, *Aedificia Justiniani*, ed. H. B. Dewing and G. Downey (Loeb; London and Cambridge, Mass., 1961).

RUFINUS, *Historia Ecclesiastica*, ed. T. Mommsen (*GCS* 9.1–2: *Eusebius Werke* II. 1–2; 1903–9).

SAEWULF, MS 111, Corpus Christi College, Cambridge.

S. Helenae et Constantini Vitae, ed. M. Guidi (*Rendiconti della R. Accademia dei Lincei, Classe di scienze morali, storiche, e filologische XVI*, 5; Rome, 1907).

SOCRATES, *Historia Ecclesiastica*, ed. R. Hussey (Oxford, 1853).

SOPHRONIUS, *Anacreontica*, ed. M. Gigante (*Opuscula, Testi per esercitazioni accademiche* 10/12; Rome, 1957).

SOZOMEN, *Historia Ecclesiastica*, ed. J. Bidez and G. C. Hansen (*GCS* 50; 1960).

Spicilegium Syriacum, ed. W. Cureton (Leiden, 1855).

PS.-TERTULLIAN, *Carmen adversus Marcionem*, ed. R. Willems (*CCSL* 2; 1954).

THEODORET, *Historia Ecclesiastica*, ed. L. Parmentier and F. Scheidweiler (*GCS* 44; 1954).

THEODOSIUS, *De Situ Terrae Sanctae*, ed. P. Geyer (*CCSL* 175; 1965).

De Transitu Mariae Apocrypha Aethiopice, ed. V. Arras, (*CSCO* 342–3; 1973); also 'Adnotationes' in *Librum Requiei* (*CSCO* 352; 1974), 75–105.

For other medieval pilgrim accounts see the list of editions and translations published in Wilkinson (1988), 346–55. Further information about Greek patristic sources may be found in M. Geerard, *Clavis Patrum Graecorum* (Turnhout, 1974).

Modern Works (Including Translations of Ancient Sources)

ABEL, F. M. (1918), 'Mont des Oliviers: ruine de la grotte de l'Éléona', *RB* 27: 55–8.

ADAN-BAYEWITZ, D., and PERLMAN, I. (1990), 'The Local Trade of Sepphoris in the Roman Period', *IEJ* 40: 153–72.

AHARONI, Y. (1954), 'A Village of Monks in the Region of Beth ha-Shitta', *Bulletin of the Israel Exploration Society*, 209–15 (Hebrew).

—— (1962), *Excavations at Ramat Rahel, Seasons 1959 and 1960* (Rome).

—— (1964), *Excavations at Ramat Rahel, Seasons 1961 and 1962* (Rome).

ALBRIGHT, W. F. (1925), 'Bronze Age Mounds of Northern Palestine and the Hauran: The Spring Trip of the School in Jerusalem', *BASOR* 19: 5–19.

ALON, G. (1973), *History of the Jews in Eretz-Israel in the Times of the Mishnah and the Talmud*, 2 vols. (Tel Aviv) (Hebrew).

AMIRAN, R. (1956), 'A Fragment of an Ornamental Relief from Kfar Bar'am', *IEJ* 6: 239–45.

ANDERSON, R. T. (1980), 'Mount Gerizim: Navel of the World', *BA* 43: 217–22.

—— (1989), 'Samaritan History During the Renaissance', in Crown (1989), 95–112.

APPELBAUM, S. (1976), *Prolegomena to the Study of the Second Jewish Revolt (AD 132–135)* (Oxford).

ARAKELIAN, B. N. (1978), 'Armenian Mosaic of the Early Middle Ages', *Atti del primo Simposio Internationale di Arta Armena* (Venice, 1978), 1–9.

AUGUSTONOVIC, A. (1971), '*El-Khader' e il Profeta Elia* (Jerusalem).

AVI-YONAH, M. (1934), 'Mosaic Pavements in Palestine', *QDAP* 3: 26–73.

—— (1940), *Abbreviations in Greek Inscriptions: The Near East, 200 BC–AD 1100* (*QDAP* Suppl. to vol. 9; Jerusalem).

—— (1946), *Map of Roman Palestine*, 2nd edn. (Jerusalem).

—— (1952), 'Mount Carmel and the God of Baalbek', *IEJ* 2: 118–24.

—— (1954), *The Madaba Mosaic Map* (Jerusalem).

—— (1957a), 'Christian Archaeology in Israel, 1948–54', in *Actes du 5e Congrès International d'Archéologie Chrétienne, Aix-en-Provence, 1954* (Vatican and Paris), 117–23.

—— (1957b), 'Places of Worship in the Roman and Byzantine Periods', *Antiquity and Survival* 2 (2/3): 262–72.

—— (1958), 'The Economics of Byzantine Palestine', *IEJ* 8: 39–51.

—— (1959), 'Syrian Gods at Ptolemais-Acco', *IEJ* 9: 1–12.

—— (1961a), *Oriental Art in Palestine* (Rome).

—— (1961b), review of Bagatti and Milik (1958), *IEJ* 11: 91–4.

—— (1962), 'A List of Priestly Courses from Caesarea', *IEJ* 12: 137–9.

—— (1966), *The Holy Land from the Persian to the Arab Conquests: An Historical Geography* (Grand Rapids).

—— (1970), 'The Caesarea Porphyry Statue', *IEJ* 20: 203–8.

—— (1973), 'Editor's Note', *IEJ* 23: 43–5.

—— (1975–8) (ed.), *Encyclopaedia of Archaeological Excavations in the Holy Land*, 4 vols. (London).

—— (1976a), *A Gazetteer of Roman Palestine* (Jerusalem).

—— (1976b), *The Jews of Palestine: A Political History from the Bar Kochba War to the Arab Conquest* (Oxford); also published as *The Jews under Roman and Byzantine Rule* (Jerusalem, 1976).

AVIRAM, M. (1985), 'The Roman Temple at Kedesh in the Light of Certain Northern Syrian City Coins', *Tel Aviv* 12: 212–14.

BAGATTI, B. (1937), 'La capella sul Monte delle Beatitudini', *RAC* 14: 43–91.

—— (1938), 'Tempera dell'antica basilica di Getsemani', *RAC* 15: 153–62.

—— (1940), 'Il cristianesimo a Kerak in Transgiordania', *TS* 20: 1–4.

—— (1948), 'Il cristianesimo nella capitale della Transgiordania ('Amman)', *TS* 23: 35–9.

—— (1950), 'Resti cristiani in Palestina anteriori a Costantino?', *RAC* 26: 117-31.

—— (1952), *Gli antichi edifici sacri di Betlemme in seguito agli scavi e restauri praticati dalla Custodia di Terra Santa (1948-1951)* (Jerusalem).

—— (1953a), 'Espressioni bibliche nelle antiche iscrizione cristiane della Palestina', *LA* 3: 111-48.

—— (1953b), 'Scoperta di un cimitero giudeo-cristiano al "Dominus Flevit" (Monte Oliveto—Gerusalemme)', *LA* 3: 149-84.

—— (1954), 'Origine e svilluppo dell'iconografia cristiana in Palestina', *LA* 4: 277-309.

—— (1955), 'Ritrovamenti nella Nazaret evangelica', *LA* 5: 5-44.

—— (1956), 'Il "Min" Giacobbe in Kafar Soma delle fonti rabbiniche', *TS* 32: 170-1.

—— (1957a), 'Gli altari paleo-cristiani della Palestina', *LA* 7: 64-94.

—— (1957b), 'I battisteri della Palestina', in *Actes du 5e Congrès International d'Archéologie Chrétienne, Aix-en-Provence, 1954* (Vatican and Paris), 213-27.

—— (1957c), 'Kaukab: in questo paese vissero i parenti del Signore', *TS* 33: 140-3.

—— (1958), 'Resti Romani nell'area della Flagellazione in Gerusalemme', *LA* 8: 309-52.

—— (1961), 'Ricerche su alcuni antichi siti giudeo-cristiani', *LA* 11: 288-314.

—— (1963a), 'Gerusalemme e Betlemme negli antichi mosaici', *TS* 39: 101-5.

—— (1963b), 'Le origini della "tomba della Vergine" al Getsemani', *Rivista biblica*, 11: 38-52.

—— (1964a), 'Al centro degli Arcontici, Kh. Kilkish presso Hebron', *TS* 40: 264-9.

—— (1964b), 'Le origini delle tradizioni dei luoghi santi in Palestina', *LA* 14: 32-64.

—— (1964c), 'Probabile figura del Precursore in un graffito di Nazaret', *Oriens Antiquus*, 3: 61-6.

—— (1965), 'Le antichità di Kh. Qana e di Kefr Kenna in Galilea', *LA* 15: 251-92.

—— (1966), 'I parenti del Signore a Nazaret', *Bibbia e Oriente*, 8: 259-63.

—— (1967), 'Alla ricerca della tomba del Min Giacobbe', *TS* 43: 74-7.

—— (1968a), 'Ancora sulla data di Eteria', *Bibbia e Oriente*, 10: 73-5.

—— (1968b), 'Recenti scavi a Betlemme', *LA* 18: 181-237.

—— (1969), *Excavations in Nazareth* (Jerusalem), trans. by E. Hoade of *Gli scavi di Nazaret* (Jerusalem, 1967).

—— (1970a), 'Le due redazione del "Transitus Mariae"', *Marianum*, 32: 272-87.

—— (1970b), *Guida di Cafarnao* (Jerusalem).

BAGATTI, B. (1971*a*), 'Altre medaglie di Salomone Cavaliere e loro origine', *RAC* 47: 331–42.

—— (1971*b*), *Antichi villaggi cristiani della Galilea* (Jerusalem).

—— (1971*c*), *The Church from the Circumcision* (Jerusalem; repr. 1984), Eng. edn. of an Italian manuscript trans. by E. Hoade; first published as *L'Église de la Circoncision*, trans. by A. Storme (Jerusalem, 1965).

—— (1971*d*), *The Church from the Gentiles in Palestine* (Jerusalem), Eng. edn. of an Italian manuscript trans. by E. Hoade; first published as *L'Église de la Gentilé en Palestine*, trans. by A. Storme (Jerusalem, 1968).

—— (1971*e*), 'Ricerche sulla tradizioni della morte della Vergine', *Bibbia e Oriente*, 13: 185–214.

—— (1971*f*), 'S. Pietro nella "Dormitio Mariae"', *Bibbia e Oriente*, 13: 42–8.

—— (1972*a*), 'I giudeo-cristiani a l'anello di Salomone', *RSR* 60: 151–60.

—— (1972*b*), 'Nuove scoperte alla Tomba della Vergine a Getsemane', *LA* 22: 236–90.

—— (1972*c*), 'Scoperte archeologiche alla Tomba di Maria a Getsemani', *Marianum*, 34: 193–9.

—— (1973*a*), 'L'apertura della Tomba della Vergine a Getsemani', *LA* 23: 318–21.

—— (1973*b*), 'Tombeau de la Vierge', *RB* 80: 581–2.

—— (1977*a*), 'Una grotta bizantina sul Monte Tabor', *LA* 27: 119–22.

—— (1977*b*), 'Note sull'iconografia di "Adamo sotto il Calvario"', *LA* 27: 5–32.

—— (1981), 'Ritrovamento archeologico sul Sion', *LA* 31: 249–56.

—— (1981–2), *Alle origini della chiesa*: 1 *Le comunità giudeo-cristiane*; 2. *Le comunità gentilo-cristiane* (Vatican).

—— and MILIK, J. T. (1958), *Gli scavi del 'Dominus Flevit'*, pt. i. *La necropoli del periodo romano* (Jerusalem).

—— PICCIRILLO, M., and PRODOMO, A. (1975), *New Discoveries at the Tomb of Virgin Mary in Gethsemane* (Jerusalem).

—— and TESTA, E. (1978), *Il Golgota e la croce* (Jerusalem).

—— (1982), *Corpus Scriptorum de Ecclesia Matre*, iv. *Gerusalemme: la rendenzione secondo la tradizione biblica dei SS. Padri* (Jerusalem).

BAHAT, D., and BROSHI, M. (1976), 'Excavations in the Armenian Garden', in Yadin (1976), 55–6.

BALDI, D. (1955), *Enchiridion Locorum Sanctorum*, rev. edn. (Jerusalem).

BARAG, D. (1970–1), 'Glass Vessels from Jerusalem', *Journal of Glass Studies*, 12 (1970): 35–63 (pt. 1); 13 (1971): 45–63 (pts. 2 and 3).

—— (1974), 'An Epitaph of the Fifth Century AD from the Raphia Area', *IEJ* 24: 128–31.

BARDY, G. (1952) (trans.), *Eusèbe de Césarée: Histoire ecclésiastique* (Paris).

BARKAY, G. (1984), 'The "Garden Tomb" in Jerusalem', in Schiller (1984), 195–203 (Hebrew).

——ILAN, Z., KLONER, A., MAZAR, A., and URMAN, D. (1974), 'Archaeological Survey of the Northern Bashan (Preliminary Report)', *IEJ* 24: 173–84.

BARKAY, R. (1987–8), 'A Roman-Period Samaritan Burial from Talluze', *BAIAS* 7: 8–20.

BARNES, T. D. (1981), *Constantine and Eusebius* (Cambridge, Mass.).

——(1985), 'Constantine and the Christians of Persia', *JRS* 75: 126–36.

BARTLETT, J. R. (1979), 'From Edomites to Nabataeans: A Study in Continuity', *PEQ* 111: 53–66.

BASSER, H. W. (1981), 'Allusions to Christian and Gnostic Practices in Talmudic Tradition', *JSS* 12: 87–105.

BAUCKHAM, R. (1990), *Jude and the Relatives of Jesus in the Early Church* (Edinburgh).

BAUDISSIN, W. W. (1855), *Adonis und Esmun* (Leipzig).

BAUER, W. (1971), *Orthodoxy and Heresy in Earliest Christianity* (London); trans. of *Rechtgläubigkeit und Keterei im ältesten Christentum* (Tübingen, 1964).

BAUR, F. C. (1831), 'Die Christuspartei in der korinthischen Gemeinde, der Gegensatz des petrinischen und paulinischen Christentums in der ältesten Kirche, der Apostel Paulus in Rom', *Tübinger Zeitschrift für Theologie*, 5.4: 61–206.

BAYNES, N. H. (1930), 'Constantine the Great and the Christian Church' (Raleigh Lecture on History, 1929), in *Proceedings of the British Academy*, 15 (London), 95–103; 2nd edn. as separate vol. (London, 1972).

BEAULIEU, A., and MOUTERDE, R. (1947–8), 'La grotte d'Astarte à Wastra', *Mélanges de l'Université Saint-Joseph, Beirut*, 27: 1–20.

BEN ARIEH, Y. (1962), 'Caves and Ruins in the Beth Guvrin Area', *IEJ* 12: 47–61.

BEN DOV, M. (1974), 'A Lintel from the Bashan Depicting Three Deities', *IEJ* 2: 185–6.

BENNETT, C., and HUMPHREYS, S. C. (1974), 'The Jerusalem Ship', *The International Journal of Nautical Archaeology and Underwater Excavation*, 3/2: 307–10.

BENOIT, P. (1971), 'L'Antonia d'Hérode le Grand et le forum oriental d'Aelia Capitolina', *HTR* 64: 135–67.

——(1975), 'L'emplacement de Bethléem au temps de Jésus', *Dossiers de l'archéologie*, 10/3: 58–63.

——(1976), 'The Archaeological Reconstruction of the Antonia Fortress', in Yadin (1976), 87–9.

——and BOISMARD, M. E. (1951), 'Un ancien sanctuaire chrétien à Bethanie', *RB* 58: 200–51.

BERDER, M. (1988), 'Un itinéraire au Mont des Oliviers', *Le monde de la Bible*, 55: 10–31.

BERTHIER, A., and CHARLIER, R. (1955), *Le sanctuaire punique d'El-Hofra à Constantine* (Paris).

BETZ, H. D. (1986), *The Greek Magical Papyri in Translation* (Chicago and London).

BIRGER, R., and NETZER, E. (1987), 'The Churches of Herodion', *Qadmoniot* 20: 32–44 (Hebrew).

BLISS, F. J., and MACALISTER, R. A. S. (1902), *Excavations in Palestine* (London).

BOISSIER, G. (1898), *La fin du paganisme* (Paris).

BONNER, C. (1950), *Studies in Magical Amulets: Chiefly Graeco-Roman* (Michigan).

BOVINI, G. (1978), *Ravenna Mosaics* (Oxford).

BOWERSOCK, G. W. (1983), *Roman Arabia* (Cambridge, Mass.).

BOWSHER, J. (1987), 'Architecture and Religion in the Decapolis: A Numismatic Survey', *PEQ* 119: 62–9.

BRANDON, S. G. F. (1957), *The Fall of Jerusalem and the Christian Church* (London).

—— (1967), *Jesus and the Zealots* (Manchester).

BRAUDE, W. G., (1959) (ed.), *The Midrash on Psalms* (New Haven).

BRAUN, J. (1924), *Der christliche Altar in seiner geschichtlichen Entwicklung* (Munich).

BRIAND, J. (1973), *Sion* (Jerusalem).

—— (1982), *The Judeo-Christian Church of Nazareth* (Jerusalem), trans. by M. Deuel of *L'Église judéo-chrétienne de Nazaret* (Jerusalem, 1979).

BROSHI, M. (1976a), 'Excavations in the House of Caiaphas, Mount Zion', in Yadin (1976), 57–60 (and pl. III).

—— (1976b), 'Excavations on Mt Zion, 1971–1972: Preliminary Report', *IEJ* 26: 81–8.

BROWN, P. R. L. (1983), *The Cult of the Saints* (London).

BROWN, R. E. (1983), 'Not Jewish Christianity and Gentile Christianity but Types of Jewish/Gentile Christianity', *CBQ* 45: 74–9.

—— and MEIER, E. (1983), *Antioch and Rome* (London).

BROWNING, I. (1982), *Jerash and the Decapolis* (London).

BROWNING, R. (1975), *The Emperor Julian* (London).

BÜCHLER, A.(1956), *Studies in Jewish History* (London).

BUDGE, W. (1927), *The Book of the Cave of Treasures* (London).

BULL, R. J. (1968), 'The Excavation of Tell er Ras on Mt Gerizim', *BA* 31: 58–72.

—— (1974), 'A Mithraic Medallion from Caesarea', *IEJ* 24: 187–90.

BURCKHARDT, J. (1880), *Die Zeit Constantine des Grossen*, 2nd edn. (Leipzig).

BURKITT, F. C. (1924), *Christian Beginnings* (London).

BURNEY, C., and MARSHALL, D. (1971), *The Peoples of the Hills* (London).

BURY, J. B. (1899), *History of the Later Roman Empire*, i. (1st edn. repr., New York, 1958).

CANAAN, T. (1927), *Mohammedan Saints and Sanctuaries in Palestine*, (Jerusalem).

CARDMAN, F. (1982), 'The Rhetoric of Holy Places', in E. A. Livingstone (ed.), *Studia Patristica XVII: Papers of the 1979 Patristic Studies Conference, Oxford* (Oxford), 18–25.

—— (1984), 'Jerusalem and the Sanctification of Place: Christian Holy Places in the Fourth and Fifth Centuries', in P. Henry (ed.), *Schools of Thought in the Christian Tradition* (Philadelphia), 49–64.

CHADWICK, H. (1953), *Origen: Contra Celsum* (Cambridge).

CHARLESWORTH, J. H. (1981), *The Pseudepigrapha and Modern Research, with a Supplement* (Missoula).

CHASTEL, E. (1850), *Histoire de la destruction du paganisme dans l'Empire Orient* (Paris).

CHIAT, M. J. S. (1982), *Handbook of Synagogue Architecture* (Brown Judaic Studies 29; Chico, Calif.).

CLEMENTS, R. E. (1965), *God and Temple* (Oxford).

CLERMONT-GANNEAU, C. (1883), 'Épigraphes hébraïques et grecques sur des ossuaires juifs inédits', *RA* (3rd ser.) 1: 257–68.

—— (1899), *Archaeological Researches 1873–1874*, i (London).

COHEN, J. M. (1981), *A Samaritan Chronicle: A Source-Critical Analysis of the Life and Times of . . . Baba Rabbah* (Leiden).

COLELLA, P. (1973), 'Les abréviations et *XP*', *RB* 80: 547–58.

COLLEDGE, M. A. R. (1986), 'Interpretatio Romana: The Semitic Position of Syria and Mesopotamia', in Henig and King (1986), 221–30.

CONANT, J. (1956), 'The Original Buildings at the Holy Sepulchre in Jerusalem', *Speculum*, 31: 1–48.

CORBO, V. C. (1956), *Gli scavi di Kh. Siyar El-Ghanam (Campo dei Pastori) e i monasteri dei dintorni* (Jerusalem).

—— (1960), 'Scavo archeologico a ridosso della basilica dell'Ascensione', *LA* 10: 205–48.

—— (1965), *Ricerche archeologiche al Monte degli Ulivi, Gerusalemme* (Jerusalem).

—— (1969), *The House of St Peter at Capernaum* (Jerusalem), trans. by S. Saller of 'La casa di San Pietro a Cafarnao', *LA* 18 (1968): 5–54.

—— (1970), 'Nuovo scavi archeologici nella sinagoga di Cafarnao', *LA* 20: 7–52.

—— (1972), 'La sinagoga di Cafarnao dopo gli scavi del 1972', *LA* 22: 204–35.

CORBO, V. C. (1975), *Cafarnao*, i. *Gli edifici della città* (Jerusalem).

—— (1981–2), *Il Santo Sepolcro di Gerusalemme*, 3 vols. (Jerusalem).

—— (1982), 'Resti della sinagoga del primo secolo a Cafarnao', in *Studia Hierosolymitana*, iii (Jerusalem), 313–57.

—— (1987), 'La chiesa-sinagoga dell'Annunziata a Nazaret', *LA* 37: 333–48.

—— (1988), 'Il Santo sepolcro di Gerusalemme—*Nova* et *Vetera*', *LA* 38: 391–422.

—— and LOFFREDA, S. (969), *New Memories of Saint Peter by the Sea of Galilee* (Jerusalem).

—— —— and SPIJKERMAN, A. (1970), *La sinagoga di Cafarnao dopo gli scavi del 1969* (Jerusalem).

CORNFELD, G. (1976), *Archaeology of the Bible: Book by Book* (London).

COÜASNON, C. (1974), *The Church of the Holy Sepulchre, Jerusalem* (British Academy Schweich Lectures, 1972; London).

CROWFOOT, J. W. (1941), *Early Churches in Palestine* (British Academy Schweich Lectures, 1940; London).

CROWN, A. D. (1986), 'Samaritans in the Byzantine Orbit', *Bulletin of The John Rylands Library of Manchester*, 69: 96–138.

—— (1989) (ed.), *The Samaritans* (Tübingen).

CRUSÉ, C. F. (1838), *An Ecclesiastical History (to the Year 324 of the Christian Era etc.)* (London).

CURETON, W. (1861), *Eusebius, Bishop of Caesarea: History of the Martyrs in Palestine* (London and Edinburgh).

DALMAN, G. (1935*a*), *Arbeit und Sitte in Palästina*, 8 vols. (Gütersloh).

—— (1935*b*), *Sacred Sites and Ways* (London), trans. by P. P. Levertoff of *Orte und Wege Jesus*, 3rd edn. (Gütersloh, 1932).

DANBY, H. (1933), *The Mishnah* (Oxford).

DANIÉLOU, J. (1949), 'Symbolik des Taufritus', *Liturgie und Monchtum*, 3: 45–68.

—— (1951*a*), *Bible et liturgie* (Paris).

—— (1951*b*), 'Le symbolisme du Jour de Pâque', *Dieu Vivant*, 18: 45–56.

—— (1952), 'Le symbolisme des quarante jours', *La Maison-Dieu*, 31: 19–33.

—— (1954), 'La carrue symbole de la croix', *RSR* 42: 193–203.

—— (1961), *Les symboles chrétiens primitifs* (Paris).

—— (1964), *The Theology of Jewish-Christianity* (London), trans. by J. A. Baker of *Théologie du judéo-christianisme* (Histoire des doctrines chrétiennes avant Nicée, 1; Tournai, 1958).

—— (1971), 'Le traité de centesima, sexegesima, tricesima et le judéo-christianisme latin avant Tertullian', *VC* 25: 171–81.

DAR, S. (1988), 'The History of the Hermon Settlements', *PEQ* 120: 26–44.

—— and MINTZKER, J. (1987), 'A Roman Temple at Senaim, Mount Hermon', *EI* 19: 30–45 (Hebrew).

DAUPHIN, C. M. (1978), 'Chronique archéologique: Shelomi', *RB* 85: 108–9.

—— (1982), 'Jewish and Christian Communities: A Study of Evidence from Archaeological Surveys', *PEQ* 114: 129–42.

—— (1984), 'Farj en Gaulanitide: refuge judéo-chrétien?', *Proche-Orient chrétien*, 34: 233–45.

—— and EDELSTEIN, G. (1984), *L'Église byzantine de Nahariya (Israël): étude archéologique* (Thessalonika).

—— and SCHONFIELD, J. J. (1983), 'Settlements of the Roman and Byzantine Periods on the Golan Heights: Preliminary Report on Three Seasons of Survey (1979–1981)', *IEJ* 33: 189–206.

DAVIES, J. G. (1968), *The Secular Use of Church Buildings* (London).

DE LANGE, N. R. M. (1976), *Origen and the Jews* (Cambridge).

DE MARCO, A. R. (1964), *The Tomb of St Peter* (Leiden).

DENIS, A. M. (1970), *Introduction aux pseudépigraphes grecs d'Ancien Testament* (Leiden).

DE ROSSI, G. B. (1864–7), *Roma sotterranea cristiana*, 3 vols. (Rome).

DE VAUX, R. (1970), 'On Right and Wrong Uses of Archaeology', in J. Sanders (ed.), *Near Eastern Archaeology in the Twentieth Century* (New York), 64–80.

DÍEZ FERNÁNDEZ, F. (1984), 'La recherche archéologique (dans Saint Sépulcre)', *Le monde de la Bible*, 33: 28–36.

DIPLOCK, P. R. (1971), 'The Date of Askalon's Sculptured Panels and an Identification of the Caesarea Statues', *PEQ* 103: 13–16.

—— (1975), 'Further Comment on "An Identification of the Caesarea Statues"', *PEQ* 107: 165–6.

DIRINGER, D. (1958), *The Aleph-Beth* (London).

—— (1968), *The Alphabet*, 2 vols. (London).

DÖLGER, F. (1929–50) (ed.), *Antike und Christentum* (Münster).

DOTHAN, M. (1981), 'The Synagogue at Hammath-Tiberias', in Levine (1981*b*), 63–9.

DOWNEY, G. (1961), *The History of Antioch in Syria from Seleucus to the Arab Conquest* (Princeton, NJ).

DRAKE, H. A. (1985), 'Eusebius on the True Cross', *JEH* 36: 1–22.

DRIJVERS, J. W. (1992), *Helena Augusta: The Mother of Constantine the Great and the Legend of her Finding of the True Cross* (Leiden).

DULING, D. C. (1983), 'Testament of Solomon', in J. H. Charlesworth, (ed.), *The Old Testament Pseudepigrapha*, i (London), 935–87.

EISENBERG, E., (1984), 'Jerusalem: Church of the Dormition', in *Excavations and Surveys in Israel* (Jerusalem), Eng. trans. of *Hadashot Arkheologiyot*, 84–5, p. 47.

EVANS, H. (1982), 'Nonclassical Sources for the Armenian Mosaic near the Damascus Gate in Jerusalem', in N. G. Garsoian, T. F. Matthews, and R. W. Thomson, (eds), *East of Byzantium: Syria and Armenia in the formative period* (Dumbarton Oaks), 217–22.

FERGUSON, J. (1970), *The Religions of the Roman Empire* (London).

FERRUA, A. (1954), review of Bagatti and Milik (1958), *RAC* 30: 268.

FIGUERAS, P. (1974), 'Jewish and Christian Beliefs on Life after Death in the Light of Ossuary Decoration', Ph.D. thesis (Hebrew University of Jerusalem).

—— (1984–5), 'Jewish Ossuaries and Secondary Burial: Their Significance for Early Christianity', *Immanuel*, 19: 41–57.

FINEGAN, J. (1969), *The Archaeology of the New Testament* (Princeton, NJ).

FINKELSZTEJN, G. (1986), '*Asklepios Leontoukhos* et le mythe de la coupe de Césarée Maritime', *RB* 93: 419–28.

FISCHER, M. (1986), 'The Corinthian Capitals of the Capernaum Synagogue: A Revision', *Levant*, 18: 131–42.

FISHWICK, D. (1963–4), 'The Talpiot Ossuaries Again', *NTS* 10: 49–61.

FLUSSER, D. (1975), The Great Goddess of Samaria', *IEJ* 25: 13–20.

—— (1976), 'Paganism in Palestine' in Safrai and Stern (1976), 1065–94.

—— (1983–4), 'The Jewish–Christian Schism (pt. II)', *Immanuel*, 17: 30–9.

FOERSTER, G. (1971*a*), 'Notes on Recent Excavations at Capernaum (Review Article)', *IEJ* 21: 207–11.

—— (1971*b*), 'The Recent Excavations at Capharnaum', *Qadmoniot*, 4: 126–31 (Hebrew),

—— (1972), 'Galilean Synagogues and their Relationship to Hellenistic and Roman Art and Architecture', Ph.D. thesis (Hebrew University of Jerusalem).

—— (1981), 'Architectural Models of the Greco-Roman Period and the Origin of the "Galilean" Synagogue', in Levine (1981*b*), 45–8.

—— (1986), 'A Christian Painted Burial Cave near Kibbutz Lohamei-Ha-gettaot', in M. Yedaya (ed.), *Western Galilee Antiquities* (Tel Aviv), 416–31 (Hebrew).

—— (1987), 'The Zodiac in Ancient Synagogues and its Place in Jewish Thought and Literature', *EI* 19: 225–34 (Hebrew).

FORABOSCHI, D. (1966), *Onomasticon Alterum Papyrologicum: Supplemento al Namenbuch di F. Preisigke* (Milan).

FOWDEN, G. (1988), 'Between Pagans and Christians', *JRS* 78: 173–82.

FRANKEL, B. (1981), 'Critical Remarks on the Production of Olive Oil in Judaea', *Teva Va'Aretz*, 23: 183 (Hebrew).

FRÄNKEL, E. (1886), *Die Aramäische Fremdwörter in Arabisch* (Leiden).

FRANKEL, R. (1981), 'The History of the Processing of Wine and Oil in Galilee in the Period of the Bible, the Mishnah and the Talmud', Ph.D. thesis (Tel Aviv University) (Hebrew).

FREEMAN-GRENVILLE, G. S. P. (1987), 'The Basilica of the Holy Sepulchre, Jerusalem: History and Future', *Journal of the Royal Asiatic Society*, 2: 187–207.

FREYNE, S. (1980), *Galilee from Alexander the Great to Hadrian 323BCE to 135CE* (Notre Dame).

FRIEDMAN, J. B. (1967), 'Syncretism and Allegory in the Jerusalem Orpheus Mosaic', *Traditio*, 23: 1–13.

GAGER, J. G. (1972), 'Some Attempts to Label the *Oracula Sibyllina*', *HTR* 65: 91–7.

GARITTE, G. (1958), *Le caldendrier palestino-géorgien du Sinaiticus 34* (Subsidia Hagiographica 30; Brussels).

GATH, J., and RAHMANI, L. Y. (1977), 'A Roman Tomb at Manahat, Jerusalem', *IEJ* 27: 209–14.

GEFFCKEN, J. (1978), *The Last Days of Graeco-Roman Paganism* (Amsterdam and New York), trans. by S. MacCormack of *Der Ausgang des griechisch-römischen Heidentums* (Heidelberg, 1929).

GERMER-DURAND, J. (1895), 'Inscriptions romaines et byzantines de Palestine', *RB* 4: 68–77.

GERSHT, R. (1984), 'The Tyche of Caesarea Maritima', *PEQ* 116: 110–4.

GIBSON, S. (1985–6), 'Ras et-Tawil: A Byzantine Monastery north of Jerusalem', *BAIAS* 5: 69–73.

GICHON, M. (1980), 'The Upright Screw-Operated Pillar Press in Israel', *Scripta Classica Israelica*, 5: 209–20.

GIFFORD, E. H. (1894), *Cyril of Jerusalem* (A Select Library of Nicene and Post-Nicene Fathers of the Christian Church, vii; Oxford).

GINZBERG, L. (1955), *The Legends of the Jews*, 7 vols. (Philadelphia).

GISLER, M. (1935), 'Sancta Sion und Dormitio Dominae. Ihre Verbundenheit im Grundplan', *Das Heilige Land*, 79: 6–9.

GLUCKER, C. A. M. (1987), *The City of Gaza in the Roman and Byzantine Periods* (British Archaeological Reports, S325; London).

GLUECK, N. (1965), *Deities and Dolphins* (London).

GOMBRICH, E. H. (1966), *The Story of Art*, 11th edn. (London).

GOODENOUGH, E. R. (1953–8), *Jewish Symbols in the Greco-Roman Period*, 13 vols. (New York).

GOODMAN, M. (1983), *State and Society in Roman Galilee, AD 132–212* (Totowa, NJ).

GORANSON, S. C. (1990), 'The Joseph of Tiberias Episode in Epiphanius: Studies in Jewish and Christian Relations', Ph.D. thesis (Duke University).

GOUSSEN, H. (1923), 'Über georgische Drucke und Handschriften', in id. *Liturgie und Kunst* (Mönchen-Gladbach).

GRABAR, A. (1946), *Martyrium: recherches sur le culte des reliques et l'art chrétien antique*, 2 vols. (Paris).

—— (1958), *Ampoules de Terre Sainte* (Paris).

GRAVES, R. (1955), *The Greek Myths*, 2 vols. (Harmondsworth).

GRAY, B. E. (1973), 'The Movements of the Jerusalem Church During the First Jewish War', *JEH* 24: 1–7.

GREGO, I. (1982), *I giudeo-cristiani nel IV secolo: reazione—influssi* (Jerusalem).

GROH, D. E. (1988), 'Jews and Christians in Late Roman Palestine: Towards a new chronology', *BA* 51: 80–96.

GUARDUCCI, M. (1960), *The Tomb of St Peter* (London).

—— (1978), *La cappella eburnea di Samagher* (Padua).

HAJJAR, Y. (1977–85), *La Triade d'Héliopolis/Baalbek*, 3 vols. (Leiden).

HALL, B. (1989), 'From John Hyrcanus to Baba Rabbah', in Crown (1989), 33–54.

HALL, S. G. (1979) (ed. and trans.), *Melito of Sardis on Pascha and Fragments* (Oxford).

HAMILTON, R. W. (1947), *The Church of the Nativity, Bethlehem* (Jerusalem).

HAMMERSCHMIDT, E. (1973), 'Die Marienkirche in Gethsemane und das äthiopische Ta'amra Maryam', in *Theokratia: Jahrbuch des Institutum Judaicum Delitzschianum*, 2: *1970–2* (Leiden), 3–6.

HAMRICK, E. W. (1977), 'The Third Wall of Agrippa I', *BA* 40: 18–23.

HANOZIN, P. (1935), *Le geste des Martyrs* (Paris).

HANSON, R. P. C. (1978), 'The Transformation of Pagan Temples into Churches in the Early Christian Centuries', *PEQ* 110: 257–67.

HARVEY, A. E. (1966), 'Melito and Jerusalem', *JTS* 17: 401–4.

HARVEY, W. (1935), *Church of the Holy Sepulchre, Jerusalem* (London).

—— (1937), *Structural Survey of the Church of the Nativity, Bethlehem* (Oxford).

HAYES, J. W. (1972), *Late Roman Pottery* (London).

HEIBACH-REINISCH, M. (1962), *Ein neu 'Transitus Mariae' des Pseudo-Melito* (Rome).

HEISENBERG, A. (1908), *Grabeskirche und Apostelkirche: zwei Basiliken Konstantins*, 2 vols (Leipzig).

HELTZER, M., and EITAM, D. (1987) (eds.), *Olive Oil in Antiquity: Papers of the Conference held in Haifa, 1987* (Haifa).

HENIG, M., and KING, A. (1986) (eds.), *Pagan Gods and Shrines of the Roman Empire* (Oxford).

HENNECKE, E. (1963), *New Testament Apocrypha*, i, rev. W. Schneemelcher, trans. by R. McL. Wilson (London).

—— (1965), *New Testament Apocrypha*, ii, rev. W. Schneemelcher, trans. by R. McL. Wilson (London).

HERFORD, R. T. (1903), *Christianity in Talmud and Midrash* (London).

HILGENFELD, A. (1886), *Judentum und Judenchristentum* (Leipzig).

HILLGARTH, J. N. (1986a), 'The Attempt to Convert the Countryside', in id. (1986b), 50–9.

—— (1986*b*) (ed.), *Christianity and Paganism 350–750* (Philadelphia).

HINTLIAN, K. (1976), *History of the Armenians in the Holy Land* (Jerusalem).

HIRSCHFELD, Y. (1985), 'Khirbet el-Kuneitrah: A Byzantine Monastery in the Desert of Ziph', *EI* 18: 243–55 (Hebrew).

—— (1987), 'The Judaean Monasteries in the Byzantine Period, their Development and Internal Organisation in the Light of Archaeological Research', Ph.D. thesis (Hebrew University of Jerusalem).

—— and SOLAR, G. (1981), 'The Roman Thermae at Hammat Gader: Preliminary Report of Three Seasons of Excavations', *IEJ* 31: 197–219.

HIRSHBERG, J. W. (1968), 'The Remains of Ancient Synagogues in Jerusalem', *Qadmoniot*, 1: 56–62 (Hebrew).

—— (1976), 'The Remains of an Ancient Synagogue on Mount Zion', in Yadin (1976), 116–17.

HOLUM, K. G., HOHLFELDER, R. L., BULL, R. J., and RABAN, A. (1988), *King Herod's Dream: Caesarea on the Sea* (New York and London).

HORBURY, W. (1982), 'The Benediction of the *Minim* and Early Jewish Christian Controversy', *JTS* 33: 19–61.

HOWARD, G. (1981), *The Teaching of Addai* (Early Christian Literature, 4; SBL Texts and Translations, 168; Chico, Calif.).

HUNT, E. D. (1984), *Holy Land Pilgrimage in the Later Roman Empire, AD 312–460* (Oxford).

JACKSON, H. M. (1989), 'The Origin in Ancient Incantatory *Voces Magicae* of Some Names in the Sethian Gnostic System', *VC* 43: 69–79.

JACOBSEN, T. (1970), *Toward the Image of Tammuz and Other Essays on Mesopotamian History and Culture*, ed. W. L. Moran (Cambridge, Mass.).

JACQUES, A. (1987), 'A Palestinian-Syriac Inscription in the Mosaic Pavement at Evron', *EI* 19: 54–6.

JAMES, E. O. (1958), *Myth and Ritual in the Ancient Near East* (London).

JAMES, M. R. (1924), *The Apocryphal New Testament* (Oxford).

JASTROW, M. (1950), *A Dictionary of the Targumim, The Talmud Babli and Yerushalmi, and the Midrashic Literature* (New York).

JEREMIAS, J. (1926), *Golgotha* (Leipzig and Göttingen).

—— (1958), *Heiligengräber in Jesu Umwelt* (Göttingen).

—— (1966), *The Rediscovery of Bethesda* (Louisville, Kentucky).

JIDEJIAN, N. (1969), *Tyre through the Ages* (Beirut).

JOHNS, C. N. (1939), 'The Abbey of St Mary in the Valley of Jehoshaphat, Jerusalem', *QDAP* 8: 117–36.

JONES, A. H. M. (1949), *Constantine and the Conversion of Europe* (London).

—— (1964), *The Later Roman Empire, 284–602*, 2nd edn. (Oxford).

JONES, T. B. (1978), *In the Twilight of Antiquity* (Minneapolis).

KADMAN, L. (1956), *The Coins of Aelia Capitolina* (Jerusalem).

KANE, J. P. (1971), 'By No Means, "The Earliest Records of Christianity"—with an Emended Reading of the Talpioth Inscription *IHΣOYΣ IOY*', *PEQ* 103: 103–8.

—— (1978), 'The Ossuary Inscriptions of Jerusalem', *JSS* 23: 268–82.

KAPLAN, J. (1967), 'Two Samaritan Amulets', *IEJ* 17: 158–60.

—— (1975), 'A Second Samaritan Amulet from Tel Aviv', *IEJ* 25: 157–9.

—— (1980), 'A Samaritan Amulet from Corinth', *IEJ* 30: 196–8.

KAPLAN, R. D. (1979), 'Looking at Some Recent Excavations', *Christian News from Israel*, 27/1: 18–22.

KASHER, A. (1982), 'Gaza During the Greco-Roman Era', in L. I. Levine (ed.), *The Jerusalem Cathedra*, ii (Jerusalem and Detroit), 63–78.

—— (1988), *Jews, Idumaeans, and Ancient Arabs* (Tübingen).

KATSIMBINIS, C. (1977), 'The Uncovering of the Eastern Side of the Hill of Calvary and its Base', *LA* 27: 197–208.

KAUFMANN, C. M. (1922), *Handbuch der christlichen Archaeologie*, 3rd edn. (Paderborn).

KEE, A. (1982), *Constantine versus Christ* (London).

KENYON, K. (1974), *Digging up Jerusalem* (London).

KERESZTES, P. (1985), 'Constantine: Called by Divine Providence', in E. A. Livingstone (ed.), *Studia Patristica XVIII: Papers of the 1983 Oxford Patristics Conference*, i (Kalamazoo, Mich.), 48–54.

KIMELMAN, R. (1981), '"Birkat ha-Minim" and the Lack of Evidence for an Anti-Christian Prayer in Late Antiquity', in Sanders, Baumgarten, and Mendelson (1981), 226–44.

KITTEL, G. (1964–76) (ed.), *Theological Dictionary of the New Testament* (Grand Rapids, Mich. and London).

KLEIN, C. S. (1909), *Beiträge zur Geographie und Geschichte Galilaeas* (Leipzig).

KLIJN, A. F. J. (1972), 'Jerome's Quotations from a Nazarene Interpretation of Esaiah', *RSR* 60: 241–55.

—— (1973–4), 'The Study of Jewish Christianity', *NTS* 20: 419–31.

—— (1977), *Seth in Jewish, Christian and Gnostic Literature* (Leiden).

—— and REININK, G. J. (1973), *Patristic Evidence for Jewish-Christian Sects* (Leiden).

KLONER, A. (1978), 'Horvat Midras', *Qadmoniot*, 11: 115–19 (Hebrew).

—— (1980), 'The Necropolis of Jerusalem in the Second Temple Period', Ph.D. thesis (Hebrew University of Jerusalem).

—— (1983), 'Underground Hiding Complexes from the Bar Kochba War in the Judaean Shephalah', *BA* 46: 210–22.

—— (1985*a*), 'The Amphitheatre of Beth Gubrin/Eleutheropolis', *Qadmoniot*, 18: 38–43 (Hebrew); Eng. trans. in *IEJ* 38: 15–24.

—— (1985*b*), 'A Burial Monument of the Second Temple Period West of the Old City of Jerusalem', *EI* 18: 58–64.

—— and HIRSCHFELD, Y. (1987), 'Khirbet el-Qasr: A Byzantine Fort with an Olive Press in the Judaean Desert', *EI* 19: 132–41 (Hebrew).

—— and SAGIN, N. (1987), 'The Technology of Oil Production in the Hellenistic Period: Studies in the Crushing Process at Maresha', in Heltzer and Eitam (1987), 133–8.

—— and TEPER, Y. (1987), *The Hiding Complexes in the Judaean Shephalah* (Tel Aviv) (Hebrew).

KOCHAVI, M. (1973), *Judea, Samaria and the Golan* (Archaeological Survey of Israel, no. 53; Jerusalem) (Hebrew).

—— (1981), 'The History and Archaeology of Aphek/Antipatris: A Biblical City in the Sharon Plain', *BA* 44: 75–86.

KOESTER, C. (1989), 'The Origin and Significance of the Flight to Pella Tradition', *CBQ* 51: 90–106.

KOHL, H., and WATZINGER, C. (1919), *Die antike Synagogen in Galiläa* (Leipzig).

KOPP, C. (1938), 'Beiträge zur Geschichte Nazareths', *JPOS* 18: 191–228.

—— (1963), *The Holy Places of the Gospels* (Freiburg) trans. by R. Walls of *Die heiligen Stätten der Evangelien* (Regensburg, 1959).

KÖTZSCHE-BREITENBRUCH, L. (1968–9), 'Zur Ikonographie des Bethlehemitischen Kindermordes in der frühchristlichen Kunst', *JAC* 11/12: 104–15.

KRAABEL, A. T. (1984), 'New Evidence of the Samaritan Diaspora has been Found on Delos', *BA* 47: 44–6.

KRAELING, C. H. (1938), *Gerasa, City of the Decapolis* (New Haven, Conn.).

—— (1946), 'Christian Burial Urns', *BA* 9: 16–20.

KRAFT, R. A. (1972), 'In Search of "Jewish Christianity" and its "Theology": Problems of Definition and Methodology', *RSR* 60: 81–96.

LACHS, S. T. (1969–70),'Rabbi Abahu and the Minim', *JQR* 60: 197–212.

LAKE, K. (1949), *Eusebius: Ecclesiastical History*, 2 vols. (Loeb; Cambridge, Mass. and London).

LAMPE, G. W. H. (1961), *A Patristic Greek Lexicon* (Oxford).

LANE FOX, R. (1986), *Pagans and Christians* (Harmondsworth).

LANGDON, S. (1914), *Tammuz and Ishtar* (Oxford).

LAUFFRAY, J. (1962), 'La memoria Sancti Sepulchri du Musée de Narbonne et le temple rond de Baalbeck', *Mélanges de l'Université Saint-Joseph, Beirut*, 38: 199–217.

LAWLOR, H. J., and OULTON, J. E. L. (1927) (eds.), *Eusebius: The Ecclesiastical History and the Martyrs of Palestine*, 2 vols. (London).

LEIBERMAN, S. (1946), 'Palestine in the Third and Fourth Centuries', *JQR* 36: 329–70 (pt. 1); 37: 31–54 (pt. 2).

LEVINE, L. I. (1975a), *Caesarea under Roman Rule* (Leiden).

—— (1975b), *Roman Caesarea* (Jerusalem).

LEVINE, L. I. (1981a), 'Ancient Synagogues—A Historical Introduction', in id. (1981b), 1–10.

—— (1981b) (ed.), *Ancient Synagogues Revealed* (Jerusalem).

LEWIS, C. T., and SHORT, C. (1879), *A Latin Dictionary* (Oxford).

LIDDELL, H. G., SCOTT, R., and JONES, H. S. (1968), *A Greek–English Lexicon*, 9th edn. with suppl. (Oxford).

LIMOR, O. (1978), 'Christian Tradition on the Mount of Olives in the Byzantine and Arab Periods', Ph.D. thesis (Hebrew University of Jerusalem).

LIVIO, J.-B. (1967), 'Nazareth: les fouilles chez les religieuses de Nazareth', *Le monde de la Bible*, 16: 26–34.

LOFFREDA, S. (1970a), 'La ceramica della sinagoga di Cafarnao', *LA* 20: 53–105.

—— (1970b), *Scavi di et-Tabgha* (Jerusalem).

—— (1972), 'The Synagogue of Capernaum: Archaeological Evidence for its Late Chronology', *LA* 22: 5–29.

—— (1973), 'The Late Chronology of the Synagogue of Capernaum', *IEJ* 23: 36–72, and 'A Reply to the Editor', 184.

—— (1974a), *Cafarnao* ii. *La ceramica* (Jerusalem).

—— (1974b), *A Visit to Capharnaum*, 2nd edn. (Jerusalem).

—— (1978), *Cafarnao, la città di Gesù* (Jerusalem).

—— (1979), 'Potsherds from a Sealed Level of the Synagogue at Capharnaum', *LA* 29: 215–20.

—— (1981), 'The Late Chronology of the Synagogue of Capernaum', in Levine (1981b), 52–6.

—— (1985a), *Recovering Capernaum* (Jerusalem).

—— (1985b), 'Resti archeologici nell'area della Flagellazione in Gerusalemme', *LA* 35: 313–27.

LOUKIANOFF, E. (1939), "ὁ Ἐλαιών", *the Basilica of Eleon in Constantine's Time at the Mount of Olives, 326–330 AD* (Cairo).

LÜDEMANN, G. (1980), 'The Successors of Pre-70 Jerusalem Christianity: A Critical Evaluation of the Pella Tradition', in E. Sanders (ed.), *Jewish and Christian Self-Definition*, i (Philadelphia), 161–73.

LUTTIKHUIZEN, G. P. (1985), '*The Revelation of Elchasai*' (Tübingen).

LUX, V. (1972), 'Vorläufiger Bericht über Ausgrabung unter der Erlöserkirche im Muristan in der Altstadt von Jerusalem in den Jahren 1970 und 1971', *ZDPV* 88: 185–201.

MACALISTER, R. A. S. (1899), 'The Rock Cuttings of Tell Zakariya', *PEFQSt*, 25–36.

—— (1900a), 'Further Notes on the Rock-Cuttings of Tell Zakariya', *PEFQSt*, 39–53.

—— (1900b), 'The Rock-Cut Tombs in Wady er-Rababi, Jerusalem', *PEFQSt*, 225–248.

—— (1901), 'On a Rock-Cut Chapel at Beit Leyi', *PEFQSt*, 226–9.

McGIFFERT, A. C. (1890), *The Church History of Eusebius* (A Select Library of Nicene and Post-Nicene Fathers of the Christian Church, 2nd series, i; London).

MACMULLEN, R. (1984), *Christianizing the Roman Empire (AD 100–400)* (New Haven and London).

MADER, E. (1957), *Mambre: Die Ergebnisse der Ausgrabungen im Heiligen Bezirk Ramat el-Halil in Sudpalästina 1926–1928*, 2 vols (Freiburg im Breisgau).

MAGEN, Y. (1983), 'Qedumim—A Samaritan Site of the Roman-Byzantine Period', *Qadmoniot*, 16: 76–83 (Hebrew).

—— (1986), 'A Fortified City from the Hellenistic Period on Mount Gerizim', *Qadmoniot*, 19: 91–101 (Hebrew).

—— (1990a), 'The Church of Mary Theotokos on Mount Gerizim', in *Christian Archaeology in the Holy Land, New Discoveries—Archaeological Essays in Honour of Virgilio C. Corbo* (Jerusalem), 333–42.

—— (1990b), 'Mount Gerizim—a Temple City', *Qadmoniot*, 23: 70–96 (Hebrew).

MAGNES, J. (1990), 'Some Observations on the Roman Temple at Kedesh', *IEJ* 40: 173–81.

MAIURI, M. (1939), 'La croce di Ercolano', in *Rendiconti della Pontificia Accademia Romana di Archaeologia*, 15: 193–218.

MALINA, B. J. (1973), 'Jewish Christianity: A Select Bibliography', *AJBA* 1: 60–5.

—— (1976), 'Jewish Christianity or Christian Judaism: Toward a Hypothetical Definition': *JSJ* 7: 46–57.

MANCINI, I. (1965), 'Adamo sotto il Calvario', *TS* 41: 277–82.

—— (1966), 'A proposito della profanazione pagana della Grotta della Natività', *TS* 42: 265–8.

—— (1984), *Archaeological Discoveries Relative to the Judaeo-Christians* (rev. edn.; Jerusalem), trans. by G. Bushell of *Le scoperte archeologiche sui giudeo-christiani—note storiche* (Collectio Assisiensis, 6; Assisi, 1968).

MANN, J. C. (1983), *Legionary Recruitment and Veteran Settlement During the Principate* (Inst. Arch. Occ. Pub. 7; London).

MANNS, F. (1977), 'Un centre judéo-chrétien important: Sepphoris', in id., *Essais sur le judéo-christianisme* (Jerusalem), 165–90.

—— (1979), *Bibliographie du judéo-christianisme* (Jerusalem).

MAOZ, R. (1990), 'Une église en plein désert', *Le monde de la Bible*, 63: 58–9.

MAOZ, Z. U. (1981a), 'The Art and Architecture of the Synagogues of the Golan', in Levine (1981b), 98–115.

—— (1981b), 'The Synagogue at Capernaum—A Christian Pilgrimage

Site?', in *Proceedings of the Eighth Archaeological Conference in Israel* (Jerusalem), 21 (Hebrew).

MAOZ, Z. U. (1985), 'Comments on Jewish and Christian Communities in Byzantine Palestine', *PEQ* 117: 59–68.

—— (1988), 'Ancient Synagogues of the Golan', *BA* 51: 116–28.

MARAVAL, P. (1985), *Lieux saints et pèlerinages d'Orient* (Paris).

MARCHI, G. (1844), *Monumenti delle arti cristianae primitive nella metropoli del cristianismo* (Rome).

MARGALIT, S. (1989), 'Aelia Capitolina', *Judaica*, 1: 45–56.

MARTIN, R. (1956), *L'urbanisme dans la Grèce antique*, 2nd edn. (Paris).

MAZAR, B. (1973), *Beth Shearim: Report on the Excavations during 1936–1940*, i. *Catacombs* (Jerusalem).

MEIMARIS, Y. E. (1986), *Sacred Names, Saints, Martyrs and Church Officials in the Greek Inscriptions and Papyri Pertaining to the Christian Church of Palestine* (Μελήματα, 2; Athens).

MEINARDUS, O. F. (1980), 'The Site of Apostle Paul's Conversion at Kaukab', *BA* 44: 57–9.

MEISTERMANN, B. A. (1903), *Le tombeau de la Sainte Vierge à Jérusalem* (Jerusalem).

—— (1920), *Gethsémani: notices historiques et descriptives* (Paris).

—— (1921), *Capharnaüm et Bethsaïde* (Paris).

MESHORER, Y. (1975), *Nabataean Coins* (Jerusalem).

—— (1979), 'A Ring from Gadara', *IEJ* 29: 221–2.

—— (1989), *The Coinage of Aelia Capitolina* (Jerusalem).

MEYER, A., and BAUER, W. (1963), 'The Relatives of Jesus', in Hennecke (1963), 413–32.

MEYERS, E. M. (1988), 'Early Judaism and Christianity in the Light of Archaeology', *BA* 51: 69–79.

—— NETZER, E., and MEYERS, C. L. (1986), 'Sepphoris, "Ornament of all Galilee"', *BA* 49: 4–19.

—— —— (1987), 'Artistry in Stone: The Mosaics of Ancient Sepphoris', *BA* 50: 223–31.

—— and STRANGE, J. F. (1981), *Archaeology, The Rabbis and Early Christianity* (London).

MILLAR, F. G. B., (1990*a*), 'Reflections on the Trials of Jesus', in P. R. Davies and R. T. White (eds.), *A Tribute to Geza Vermes: Essays on Jewish and Christian Literature and History* (*Journal for the Study of the Old Testament*, suppl. series, 100; Sheffield).

—— (1990*b*), 'The Roman *Coloniae* of the Near East: A Study of Cultural Relations', in H. Solin and M. Kajava (eds.), *Roman Eastern Policy and Other Studies in Roman History* (Proceedings of a Colloquium at Tvärminne, 2–3 October 1987; Helsinki), 7–58.

MITCHELL, S. (1988), 'Maximinus and the Christians in AD 312: A New Latin Inscription', *JRS* 78: 105–24.

MONTGOMERY, J. A. (1907), *The Samaritans: The Earliest Jewish Sect, their History, Theology and Literature* (Philadelphia).

MOORGATE, A. (1949), *Tammuz* (Berlin).

MOULTON, W. J. (1921–2), 'A Painted Christian Tomb at Beit Jibrin', *AASOR* 2–3: 93–101.

MUNCK, J. (1959–60), 'Jewish Christianity in Post-Apostolic Times', *NTS* 6: 103–16.

MURPHY-O'CONNOR, J. (1986), *The Holy Land*, 2nd edn. (Oxford).

MURRAY, R. (1974), 'Defining Judaeo-Christianity', *Heythrop Journal*, 15: 303–10.

—— (1982), 'Jews, Hebrews and Christians: Some Neglected Distinctions', *NT* 24: 194–208.

NARKISS, B. (1979), 'The Armenian Treasures of Jerusalem', in id. (ed.), *Armenian Art Treasures of Jerusalem* (Jerusalem), 21–8.

NAVEH, J. (1981), 'A Greek Dedication in Samaritan Letters', *IEJ* 31: 220–2.

—— (1982a), 'An Ancient Amulet or a Modern Forgery?', *CBQ* 44: 282–4.

—— (1982b), *Early History of the Alphabet* (Jerusalem and Leiden).

—— (1988), 'Lamp Inscriptions and Inverted Writings', *IEJ* 38: 36–43.

—— and SHAKED, S. (1985), *Amulets and Magic Bowls* (Jerusalem).

NEGEV, A. (1963) (ed.), 'The Chronology of the Seven-Branched Candelabrum', *EI* 8: 193–210 (Hebrew).

—— (1971), 'The Nabataean Necropolis of Mampsis (Kurnub)', *IEJ* 21: 110–29.

—— (1977), *Inscriptions of Wadi Haggag, Sinai* (Qedem, 6; Jerusalem).

—— (1986a) (ed.), *Archaeological Encyclopaedia of the Holy Land*, rev. edn. (Nashville and Camden, NY).

—— (1986b), *Nabataean Archaeology Today* (New York).

NEUSNER, J. (1973), *Eleazar ben Hyrcanus: The Tradition and the Man*, 2 vols. (Leiden).

—— (1975) (ed.), *Christianity, Judaism and Other Graeco-Roman Cults*, 4 pts. (Leiden).

—— and FRERICHS, E. S. (1985) (eds.), *To See Ourselves as Others See Us* (Chico, Calif.).

NEWMAN, J. H. (1838), *The Catechetical Lectures of S. Cyril, Archbishop of Jerusalem* (A Library of Fathers of the Holy Catholic Church; Oxford).

NORDSTRÖM, C.-O. (1953), 'Der leere Thron und die Symboltiere', in id. (ed.), *Ravennastudien* (Uppsala), 46–54.

ODEBERG, H. (1928), *3 Enoch or the Hebrew Book of Enoch* (Cambridge).

OREN, E. (1965), 'The Caves of the Palestinian Shephalah', *Archaeology*, 18: 218–24.

ORFALI, G. (1922), *Capharnaum et ses ruines* (Paris).

—— (1924), *Gethsémani: notice sur l'Église de l'Agonie ou de la Prière, d'après les fouilles récentes accomplies par la Custodie Franciscaine de Terre Sainte (1909 et 1920)* (Paris).

OULTON, J. E. L. (1927), *Eusebius: The Ecclesiastical History and the Martyrs of Palestine* (London).

OVADIAH, A. (1970), *A Corpus of the Byzantine Churches in the Holy Land* (Bonn).

—— (1981a), 'The Synagogue at Gaza', in L. I. Levine (ed.), *The Jerusalem Cathedra*, ii (Jerusalem and Detroit), 129–32.

—— (1981b), 'Was the Cult of Dushara-Dusares Practised in Hippos-Susita?', *PEQ* 113: 101–4.

—— FISCHER, M. and ROLL, I. (1984), 'The Roman Temple at Kedesh, Upper Galilee: A Preliminary Study', *Tel Aviv*, 11: 146–72.

—— and MUCZNIK, S. (1981), 'Orpheus from Jerusalem—Pagan or Christian Image?', in L. I. Levine (ed.), *The Jerusalem Cathedra*, i (Jerusalem and Detroit), 152–66.

—— and ROLL, I. (1987), 'A Greek Dedicatory Inscription to Azeizos', *EI* 19, 270–1 (Hebrew); Eng. trans. in *IEJ* 38: 270–1.

PARROT, A. (1955), *Golgotha et Saint-Sépulcre* (Paris).

PATON, L. B. (1919–20), 'Survivals of Primitive Religion in Modern Palestine', *AASOR* 1: 51–65.

PATRICH, Y. (1986), 'Caves of Refuge and Jewish Inscriptions on the Cliffs of Nahal Michmas', *EI* 18: 153–66 (Hebrew).

—— and DI SEGNI, L. (1987), 'New Greek Inscriptions from the Monastery of Theoctistus in the Judaean Desert', *EI* 19: 272–81 (Hebrew).

PAYNE-SMITH, R. (1891), *Thesaurus Syriacus*, 2 vols. (Oxford).

PELEG, Y. (1980), 'Ancient Oil Presses and the Way they Function', *Teva Va'Aretz*, 22: 189–90 (Hebrew).

PETERSEN, E. (1926), *ΕΙΣ ΘΕΟΣ* (Göttingen).

PHARR, C. (1952), *The Theodosian Code and Novels and the Sirmondian Constitutions* (Princeton, NJ).

PIEROTTI, E. (1864), *Jerusalem Explored*, 2 vols. (London and Cambridge).

PIGANIOL, A. (1932), *L'empereur Constantin* (Paris).

PINKERFELD, J. (1957), *In the Paths of Jewish Art* (Tel Aviv), 128–30 (Hebrew).

—— (1960), 'David's Tomb: Notes on the History of the Building, Preliminary Report', *Bulletin of the Louis M. Rabinowitz Fund for the Exploration of Ancient Synagogues*, 3 (Jerusalem), 41–3.

PIXNER, B. (1981), 'Das Essenerquarter in Jerusalem und dessen Einfluss auf die Urkirche', *Das Heilige Land*, 113: 3–14.

—— (1986), 'An Essene Quarter on Mount Zion?' in *Studia Hierosolymitana in onore di P. Bellarmino Bagatti* (Jerusalem), 245–87.

—— (1990), 'Church of the Apostles Found on Mt. Zion?' *BAR* 16/3: 16–35, 60.

PRAUSNITZ, M., AVI-YONAH, M., and BARAG, D. (1967), *Excavations at Shavei Zion: The Early Christian Church* (Rome).

PREISIGKE, F. (1922), *Namenbuch* (Heidelberg).

PRITZ, R. A. (1981), 'On Brandon's Rejection of the Pella Tradition', *Immanuel*, 13: 39–43.

—— (1988), *Nazarene Jewish Christianity* (Jerusalem and Leiden).

PUECH, H. C. (1950), 'Archontiker', in F. J. Dölger, H. Lietzmann (eds.) with J. H. Waszink, L. Wenger, and T. Klauser, *Reallexikon für Antike und Christentum*, i (Stuttgart), 634–43.

PUMMER, R. (1979), 'New Evidence for Samaritan Christianity?', *CBQ* 41: 107–12.

—— (1987*a*), 'Samaritan Amulets from the Roman-Byzantine Period and their Wearers', *RB* 94: 251–63.

—— (1987*b*), *The Samaritans* (Leiden).

—— (1989), 'Samaritan Material Remains and Archaeology', in Crown (1989), 135–77, 190–4.

QUISPEL, G. (1968), 'The Discussion of Judaic Christianity', *VC* 22: 81–93.

RAHMANI, L. Y. (1967), 'Jason's Tomb', *IEJ* 17: 61–100.

—— (1981), 'A Roman Patera from Lajjun', *IEJ* 31: 190–6.

REIGEL, S. K. (1977–8), 'Jewish Christianity: Definition and Terminology', *NTS* 24: 410–15.

RENARD, H. (1900), 'Die Marienkirche auf dem Berge Sion in ihrem Zusammenhang mit dem Abendmahlssaale', *Das Heilige Land*, 44: 3–23.

ROBERT, L. (1937), *Études anatoliennes: recherches sur les inscriptions grecques de l'Asie Mineure* (Paris).

ROKEAH, D. (1982), *Jews, Pagans and Christians in Conflict* (Jerusalem and Leiden).

ROSEN, B. (1985), 'Reidentified Animals in the "Orpheus Mosaic" from Jerusalem', *IEJ* 35: 182–3.

ROSENTHAL, E. S. (1973), 'The Giv'at ha-Mivtar Inscription', *IEJ* 23: 82–91.

ROSENTHAL, R. (1976), 'Late Roman and Byzantine Bone Carvings from Palestine', *IEJ* 26: 96–103.

ROSENTHALER, M. (1975), 'A Paleo-Hebrew Ossuary Inscription', *IEJ* 25: 138–9.

ROSTOVTSEV, M. (1938), *Dura Europos and its Art* (Oxford).

RUSSELL, K. W. (1985), 'The Earthquake Chronology of Palestine and Northwest Arabia from the 2nd through the mid-8th Century AD', *BASOR* 260: 37–59.

SACHS, C. (1944), *The Rise of Music in the Ancient World: East and West* (London).

SAFRAI, S. (1973), 'The Holy Congregation in Jerusalem' (Scripta Hierosolymitana; Jerusalem), 62–78.

—— and STERN, M., (1976) (eds.), with D. Flusser and W. C. Van Unnik, *The Jewish People in the First Century*, ii (Assen and Amsterdam).

SALLER, S. (1946), *Discoveries at St. John's, Ein Karim 1941–1942* (Jerusalem).

—— (1957), *Excavations at Bethany* (Jerusalem).

—— (1961), 'The Archaeological Setting of the Shrine of Bethphage', *LA* 11: 172–250; repr. in Saller and Testa (1961), 5–83.

—— (1965), 'The Tombstone Inscription in the Church of Mary's Tomb at Gethsemani', in Corbo (1965), 76–80.

—— and TESTA, E. (1961), *The Archaeological Setting of the Shrine of Bethphage* (Jerusalem).

SANDERS, E. P., BAUMGARTEN, A. I., and MENDELSON, A. (1981) (eds.), *Studies in Jewish and Christian Self-Definition*, 2 vols. (London).

SANJIAN, A. K. (1979), 'The Armenian Communities of Jerusalem', in B. Narkiss (ed.), *Armenian Art Treasures of Jerusalem* (Jerusalem), 11–20.

SAPIR, D., and NE'EMAN, D. (1967), *Capharnaum* (Tel Aviv).

SAUVAGET, J. (1941), *Alep: essai sur le développement d'une grande ville syrienne* (Paris).

SCHEIN, B. E. (1981), 'The Second Wall of Jerusalem', *BA* 44: 21–6.

SCHILLER, E. (1984) (ed.), *Zev Vilnay's Jubilee Volume* (Jerusalem), (Hebrew).

SCHNEIDER, A. M. (1937), *The Church of the Multiplying of the Loaves and Fishes* (London).

—— (1951), 'Beiträge zur biblischen Landes- und Altertumskunde hervorgegangen aus der: Römische und Byzantinische Bauten auf dem Garazim', *ZDPV* 68: 211–34.

SCHOLEM, G. (1960), *Jewish Gnosticism, Merkabah Mysticism and Talmudic Tradition* (New York).

SCHUMACHER, G. (1886), *Across the Jordan* (London).

—— (1888), *The Jaulan* (London).

SCHUR, N. (1989), *History of the Samaritans* (Beiträge zur Erforschung des Alten Testamentes und des Antiken Judentums, 18; Frankfurt am Main).

SCHÜRER, E. (1973), *A History of the Jewish People in the Age of Jesus Christ*, i, ed. G. Vermes, F. Millar, and M. Black (Edinburgh).

—— (1979), *A History of the Jewish People in the Age of Jesus Christ*, ii, ed. G. Vermes, F. Millar, and M. Black (Edinburgh).

—— (1986), *A History of the Jewish People in the Age of Jesus Christ*, iii/1, ed. G. Vermes, F. Millar, and M. Goodman (Edinburgh).

SEGAL, A. (1986), 'Gerasa—An Archaeological–Historical Review', *Qadmoniot*, 19: 12–22 (Hebrew).

SEGAL, A. F. (1977), *Two Powers in Heaven: Early Rabbinic Reports about Christianity and Gnosticism* (Leiden).

SEGAL, J. B. (1963), *The Hebrew Passover from Earliest Times to AD 70* (London).

SHANKS, H. (1979), *Judaism in Stone* (New York and Washington, DC).

—— (1984), 'Clumsy Forger Fools the Scholars—but Only for a Time', *BAR* 10: 71–2.

SHATEL, A. (1980), 'The Production of Olive Oil in Judaea', *Teva va'Aretz*, 23: 80–1 (Hebrew).

SIMON, M. (1964), *Verus Israel: étude sur les relations entre chrétiens et juifs dans l'empire romain, 135–425* (Paris).

—— (1965), 'Problèms du judéo-christianisme' in *Aspects du judéo-christianisme: Colloque de Strasbourg, 23–25 avril, 1964* (Paris), 1–17.

—— (1972), 'La migration à Pella: légende ou réalité?', *RSR* 60: 37–54.

—— (1975), 'Réflexions sur le judéo-christianisme' in Neusner (1975), pt. 2, 53–76.

SMALLWOOD, E. M. (1976), *The Jews under Roman Rule from Pompey to Diocletian* (Leiden).

SMITH, M. (1975), 'On the Wine God in Palestine', in *Salo Wittmayer Bamon Jubilee Volume* (American Academy for Jewish Research; Jerusalem), 815–29.

—— (1978), *Jesus the Magician* (London).

SMITH, R. H. (1974), 'The Cross Marks on Jewish Ossuaries', *PEQ* 106: 53–66.

SNYDER, G. F. (1985), *Ante Pacem: Archaeological Evidence of Church Life before Constantine* (Macon, Ga.).

SOPHOCLES, E. A. (1870), *Greek Lexicon of the Roman and Byzantine Periods (from BC 146 to AD 1100)* (Boston).

SOYEZ, B. (1977), *Byblos et la fête Adonies* (Leiden).

SPERBER, D. (1978), *Roman Palestine 200–400: The Land* (Ramat Gan).

SPIJKERMAN, A. (1970), 'Monete della sinagoga di Carfarnao', *LA* 20: 106–16.

—— (1975), *Cafarnao, iii. Catalogo della monete della città* (Jerusalem).

STERN, M. (1980), *Greek and Latin Authors on Jews and Judaism*, 2 vols. (Jerusalem).

STONE, M. E. (1982), *The Armenian Inscriptions from the Sinai* (Cambridge, Mass.).

—— (1986), 'Holy Land Pilgrimage of Armenians before the Arab Conquest', *RB* 93: 93–110.

STRACK, H. L. (1910), *Jesus, die Häritiker und Christen, nach den ältesten jüdischen Angaben* (Leipzig).

STRANGE, J. F. (1977), 'The Capernaum and Herodium Publications (Part 1)', *BASOR* 226: 65–73.

—— (1983), 'Diversity in Early Palestinian Christianity', *ATR* 65: 14–24.

STRAUBINGER, J. (1912), *Die Kreuzauffindungslegende* (Paderborn).

STRECKER, G. (1958), *Das Judenchristentum in den Pseudoklementinen* (TU 70; Berlin).

STRECKER, G. (1971), 'On the Problem of Jewish Christianity', app. 1 in Bauer (1971), 241–85.

STRONG, H. A., and GARSTANG, J. (1913), *The Syrian Goddess* (London).

STRUGNELL, J. (1967), 'Quelques inscriptions samaritaines', *RB* 74: 556–9.

SUKENIK, E. L. (1919), 'The Samaritan synagogue at Salbit: Preliminary Report', *Bulletin of the Louis M. Rabinowitz Fund for the Exploration of Ancient Synagogues*, 1 (Jerusalem), 26–9.

—— (1934), *Ancient Synagogues in Palestine and Greece* (British Academy Schweich Lectures, 1930; London).

—— (1947), 'The Earliest Records of Christianity', *AJA* 51: 351–65.

SUSSMAN, J. (1981), 'The Inscription in the Synagogue at Rehob', in Levine (1981*b*), 146–53.

SUSSMAN, V. (1978), 'Samaritan Lamps of the Third and Fourth Centuries AD', *IEJ* 28: 238–50.

—— (1983), 'The Samaritan Oil Lamps from Apollonia-Arsuf', *Tel Aviv*, 10: 71–96.

TARN, W., and GRIFFITH, G. T. (1952), *Hellenistic Civilisation*, 3rd edn. (London).

TARSCHNICHVILI, M. (1959), *Le Grand Lectionnaire de l'Église de Jérusalem* (CSCO 189: Louvain).

TAYLOR, J. E. (1987*a*), 'The Cave at Bethany', *RB* 94: 120–3.

—— (1987*b*), 'A Graffito Depicting John the Baptist in Nazareth?', *PEQ* 119: 142–8.

—— (1989), 'A Critical Investigation of Archaeological Material Assigned to Palestinian Jewish-Christians of the Roman and Byzantine Periods', Ph.D. thesis (University of Edinburgh).

—— (1990), 'The Phenomenon of Early Jewish-Christianity: Reality or Scholarly Invention?', *VC* 44: 313–34.

—— (1990–1), 'Capernaum and its "Jewish-Christians": A Re-examination of the Franciscan Excavations', *BAIAS* 10: 7–28.

TEIXIDOR, J. (1977), *The Pagan God* (Princeton, NJ).

TELFER, W. (1955*a*), *Cyril of Jerusalem and Nemesius of Emesa* (Library of Christian Classics, iv; London).

—— (1955*b*), 'Constantine's Holy Land Plan', *Studia Patristica*, 1 (TU 63; Berlin), 696–700.

TEPER, Y. (1987), 'The Oil-Presses at Maresha Region', in Heltzer and Eitam (1987), 25–46 (Hebrew).

TESTA, E. (1957), 'Hgll'ym—nome dispregiativa dei giudeo-cristiani', *Euntes Docete*, 10: 281–4.

—— (1961), 'The Graffiti of Tomb 21 at Bethphage', *LA* 11: 251–87; repr. in Saller and Testa (1961), 84–120.

—— (1962*a*), 'Le grotte mistiche dei Nazareni e i loro riti battesimali', *LA* 12: 5–45.

—— (1962*b*), *Il simbolismo dei giudeo-cristiani* (Jerusalem).

—— (1964*a*), 'Le "Grotte dei Misteri" giudeo-cristiane', *LA* 14: 65–144.

—— (1964*b*), 'La piscina probatica, monumento pagano o giudaico?' *TS* 40: 311–16.

—— (1965), 'Le céne del Signore', *TS* 41: 116–21.

—— (1967), 'I Targum di Isaia 55, 1. 13 scoperto a Nazaret e la teologia sui pozzi dell'Acqua Viva,' *LA* 17: 259–89.

—— (1969), *Nazaret giudeo-cristiana* (Jerusalem).

—— (1972), *Cafarnao*, iv. *I Graffiti della Casa di S. Pietro* (Jerusalem).

—— (1973), 'La mitica rigenerazione della vita in un amuletto samaritano-cristiano del IV secolo', *LA* 23: 286–317.

—— (1983), 'L'angelologia dei giudeo-cristiani', *LA* 33: 273–302.

—— (1985), 'La settimana santa dei giudeo-cristiani e i suoi influssi nella Pasque della Grande Chiesa', *LA* 35: 163–202.

TESTINI, P. (1958), *Archeologia cristiana* (Rome).

THEE, F. C. R. (1984), *Julius Africanus and the Early Christian View of Magic* (Tübingen).

THOMAS, C. (1971), *The Early Christian Archaeology of North Britain* (London).

THOMPSON, E. M. (1912), *Introduction to Greek and Latin Palaeography* (Oxford).

TRISTAM, H. P. (1894), *Eastern Customs in Bible Lands* (London).

TSAFRIR, Y. (1987), 'More Evidence for the Cult of Zeus Akraios at Beth Shean', *EI* 19: 282–3 (Hebrew).

TURNER, C. H. (1900), 'The Early Episcopal Lists: The Lists of Jerusalem', *JTS* 1: 529–53.

TYSON, J. B. (1973), *A Study in Early Christianity* (New York).

TZAFERIS, V. (1971), 'Christian Symbols of the 4th Century and the Church Fathers', Ph.D. thesis (Hebrew University of Jerusalem).

—— (1975), 'The Archaeological Excavations at Shepherds' Field', *LA* 25: 5–52.

—— (1983*a*), *The Excavations at Kursi-Gergesa* (*Atiqot*, Eng. series, 16; Jerusalem).

—— (1983*b*), 'New Archaeological Evidence on Ancient Capernaum', *BA* 46: 198–204.

—— (1987), 'The Greek Inscriptions from the Early Christian Church at Evron', *EI* 19: 36–53.

—— *et al.* (1989), *Excavations at Capernaum* i. *1978–82* (Winona Lake).

—— MEIDONIS, K., and KESSIN, E. (1979), 'What became of Ancient Capernaum?', *Christian News from Israel*, 27/2: 74–7.

—— and URMAN, D. (1973), 'Excavations at Kursi', *Qadmoniot*, 6: 62–4.

URBACH, E. E. (1959), 'The Rabbinical Laws of Idolatry in the Second and Third Centuries in the Light of Archaeological and Historical Facts', *IEJ* 9: 149–65, 229–45.

URMAN, D. (1985), *Golan: A Profile of a Region during the Roman and Byzantine Periods* (British Archaeological Reports, S269; London).

—— (1988), 'Beth Guvrin: a History of a Mixed Population', in E. Stern and D. Urman (eds.), *Man and Environment in the Southern Shephalah* (Tel Aviv), 151–62.

VAN DER MEER, F., and MOHRMANN, C. (1958), *Atlas of the Early Christian World* (*Atlas van de Oudchristlijke Wereld*), trans. and ed. by M. F. Hedlund and H. H. Rowley (Amsterdam and London).

VAN ESBROECK, M. (1975), *Les plus anciens homéliaires géorgiens* (Louvain).

—— (1984), 'Jean II de Jerusalem et les cultes de S. Étienne, de la Sainte-Sion et de la croix', *Analecta Bollandiana*, 102: 99–134.

VAN-LENNEP, H. J. (1875), *Bible Lands, their Modern Customs and Manners Illustrative of Scripture* (London).

VAN UNNIK, W. C. (1939), 'De betekenis van de mozaische wet voor de kerk van Christus volgens de syrische Didascalia', *Nederlandsch Archief voor Kerkgeschiedenis*, 31: 65–100.

VELLAY, C. (1904), *Le culte et les fêtes d'Adonis-Thammouz dans l'Orient Antique* (Annales du Musée Guimet, Bibl. d'Études, xvi; Paris).

VERMES, G. (1961), *Scripture and Tradition in Judaism: Haggadic Studies* (Leiden).

—— (1975), *Post-Biblical Jewish Studies* (Leiden).

VERMEULE, C., and ANDERSON, K. (1981), 'Greek and Roman Sculpture in the Holy Land', *Burlington Magazine*, 123: 7–19.

VIAUD, P. (1910), *Nazareth et ses deux Églises de l'Annonciation et de Saint-Joseph d'après les fouilles récentes* (Paris).

VINCENT, L.-H. (1908), 'L'Éleona, sanctuaire primitif de l'Ascension', *RB* 17: 122–5.

—— (1911), 'L'Église de l'Éleona', *RB* 20: 219–65.

—— (1936), 'Bethléem: le sanctuaire de la Nativité', *RB* 45: 544–74.

—— and ABEL, F. M. (1914a), *Bethléem, le sanctuaire de la Nativité* (Paris).

—— (1914b), *Jérusalem: recherches de topographie, d'archéologie et d'histoire*, ii. *Jérusalem nouvelle* (Paris).

VLAMINCK, B. (1900), *A Report of the Recent Excavations and Explorations conducted at the Sanctuary of Nazareth* (Washington).

VOGT, J. (1963), 'Pagans and Christians in the Family of Constantine the Great', in A. Momigliano, (ed.), *The Conflict between Paganism and Christianity in the Fourth Century* (Oxford).

VREIZEN, K. J. H. (1977), 'Zweiter vorläufiger Bericht über die Ausgrabung unter der Erlöserkirche im Muristan in der Altstadt von Jerusalem (1971–74)', *ZDPV* 93: 76–81.

WALKER, P. W. L. (1990), *Holy City, Holy Places?* (Oxford).

WARREN, C., and CONDER, C. R. (1884), *The Survey of Western Palestine* (Jerusalem).

WEINBERG, W. (1975), 'The History of Hebrew *Plene* Spelling: From Antiquity to Haskalah', *HUCA* 46: 457–87.

WEIR SCHULTZ, R. (1910) (ed.), *The Church of the Nativity at Bethlehem* (London).

WEITZMANN, K. (1982), *Studies in the Arts at Sinai* (Princeton, NJ).

WELLES, C. B. (1967) (ed.), *The Excavations at Dura Europos*, viii.2 (New Haven, Conn.).

WELTEN, P. (1983), 'Bethlehem und die Klage um Adonis', *ZDPV* 99: 189–203.

WENGER, A. (1955), *L'Assomption de la T. S. Vierge dans la tradition byzantine du VIIe au Xe siècle* (Paris).

WENNING, R. (1987), *Die Nabatäer: Denkmäler und Geschichte* (Freibourg).

WHITBY, M., and WHITBY M. (1989), *Chronicon Paschale* (Liverpool).

WHITE, L. M. (1990), *Building God's House in the Roman World* (Baltimore, Md.).

WILKEN, R. (1983), *John Chrysostom and the Jews* (Los Angeles).

—— (1985), 'The Restoration of Israel in Biblical Prophecy', in Neusner and Frerichs (1985), 443–71.

WILKINSON, J. (1972), 'The Tomb of Christ: An Outline of its Structural History', *Levant*, 4: 83–97.

—— (1976), 'Christian Pilgrims in Jerusalem during the Byzantine Period', *PEQ* 108: 74–101.

—— (1977), *Jerusalem Pilgrims Before the Crusades* (Warminster).

—— (1978), *Jerusalem as Jesus Knew it* (London).

—— (1981), *Egeria's Travels*, rev. edn. (Warminster).

—— with HILL, J., and RYAN, W. F. (1988), *Jerusalem Pilgrimage 1099–1185* (London).

WILLIAMS, F. (1987), *The Panarion of Epiphanius of Salamis* (Leiden).

WILLIAMSON, G. A. (1965), *Eusebius: The History of the Church from Christ to Constantine* (Harmondsworth).

WILSON, C. M. (1869), 'Notes on the Jewish Synagogues in Galilee', *PEFQSt*, 37–41.

—— (1906), *Golgotha and the Holy Sepulchre* (London).

WINSTRAND, E. K. H. (1952), *Konstantins Kirche am heiligen Grab in Jerusalem nach den ältesten literarischen Zeugnissen* (Göteborgs Högskolas Årsskrift, 58; Gothenburg).

WORTH, W. (1908), *Catalogue of the Imperial Byzantine Coins in the British Museum* (London).

WRIGHT, W., MCLEAN, N., with MERX, A. (1988) (eds.), *The Ecclesiastical History of Eusebius in Syriac* (Cambridge).

YADIN, Y. (1976) (ed.), *Jerusalem Revealed: Archaeology in the Holy City 1968–1974* (Jerusalem).

YEIVIN, Z. (1966), 'Two Ancient Oil Presses', *Atiqot*, 3: 52–63 (Hebrew).

Index

graffiti (*cont.*):
  Nazareth 233, *234*, 244–6, *247*,
    251–2, 254–5, 258–64, *263*, 338
  on ossuaries 5–6, *6*, *7*, *8*, 9
Greek, in graffiti and inscriptions 5, 41,
    176–7, 184, 190, 216, 233–4,
    260–1, 275, 284–7

Hadrian 42, 54, 77, 113–16, 132, 141–
    2, 211, 318
Hall, B. 65 n. 57
Hammath, Jews in 53–4
Hanson, R. P. C. 319 n. 57
Hauran, pagan settlements 72, 335
Hayes, J. W. 251
Hayman, Peter 25 n. 20
Hebrew, use in inscriptions and graffiti
    46, 252, 263–4
Hebron:
  and burial of Adam 130
  Jewish–Christians in 13
  Jews in 49
  Tombs of the Patriarchs 105, 322,
    324, 327
Hegesippus 27, 34–6, 42, 44, 243
Helena:
  and Bethlehem 110
  and discovery of true cross 138–9
  and Eleona Church 143, 148
  and foundation of churches 213, 307,
    309
  and pilgrimage 307–8, 310, 312–13,
    339
Heraclius 229, 266
herms, veneration 83
Hesychius (?Ps.-) 207
Hesychius of Jerusalem 195
Hilgenfeld, W. A. 20
Hinterkeuser, Wendelin 268
Hirschfeld, Y. 190
History of Joseph 146, 223–4
holiness of place vii–viii, xi, 92–3,
    154–5, 296, 311–15, 326, 331,
    340–1
holy places:
  authenticity ix, 333
  Christian 84–5, 154, 295–32, 335–6
  and Constantine 296–300, 310,
    314–17, 335, 337, 339
  contamination vii, xi, 113–14, 163–4
  Jewish 87–8, 94, 106, 315–16,
    321–8, 339–40

maintained by Jewish–Christians
    1–4, 17, 335
  Muslim 81, 82, 158
  pagan 81–4, 86–90, 96–9, 123–4,
    314, 316–17, 318–32
  'restoration' by Christians 1, 92–4,
    98–9, 113, 163, 295–6, 318–12,
    330–2, 335–6, 339–40
  Samaritan 67, 69, 82, 84, 316, 321–2,
    329
  and scholars 310–13, 317, 338–9
  see also Bethlehem; Capernaum;
    Gethsemane; Golgotha; Mamre;
    Mount of Olives; Nazareth; Rock
    of Calvary
Horbury, William 27
hospitium, Bethany cave as 190–1,
    205, 337
house-churches:
  Capernaum 17, 268, 269, 338
  Mount Zion 210, 211–12, 215,
    217–18, 219–20, 337
Hugeburc, *Life of Willibald* 196, 198,
    273, 289
Hunt, E. D. 90, 130 n. 33, 229

Iamblichus 78
iconoclasm, evidence of 188–9
iconography:
  Christian 2, 86–7, 96–7, 186–9
  Jewish 55–6
Idumaeans 70, 75, 88, 95, 108
Ignatius 21
imagination, role viii–ix
inscriptions:
  Christian 167, 169, 170–1, 180–1,
    260–2, *261*, *262*
  at Farj 39–41, *40*, *41*
  Jewish 154 n. 38, 166, 172–9
  Jewish–Christian 5–6, *6*, *7*, 45, 172
  magical 172
  Samaritan 67–9, 172–9
  see also graffiti; Khirbet Kilkish,
    funerary stelai
Irenaeus 22, 257, 260
Isidore of Pelusium 159
Islam, and ancient venerated sites 81,
    158
Ituraeans 70, 71

James:
  as leader of Jerusalem church 1, 224
  throne of 209, 219